LOST *for* WORDS?

A homily resource for the Catholic three-year cycle

Compiled and edited by Peter Edwards
Editor of The Living Word

with a foreword by Denis McBride C.Ss.R.

A Redemptorist Publication

Published by **Redemptorist Publications**
A Registered Charity limited by guarantee. Registered in England 3261721.

Copyright © Redemptorist Publications 2009

First published November 2009

Layout: Rosemarie Pink
Cover design: Chris Nutbeen

ISBN 978-0-85231-368-8

A CIP catalogue record for this book is available from the British Library

Printed by Stanley L Hunt (Printers) Limited, Northamptonshire, NN10 9UA

Redemptorist
PUBLICATIONS
Alphonsus House Chawton Hampshire GU34 3HQ
Telephone 01420 88222   Fax 01420 88805
rp@rpbooks.co.uk   www.rpbooks.co.uk

Contents

Foreword

Dear Friends,

Some days words come easily to us, and insights seem to spring up from some secret sanctuary to surprise and delight, leaving us wondering at hidden resources within. On other days we feel lost for words, with insight buried under a mountain of routine concerns. The telephone keeps ringing, people lean on the door with a litany of demands, the diary looks stuffed with tedious meetings, and the slates are slipping from the sacristy roof.

Sunday is approaching. Again. A congregation will assemble to hallow the name of the Lord, hoping that they might hear some good news. From you. You take a deep breath.

Having a word for your congregation, in season and out of season, for the high feast days and the spread of ordinary time, is no mean feat. Sometimes you might feel in sympathy with a tired priest who said to me: "People keep coming to me, but at the moment I feel like a shopkeeper with nothing on the shelves behind me. Sold out."

We all need help on dull days when reserves are low. This volume has been assembled not as a substitute for your best thinking, but as a humble help for those days when you feel a bit weary and out of luck. It aims to provide a line, an image, a thought – a trigger to set the mind in movement towards Gospel.

If this book achieves this, it will have fulfilled a wonderful pastoral purpose – helping you to minister to the people charged to your care.

Sincerely,

Denis McBride, C.Ss.R.
Publishing Director
Redemptorist Publications
Chawton
Alton
Hants GU34 3HQ

Editor's Preface

Faith, in the words of the Second Vatican Council, "is born of the word and is nourished by it" (*Presbyterorum Ordinis*, 4). In Catholic churches throughout the world, over the course of the three-year liturgical cycle, we get to hear a great deal of the word of God in the scripture readings. Some of the readings have become very familiar to us, while others seem to strike us anew each time we hear them.

The same document of the Council also describes the preaching of the Gospel as the "first task" of priests, in response to Jesus Christ's command to "proclaim the Good News to all creation" (Mark 16:15). Much of the most effective preaching comes from the heart, and from reflection on local and pastoral issues; yet it also needs to be rooted in the word of God and in prayer. The power of Jesus' own words as he proclaimed the Good News of the kingdom, and the authority and authenticity that the people who heard those words recognised in them, were founded on the integrity that his listeners observed in his own life; and a vital part of that life, as we can ourselves observe from the Gospels, was Jesus' own knowledge of the scriptures and his prayerful relationship with his Father.

As we seek to open and understand the scriptures ourselves – and to open them and bring understanding of them to others – prayer and study, reading and reflection, will be important elements. They can help us to see with fresh eyes words that have long been familiar, and cast new light on others that may have been obscure.

The tradition of the publication of aids for those called on to preach homilies has a long, often distinguished and sometimes colourful history, stretching back through the centuries. Since 1973, Redemptorist Publications have produced the quarterly publication *The Living Word* as a resource for those who preach and lead the liturgy. At the heart of this publication are the homily reflections written for each Sunday and feast day. One of the strengths of these throughout the years is that they have been written by a variety of people – priests, religious and lay – from a wide range of different backgrounds and with a diversity of pastoral and personal experience.

In this volume, we have brought together a selection of homilies and reflections on the scriptures from *The Living Word*. Most of them have been previously published as part of the quarterly edition, though a few have been newly written specifically for this volume. This book covers each of the Sundays and solemnities in the three-year cycle of the Catholic Lectionary, as well as those feast days of the universal Catholic calendar that can, on occasion, take the place of a Sunday in the liturgy. It is not intended to be a sort of "Best of...", but rather a compilation that it is hoped will be helpful to those preparing homilies and those who simply want to explore and reflect on the scriptures.

Thanks are due to all those who, over the years, have contributed to *The Living Word*, which remains an important and ongoing part of the mission of Redemptorist Publications; and also to those who have supported it by subscription and in other ways. Special thanks also to Rosemarie Pink, for her tireless typesetting, and to all the other staff at Chawton for their support.

Peter Edwards
Editor

The Season of Advent

"So stay awake, because you do not know the day when your master is coming."

Illustration

"I woke up to find the message in my left hand. It had me trembling. It wasn't a fax, telegram, memo, or the usual sort of missive bringing disturbing news. In fact, my hand held nothing at all. The trembling was the message." This is how Michael J. Fox begins his autobiography, *Lucky Man*. This popular film and comedy star was devastated when, at a very young age, he was diagnosed with the early onset of Parkinson's disease. While incredibly successful and wealthy, he was also going through a very difficult period – he had been drinking more and more, and neglecting his relationship with his wife.

The trembling and subsequent diagnosis were to act as a "wake-up call" for Michael. Amazingly, in his book, he describes the emergence of Parkinson's as one of the best things that ever happened to him – because it made him completely re-evaluate every aspect of his life. His perception shifted from "life is about what happens to me" to "now I know that life is about what I can do in the world". Family, love and helping others replaced the idols of fame and fortune that once dominated and nearly destroyed his life.

Michael J. Fox is not alone in having an experience, sometimes disturbing, sometimes invigorating, that leads to a complete turnaround in lifestyle and priorities. It has been said that on their deathbed no one has ever been heard saying, "I wish I'd spent more time at the office", whereas "I wish I'd spent more time with my family" has been heard time and time again. Some people manage to recognise the true priorities before it is too late.

Gospel Teaching

We can be uncomfortable today with the sections of the Gospel that speak about the "Last Things", yet they need not hold any fear for those who trust in God's plan. Those who were living in the time of Noah were so caught up in their daily activities, eating and drinking, that they were neglectful of the consequences of their sins and were caught unawares by the flood. Disciples of the Lord Jesus are called to a constant awareness that we are no longer simply to focus on the daily activities of eating and drinking. We have the challenge of living life purposefully. We have a mission that is supposed to influence us at all times and direct our words and actions in all circumstances.

We are challenged by Jesus to be alert and vigilant in living out the Gospel message. We never know the day nor the hour when our presence may bring life to another or, through our inattention, allow them to remain in need or pain.

If we live our lives with passion and purpose, with a wholehearted dedication to God's kingdom, then when "one [of us] is taken" it will not be an experience of disaster or catastrophe. Rather, it will be the joyful entry into the fullness of life that God has promised us in Jesus. God's plans for us are plans of fullness, not of harm.

Application
In his letter to the Romans, Paul gives us the wake-up call that we need today as we begin this season of Advent. Now is the time to wake up. Now is the time to be alert. Now is the time to be active, for we are called to live in the light and not to skulk around in the darkness. Anything in our lives that we would rather keep as a guilty secret should be disposed of and left behind. As part of our Advent preparations we could reflect on the hidden areas of our life and ask the Lord for the courage to live more freely in the light.

In our workplaces, in our homes, in our communities: how committed are we to living life purposefully? When people meet us, do they meet prophets of doom or prophets of eternal life?

Michael J. Fox had a dramatic conversion experience through a very painful experience of illness and weakness in his own life. His priorities and his purpose were turned upside down as he rediscovered enduring, life-giving values. This time of preparation for the coming of the Christ-child at Christmas is a wonderful opportunity for us to rediscover our true priority and purpose. A trembling hand was the first indication of a new world for Michael J. Fox. In our lives what are the indicators calling us to life with God?

"Our Redeemer is your ancient name."

Illustration

Every year on Advent Sunday there is a procession with carols at King's College Chapel, Cambridge, England. The famous chapel was founded by King Henry VI in 1441 and among its many glories is the fan-vaulted roof described by the poet William Wordsworth as "self-poised, and scooped into ten thousand cells, where light and shade repose, where music dwells lingering – and wandering on as loth to die".

The music that is heard in the chapel on this day begins with the gentle sound of the organ and then, in the distance, the voices of the choristers intoning the responsory which begins, "I look from afar: and lo, I see the power of God coming, and a cloud covering the whole earth." As the procession moves from the west door the choristers sing, "Come, thou Redeemer of the Earth", a hymn written by St Ambrose in the fourth century. It continues, "Come, testify thy virgin birth: All lands admire, all times applaud! Such is the birth that fits a God." The words and the music are haunting and sublime. They send a tingle from your head to your toes. Advent is here again!

The season of Advent has been celebrated in the Church probably since the fourth century. The word "advent" comes from the Latin *adventus*, a word used in ancient times to describe the arrival or presence of a king who had come to visit a part of his kingdom. The Church adopted this word as fitting for the season that has now begun.

Gospel Teaching

Through the incarnation God has visited the world and dwelt among us. Christ remains with us always, though now we see him only with the eyes of faith. But, as we proclaim in the liturgy, "Christ has died, Christ is risen, Christ will come again." Advent is a period of waiting and preparation for the Lord's coming, not only in the celebration of Christ's birth – the coming of Emmanuel, God-with-us – but also the second coming of Christ on the last day.

This "day" is alluded to by Jesus in the verse immediately preceding today's Gospel, when he says that of that day or hour "nobody knows… neither the angels of heaven, nor the Son; no one but the Father". He exhorts his disciples to be like the doorkeeper in the parable who awaits the return of the master of the house – awake and vigilant at "evening, midnight, cockcrow, dawn".

As in the Gospel, so in the other readings of the day there is hope of a future coming. Our first reading, from Isaiah, recalls that it was as Redeemer – God's "ancient name" – that God became the Father of Israel. With a vision that sees beyond the feelings of hopelessness and guilt experienced by the people of Israel at that time, Isaiah pleads that God will come again as Redeemer. Paul puts his hope in the second coming of Christ as he assures the Christian community in Corinth that God's faithfulness will keep them true to the gifts of the Spirit as they wait for the last day, the "day of our Lord Jesus Christ".

Application

Wordsworth saw what others did not see. He gazed at the lofty pillars and the branching roof of King's College Chapel and saw its self-possession, its myriad cells where light and shade were at rest, and where, as the poet wrote, music lingered like thoughts whose "very sweetness" yielded proof that they "were born for immortality". This is the poet who "wandered lonely as a cloud", for whom daffodils danced and daisies glittered from afar like stars, and a cuckoo was "no bird, but an invisible thing, a voice, a mystery".

If we do not have Wordsworth's unique vision or eloquence, as Christians we do have the gift of faith; and this enables us to see beyond this world. Let us renew our faith this Advent so that our eyes may see and our ears may hear the wondrous truth that we are "born for immortality". In the season's light and shade, words and music, holly and ivy, candles and wreaths of greenery, may we see and hear the joyful proclamation of the coming of our Redeemer. Let us be ready to meet him so that, whatever our weaknesses, strengths, hopes, fears, joys, or disappointments, when at last our Redeemer comes to us, our eyes shall be fully opened and we shall recognise the One who has loved us from all eternity.

"And then they will see the Son of Man coming in a cloud with power and great glory."

Illustration

Today's scripture readings seem to come from another world. Jeremiah looks forward to honesty and integrity in the land. Paul expects us to live a completely blameless life. And Jesus speaks of a day when "the powers of heaven will be shaken". Jeremiah and Paul, and even Jesus himself, may appear so much concerned with another world that they seem irrelevant to the world in which we actually live today.

Nothing could be further from the truth! Their world was as disordered as ours. Jeremiah preached as the Babylonian armies began their destruction of Jerusalem. Paul wrote when the first Christians were beginning to despair under the pressure of persecution. And Jesus' words are his last before his passion. Their message was for a world like ours.

But how, in the midst of such chaos and suffering, could the visions of today's readings be recognised as real and relevant? The answer is illustrated in the lesson given in a simple way by an elderly lady in a nursing home. She had been paralysed for years but had retained the use of her hands. With these hands she produced the most beautiful embroidery one could ever wish to see. One day she showed a visitor her latest creation, a beautiful pattern of flowers and birds. "This", she said, "is the way God sees our world: a thing of beauty, ordered and harmonious."

Then, reversing the material, she showed the other side: the little tufts and loose ends, the irregular patterns. "And this", she added, "is the world we see: disordered, problems unresolved, questions unanswered. But it will not always be like this. Next time you come I will have tidied up that side too and it will be as good as the other. This is what God will do at the end of time. God will tidy up what human beings have disturbed, and put right what has gone wrong."

Gospel Teaching

Jesus Christ taught us to look at the world through his own eyes – the eyes of God. When we look at the world using our own eyes we can be filled with confusion. But using Christ's vision we recognise something ordered and beautiful. We see a purpose in life; we are given true insight. The necessary "tidying up" comes, of course, at the end of time when the Son of Man appears "with power and great glory", but the picture can already be recognised.

The season of Advent prepares us to look at the world through Christ's eyes: it prepares us for his coming into our life in a richer and more realistic way. Sometimes we think that we prepare by ignoring the world we live in; or we imagine that the difficulties of this life are somehow an obstacle between ourselves and God. But Christ makes it plain that we prepare for his coming precisely by taking a searching look at *this* world and perceiving, through the disorder, the guiding hand of God. With Christ's insight we can enjoy the vision of Jeremiah and Paul: we can recognise that God is truly with us.

Application

How can we absorb that assurance of God's presence enjoyed by Jeremiah and Paul? How can we learn to look at the world through Christ's eyes? These are tasks for life. But Advent is a time set aside to stop and reflect in a special way on how Christ comes into our life.

First, Advent directs us to the birth of Christ in Bethlehem. Our faith is not founded on feelings or emotions. It is founded on one clear fact: that in the birth of Jesus Christ, God came into the world as a human being.

Second, Advent directs our attention to Christ's coming in our everyday life. He comes when we least expect him: in the awkward person we have to deal with; when we are feeling unwell and are tired with the difficulties of life. Our daily prayer helps us to prepare for those moments.

Finally, Advent directs us to Christ's coming for the last time – the "day [that] will be sprung on you suddenly, like a trap". If we have contemplated his coming at Christmas and in our daily life, this final coming will be no fearful scanning of the horizon, hoping we will not be caught unawares. On the contrary, it will be a welcoming of a God who has been as close to us as he is in our celebration of the Eucharist: a God with whom we have been in such close communion that we have learned to see the world through his eyes.

A

"Prepare a way for the Lord."

Illustration

In 1997, Jesus was born again in Cuba. Or at least that is how it seemed to many Cubans, who, for the first time in the thirty or so years since the Cuban revolution, celebrated Christmas as a public holiday. Some Christians had managed to celebrate the birth of Christ in a quiet way each year, but for most people the Christmas Gospel was something long forgotten, or something entirely new. It must have seemed strange to find out about events that took place two thousand years ago, and to learn of their continued importance to hundreds of millions of Christians worldwide. People were discovering something new, and at the same time discovering something two thousand years old.

Cuba's first public Christmas holiday in years was called in honour of Pope John Paul II's visit to the country. The Cuban experience, though particular to that country, is part of a wider pattern of human encounter with God. God's mercy is announced to us again and again; with joy we discover, we rediscover, what we have known all along: God's mercy is faithful and sure.

John the Baptist appeared in the wilderness as though he had stepped straight out of the Old Testament. The past had come into the present. But John's message was not about the past. It was about the future: a radical challenge to each and every person to prepare for the coming of the Lord. John was announcing anew what people had known all along.

John proclaimed the coming of Jesus. The people knew God, and had heard of God's salvation, but they had become blind to what was before their eyes. John did not give the people a new religion, but called them to greater faithfulness to their own tradition.

Gospel Teaching

Like all true prophets, John distinguished between the truth and all the cultural clutter that inevitably surrounds it. He had no patience with what was not important, and pronounced urgently on what really mattered: preparing the Lord's way by repenting from sin. What Isaiah foretold, John proclaimed again. What John foretold, Jesus announced too. What Jesus announced, we proclaim anew. The Gospel of Jesus Christ, always the same, always new.

The easiest way to discover what John the Baptist represents is to imagine him preaching to us, in our own time, "Prepare a way for the Lord." His message is from the past, spoken to the present, for the future.

We meet John the Baptist in the Gospel reading today. It begins with the man himself: who he is, his personal qualities and how he lives. Then we have the strands of his message. He announces the same salvation of God as Isaiah announced, so he preaches continuity with the past. He predicts the coming of Jesus, the Messiah, and is thus telling the people that the former times have come to an end. He condemns hypocrisy and sin, but offers freedom through repentance. He is a powerful messenger of God, but regards himself merely as a sign, a pointer to Jesus. And he says that we will be judged by the fruit that we bear.

Application

Most of us are not prophets or preachers as John the Baptist was. But each of us can seek to do as the Baptist demands. Through repentance we can rediscover the mercy of God. Through sorrow for our sinful ways, a sorrow that is eager to put right what we have disrupted, we can make straight the way of the Lord. The best way to judge ourselves is not by what rules we do or do not keep, but by the fruits of the Spirit growing within us.

We rejoice that soon we will once again celebrate the coming of Jesus, while never forgetting he is with us always. What we have always known, we come to know again, and find ourselves renewed in Spirit.

The experience of Christians in Cuba, and in other parts of the world where public celebrations of Christmas are rare or entirely absent, can make us pause for thought. We can take our faith for granted, overlooking the fact that John the Baptist was announcing something powerful, something radical, something new. And when we realise what Jesus signifies, as John realised, then it begins to challenge us to a new way of life.

We will not rely on our religious inheritance: we will rely instead on a living faith. We will not presume that we are secure, but will judge ourselves by the fruit we bear.

"The Lord is not being slow to carry out his promises…
but he is being patient with you all."

Illustration

Do you remember your first day at school? For some people new beginnings represent opportunities and are full of adventure. For others, change is difficult and is associated with fear and anxiety. Some changes are chosen: for example, a new school, a new job, a move of house. Others are forced upon one by circumstances: redundancy, death, becoming a refugee, seeking asylum from those who seek to punish and kill. Not even the Church is free from change today. Many dioceses are discussing the changing of Mass times, perhaps the clustering or amalgamation of parishes, maybe even celebrating Sunday with a service in the absence of a priest. What seemed impossible in the past is now being discussed. The old certainties are disappearing. Whilst some may see opportunities in the new situation, others are fearful and seek security.

Change is always difficult, even when it is chosen. Forced change is painful and shatters life. It may take a long time to recover. Refugees and asylum seekers, the victims of warfare and conflict, did not choose their situation: it happened, and now they have to carry the pain of it. Men or women who have been made redundant know the pain of forced change, which has dramatically altered their lives, relationships and financial situations. Life is often unpredictable and we long for some stability and order in the midst of the confusion. In a situation of change it can be difficult to remain hopeful, and God can seem very distant and uncaring. People ask, "Why is God silent?" or "Why did this happen to me?"

Gospel Teaching

Today's scripture readings give hope to people who are beginning to despair and doubt God's promise. They think and feel that God is acting too slowly. Has God abandoned them? The prophet Isaiah offers the exiled Jewish people in Babylon the promise of consolation. Being taken as prisoners into exile was a catastrophe for the people of Israel. It meant becoming slaves again, dispossession and the loss of homeland. All their hopes and expectations were shattered. As they recognise their failings and sin, Isaiah tells his people to continue to trust in God who will lead them from slavery and exile back to the Promised Land. From the wilderness of Babylon, the Lord will lead his people to freedom.

The second letter of Peter gives encouragement to those who despair about the timing of the Lord's second coming. The author warns against being impetuous for the last days. Christians are commended to live faithful and holy lives while they wait for God. Some people think that God is working too slowly. But the purpose of God's plan is to give people time to change. God is patient and works slowly. God respects human freedom and allows growth to happen in small, often imperceptible, ways. It is only over a period of years that one can see the changes that have occurred.

The Gospel offers the hope of a new beginning. This beginning is the birth of Jesus Christ, who is the Son of God. The birth of a child in a manger at Bethlehem changes the meaning of life and the purpose of time. Jesus Christ offers a new life to those who choose to follow him: a life that culminates in friendship with God. There is no greater purpose in life than to become a friend of God.

Application

God is not silent. God is gentle, like a caring shepherd who loves his flock intimately, and is a loving presence in adversity. The hope of Christians is that God will bring freedom from whatever enslaves a person. In God's plan this will happen at the right time for each person. We might feel impatient, but we are called to trust. We may not understand the meaning of an event or the timing, but we are called to believe in God.

To trust in God's providence requires great faith. The disciples who knew Jesus in the flesh struggled to believe in him. Many people pray, "Lord, I believe; help my unbelief." One should not lose heart if doubt persists. It can be a period for deepening faith. The path to becoming a friend of God needs time; different people are at different stages of the journey. God is gentle and does not rush persons but allows each to respond in his or her own time. God works in God's own time in ways that are deeply mysterious.

2nd Sunday of Advent

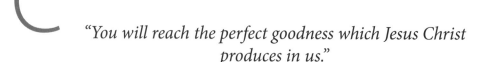

"You will reach the perfect goodness which Jesus Christ produces in us."

Illustration

At the time of the London Blitz during the Second World War, in 1940, Coral Atkins, like thousands of other children, was evacuated to the countryside for her own safety. The people she stayed with were strict and cruel towards her, and this disrupted childhood experience haunted her adult years. She grew up to become a British theatre and television actress, and it was while making a celebrity appearance for charity one day that she saw Jessica, a little girl with a haunted face, living in a children's home.

This event triggered a deep impulse in Coral that she should do more than just make appearances at charity events. She decided to dedicate her life to lost children. She opened her own children's home. Disruptive, disturbed children, she said, are just children who need a lot of love, because they have had disruptive, disturbed experiences.

One day, one of Coral's helpers, a qualified assistant very much given to discipline, expressed her despair at Coral's simple method of love and patience. "I must protest," she said, "or else something terrible will happen." Coral was exasperated. "You just don't get it, do you?" she replied. "Something terrible has already happened to these children."

Coral's simple method was a profound understanding of these children's pain and needs. She instinctively knew what was going on inside their hearts, and she gave them unfailing love and attention and her utmost honest endeavour. By her integrity she gave them peace. By her devotedness she gave them honour. She helped them to recovery and to the restoration of their lives.

Gospel Teaching

This is the experience of the prophet Baruch in our first reading today. Something terrible has happened. The Jewish people are forced from their homes into exile, but Baruch can see a day of liberation in the future, when something wonderful will happen. Jerusalem will be restored, and the glory of God will shine for all to see.

This future day is given definition for us in the Gospel when Luke says exactly when it was that John the Baptist began his preaching along the

Jordan valley. "In the fifteenth year of Tiberius Caesar's reign" is when John came; and John's coming was a definite sign that something was about to happen, something wonderful. Someone was coming. The day that the prophet had longed for is the day of Jesus Christ.

This good news was preached most powerfully by the apostle Paul. It was an amazing conversion that Saul of Tarsus – so fierce, forceful and even violent in protecting his rigid version of religion – should now spend his life preaching the love of Jesus Christ. He tells his people in Philippi that he loves them "as Christ Jesus loves you", and he prays that their love for each other "may increase more and more".

This is not a pious platitude that Paul is speaking. He has come to realise that the love of God in a person does powerful things. It improves our knowledge and our understanding. It deepens our perception so that we can always recognise what is best in life. More, it makes us pure. It brings us to the condition of being like Jesus himself; and that is the glory of God, present in our world.

Application

When this happens to us, something wonderful has happened; and, no matter how terrible some of our experiences may be, no matter what has happened to us in this life, this love, this persevering love, is stronger and deeper and greater. It restores to life, where once there was only death.

Coral Atkins had one little girl in her care who never spoke, but who crawled into a pram, and hugged her dolly for love. Coral never forced this child to be better. She just loved her and cared for her and protected her. Then one day, during a noisy party, the little girl spoke and brought the room to a shocked silence. "I don't like turkey," she whispered. A stunned and surprised Coral pretended not to hear properly. Eventually the little girl roared, "Can nobody in this room hear me? I don't like turkey."

"Oh yes, we can hear you," Coral answered with a beam of happiness on her face. "Oh yes, we can hear you very well."

A

"Are you the one who is to come, or have we got to wait for someone else?"

Illustration

Many people all over the world are unjustly imprisoned for reasons of conscience, or for crimes they did not commit. They may face torture, or even being put to death. In places from the Americas to Africa, the Middle and Far East, China, Russia and many European countries, people have had their human rights abused. In recent years in various parts of the world we have seen how easily injustice and violence can take over, and how innocent people suffer as a result.

The Gospel story of John the Baptist reminds us that this is not new. John had done nothing wrong. He had simply preached the truth, and announced the coming of the Messiah, the Anointed One of God. In doing so he criticised the immorality of the ruler, Herod Antipas. For his fearless speaking of the truth, John was put in prison and finally had his head cut off.

We also have some details about John's story that do not appear in the Gospels. There was a Jewish historian called Josephus, writing just after the time of Jesus and John. He tells us how Herod was jealous of John, because the people flocked to hear him preach and to be baptised. This confirms what we read in the Gospels. Josephus tells us that John was put in prison in Herod's fortress called Machaerus. This was a grim hilltop fortress to the east of the Dead Sea, and its remains can be seen to this day.

On a clear day, it is possible to look from Machaerus and see the Mount of Olives and Jerusalem. It is touching to think that perhaps the last time John saw the light of day he looked towards the holy city, towards the place where Jesus, the one he had hailed as the Lamb of God, was going to suffer and die.

Gospel Teaching

John sends messengers to ask Jesus "Are you the one who is to come, or have we got to wait for someone else?" The phrase, "the one who is to come", was one of the many titles for the Messiah at the time. In John's Gospel the Baptist cries out when he sees Jesus, "Look, there is the lamb of God that takes away the sin of the world." "Lamb of God" was another

22

title for the coming Messiah. We know Israel was alive with expectation of the coming of the Messiah, the divine Redeemer. Many people even went into the desert and lived there in communities to watch and pray for his arrival. What all this means, in the context of the time, is that people were waiting for the one who would be both truly God and truly human.

It is very interesting to note what Jesus does not do in reply to the question posed by John's disciples. He does not say yes or no, but points out what has been happening. The blind see, the lame walk, the dead are raised to life and so forth. These were the signs prophesied by Isaiah, and they are being fulfilled by Jesus. We can appreciate how wise Jesus' response is. Surely our first reaction to anyone claiming to be the Messiah would be to think that this person is blowing their own trumpet? To rephrase a modern saying, Jesus does not even try to "talk the talk", but he does "walk the walk". He lets his actions, in the context of Israel's sacred scriptures, speak for themselves. He knows John will understand this, and says of him, "happy is the man who does not lose faith in me".

Application

This story of John in prison can encourage us all. Jesus tells the crowds that no one born of woman is greater than John the Baptist. John is one of the first to recognise Jesus as the Messiah. But even he, in the darkness of his prison, has doubts and needs reassurance.

There may be times in our lives when our faith is weakening, our hope is dying, and our charity is running low. This does not mean we should despair. Even a great saint like John had his troubled times. John gives us an example of what we are called to do: to turn again to Christ. Not because we expect him to magically make everything better. What he will do is give us renewed faith and the courage to go on witnessing to him, just as John witnessed to Christ by the shedding of his blood.

B

"There stands among you – unknown to you – the one who is coming after me."

Illustration

The monastery was experiencing a crisis: monks were leaving and no new monks were joining. The abbot decided to consult a respected hermit living nearby. The hermit told him a secret: one of the monks in the community was actually the Messiah, though he was living in such a way that no one would recognise him.

The abbot returned to the community and told his brothers. All the monks were amazed but had no idea which of them it could be. All they knew was that one of them could be the Christ. Knowing this led to an amazing change in the monastery. They all began to show more reverence and love for each other, and their common prayer became more sincere and fervent. People noticed; and the monastery began to grow again in numbers as the monks grew in holiness. All of this happened because a man of God pointed to the truth that Christ was indeed living among them.

Gospel Teaching

Like the holy hermit, John the Baptist directs our gaze to the presence of Christ among us. In today's Gospel we are given a wonderful sense of the fulfilment of prophecy. Everything promised in the scriptures is about to be fulfilled. All the hopes contained in the old covenant are soon to be accomplished. Into this picture of hope and promise steps the powerful figure of Jesus' cousin, John the Baptist.

Even before his birth, when he leaped for joy in his mother's womb, John had recognised Jesus as the promised Messiah. In the best sense of the phrase he was somebody who "knew his place". It was not that John fully understood from the very start exactly what were God's plans and purposes for him. What John knew, though, without any doubt was that God had a plan and purpose for his life. This divine purpose, his vocation, lay in fulfilling the words spoken many years earlier through the prophet Isaiah, to be "a voice that cries in the wilderness: Make a straight way for the Lord."

John was a prophet of God and his role in salvation history was pivotal. In the Gospel we are given a clear glimpse into John the Baptist's heart, and his extraordinary openness and willingness to play his part in God's wonderful plan of salvation for the world. He knows that his joy and privilege do not lie in proclaiming himself but instead in pointing clearly to Jesus, the promised Messiah, who is the light and source of our hope: "I baptise you with water; but there stands among you – unknown to you – the one who is coming after me; and I am not fit to undo his sandal-strap." Jesus is the only one with the power to save his people.

It is this recognition of the Messiah, Jesus, already standing among his people that forms the heart of John's prophetic proclamation. As, effectively, the last of the Old Testament prophets, John bears witness to Christ in his preaching, his fearless truthfulness, his ministry of baptism and repentance. Finally, he will witness with the ultimate sacrifice in the shedding of his own blood.

Application

We can be like any of the crowd who gathered around John the Baptist. We can be alert to his message, that the Messiah is already among us, or we can be blind to this saving presence. We can also be like the "interrogators" sent by the Pharisees with many questions but not really listening attentively to the answers.

The readings in these days of Advent, especially today, are full of joy and hope. The joy and hope are found in the fact that the promises of God are being fulfilled before our very eyes, even as we listen. The Lord calls on each of us to play our part in the unfolding of his plan of salvation. Our part may feel small. We may wonder, as John himself would have done, what exactly God is asking us to do and say that will make a difference. But what matters is that we try to help each other to see and recognise Jesus standing among us. This is the Good News; and our joy and privilege, like John's, lie in proclaiming this to others.

Always we take heart not from our own abilities or worthiness but from the simple fact of God's love and faithfulness. The words of St Paul in today's second reading give us great encouragement as we try to live our Christian lives generously: "May the God of peace make you perfect and holy... God has called you and he will not fail you."

"What must we do?"

Illustration

Father Michael finally sat down at his computer. He'd been interrupted several times that day as he tried to write a school report that was already a week late. Just as he was beginning to put his fingers to the keyboard, the doorbell rang. He was tempted to ignore it, but out of duty he stomped towards the front door and yanked it open. It was Patrick. Father Michael knew his caller very well. Patrick was a "gentleman of the road" who liked a drink now and then. The priest would usually pass the time of day with Patrick, who would then happily move on, having gained the price of a cup of tea. Today, however, was different. Angry that he'd been disrupted, Father Michael snapped: "And what do you want?" Patrick began his usual story, building up to the request for a little money. But Father Michael was not in the mood. Before Patrick had the chance to ask, he was sent away and the door was slammed shut behind him.

Father Michael returned to his computer and started to type. But now he was even more frustrated, not because he'd been disturbed, but because he'd been so unkind. All he could think about was Patrick's stooped figure walking down the presbytery path. To make things worse, it was a few weeks before Christmas and the snow was gently falling. He imagined himself as Scrooge in Charles Dickens' book *A Christmas Carol*.

Then the doorbell rang again. Unable to concentrate on writing his report, Father Michael went to see who it was. There stood another gentleman of the road. Immediately, Father Michael pulled one of his coats off its hook and thrust it towards the man. The visitor was slightly bemused by the priest's gesture, particularly because he hadn't even had time to ask for anything. Wearing his new coat, and with the price of a meal in his pocket, the man set off on his way. Father Michael returned to his computer. As he began to type, he smiled knowingly to himself. Had God taught him a lesson? If only he'd been generous when he first had the chance, it would have cost him the price of a cup of tea and not his best overcoat.

Gospel Teaching

At the beginning of today's Gospel, the people put a question to John the Baptist: "What must we do?" It doesn't really make sense unless we remember what John was telling them, and us, earlier in the text. Last

Sunday we heard John announce the coming of the Lord. A path must be prepared for the one who brings salvation. It's almost as if the people who heard John's message wanted to know what it meant in practice: how do we smooth and straighten our lives into a welcoming highway for the Lord? Today we hear John's answer. We can make our hearts ready to receive Christ by sharing what we have with those who have nothing and by treating others with fairness and respect. Jesus will reveal God's love to us. Our faith-response to that loving presence requires that we act according to the ways of justice and always with the greatest kindness and charity.

How we behave towards others is a measure of how deeply we have welcomed Christ into our hearts. But, as well as reflecting on what we do, we are also invited to think about the spirit in which we act. Zephaniah speaks of the joy that proclaims God's presence among us. St Paul invites his hearers always to be happy in the Lord. It's one thing to share what we have begrudgingly or out of duty; it's another thing completely to do so happily and joyfully.

Application

Advent is a time of waiting in joyful hope. We are looking forward to celebrating the fulfilment of God's promise. It's a time of thankfulness for God's generous love, made real for us in Jesus. John the Baptist knew that this love was a free and undeserved gift. He was not even worthy to bend low and undo Christ's sandals. We do not have to be worthy to welcome Jesus, but we are called to be willing to let his presence change our attitudes and behaviour.

The Gospel shows us what this means in practice. Whatever shape they take, genuine Christian generosity and kindness will always be expressed with happiness and joy. We rejoice in God's gifts to us; let's also be joyful in happily sharing them with others.

"Joseph son of David, do not be afraid to take Mary home as your wife."

Illustration

All of us are getting ready for Christmas – perhaps this is our last chance to pause and reflect before the day itself. And so these may be very precious moments for us! Last-minute preparations feel both exciting and a bit stressful. Some of us will be trying to recreate for our children the excitement we remember from our own childhood Christmases years ago. Family traditions at this time of year are very special, and very important to us. As we decorate the house and dress the Christmas tree, as we hang up the stockings and leave out refreshments for reindeer, we may bring back happy memories from our own childhood days of giggling with excitement and picturing Father Christmas on his way.

As children we feel the slight tingle of fear, alongside the incredible wish to actually see Santa Claus coming down the chimney and leaving us all the things we have dreamed of and asked for. All our dreams are sweet, and every Christmas is special.

As adults, however, we may have a problem. The rush and the stress of getting ready for the feast, all of the efforts that we make to try to ensure that our Christmas celebrations are perfect, may get in the way of the meaning of what we are celebrating. And even when we try to focus on its real meaning, we may find that we have heard all the Christmas stories in church so often that they have become a bit like a fairy story. We hear of the census, the trip to Bethlehem, the "no room at the inn", the stable, angels and shepherds – all very familiar and rather comforting. Have we let them become just "traditional", like Christmas pudding and mince pies?

Gospel Teaching

Today's Gospel actually brings us back to a harsh reality. Joseph is facing a moral dilemma. Mary is expecting a child, and Joseph knows it is not his. He does not want to expose Mary to the full wrath of the law, but he also does not feel that he can continue with their betrothal and marriage.

Joseph hears what God wants him to do when an angel speaks to him in a dream: "Joseph son of David, do not be afraid to take Mary home as your wife." When he wakes up, Joseph does what the angel has commanded. He trusts God so much that all other considerations are put aside. Joseph listens to God, and makes the right decision, even though it is a difficult one. We do not hear much more about Joseph in the Gospels. But his character and his faith come through very strongly here. He is compassionate – he does not condemn harshly. He has the moral courage to seek to do the right thing, even when it is not necessarily what is laid down by the law. He discerns the right path forward by listening to what God wants.

Application

Christmas is a time of traditions, of excitement; of Santa Claus, chimneys, reindeer and presents. But this Christmas, let's try to listen to the real story of Christmas more closely and take the time to seek out God's voice among the incessant chatter and hubbub of everyday life. Could we love more compassionately? Are we too quick to condemn? Are we really always seeking out what God wants and trying to bring about God's will? Do we listen for the Lord's voice, or is it drowned out by all our own wants and wishes? We need not be afraid. We are all called to God's service; we all belong to God.

The feeling of having to do what somebody else wants often induces a resistance in us, because our ego is very powerful and very loud. But wouldn't we want more love, more peace, more joy? God is love, peace and joy, so if we mould ourselves to God's will then that is what we bring to the world. And ours is a world in desperate need, a world with its priorities firmly fixed on material wealth and status, a world where everyone appears to be "grasping" – holding on tight to everything they've got in the hope that it will bring them the peace they are so desperate for. We are called to a different way, a way of life where listening to the voice of God is our priority – somewhere in the chaos of Christmas, let's try to listen to the quiet voice of the truth of Christ's birth and what it means for us.

B

"The revelation of a mystery kept secret for endless ages."

Illustration

In the misery of a Nazi prison camp shortly before Christmas, a group of Christians turned to one of their companions. They wanted him to write something to celebrate the birth of Christ. He was the celebrated philosopher Jean-Paul Sartre, and his contribution took the form of a play in which the meaning of Christ's birth is presented through the eyes of Mary.

One of its main characters is a blind man, a would-be painter, who tries to explain what he would like to capture in his portrayal of her. "No woman", he comments, "has possessed her God… in such a way, a tiny God whom one can take in one's arms and cover with kisses, a God who is very warm and who smiles… a God who can be touched and who laughs. It is in one of these moments that I would paint Mary if I were an artist."

Poignantly, there's a way in which Sartre himself was unable to see, in the sense that he was a confirmed atheist. And yet, as a modern theologian has said, it is "a blind man [Sartre], more than anyone else perhaps, [who] has helped me to see the mystery of Christmas as portrayed in the Gospels".

Gospel Teaching

One of the most memorable of the Gospel stories is, of course, the one we heard this morning: the one that tells how the greatest event of all time took place at a particular date in history, in the midst of a particular people – a people who since before the days of King David had kept alive the conviction that a saviour would one day come. Above all, it took place in the person of a particular woman, a real woman who could be "deeply disturbed", who could feel afraid and yet who had an unbreakable trust in God, an overwhelming desire that God's plans should be fulfilled.

It is in Mary that God chooses to dwell: of her, God takes our flesh and blood; through her, in Paul's words, the great "mystery kept secret for endless ages" is revealed. It's Paul's way of telling us that in Mary's little house in Nazareth God's mighty plan for our salvation first began to be uncovered. In a sense it had been hidden away in God – it was God's secret – but now in the unborn child in Mary's womb it is being disclosed. God has become one of us, has entered into our humanity and our history.

But it is not just a romantic story: God's helplessness and fragility as an unborn babe reflect the helplessness and vulnerability that will one day be his again as he lies dying on a cross. He has come as saviour, and that means he has come to die; he has come for the whole human race, Gentiles as well as Jews. No wonder Paul cries out: "give glory therefore to him through Jesus Christ for ever and ever".

Application
Did the annunciation to Mary take place in the space of a few minutes, as the Gospel suggests? Or could we think of it as having taken place over the course of many months – even a couple of years? Unlike our busy world, which wants instant results, there is no rush with God; the one chosen is like a flower that opens up to the sun slowly, gently, without any kind of fanfare.

According to an old tradition, when the angel saluted Mary it was not in her home while she was at prayer but at the local fountain where she'd gone to draw water. And why not? It was through prayer and reflection, and also through the ordinary events of life, that she completed that first Advent, slowly growing into the sort of person God wanted her to be, living out the implications of her response to the angel: "You see before you the Lord's servant; let it happen to me as you have said." She invites us to follow her example, to put our lives at the Lord's service.

This is the time of year when the noisy world cries out: "Only four more days to go!", "Only three more days to go!" But Mary, the perfect Advent model, gently says: "Seek a little silence, be still, ponder in your heart." And if we do, we shall not be taken by surprise: we shall be ready to receive him who is our friend, our brother, our long-awaited saviour, the revelation of God's great secret.

"The moment your greeting reached my ears, the child in my womb leapt for joy."

Illustration

Amazing progress has taken place in our ability to view the unborn child as it develops in its mother's womb. From a certain stage in her baby's growth, a mother has always been able to feel the child moving inside her. Fathers too have been able to place a hand on the mother's stomach and feel their child as it kicks and jumps. However, ultrasound technology has revolutionised how people understand and think about human life in the womb. Now, rather than just feeling their child move, a mother and father can actually see it. They can watch as it sucks its thumb, as it turns and stretches. An incredible video called *Window to the Womb* even shows an unborn child doing somersaults inside its mother's womb!

It has also become common practice for expectant parents to be given ultrasound pictures of their unborn children. They rightly consider these to be the first photographs of their child. Sometimes they even put them in frames or save them in photo albums. They provide a record of the first nine months of life.

We now know that much more is going on in the womb than we previously imagined. We can see the unborn child living in harmony and security with its mother and, through her, with the outside world. Ultrasound enables us to see and appreciate what God has always known: the beauty and wonder of human life as it grows and develops.

Gospel Teaching

The meeting between Mary and Elizabeth, as recounted to us by St Luke, is often referred to as the visitation. But more is going on than just one expectant mother visiting another. Both of these women have been caught up into God's plan to send his Son into the world. Both women are pregnant. Mary carries the unborn Christ child in her womb; Elizabeth carries John the Baptist, the one who will announce his coming. Here, two women meet; and both of their lives have been touched in different ways by the Holy Spirit. They are crucial to God becoming Emmanuel, to God dwelling among us as one who is truly like us.

Yet, as well as two mothers encountering each other in this act of visitation, two unborn children also encounter each other. When Mary greets Elizabeth, the child in Elizabeth's womb leaps for joy. Both she and her unborn child know they are in the presence of the Lord. Jesus is there among them, hidden in Mary's womb. Mary is blessed because she is pregnant with the saviour of the world. Elizabeth rightly calls her the mother of the Lord: the fruit of her womb is the one who will take away the sins of the world.

We speak of God's coming to live a human life as the incarnation. This word literally means "taking flesh". It's a very physical reality; it's about God working in and through a real body and real people. The Israelites had long described God in human ways. Today the prophet Micah and the psalmist foretell how God would come as a shepherd, but one with divine power and majesty. In the same way, God would descend from heaven and protect the people like a gardener caring for a vine. God's hand would stretch over them. God had promised to be close to the people. In becoming one flesh with us, Jesus fulfils this promise, standing beside us. His physical body becomes the place where people can meet the living God, and in the sacrifice of that body on the cross our sins are forgiven.

Application
Very soon we shall be placing the child Jesus in the manger of our Christmas cribs. The figure of that tiny baby reminds us that God has not only blessed us by creating us but also chose to become one with us. God can work through human lives and make them extraordinary. Mary and Elizabeth had faith to believe God's promises; they were prepared to trust God's word.

The visitation is more than a nice story. It's an invitation to deepen our faith and trust in God's love. It's a call to recognise the presence of Christ in the people we meet and to allow Christ to shine through our often fragile human lives. Mary and Elizabeth were unique in what God asked of them. We too have a unique calling. As someone once said, we are all meant to be mothers of God, because Jesus needs to be continually born in our lives.

The Season of Christmas

"You will find a baby wrapped in swaddling clothes and lying in a manger."

Illustration

Not far from the Colosseum in Rome, and perched on the edge of what remains of the Imperial Forum, stands the Church of Ss Cosmas and Damian. This ancient building was originally a pagan temple and was converted into a church in the sixth century. For both tourists and pilgrims, it's a magnet. They come to gaze at the stunning mosaic of Christ flanked by the saints which adorns the ceiling behind the altar. But the church also houses another attraction. Near the entrance is a beautifully carved crib, originally from Naples and dating back to the eighteenth century.

Neapolitan cribs are not so much stables as hillsides. The one at Ss Cosmas and Damian fills a whole room. Whereas many modern cribs focus solely on the Holy Family, the shepherds and the kings, Neapolitan cribs show life in all its variety, its busyness and its ordinariness. Often, an entire village is displayed complete with streets, houses and shops. There are knife-grinders, shoemakers, blacksmiths and butchers. People are eating and drinking, chatting and shopping. Then, somewhere amongst all of this, almost hidden, there is the simplicity of the nativity scene. You have to look carefully to find it, but there in the midst of the world's activity a mother and father watch over a newborn child. Onto the stage of humanity has stepped the Prince of peace, the mighty God, the Word made flesh, our saviour.

Gospel Teaching

St Luke's account of Jesus' birth captures a timeless truth. In the words of the angel to the shepherds, the birth of Jesus is a sign for us. It's a sign of God's faithfulness, sending the Messiah long promised by the prophets. It's a sign that God has sanctified human life by becoming one of us in Christ, truly God and truly human. It's a sign that we never have anything to fear, that God is with us, Emmanuel, now and always.

Into the poverty of a stable, and the fragility of a human life, a saviour is born for us, wrapped in simple blankets and laid in a trough full of hay. His coming once in time is echoed again in our celebration. Into the poverty and fragility of our human lives Christ is born for us tonight. Into the poverty of war, of violence and of injustice, Jesus is born anew to bring peace, harmony and love. Into the fragility of sickness, anxiety and sin, he comes to minister healing, security and forgiveness. Into whatever is happening in our world or in our lives, Christ is born to bring reconciliation, to bring courage, to bring joy and new hope. This is the Good News that God destined to be shared by all people.

Application

In the traditional cribs of Naples it's not always obvious to the onlooker where Christ actually is. He's obscured by all the busyness of life, so much so that some of the characters carry on as if he's not there at all. It's into our often disbelieving world that Christ is born again this Christmas: to reassure us, to make us certain of who he is and where he is. Our celebration of Christmas reaffirms our faith that Jesus is the only Son of God, sent because God loves us, sent not to condemn the world but to bring it salvation. In Christ, God is with us always – in our fears and worries, in our losses and in all that makes us less than perfect. The presence and power of God may not always appear obvious to us, but are always there and at work. Sometimes we struggle to make sense of what happens. We find it hard to really believe that a loving God has all things in hand and holds us safely. This feast of Christmas invites us to renew our trust that God is with us in Jesus, at all times and in all places, dwelling within the crib of our heart.

As we reflect and gaze upon the nativity scene, let us be certain that the Christ who was born in Bethlehem is with us always. In the outstretched arms of a tiny babe we see the arms that grew to embrace the cross. In this new birth in a stable we see the one who was born anew by rising from the empty tomb. As we ponder with love, may the words of the angel host fill our minds and hearts: "Glory to God in the highest, and peace to all people on earth."

A B C

"For no reason except his own compassion."

Illustration

The story is told of a church organist who played devotedly for his parish for over fifty years. He then retired and moved to another district; but the parishioners were determined that his years of faithful service should be suitably acknowledged. A parish party was arranged at which a handsome cheque would be presented to the ex-organist. A huge crowd filled the parish hall, thanks to many weeks of extremely hard work by the organisers. It was only at the last moment that the embarrassing truth dawned on them – in the busyness of their preparations they had forgotten to invite the principal guest himself.

There's a sense in which that story is re-enacted every Christmastime. After months of hectic preparations for a grand celebration, many people seem to be unaware of the One in whose honour the celebration takes place: to all intents and purposes, he is not invited. The situation is highlighted in stationery shops that display shelves labelled "Christmas cards" and at the end a subsection entitled "Religious cards". The implication is that the latter group is intended for those extremists who want to drag religion into Christmas.

Gospel Teaching

However, as today's readings make clear, leaving Jesus out of Christmas is not simply a sad oversight. It's a tragedy. It means that we are bypassing the supremely important event in human history, bypassing God's extraordinary love for us, bypassing the dazzling destiny that awaits us. These truths are powerfully presented in today's excerpt from St Paul's letter to Titus. Titus was leader of the infant church on the island of Crete. Paul reminds him (and us) that the birth of Jesus is not just a romantic story of days gone by: it is an earth-shattering event which affects us still; it is the visible expression of God's "kindness and love". It is something totally undeserved by us, so that Paul can say that Jesus' coming was "for no reason except [God's] own compassion": there is no explanation for it other than God's boundless mercy.

Through Mary, Jesus Christ, our saviour, has taken upon himself our humanity in its entirety; he has entered into our history, become one of us. In doing so, he has made us heirs to his Father's kingdom. Christmas

Day is not only the birthday of Christ: it is our birthday, too, our birth into eternal life. How appropriate that the first recorded visitors to the newborn child of Bethlehem were a group of mountain shepherds, men generally regarded by their contemporaries as outcasts and ne'er-do-wells. Their presence shows, if ever we had any doubt about it, that there is a place for all of us at the stable in Bethlehem, no matter how small, how ordinary, or even how sinful we may be, provided only that we come with humble, loving hearts.

Application

Mary, always so alert to the ways of the Lord, is described in today's Gospel as treasuring and pondering in her heart the wonder of Christ's birth and the events surrounding it. Today we are invited to follow her example – to spend a little time pondering on the real meaning of Christmas, trying to appreciate what it means that our God should have such immense love for us. It is that prayerful pondering of God's compassion and generosity that inspires many people at Christmastime to try to offer their less fortunate sisters and brothers something of the divine love. And so, on Christmas Day, bishops often visit people in prison, some Christians call upon those who are sick and housebound, others look after those who are homeless, families invite a lonely person into their home for a meal.

Christmas is, for many people, a time of family celebration; and while such get-togethers can be gloriously happy occasions, a wonderful way to celebrate Christ's birth, it is no secret that they can be fraught occasions too, giving rise to tensions and worse. According to a Latin hymn, wherever there is love and loving kindness, there is God: the implication being that where such love is absent, so too God is absent. That is why we who appreciate the wonder of Christmas will do all in our power during this season to promote love and friendship and goodwill, wherever we may be. We'll do it not just because it makes life more pleasant all round, but because it is a way of ensuring that Jesus will indeed be present in the midst of our Christmas, his birthday celebrations.

"The Word was made flesh, he lived among us."

Illustration

One of the most distinctive things about human animals is that we have language: this makes us different from other creatures. It is so essential to us that we often forget how much a part of our nature it is. When we are babies, we are still learning, and don't have the words we have later on. By hearing our parents and family tell us stories of what we were like or what we did when we were young, we come to understand who we are and our place in the world.

Part of our identity, then, is built up with words and stories. When we are older we do all sorts of things with words, not just passing on information or describing. We can make agreements, we can give names to children or things, we can make jokes, we can create imaginary worlds in novels or poetry. We can encourage people and build them up; we can tell them that we love them. We can, in fact, be creative with language. When we are creative and create goodness, we share in the very creative power of God.

Since we live in a fallen world, however, we can also use words to cause hurt and darkness, instead of love and light. As the letter of James says, no one can tame the tongue; it can be "a pest that will not keep still", capable of deadly poison. As we are rational creatures, we need the truth to flourish; but often language is used to spread lies. This can be the case on a personal level but also on a much larger scale. Governments can deliberately lie to their people to retain power. So our words can be a force for very great good, and very great evil.

Gospel Teaching

From the very first words of scripture, we are told about the creative Word, Christ. Genesis tells us that the world was made when God the Father spoke his eternal Word: "God said, 'Let there be light.'" As the letter to the Hebrews tells us, throughout the history of God's people, God gave words to the prophets to announce the divine plan of salvation which would one day come about. As Isaiah puts it, the people of Jerusalem will one day "see the Lord face to face, as he returns to Zion". These words of God all point towards the great moment when God would reveal not only divine words, but the Word himself, the eternal Son of the Father.

The Gospel tells us the most important truth about God and us. God the Father does not only eternally speak the Word outside time, but the Word was sent into time to share our very nature. "The Word was made flesh, he lived among us." The Word, who is the source of our language, of our very existence, takes on our nature to speak with us, face to face. This is a sign of God's love for us. God creates and sustains everything there is in existence through the eternal Word. In the incarnation, however, the eternal Word becomes a baby who learns human language from his mother. As St Jerome wrote long ago, the eternal Word does not come to us in power and might but humility. His earthly life begins in the tears of the crib, and ends in silence on the cross.

Jesus, as the Word of God, is the source of our human language. As a human, he is also the fulfilment of our human language since by his very nature he is "full of grace and truth". Every word and action of his communicates truth and goodness.

Application
All babies are demanding; this is especially true of the Christ child in the manger of Bethlehem. By sharing his divine life with us, he challenges us to imitate him, to be "full of grace and truth". By living a sacramental life in the Church we hear God's saving words and make them part of our lives. We hear the words of Christ through which bread and wine are transformed into his own body and blood. Despite the complexity and troubles of our lives, we can be transformed too, to act and speak justly and creatively. Like Christ we can speak words of peace and mercy; we can pray for those who persecute us. We can become living words who make the presence of the eternal Word visible to the world.

A

"Get up, take the child and his mother with you, and escape into Egypt, and stay there until I tell you, because Herod intends to search for the child and do away with him."

Illustration

Posada is a Spanish word meaning "shelter". It is also the name of a Christmas commemoration popular in towns close to the border between Mexico and the USA. Neighbours play the roles of Joseph and Mary and go from door to door asking for shelter. Each time they are sent on their way.

"The Posada on the Border" doesn't simply recall the experience of the Holy Family seeking safety in Bethlehem and, later, on the journey to Egypt. It draws attention to the plight of modern-day migrants from Mexico trying to enter the USA. Many have crossed a hostile desert in scorching temperatures seeking security, jobs and a better life. Some have died in the wilderness and many border churches have erected monuments in their memory. Migration puts families under great pressure and they can be torn apart for years.

Recently, a Presbyterian minister in a church at the border described watching a young family, water jug in hand, begin a perilous trip across the Arizona desert. "The family – a man, a woman and a baby propped on her hip – were Mexican migrants desperate to flee and give the child a better life," he recalled. "Like Mary, Joseph and Jesus on their way to Egypt, they set out on a treacherous journey, vulnerable and poor," the minister added.

Gospel Teaching

Matthew narrates that, shortly after the birth of Jesus, Joseph was warned to prepare his family in the middle of the night and flee into Egypt to escape the persecution of King Herod. Their arduous journey was fraught with hazards every step of the way. There were several known routes for travellers to cross Sinai from Palestine to Egypt, but the Holy Family probably had to avoid the beaten tracks altogether, and pursue unknown paths. They would have picked their way, day after day, through hidden valleys and across uncharted plateaus in the rugged wastelands of Sinai, enduring the scorching heat of the sun by day and the bitter cold of the desert nights, all the time fearing for their precious infant – Herod might have sent assassins after them.

As we celebrate Christmas, we tend to forget the harsh side of the story. We underplay the fact that the pregnant Mary and her husband, Joseph, were turned away from the inn. We forget the slaughter of the Holy Innocents – and that the infant Jesus was spared their fate only through the hurried flight into Egypt where the Holy Family lived for some years as what today we would call "political refugees". Mary and Joseph were clearly strong for each other, raising Jesus in exile for several years before being given the all-clear to return home to Galilee.

Application

"The family of Nazareth in exile, taking refuge in Egypt to escape the fury of an evil king, are the model, the example and the support of all refugees compelled by persecution and need to abandon their homeland, their beloved relatives, their neighbours, their dear friends, and move to a foreign land" – so spoke Pope Benedict in his message for the World Day of Migrants and Refugees in 2007. There are Christian groups within our society, such as the Jesuit Refugee Service, who support migrants, but all of us can play a part in welcoming and assisting those forced to seek a better life in our country. Indeed, many of our parishes are blessed with the presence of migrants who have made their home among us. On this day, we reflect on the needs of migrant families and consider our own roles in promoting their welfare.

In this Christmas season we celebrate the incarnation, which is a divine border-crossing in which God became human to dwell among us. Jesus crossed borders throughout his ministry, with those of other regions, with poor people and rich people, with women, with children, with those in authority. His life began when no one would make room for his family. The rest of his life was spent making room for outsiders to be included in the fullness of God's love. We are called to follow this generous outreach to others.

And it is difficult to reach out in love to others without having the stability of loving relationships within our own families. We have the role model of the Holy Family, and we can all work towards holiness in our own families, recognising the sacredness in everything we do together – from our meals shared to our reconciliations after tensions. Through finding ordinary ways of deepening our relationship with our extraordinary God we become families of faith.

The Holy Family of Jesus, Mary and Joseph

"She believed that he who had made the promise would be faithful to it."

Illustration

Every night at bedtime young Michael likes to be read to. It is a lovely way to fall asleep, tucked up in bed, warm and cosy, with favourite toys beside his pillow. He even keeps his grandfather's dressing gown rolled up beside him in the bed. It is the dressing gown of a grandfather he never knew, who died before Michael was born. But Michael knows all about his grandfather and cherishes the contact with him that the dressing gown represents.

Surrounded by these tokens of love and security, Michael drifts off to sleep and to dreamland, while his father reads to him the adventures of Harry Potter, or the stories of Roald Dahl. Occasionally his father feels too tired to read, and then a war of words might ensue: "If you won't read to me tonight, then promise that you will read tomorrow night!" Extracting the promise is the guarantee that tomorrow all will be well and that the reading will resume. Children learn very quickly how powerful a promise can be, and that if a promise is made, then a promise must be kept. Faith in the future is founded upon the power of the promise.

Gospel Teaching

In the story of Israel's beginnings, the future of the nation is founded on the promise made by God to Abraham: "I will make you the father of many nations. Your descendants will be as many as the stars of heaven." Believing in the promise and trusting fully in God's faithfulness, Abraham set out for a future and for a foreign land. Both were given to him.

This story, told over and over again to succeeding generations, teaches us to have faith in God, to believe in the power of those promises, in that love and care for each one of us. The lesson is far from easy. For Abraham, at the time, it must have seemed impossible that he should have children, and that from him a great nation would grow. Abraham could see none of these things, but he believed in God, and God is the Lord of the future. In a little while a son was born to him, and the future had begun. The rest lay in the "far distance", but its time would come, and Abraham would welcome that. As Jesus said, "He rejoiced to see my day."

The great offspring of Abraham, the child of the future, was born to Mary and Joseph – Jesus Christ. In the name of the great nation of Israel, Jesus was welcomed into this world by the holy man Simeon and by the prophetess Anna. "Now I can die in peace," Simeon says, "just as you promised. For I have seen your salvation." The parents of this child, Mary and Joseph, stand there wondering at all the things that are being said. What will the future hold for this beloved son of theirs? What will the future hold for them? There is no way of knowing. Joy and sorrow, surely. Peace and pain. Worry and wonderment. Life gives us no guarantees or sureties regarding the weal and woe of this world. We will all have our fair share of suffering, a sword to pierce the soul.

But this we do know: that faith in God finds its expression in love, and lives of love will mean that our children will grow to maturity, with God's wisdom and grace upon them. A holy family is a family of faith, where love and tenderness abound; where people feel secure because others care about them; where people feel confident because others believe in them; where people feel hopeful because others encourage them.

Application

The child that was born to Abraham was called Isaac, and that name means "God smiles upon you, God is kind to you". It is a true description of children. They are the smile of God upon us. Now we too are children of God, and it is for us to show God's smile, God's kindness to the world. The signs are not hopeful. Wars and rumours of war fill the world, and terrible things are done. It is not easy to believe. We are invited to go into the foreign land of the future, believing in God's promises.

Young Michael looks forward to tomorrow. His past is wrapped safely in his grandfather's cloak. His present is protected by his parents' love. His future bursts out of his eager young heart. In our very being we are all the promise of God. And God keeps his promises.

C

"My child, why have you done this to us?"

Illustration

In the Holy Land, there is a basilica dedicated to Jesus the Adolescent. It is the chapel of a trade school run by the Salesians of Don Bosco, set high in the hills above Nazareth. Here teenage Palestinians are trained for a variety of occupations, including carpentry. The basilica is dedicated to a boy of their age and within it is a statue of the teenage Jesus. This is a rare sight. The notion of Jesus as an adolescent is one that is difficult for Christians to imagine. We are able to picture Jesus as a baby, and there are numerous images of Jesus as an adult, but a teenage Jesus, neither child nor adult, an adolescent Jesus, is somehow beyond our imagination. Why is this?

Gospel Teaching

In the Gospel today, Mary and Joseph have been with the twelve-year-old Jesus to the Temple in Jerusalem. It was a custom for all Jewish males to visit the Temple three times a year, to commemorate three major festivals: Passover, Pentecost and the feast of Tabernacles. By recording this journey, Luke shows us the commitment that Mary and Joseph had to the practice of their faith and their fidelity to its law.

Jesus, perhaps unwittingly, causes them huge anxiety when he goes missing. Such is his interest in spiritual matters that he stays behind in the Temple to continue talking to the elders. He seems oblivious to the concern of his parents when they express their distress at having lost him. As far as Jesus is concerned, he is doing what he simply needs to do. His words to his parents may seem rather brusque and dismissive: "Why were you looking for me? Did you not know that I must be busy with my Father's affairs?"

Apart from this story of Jesus in the Temple, the Gospels remain silent about his life between infancy and baptism. In this account Jesus is on the cusp of becoming a teenager, an unpredictable time when family life can be thrown into turmoil and confusion. Staying behind to talk "religion" is not, perhaps, the most predictable activity of a teenager.

Application

Sadly, we often hear only negative things about young people. The media portray knife crime, gang warfare and binge drinking as being what young people are about. Yes, of course adolescents can at times be remote, moody and argumentative – as, if we're honest, all of us can. But rarely do our newspapers report the magnificent things that young people are doing and are involved in and are thinking about.

Each stage of life has its own spirituality – teenagers don't simply fall into some spiritual black hole. This is the time when many are questioning assumptions and choosing to find their own way and practise their hopes for the future. Caring about the environment, oppression, the impact of natural disasters and atrocities – things that many young people are passionate about – are ways of expressing their desire for a world that is just and compassionate. Far from being spiritually vacuous, young people may have their own ways of praying and loving – briefer, more intense perhaps than the ways of those of us who are older, but possessing their own integrity. Just like people of any age they make mistakes and can be difficult, but they are as much in need of a sense of forgiveness and the love of God as the rest of us.

The "holy" family is a family that is willing patiently and lovingly to bear with each other at every stage of life. Knowing that Jesus was himself an adolescent is a matter for hope. It does not provide a blueprint of adolescent conduct but does confer infinite worth on this stage of life as on every other. If Jesus was as much at one with God in adolescence as in infancy and in adulthood, then it must be affirmed that there is, for all young people, the potential to have a life in relation to God that is no less complete.

As we celebrate this feast of the Holy Family, let us pay particular attention to the young people in our midst; and pray that as families and as a society we will have the confidence to embrace them warmly and generously and with understanding, remembering that we are all, as St John says, "the children of God". Those of us who are parents may have every sympathy with Mary and Joseph in today's Gospel. But let us see in each of our young people the face of the young Christ who himself wandered off, failing to tell anyone where he was.

"God sent his Son, born of a woman."

Illustration

The sound of gunfire and the noise of tanks could be heard. The Russians were coming! In East Prussia and Pomerania in 1945, the civilian population was being mercilessly brutalised by the avenging Red Army. After the suffering of Stalingrad, it was payback time. Stalin's men were heading for Berlin and Hitler's last days had come.

In a little village in Pomerania an old woman retired to bed for the night. As she settled down to sleep, suddenly the door of her bedroom burst open and a very drunk young Russian soldier came in. He signalled for her to get out of the bed so that he could sleep there. But the old woman refused. It was her bed. He could sleep on the floor, on the bedside rug. She would give him a pillow. Then the old woman put her hands together and began to say her prayers. The young soldier, too befuddled to argue, lay down and slept where he had been told.

That night two children of God slept soundly and peacefully, while all around them murder and mayhem were engulfing the world. The old woman, experienced in life, knew that she had nothing left in all the world save her faith in God. She was a child of God and would remain so until her dying day. The young soldier, sent out to capture and to kill, heard a mother's voice telling him what to do, and was happy to obey. A simple human interchange that night released both parties from fear, and reminded them of a humbler truth, that we are all God's children. For a brief moment in an hour of the world's madness, the blessing of peace and human communication settled on that house and gave its occupants rest. Tomorrow the guns would start again.

Gospel Teaching

Since those days of 1945 the guns have hardly stopped. War and the threat of war are never far away. In our violence we reveal a great truth about ourselves. We do not know who we are. We have no deep appreciation of what it means to be children of God. In fact, all the evidence of life seems to point the other way. We are strangers to each other. We have little in common and our friendships are very fragile. Whatever else we are, we are not children of God.

When the child of God, Jesus Christ, was born into this world, he would show us how to be God's true children. Great things were said about him at his birth. He would be a light of God's glory and a bringer of peace to people of goodwill. Listening to these things, Mary was given much to rejoice in and much to think about. This child of hers, so beautiful and so mysterious, would be her joy, her sorrow, her love, her life and a source of constant wonderment. This child is a son of God. From him Mary would learn many things, even as she taught him many things. In later years she would tell others, "Do whatever he tells you."

This child, Jesus Christ, born of Mary, in the fullness of time, teaches us how to live as God's true children. Creatures of God, we have been made in God's image, and we have been adopted as children. But, like all children growing up, we have to learn how to be good children, members of a family, brothers and sisters to one another. It takes time and it takes effort. We are called to heed the loving experience of our elders, the straight word and the occasional rebuke.

Application

When we were adopted as God's children, we were given the Holy Spirit to dwell in us. It is this Spirit that inspires us to say, "Our Father". The same Spirit will teach us how to treat others as brothers and sisters. We are heirs to God's promises, and God calls us to help one another to understand that.

The old woman in Pomerania had lost everything that makes life beautiful. But she had not lost her sense of herself. She knew she was a daughter of God. She prayed for the Lord's protection and spoke to the young soldier as though to her own son. It brought some sense into a senseless world, a moment of order into chaos, and truth into a world of lies.

May Mary, the Mother of God, teach us this same wisdom.

"We saw his glory, the glory that is his as the only Son of the Father, full of grace and truth."

Illustration

When something new is invented, we have an innate tendency to say, "It will never catch on!" People have said it about railways, the combustion engine, powered flight, television… the list is endless. Later, looking back, we find it hard to think of a world in which these inventions did not exist.

Human inventions have taken over from nature in providing us with the background to our lives. Even if we live away from town or city life, there is no escaping the hum of traffic, the vapour trails in the sky or the insidious presence of chemicals in our air, water and food.

Possibly one of our greatest inventions is our capacity to record all that happens around us. We began as human beings with the great gift of memory, and for a long time we relied on spoken traditions and copied practices to pass on our culture and beliefs. Then came the written word and pictures, codifying our lives but also continuing the work of imagination in art, poetry and song. Later came the world of radio, telephone and television. Now, with the microchip's extraordinary abilities, we can record everything and communicate everything. The question is whether this creative blitz, with all the power of modern technology, overwhelms our human receivers – our ears, eyes and feelings. How do we discern what is true and what is good in all this glittering world?

Gospel Teaching

The whole of John's Gospel is the evangelist's attempt to answer this question of discernment. Jesus is portrayed as the healer and teacher who embodies in himself the truth for which we search. As he says to Thomas at one point: "I am the way, the truth and the life." In the Prologue to his Gospel John summarises the historical sweep of this act of revelation. The Word was always in the world. It was there before the world began, intimately involved with its creation. It was there in creation itself, but people failed to recognise it, even though it was the life and light by which they existed.

John the Baptist came to announce that the Word was coming into the world in a new way. The Word became flesh. He became a human being, not through purely human action but by the power of God. He did this so that we in our turn might become children of God. If we accept him, if we believe in him, then we see and share in his glory.

In the stages of salvation the Law may have come through Moses, but grace and truth come through the person of Jesus Christ. In the Gospel, Jesus will fill out this unfolding story of salvation. He will show signs, he will heal, he will teach, each word and event pointing out how he offers us what God offers, calling us to believe in him so that we may have the gift of eternal life. This is our sharing in his glory, our being with him in the love he shares with his Father.

Application

We have different ways of knowing, different ways of understanding in our world. We have truths of the heart and truths of the mind. Ultimately they all come together in harmony, but from our very partial viewpoints the threads that link and unite may be invisible. We often see more easily the differences, the conflicts between beliefs, truths and convictions. This affects not just the way we think but the way we live. We may see the differences between ourselves and our neighbour as dividing us rather than building a new and greater unity.

However, in our celebration of the coming of Christ into the world we celebrate the unifying link between the threads. He is the one who brings the different colours of the spectrum into glorious unity. It is an act of faith that joins us to him, a truth of the heart that leads us to shape differently the truths of reason, heart and experience so that they blend rather than fragment. Each hand I touch is that of a friend, not an enemy. Each word I hear I use to increase my wisdom rather than to disown or disrespect its speaker. We uncover the mystery of God's love for us and in so doing discover the love that binds us together in our world. Once taken into this mystery we cannot let it go, for we have been taken into the mystery of God's own glory.

"We saw his star… and have come to do him homage."

Illustration

It is said that travel broadens the mind. It's one of the features of life in some parts of the world that people expect to have a holiday abroad at least once a year. These trips can be a welcome break from work, a change of scene, a chance to experience a different culture. Some holidays can be disasters, of course. There are many dissatisfied customers locked in legal battles with travel agents over horrible hotels, poor service or lost baggage. What we look for at such times is a bit of happiness, and it can be disappointing if the holiday does not live up to expectations.

Some people experiment with another sort of travelling: trying to "travel" into the future, or into another "dimension", by reading horoscopes or consulting mediums. People might be worried about the future. People might want to contact a deceased loved one to relieve their grief. Such activities are surprisingly common and often end in more sorrow. During the First World War many people who lost loved ones in those terrible battles turned to a booming but fraudulent clairvoyant and medium industry to look for comfort. Once again, the basic motive is happiness, the need for comfort and a desire for knowledge. It has to be said that a holiday is a more reliable and rational way of achieving happiness, if only for a short while.

Gospel Teaching

The wise men were both travellers and stargazers, but in a particular way. One of the main points of today's Gospel is that there is a real, fulfilling destination for everyone. In the Old Testament, God especially favoured the people of Israel, but with the promise that the Messiah would come for everyone. The magi represent those Gentiles who now come to faith in Christ. God's promises are for everyone; as St Paul says, we all now "share the same inheritance". The Lord prophesied by Isaiah has come, and all the nations flow to him. It is a celebration of the catholic, universal, nature of the Church.

There is a subtle addition, however. Isaiah talks about gold and incense among the gifts. But the magi bring one more gift – myrrh. Gold has been seen as indicating Christ's kingship; incense, his divinity. Myrrh, which was used to embalm dead bodies, symbolises the coming death of Christ.

So the journey to Christ and with Christ will involve us all in passing through death, but passing through death with the knowledge that Christ is waiting for us in eternity. So on the ultimate search for happiness, the search for God, we recognise that the journey is often a painful one. We may think that it is often an uncertain one too, when we cannot see the future but are called to trust in God.

Application

And yet, unlike many people in our world today, we do have the great advantage of knowing where we are going and how to get there. We have been given a glimpse of our journey's end. Even now, we have the knowledge that God loves us and became human for our sake. In the infant Christ we see the greatest example of God's providential care for all creation. Today's Gospel reminds us that it is not ultimately in this world that we will be happy but in eternity with God. The universe is not ruled by vague astrological or spiritual powers, but by the living God who creates and sustains everything there is. There is no magic or secret knowledge that fearfully governs our lives.

One early leader of the Church, St Ignatius, Bishop of Antioch, wrote about how many people believed in magic and the power of the stars to influence people's lives. Writing about the star of Bethlehem, he said:

"A star shone forth in heaven above all the other stars, the light of which was inexpressible… And all the rest of the stars, with the sun and moon, formed a chorus to this star, and its light was exceedingly great above them all… Hence every kind of magic was destroyed, and every bond of wickedness disappeared; ignorance was removed, and the old kingdom abolished, God himself being manifested in human form for the renewal of eternal life."

Let us pray for strength and hope for our journey, joy for our travelling and thanksgiving for the bread of life that sustains us on our way.

A

"This is my Son, the Beloved; my favour rests on him."

Illustration

On an October evening in 1958 Cardinal Angelo Giuseppe Roncalli – soon to be known the world over as Pope John XXIII – spoke of the shock he felt at being elected to the papacy. Yet, within a few hours, he was suggesting to his advisors that, on the very next day, he would visit the large prison, Regina Caeli, on the outskirts of Rome. It was gently suggested to him that there were one or two other things he might have to do first.

And so in fact it wasn't until Christmastime that the visit took place, but the new Pope quickly won the hearts of his prisoner audience. He told them that he had come as "Joseph your brother", and that a couple of his own relatives had done time in prison. "I want my heart to be close to yours," he told them. "I want to see the world through your eyes." Today those words are to be found inscribed on a plaque in the prison chapel.

It wasn't only what the Pope said, but the very fact that he was there, that he had come among them as one of them, that touched the hearts of many in his congregation: there were tears in the eyes of some of the prison officers, as well as in those of prisoners.

Gospel Teaching

Today we celebrate the fact that Jesus, God's own Son, has come into our world as one of us, has associated himself with sinners, has been baptised at the hands of one of his own creatures.

The baptism performed by John the Baptist was not, of course, the sacrament of baptism that we know. It was a ceremony by which people publicly expressed sorrow for their sins and a desire for God's forgiveness; but how remarkable that Jesus should have joined them, this crowd of sinners who lined the banks of the River Jordan waiting for their turn to be baptised! He, the utterly sinless one, has no need of such a ceremony and yet, without a moment's hesitation, he joins the queue, making himself one with sinful humanity; and he humbly seeks baptism from John.

John obviously senses that this shouldn't happen. "It is I", he protests, "who need baptism from you." But Jesus brushes the objection aside: "Leave it like this for the time being," he says, and goes on to explain that this is the way to fulfil "all that righteousness demands", all that God plans to do through Jesus. There is perhaps no better commentary on God's plan than the words of Isaiah in our first reading. Jesus is God's "chosen one", endowed with God's spirit, sent to bring "true justice to the nations", and always acting with gentleness and compassion, especially towards sinners: he will not "break the crushed reed, nor quench the wavering flame". Already, here at the Jordan, that mission has begun.

However, John must quickly have realised that his initial reluctance to baptise Jesus was not misplaced; for, as Jesus emerges from the Jordan, his body still glistening with water, the heavens are suddenly torn open. The Holy Spirit descends upon Jesus, and the Father's voice is heard, acknowledging him: "This is my Son, the Beloved; my favour rests on him."

Application
The prisoners, who rejoiced to see Pope John XXIII in their midst, were particularly moved by his reaction when one of their number, a murderer, fell on his knees before the Pope, crying: "Holy Father, can there be forgiveness for the likes of me?" Pope John's eloquent response was to raise the man to his feet and put his arms around him, like the father in the parable of the prodigal son, embracing his wayward boy.

Like the action of Pope John XXIII, Jesus' baptism carries a powerful message. His plunging into the waters of the Jordan, shoulder to shoulder with sinners, together with the wonders that followed, are a revelation of who Jesus is, God's beloved Son; but also of who he is for us, our saving Lord. Pope John Paul II called Christ's baptism a luminous mystery, a mystery of light. Standing as it does at the beginning of the year, today's feast is like a beacon of light, and its radiance is meant to journey with us in the months ahead, forever reminding us that Jesus is our dearest friend, he is our compassionate saviour, he is our loving brother.

The Baptism of the Lord

B

"Someone is following me, someone who is more powerful than I am."

Illustration

In 1947 a young Bedouin shepherd boy stumbled across a cave in the desert of Judaea. Inside the cave was a jar, and inside the jar was a scroll. Over the next two years, more and more scrolls were found and excavations began on a ruin near the same place. This has now become world-famous as the settlement of Qumran, with its Dead Sea Scrolls.

What do these discoveries have to do with us? The Dominican friars who excavated the site, and the scholars who examined the scrolls, concluded that in the period before and during the time of Jesus there had been a monastery of Jewish monks on this site, and they were the writers of the scrolls. The scrolls tell us a great deal about the religious life in Judaea at the time of John the Baptist and Jesus. They are copies of biblical books, and other works that tell us of the prayers of the community and their hopes for the coming Messiah. The monks led a disciplined life of prayer and work, and were obeying the words of the prophet Isaiah, "In the wilderness prepare a way for the Lord, make straight in the desert a highway for our God." They were carrying on the tradition of Elijah and Elisha, and the other sons of the prophets.

Gospel Teaching

This is part of the background of John the Baptist. He emerges from the desert wearing a prophet's habit to announce the arrival of the Messiah. This is why he is so prominent during Advent. But today there is another new beginning, the beginning of the public ministry of Jesus. John, in a way, represents the old covenant, which must now be fulfilled and give way to the new. Elsewhere, John says that he is the friend of the bridegroom, that Jesus must increase and John must decrease; John's mission is coming to an end as Jesus' ministry begins: "I have baptised you with water, but he will baptise you with the Holy Spirit."

This being the case, we might wonder why Jesus submits to being baptised by John. We believe not only that Jesus is God, the second Person of the Blessed Trinity, who creates and sustains everything there is; but also that, as a human, he is sinless, and had no need to wash for repentance. Traditionally, there are two answers to this. First, Jesus wished to be ritually washed by John to show full solidarity with us: like a good leader, he doesn't ask us to do anything he hasn't done himself. Second, by going down into the waters of the Jordan, he sanctifies the waters of the whole world, to make them fitting for his own life-giving sacrament of baptism, which he gives to us through the Church. John's baptism was in fact more like the ritual washing of the Qumran monks, not the full sacrament of baptism which Jesus instituted.

Application

One of the great strengths of the Catholic Church is its sense of history. Our faith goes all the way back to the time of Jesus and John the Baptist. It goes back to the monks of Qumran, to Elijah and Elisha, to Joshua, Moses and Abraham, who all believed in the divine Messiah, the one who was coming into the world.

Many of their adventures took place in and around the Holy Land. Moses led the people as far as the Jordan, and Joshua led them through it to enter the promised land. Elijah was taken up from Elisha beside the Jordan. This is one of the reasons Jesus goes there to be baptised: the Jordan stands between the desert and the promised land.

That symbolism is continued in the sacrament of baptism: through it we share the same faith as these ancient figures. Sacramentally, we cross the Jordan, go down into the Jordan with Christ, leaving the desert of this world, so that we can one day enter the promised land of heaven. Physically, of course, we still live in the world, in this desert. But we too can prepare a way for the Lord, by living out our baptismal vows, by letting Christ feed us in this desert with himself as heavenly food, by working with Christ to establish his kingdom of peace and justice. At his baptism in the Jordan, Jesus sums up all that history of salvation, and begins his public mission of preaching the kingdom. He passed that mission on to the apostles and the whole Church, and we carry on that mission today.

"Here is the Lord God coming with power."

Illustration

In 1977 and again in 2002, the British people celebrated important milestones in the life of the reigning monarch, Queen Elizabeth II. For both her silver and her golden jubilees, the queen travelled extensively throughout her realm, to cities, towns and villages in every part of the kingdom. As she did so, the various places she was to visit smartened up their appearance. Buildings were painted inside and out; flags and bunting festooned the streets; the national colours of red, white and blue were everywhere to be seen; new paths and roads were laid – in some places the tarmac used was even coloured a royal red for the occasion. And everywhere she went, the queen was greeted by large numbers of cheering crowds, jostling to get close, perhaps even to speak to her.

Gospel Teaching

There is something of that atmosphere in this feast of the Baptism of the Lord. Today's readings portray it as a royal visitation, a revelation of God to his people, a world-changing event. Isaiah gives a description of what used to happen when a king visited his people: everything was done to prepare for the king's arrival. The road along which the king was to travel was made smooth and level – valleys filled in and hills flattened to speed the king's journey and make his way easier. The arrival of the king is regarded as a joyous event, eagerly awaited by his people, joyfully heralded from the mountain tops. The king would come in power – as a victorious warrior. But to his people he was also a gentle shepherd, caring for those who were weak and needy – the "lambs" and "mother ewes".

These are the terms in which Jesus' first public appearance is portrayed. Indeed, Luke explicitly quotes this passage from Isaiah when he describes John the Baptist's ministry: John is the joyful herald preparing the way for the coming of the king. Luke emphasises that there is a feeling of expectancy among the people: the Baptist's ministry has heightened their awareness that something momentous is on the horizon. Then Jesus appears, but John is not even worthy to perform for him the task usually left to slaves: undoing the master's sandals.

There is a contrast between John's use of water as a symbolic cleansing, and the deeper reality of baptism by the Holy Spirit and fire, which Jesus brings. The depiction of the Spirit descending on Jesus and the divine voice acclaiming Jesus as God's beloved Son shows that everything Jesus does and says is in the power of God. As Son, Jesus is the most intimate and most perfect agent of God that there can possibly be. To say that Jesus baptises with the Holy Spirit and fire is the supreme statement of who Jesus is and what he does: he alone is able to confer the Spirit – the very life of God. He alone is able to purify, to burn away the sin and evil that separate us from God.

Application

Paul spells out what that means for us: baptism by water and the Spirit purifies us of sin and so makes us heirs of eternal life. This is the revelation of God's grace, God's love. Jesus' baptism helps us understand the meaning of our own baptism. However, perhaps we need to recapture something of the sense of expectation and joy of our baptism, by which God – the divine king – comes to us, not to visit, but to remain with us. The presence of God's Spirit ignites a fire in our souls, which burns away all impurity, and inflames us with zeal and a passion for the things of God. Through baptism, we too have become the sons and daughters of God, God's very own people, God's beloved, on whom God's favour rests.

Baptism is a true "Christ-ening", making us like Christ – making us other Christs. The Spirit given to us empowers us to reveal God's love and grace to the world. The Spirit enables us to be kingly, as Isaiah describes kingship: being victorious in the struggle with the forces of evil in ourselves and in our world; but also being pastoral – true shepherds to those who are weak, poor, needy. We can prepare for our kingly role through prayer – as Jesus prayed. Through prayer, we can reclaim our own baptism, that the Spirit's vitality and power may be stirred up and renewed within us, so that, like Christ, we can work for God's kingdom, know God as our loving Father, and offer our lives in service of others.

The Season of Lent

A

"Jesus Christ will cause everyone to reign in life."

Illustration

At the beginning of the American Civil War in 1861, a young Union soldier wrote a letter to his wife, as he prepared to go into battle. He spoke of the happiness he had found in marrying her, and of the joy of their life together. He considered the danger of his present situation and the strong possibility that he might very soon lose his life and say goodbye to this beautiful world. Faced with the threat of death, he expressed a fond farewell to his lovely bride and companion, and concluded his letter with these words: "And dear Sarah, when my last breath escapes me on the battlefield, it will whisper your name." A few days later he was killed in action.

This impulse in us to write farewell letters, letters of love to our dear ones when we are faced with death, is very strong. Our love is stronger than death, and, should we die, our words will reach our loved ones, and death will not be able to deny or to destroy such love.

Less than a hundred years after the American Civil War, other soldiers in another theatre of war set themselves to write letters of farewell and tenderness to loved ones left behind. As the great flotilla of the Normandy invasion fleet crossed over the choppy waters of the English Channel on D-Day, 6th June 1944, many men wrote their final letters to families, wives and sweethearts, to say goodbye and send their love, before they disembarked to enter the jaws of hell. So many of them met their end immediately; and their bodies littered the beaches of northern France. Their last moments may have been in the noise and smoke and darkness of battle, but their last thoughts and final messages were of light and love and a longing for home. Yes, love is stronger than death.

Gospel Teaching

In days long ago, the writer of Genesis considered these great antagonists – love and death. He was familiar with all their struggles and sought to tell their story in a way that was faithful to his experience.

The message of God's love could be seen in God's creation. This beautiful world is created out of love for us. It is a tremendous gift of God, and it is given to us, a Garden of Eden. But the beauty is marred and the joy is edged with sorrow, because of death. Death comes as the end. Not only death, but also the grievous sorrow, the spiritual death that comes wherever evil raises its ugly head: the serpent of sin that creeps in everywhere to destroy the peace and harmony of life. In the story of Adam and Eve, the ancient writer seeks to depict the history of humankind and the story of human unkindness, the story of evil. This evil touches every one of us in our lives, whether as affliction, circumstance, history, or personal temptation. We see in others "the evil that men do", and we feel in ourselves the terrible possibility of falling into such evil too.

Jesus, in his life, in his personal story and in his innermost self, was not spared the torment that temptation brings. His forty days in the wilderness bring him face to face with the evil one. His responses, when tested, give us a blueprint for wise and holy living. We do not live on bread alone, he says. We are spiritual beings, and we are called to live a spiritual life. We are not to tempt God, he says, but are to take responsibility for the conduct of our lives. We are called to worship God alone, he says, and not sell our souls to the devil.

In reviewing all this, St Paul paints a great drama of Adam and Jesus: Adam, the man who fell from grace and swamped the whole world in sin; and Jesus, the man who was raised on a cross, and raised higher than the earth, and who raised all of us up with him to heaven.

Application
As Jesus faces his own death and yields his spirit on the cross, as his dying breath escapes him, it whispers our name. His love is stronger than death, and his resurrection promises us life.

This is God's "love letter" to us, written on a cross, sealed in blood and opened in the resurrection. It is a letter to be read to all the world: "Jesus Christ has conquered sin and death."

B

"The Spirit drove Jesus out into the wilderness and he remained there for forty days."

Illustration

The noise of twenty-first-century living can prevent us from seeing our own true selves. That is why the remote Camas Centre was set up by the Iona Community on the Isle of Mull, off the west coast of Scotland. Geared towards young people, it encourages them to use the outdoors to assist their journey to spiritual awareness and to discern their role in the world. You can imagine teenage arrivals from the city trekking over moorland to reach a row of old quarry workers' cottages with no electricity, central heating, flushing toilets or running hot water. "How on earth am I going to get through a week here?" many complain as they offload rucksacks.

Yet, after a few days of food gathering in the garden, outdoor cooking, cutting and storing peat for the following year, and even emptying loos into the recycling system, most report to daily reflection sessions that they feel their spiritual life is developing. The closeness to nature makes them more aware of the loving God who created such a fruitful and diverse world. Squelching through the purple heather, they watch otters and red deer at play. Smelling the fresh sea air, they observe seals hunting for fish, gorgeous sunsets and mists rolling in off the sea. Listening to the flapping wings of golden eagles overhead, they find out a little about God's creatures.

It tends to rain a lot. When a rainbow appears after a shower, it is pointed out to the young people that the rainbow is the sign of God's covenant not only with human society, but with all living things.

Gospel Teaching

Jesus loved the natural world around him, embracing God's covenant with all of creation, highlighted in today's first reading. In the Gospel we hear that, in order to be fully open and receptive to his call, Jesus forsook the company of people and spent time with wild animals in the Judaean wilderness. At that time this would have been home to lions, leopards, bears, jackals, foxes and all kinds of antelope – this was before humans had driven most of these creatures into extinction in the Near East. It was here in the wilderness, away from human society, that Jesus came to accept and appreciate the messianic ministry he was about to embrace.

The natural world played a key role in Jesus' teachings and life. He regularly returned to the hills to pray and commune with the Father, especially before making important decisions. Much of his teaching ministry was carried out in the cathedral of nature. The Beatitudes and subsequent teachings were delivered on a mountain, and the miracle of the loaves occurred in a "lonely place". A lot of his teaching, and many of his miracles, took place on and around the shores of the Sea of Galilee. Just as God safeguarded all living things by ensuring each species had sanctuary on Noah's ark, Jesus announced a kingdom that is "good news" to the whole world.

Application

Lent is a time of repentance and new beginnings. This Lent, let us look at the signs of our times, particularly the damage being done to the community of living things on Earth by destructive human behaviour. Wilderness areas throughout the world are under threat – from Antarctica to the Himalayas to the peatlands of Europe and Asia. Human-induced global warming is disrupting agriculture and causing drought and flooding. Almost a quarter of the world's mammals currently face extinction, along with many ocean fish species. These are God's beloved creatures and express God's presence, wisdom, power and glory. Human well-being, including the spiritual dimension, is greatly impoverished as they and their habitats diminish. Organisations such as Christian Ecology Link and the Live Simply campaign can tell us about the many issues, and encourage us to get involved in working for environmental justice.

Who doesn't smile and feel hopeful when they see a rainbow? The next time you spot one, perhaps it will prompt a new sense of humility and a sense of awe that God's creation is so bountiful. This Lent, let us draw on two Christian virtues – generosity and frugality. Generosity calls us to share Earth's riches with all humanity and be more sensitive to the common good of the whole community. Frugality means opting for a new way of life based on simplicity and sufficiency rather than endless consumption and the accumulation of material possessions. Above all, let's pause and consider our own place in, and our responsibility for, God's good creation.

"The Lord heard our voice and saw our misery, our toil and our oppression; and the Lord brought us out of Egypt with mighty hand."

Illustration

On a hot, sticky summer's day, an American boy of around seven years old stands beneath the imposing figure of Abraham Lincoln. Milling around him are thousands of fellow pilgrims who have come to the Lincoln Memorial in Washington, DC. In this temple of dazzling white, the focus is an enormous statue of Abraham Lincoln seated on a huge chair looking out like a sentinel towards the Capitol where Congress and the Senate meet. Awed by this impressive spectacle, the young boy asks his mother who the man is and why there is a statue of him. His mum tells him of the terrible Civil War that ripped the country apart as it fought over the meaning of the words "all are created equal". Slavery needed to be overthrown and Lincoln was the one who led the oppressed to freedom. There, at the feet of the statue, a young boy discovers for the first time the history of his people and glimpses part of his own story.

About a quarter of a mile away there is another memorial. The Vietnam Veterans Memorial is unobtrusive, a simple wall of black stone upon which thousands of names are inscribed. Each name represents a life lost in the war. The memorial does not celebrate the war but rather cherishes some of those who were victims of it. Here, people are filing past with a sombre dignity and respect. Older men and women are placing flowers where a loved one's name is written. Some are crying, while others explain to the younger generation about the loss and tragedy of war. At this memorial the story is retold and the cry is: "Do not forget."

Gospel Teaching

As the people of Israel enter the promised land, they are given explicit instructions from Moses about what to do. First of all they should offer a thanksgiving gift to God, and then tell the story of their deliverance from Egypt. This story is to be announced in a similar way to our profession of faith in the Creed. "We were wanderers in the desert. In Egypt we multiplied but were oppressed. God acted mightily to free us from tyranny and led us through the wilderness to this land of milk and honey." This proclamation is not a one-off event. It is to be the constant reminder to Israel of its source, its history, its identity and its destiny as God's people.

When Jesus is at his lowest ebb in the desert, exhausted, disoriented and hungry, the tempter appears. In a mocking tone he challenges Jesus' self-understanding – who he is and how he relates to God and other people. The tempter seeks to distract Christ from his mission by encouraging him to trust in his own power to transform stone into bread. Jesus is tempted to lose sight of his intimate relationship with the Father, and is tempted to abandon the Father and his mission by worshipping the forces of darkness.

Jesus resists these advances. He calls to mind and proclaims the story of liberation proclaimed by faithful Jews down through the ages. "Serve the Lord your God alone; we do not live on bread alone; do not put God to the test." The story of Israel, the story of God's saving activity and faithful presence, is the bedrock upon which Jesus lives his life. From this story he discovers who he is and receives the energy to resist any distortion that the tempter would foist upon him.

Application

All of us are called to base our lives upon the story of our salvation in Jesus Christ. Nations have their founding stories from which they draw their identity and purpose. We, as followers of Jesus Christ, have a revolutionary founding story – each one of us is created in love, is redeemed by love and is united to others in love.

This Lent we have the opportunity to repent – to turn away from any voice that has distracted us from our life of faith. We have the opportunity to retell the story of Jesus Christ, to retell our own story by reading and meditating upon the scriptures. Perhaps we could spend time each day reading a small portion of the Gospel and allowing this story to become our foundation. We have the opportunity this Lent to remember who we are and what our destiny is. The little boy was caught up in his country's story; those who visit the Vietnam memorial are urged never to forget. In the life of Jesus Christ we discover our own story – may we make this our top priority during this holy season.

A

"He abolished death, and he has proclaimed life and immortality."

Illustration

It was a bright Easter morning in O'Connell Street in Dublin. A young couple were walking down the street. It was their honeymoon. They were married in April 1944, but they had to wait until now, Easter 1946, to begin their married life. The young man, a soldier, fought on the beaches of Normandy on D-Day in June 1944, and survived the war to come back home to "Civvy Street", as they called civilian life. The young woman had worked in munitions factories during those war years, and now was returning with her husband to visit family in Ireland for the first time as a married woman.

As they walked down that famous Dublin highway, a street photographer suddenly picked them out and took their photograph. The picture that they collected next day shows a crowded sidewalk, and a shy young couple with sunshine on their faces. It was a sunshine time of life for them. War was over, and family life was about to begin. Four children came along in the ensuing years, much joy, some heartache, many blessings. When that young man died, forty-four years later, his children made copies of that special photograph, to keep as a record of the day it all began.

The photographer had caught a special moment. It was not a posed photograph, but the capturing of a moment, as Dublin life bustled all around, and a young couple strolled along, with sunshine on their faces, looking into the future with bright hope and happiness. The moment is full of life, and of the promise of all that can be.

Gospel Teaching

When Jesus goes up the mountain with his three disciples, a special moment in time is about to be captured. There on the mountain the brightness of God shines out in the body of Jesus. It is a glimpse of all that can be, the promise of future glory. It is a vision of heaven, of a land that God will show to us. There was no camera, no photographer to catch this moment, but it is caught in the eyes and in the memory of those disciples. Peter, especially, will have occasion to write it down and hand it on to us as a precious possession. In a letter bearing his name, written many years later in Rome, Peter says, "We were with him on the holy mountain."

Not only did those disciples see the glory of Christ, but they heard the voice from heaven say, "This is my Son, the Beloved; he enjoys my favour. Listen to him." This is a special moment of revelation. These disciples have seen and they have heard something very precious. The sight they saw is a vision of the land that God promises to us, the glory of heaven. The words that they heard tell us the real identity of Jesus of Nazareth. He is the Son of God in our flesh.

When the moment is over, the group leave the mountain and return to earth. They return to the life that must be lived day by day in this troubled world. But they now bring with them that vision of a world to come, and that confirmation of the truth of Jesus Christ. There will be many joys and many sufferings to come, and the shock and scandal of the cross will test their faith to the limits, but they will never forget what they have seen and heard. That vision and that Good News they will hand on to us.

Application

St Paul belongs to that first generation of believers. He proclaims the great truth about Jesus: "He abolished death, and he has proclaimed life and immortality through the Good News." That is why we journey in faith. That is why we bear the hardships of life: because, in Jesus Christ, we have seen a glimpse of the "promised land". We have seen what lies ahead. Not death and disaster, but life everlasting in the presence of God.

Abraham was called away, to leave home and family and the land of his birth, for "the land that I will show you". That land we have now seen, in the face and form of Jesus Christ. So we journey through this life in a great faith. Let us hear the Lord's words to us today, the same words that he spoke to the disciples on that holy mountain: "Stand up. Do not be afraid." In the journey of our own life through this world, may Easter sunshine fall on our faces.

B

"It is wonderful for us to be here."

Illustration

Shortly after his appointment as Archbishop of Westminster in 1976, Cardinal Basil Hume was questioned by journalists. "What", they wanted to know, "is going to be your number one task?" His answer must have taken them by surprise. It wasn't to work harder for the reunion of all Christians; it wasn't to build more Catholic schools, or to fight against materialism, or to provide more aid for the people of the developing world. "I want", he said simply, "to do everything in my power to convince people that God loves them."

An unexpected answer but a magnificent one. There is no more exciting truth than this – that God loves us, that God loves me. I don't have to persuade or cajole God: God loves me already, just as I am; and nothing can change that. It's a message that rings out from the readings we've heard this morning, especially from the excerpt from the letter to the Romans. There, St Paul points to the most convincing proof of God's love: the fact that, for our sakes, God did not spare his own dear Son but allowed him to die in anguish. In the light of this, Paul says words to the effect of, "How could you ever doubt his love?"

But let's be honest: we wouldn't need such assurances if it were not that there are times when we are not too sure. It seems, it feels, as though God doesn't love us at all – or, at any rate, doesn't love us as much as God ought. What must Abraham have thought as he set out on his journey, convinced (even if mistakenly) that God wanted him to do the craziest thing – to sacrifice his only son, the boy he'd always hoped and prayed for, the son in whom all his hopes rested? Mustn't he have tussled with doubts about God's love for him – and for the boy? Of course, in the end God did intervene.

That doesn't always happen, however. All too often there's no divine intervention: tragedies happen, dear ones are snatched away from us. If God loves us, it might be argued, God certainly doesn't pamper us. Could that be because God knows that it's only by passing through dark and difficult times that we can mature as his sons and daughters? In any event it is certain that God does love us, and that therefore there is nothing that cannot work out for our ultimate good.

Gospel Teaching

In today's Gospel three apostles see the Lord transfigured in glory. They are delighted; and who wouldn't be? They've caught a glimpse of who and what their Master really is. "It's wonderful," they murmur, "just wonderful to be here. Let's stay here; let it always be like this. Let the good times last."

But the next time they see their Master transfigured, how different it will be! He will be lying prostrate in the garden of Gethsemane, his body bathed in sweat. How hard then for them to believe that this is indeed the only Son of God, the well-beloved one. But a little patience, just a few more days, and that same Jesus, now ablaze with risen glory, will stand before them; and on that Easter Sunday morning they will realise that their doubts were unfounded. God will prove his love for his Son in a way they could never have imagined – not by saving him from suffering and death, but rather by enabling him to conquer them and finally by raising him up from death itself.

Application

When we're given assurances of God's love for us, as we are today, that's like being with the apostles on the mountain of transfiguration. When we meet with tragedy, when we feel driven almost to the point of despair, finding it hard to believe that God does still care for us – that's like being with the apostles in the garden of Gethsemane.

And yet if we keep on trusting in God, keep on having patience even though God appears to have forgotten us, then for us, as for the apostles, there will be an Easter Sunday. On that day we shall be convinced, we shall know, that God does indeed love us and always has, not least in those dark moments when God seemed so far away. Then, like Peter, we shall murmur, "Lord, it's good for us to be here." Only this time the joy, the thrill, the ecstasy will never grow dull: we shall have reached the destiny for which we were made.

C

"Master, it is wonderful for us to be here."

Illustration

Alison had never been to Ireland before. Now, on holiday with her husband and brother-in-law, she was driving along the road that leads from the town, down past the harbour, to the sea. Suddenly, as the car came round the corner, an island came into view, sitting proudly in the shimmering blue sea. It was a warm and sunny afternoon in August, and the smell of the sea and the fragrance of meadow grass were everywhere: a rich aroma to match the magnificence of the scene before their eyes.

They stopped the car and got out, and sat on the stone wall that stopped the road from falling into the sea. "Oh my!" said Alison. "I could stay here for ever." It was one of those special moments when all the beauty of the world is revealed at once. The earth and sky and sea, the warm wind and the fresh air, the flowers and the animals and the birds, the island in its stillness, the water in its constant motion. Everything spoke at once, in unison and in harmony, of the loveliness of life. And those three friends were there, to witness the wonder and to share the blessing.

Gospel Teaching

Two thousand years before, on a mountainside in Palestine, three other friends found themselves witnesses to a wonderful sight. Peter, James and John had climbed Mount Tabor with Jesus. This mountain, rising six hundred metres above the green Galilean countryside, gives back stunning, panoramic views to all who make the climb. But on this occasion it was not the earthly view that captured the attention of the climbers. It was a vision of heaven, a vision of a world beyond our sight.

There, on that lofty summit, away from the everyday noise, Jesus in prayer was transformed before their eyes. The aspect of his face, the texture of his clothing, all became a shining brilliance. Moses, the lawgiver, and Elijah, the prophet, were with him, talking about strange, dark events to come. But here and now, in that moment, everything was wonderful. Peter wanted to capture the moment, to make it stay for ever. A voice was heard that confirmed for them what they were seeing with their eyes: "This is my Son, the Chosen One."

Coming back down the mountain, the three disciples kept quiet about what they had seen and about the voice that they had heard. As for the ominous conversation that they had overheard, that was beyond their understanding at that time. Only later, when they had witnessed Jesus' sufferings in Jerusalem, did those words come back in all their stark reality.

Listening to this story today, we are the inheritors of the disciples' faith. What they have seen and heard has now become our gift and possession. They have told us the story, they have shared with us their vision and experience, and it now belongs to us. By the gift of faith, we have heard the Father's voice and have come to know his beloved Son. This is the power of faith. In those disciples we were present on the mountain to witness the beauty of Christ.

Application
The world we live in, particularly in the West, is an agnostic world, a world that does not know about God. This is not to criticise the world, merely to describe it honestly. Not everyone goes up the mountain. Yet many people who have no religious faith have a great belief in the goodness of life and an instinct to live their lives in the service of others. Deep within us all, God has planted the yearning for what is good and true and loving. People live for that and search for that. This is an instinctive faith in the goodness of the world, even as we know how dark and ominous it can be.

For us, such instinctive faith has been made clear by God's gift. We believe in Jesus Christ. We see God's glory in the beauty of his face. We hear God's truth in the sound of his voice. We feel God's love in the joy of his presence. We know, as Paul reminds us today, that our bodies will be transformed into copies of his glorious risen body. So, then, let us remain full of faith, and let the light of faith shine in our world.

"If you only knew what God is offering."

Illustration

First impressions last. When we meet someone for the first time, we immediately begin to weigh them up. We pick up the signals. Is the smile sincere? Is the person loud or timid? Is their character confident, happy, interesting? Is this someone worth knowing?

Some people seem able to gain an accurate impression of an individual after only a few seconds, whereas for many of us those initial impressions can prove very wide of the mark. We all know at interviews how those first moments can be decisive in creating a good impression. So we prepare carefully: we dress appropriately; we make sure of eye contact with our interviewers; we give a firm, confident handshake; we smile, just enough; we make sure we remember our interviewers' names. We try to communicate the kind of person we are, and hope that this will be what is wanted. A favourable first impression might well tip the balance and get us that job, or win a contract, or gain a new friend.

Gospel Teaching

When Jesus met the woman at the well, they both made fairly quick assumptions about each other. The woman was instantly able to see that Jesus was a Jew, and so her natural expectation was that he would not want anything to do with her. In this, her first impression was wrong.

Jesus, in turn, was able to gain an impression of the woman – and a very accurate one at that. It was midday. Drawing and carrying water is heavy work, not normally carried out in the heat of the day. Not, that is, unless a person is an outcast, someone with something to be ashamed of. Jesus quickly works out exactly why the woman is there at that time: she is living in an adulterous relationship. She would be looked down upon by the decent people of the village, who would not associate with her in any way.

Jesus proves the woman wrong in her assumptions about him. He doesn't share the prejudices of his people, or others' judgemental attitudes. He very gently leads her on a journey of discovery. He shows that he knows who – and what – she is. He shows that he accepts her, will not condemn or dismiss her. He gives her time, treats her with respect, acknowledging her dignity. He makes her an offer, which entices her, but which she misunderstands: "Give me some of that water, so that I may never get thirsty and never have to come here again," she says.

Patiently, he leads her to a deeper understanding of what he is offering. He is not put off when she brings up the differences between her people and Jesus' own traditions. Then, when she is ready, Jesus reveals who he is, in response to her intuitive remarks about the Messiah. Finally, she is so taken with Jesus that she spreads the message and brings others to meet him, so that they also can spend time with the Lord and come to experience for themselves who he is.

Application

This story is a pattern of every believer's journey in faith. Like the woman, we too meet the Lord with our flawed personalities, our weakness, our history, our skeletons. We find in him not rejection or condemnation but acceptance and love. When we meet the Lord, we do not instantly find that we understand everything, that we have a fully developed relationship with him. Faith takes time. We misunderstand or only partially understand. We grow in our knowledge and love of him, of who he is and what he means to us.

Like the woman, we ask questions. We grapple with the consequences of our faith in Christ – what it means for our lifestyle, our values, our relationships, our priorities. He is patient with us, and as we persist, as we spend time with him, so his offer of living water begins to become a reality. We come to that spring of water more and more frequently – to be refreshed and quickened by him, as we meet him in prayer, in the sacraments, in his word, in day-to-day life. We become changed by this contact. And then the most natural thing in the world is to share that good news with others, to bring them to Christ, to let them experience for themselves the salvation that he offers. And in so doing, like that woman, we become reconciled with others, part of a community once more, a community of people who experience that Jesus is their saviour, and the saviour of the world.

B

"Destroy this sanctuary, and in three days I will raise it up."

Illustration

Sister Dorothy Stang was a woman driven by love – love for the Amazon rainforest and the poor people for whom it is their home. For nearly thirty years she worked with the Church's Pastoral Land Commission in Brazil, helping poor farmers and their families to stand up to the big businesses that plunder the forest. Already twenty per cent of the Brazilian rainforest has been destroyed, affecting global climate change and leading to the extinction of thousands of species. Cedar and mahogany trees are felled to make room for vast ranches of cattle, which soon erode the thin layer of soil, turning it barren.

Sister Dorothy was not afraid, despite numerous death threats against her and the knowledge that scores of others had been murdered by agents of the loggers. For she wanted to be a sign of hope, whatever happened to her personally. In February 2005, the gunmen came for her, killing the seventy-four-year-old American nun with six shots at close range.

Gospel Teaching

To say that Jesus loves deeply is to misuse language. He does not just love, he is love. His love for his Father informs everything he does, whatever the risks to his personal safety. Driving out the Temple money changers and sellers of animals was a bold action that works on many levels.

At the simplest level, the dignity and holiness of the Temple, God's dwelling place, had been compromised. Money changers and sellers of animals for sacrifice had been permitted to set up their stalls in the Temple's very precincts. This insult to the Father's honour could not be borne by his Son.

But, at a deeper level, Jesus' expelling the traders is a sign that an Old Testament prophecy is being fulfilled, for in the time when God's kingdom is to break into history "there will be", as the prophet Zechariah says, "no more traders in the Temple". The prophet Malachi too foresees that, on that day, "the Lord you are seeking will suddenly enter his Temple". The Messiah's reign begins publicly, in John's Gospel, with this powerful symbolic act – and, significantly, it begins right in the heart of God's house. This very house will no longer be a building of stone, but the person of

Christ and the body of Christ which will be his Church. Jesus is declaring through his actions that the messianic age begins right now with him. From now on there will be no need to exchange Roman money for Temple coins to buy animals for sacrifice. For after Christ's death on the cross no animal will ever again need to be sacrificed. His sacrifice will be sufficient for all time.

John places this scene at the beginning of Christ's ministry, whereas the other Gospels feature it later. John wants to show that this claim of Jesus of ushering in the messianic age, connected with the reference to his resurrection, is the key to understanding the whole of the rest of the Gospel. He also hints at the price Jesus will pay, the inevitable retribution from the religious leaders. So the shadow of the cross and the victory of the resurrection are both woven into this remarkable story, as they will be throughout the Gospel's account of Jesus' life.

Application

Like Jesus, Sister Dorothy risked her life for love and, like Jesus, she paid the price. Standing up for what is right and true, being prepared to speak out and act, is always going to be a threat to powerful forces. When they are challenged by individuals who love greatly, the world's great controlling powers – commerce, religion, politics – lash out and cut them down. But the spirit that gave these individuals the capacity to love cannot be cut down. The proof of that is Jesus' resurrection, and his spirit living in people like Sister Dorothy.

On a personal level, we can allow Jesus to overturn and throw out the money changers and animal-sellers in our own lives. That means that whatever despoils the dwelling place of God within each of us needs to be rooted out and destroyed. For us to be fit temples of the Holy Spirit, we are called to purify ourselves of our sins and selfishness – and that may require us to be as tough and bold on ourselves as Jesus was on the traders. Then, perhaps, we will be able to exercise something of the love for God and for others that we see in the life of Christ and of his saints.

C

"I mean to deliver them."

Illustration

The schoolteacher takes his class out of the classroom and walks them down to the imposing entrance hall of the famous old school. There he gathers his students around the photographs of students from years gone by – students who are by now long since in their graves. He gets the students to lean in to listen to what the boys in these old photos might have to say to his current students, who have their whole lives before them. "Can't you hear what they're saying to you?" the teacher whispers. "They're saying 'Carpe diem'. Seize the day, boys, seize the day."

That powerful scene from the film *Dead Poets Society* encapsulates that piece of ancient wisdom: Act now. Life is short, don't waste it. Use the opportunity life offers to you today. Who knows what tomorrow might bring? Grasp the moment. Seize the day.

Gospel Teaching

Today's readings all focus on that piece of wisdom. But curiously, in the first reading, it is the Lord himself who seems to be seizing the day. He has heard the sighs and wailing of his people. "I have seen… I have heard… I am well aware of their sufferings," God tells Moses. And so the Lord will seize the day, he is going to act on behalf of his people: "I mean to deliver them… and bring them… to a land… where milk and honey flow." From the human point of view, it is almost as if the Lord has woken from slumber, heard the cries of his people, remembered who he is: "I Am who I Am… the God of your fathers" – the Lord who has made a covenant of love with his people. And now God is going to act on that covenant.

Jesus has a very strong sense of God acting now – that the day has come. Jesus knows that, through him, God is acting to bring that covenant of love to its fulfilment. Through Christ's passion, death and resurrection, God is about to act to set all people free. And because the kingdom of God is so close – because God is acting in such a dramatic way in the person of Jesus – time is short. People have to make a choice, they have to seize the day, make a decision. In this curious passage, Jesus refers to some topical tragedies – the people killed in an accident, the Galileans who suffered such a terrible fate at the hand of the Romans – and Jesus warns people not to think that these victims did anything wrong. Rather, Jesus advises that what happened to them should be a warning: there is a far worse fate going to overtake anyone who refuses to repent.

What is at stake is eternal life. This passage concludes a whole series of warnings in which Jesus invites people to respond with urgency to his call. He tells them: "Seek God's kingdom... Let your hearts be girded and your lamps burning... Be ready for the master to return... Read the signs of the times... Settle with your accuser beforehand, lest you end up in prison." There is an urgent need to repent, Jesus tells his audience. Seize the day, time is short, act now to be saved.

Application

Seize the day. Repent. Lent is the time for us to respond to that urgent appeal of Christ. Such repentance is not simply a one-off event, but is a way of life, a daily turning of the whole of our lives to the Lord, who alone can lead us to the promised land of eternal life. Paul reminds the Corinthians to act in ways that are fitting for a repentant people. He recalls that even though the people of Israel were freed from Egypt – indeed, had a kind of baptism and spiritual communion with Christ – nevertheless, their continued disobedience meant that they perished in the wilderness: only their descendants reached the promised land.

The warning is clear: though we Christians are baptised and eat the spiritual food and drink that is Christ, we must be careful not to fall. True repentance means leading a life that reflects that communion with God. Remember the fig tree: if it fails to bear fruit, it will be cut down, removed from the vineyard, which is the ancient symbol of the promised land. In this season of grace, God is acting. We too should act now to seize the day, by turning back to God who leads us to the fullness of life.

A

"The man said, 'Lord, I believe', and worshipped him."

Illustration

Everyone told her that one day it would happen, but Karen was struggling so much with the language that she doubted it was going to happen for her. Karen was spending the summer in Paris studying French. She had always prided herself on her ability with languages, but after a few days among the Parisians she realised that her French was not nearly as good as it appeared in the classroom.

She was given much encouragement from those around her, and was constantly being told that eventually she would dream in French and it would all fall into place from then on. Every night she went to bed, praying this would be the night. Sure enough, after several weeks the night came and she dreamt in French; her brain was no longer translating from English into French. Finally, the penny had dropped and the language was coming naturally.

Gospel Teaching

Characteristic of St John's Gospel is the fact that the story operates at several different levels. There is the obvious recounting of the facts of a simple story and then there is the deeper theological message that gives real meaning to the story.

Initially the story begins with the disciples trying to understand who is to blame for the man's blindness. It was commonly understood that someone with a serious ailment could attribute it to the sins of their forebears. Sickness and disability were equated with God's displeasure and therefore regarded as a punishment. In today's passage Jesus sweeps this misconception aside and turns the popular perception on its head, saying that the man's blindness will be used to show the glory of the Lord, not the Lord's displeasure.

The story progresses as one might expect: a man has been born blind, Jesus restores his sight, people doubt he was blind in the first place, an investigation takes place, people struggle to understand what has happened. Apart from Jesus, the only person in the story who really understands what has happened is the blind man himself, although his understanding comes gradually. St John is not concerned primarily with the man's physical blindness but with his spiritual blindness and subsequent enlightenment.

Gradually the man understands. When he is first asked who cured him, he says, "The man called Jesus". When the Pharisees question him, and ask what he has to say about Jesus, he replies, "He is a prophet." Finally, when Jesus speaks with the man, the man born blind comes to the knowledge that Jesus is Lord and he makes his profession of faith, "Lord, I believe."

Application

St John recognises that each member of the Christian community struggles with spiritual blindness during their spiritual journey. Coming to know the Lord can be an instantaneous experience, like that of St Paul. However, for most of the believing faithful it is a gradual process of fully appreciating and understanding the Lord's place and power in our lives.

Often we are so familiar with the prayers of the Mass that we can automatically and with ease make our profession of faith. The words "Lord", "Son of God" and other titles readily fall from our lips, but are they born out of a real knowledge of Jesus or are they more formulaic? The man born blind has no previous knowledge of Jesus or his true identity, but meeting Jesus changes his life and his outlook on life and its purpose. His belief in Jesus and his acceptance of Jesus as Lord mean that he will never be the same again.

We have a head start on the man born blind, as we know Jesus and his true identity; however, our discipleship may be hampered by spiritual blindness and that blindness may affect our ability to call Jesus Lord and worship him. Let us ask the Lord to open our eyes to the areas of our lives that stunt our spiritual growth and knowledge. It may be that we are selfish, prejudiced, hypocritical, lacking compassion and so forth, and yet do not see it and therefore are not able to worship the Lord as we would like.

Today's Gospel gives us encouragement, as it is a reminder that the spiritual journey is a process always directed towards enlightenment. It is gradual and as we progress along the way we gain ever more insight into ourselves and into the Lord. If we engage with it seriously and sincerely, the Lord will remove our lack of vision from us and one day we shall see him face to face.

4th Sunday of Lent

"We are God's work of art, created in Christ Jesus to live the good life."

Illustration

Stephen Wiltshire became famous when he was just a young teenager. Born to West Indian parents who had emigrated to England, he had lost his father, and could barely read or write, but was discovered to have an extraordinary gift for drawing buildings and townscapes.

First of all his art teacher, Chris Marris, and then the literary agent Margaret Hewson supported and encouraged him in his special talent. He himself was passive about his ability; he just drew but at a highly technical level, even when he was but a young child. Margaret took him on drawing trips, first of all around London and then to Venice, Amsterdam, Russia and the United States.

Stephen responded immediately to these new sights, and Margaret got him commissions and sponsorships, arranged and financed exhibitions, and helped him to produce his two best-selling books, *Floating Cities* and *Stephen Wiltshire's American Dream*. She also found him a place at art school and established a trust fund to provide for his future. Her own exuberance and energetic personality seemed to inspire Stephen, as though his creativity took life from what the author and neurologist Dr Oliver Sacks, who accompanied them on some of their journeys, called "the exhilarating, whirlwind atmosphere Margaret seemed to create all around her". Without such support it is doubtful that Stephen would have fully developed his gifts or have become known to the wider world.

Gospel Teaching

We live in a limited and conditional world, whereas God is unlimited and unconditional. We are asked to accept that we can share the much more wondrous life of God, not through our own merits and abilities but only through God's great love for us. Such a leap can only be brought about through faith: the belief that God is so generous in mercy that the gap can be bridged, that God's grace is so infinitely rich that we can be saved.

The grace that is offered to us through the death and resurrection of Jesus lifts us up out of our sin and failure and gives us a place in heaven with him.

It also restores us to the possibility of living the good life we were always intended to live. The letter to the Ephesians explores how the mystery of salvation is made available to all. There is a profound conviction that Christ is the Lord of the whole of creation and that all creation is taken up into his saving death and resurrection.

We become again what we were meant to be at the world's beginning, God's work of art; but also, made in God's image and likeness, artists in our turn. We can neither fully appreciate nor practise our calling without being constantly in touch with the brush of the painter, the poet's pen, namely the presence of God, which we celebrate in word and sacrament. If the Temple was the symbol of the Lord's presence among his people in the Old Testament, we are now the new temple, the house where God lives in the Spirit, with Christ Jesus himself as the main cornerstone.

Application

People sometimes struggle with life problems because they suffer from low self-esteem. Coping with life needs a certain resilience, a certain confidence that enables us to ride the ups and downs we encounter. If we don't think we are worth much, we will tend to think that others think the same of us. We may even act in a way that gives others that impression and encourages them to ignore us or treat us with disdain. Or we might go to the opposite extreme, becoming bullying or boastful in the attempt to persuade others that we are really worth something.

But if we are convinced in our hearts that we are God's work of art, then our perception of life is very different. We are free to use our imagination more. We can explore what is old, what is new and what is different. We can be endlessly curious. The world is not hostile but somewhere we can give ourselves time to stand and stare and wonder. We can delight in others' gifts as well as our own. This is where our real imitation of God begins, when we enable others to see their gifts and use them to the full. It is a sign of God's love for us that we can move beyond our limitations and share in the splendour of creation. Our love is seen in our removing of each other's limitations, allowing our spirits to soar freely in the image and likeness of their creator.

C

"He ran to the boy, clasped him in his arms and kissed him."

Illustration

Joe knew that he'd done wrong. He was allowed to play football in the garden. But this time the game with his friends had been a bit too exciting. And they'd ended up by trampling all over the new flowers that his mum had carefully planted only a few days before. Joe was really worried about what his parents would say to him. But when his mum saw the tears in his eyes and the sorrow on his face, she simply wrapped her arms around him. "Oh Joe," she said, "I know you're feeling sorry. But you know I love you more than I love those flowers." Joe told himself that he wouldn't be so careless again.

When good parents forgive a child some fault, they do so completely. Any half measures will leave the child unable to move on, still wondering whether it is worth trying to be good, and maybe failing again. When we forgive our children their faults, our forgiveness has to be total and unconditional; when we forgive in this way we mirror the love and forgiveness of God.

Gospel Teaching

Our three readings speak in different ways of the immense generosity of God. The book of Joshua tells of the new life God gave to the people of Israel when they escaped from slavery in Egypt and entered the promised land. Here is described how they finally reached maturity as they ate the produce of the land and no longer relied, infant-like, on the heavenly manna. There, at last, they had the opportunity to live with hearts open to God. We know, however, that the attempt failed. The nation continued to sin and could only be restored to a right relationship, reconciled to God, by the Father giving his unconditional love in and through the death of Jesus.

In our second reading, Paul uses the verb "to reconcile" five times as he explores the depths of the forgiveness Christ has won for us and the implications of the new life which that brings. We are, he says, "a new creation"; God does not do things in small measure, half-heartedly: "in him [Christ] we... become the goodness of God". What a gift! What an immense calling! You and I in union with Christ can now act towards the world as "ambassadors", able to speak with others in the name of the Lord himself. We are not distant shadows of the reality, but God's intimates, sharing God's life, truly God's representatives.

The well-known tale of the prodigal son should be seen in this way. It is not fundamentally a moral story about someone fallen on hard times who pulls himself together. No, it is all about the reconciling love of God the Father. God in the story is represented by the father, and we are the prodigal son. It is not a story of justice either, for the young man doesn't deserve the forgiveness he receives. He has treated his father as if he were dead by demanding his inheritance in advance, and then added insult to injury by wasting it in a way that utterly defiled him and shamed his family. The father's outrageous love for his son is shown in the new identity he gives to the returnee: costly clothing, a ring denoting citizenship, and sandals, all signs of status and respect. As if this were not enough, he lays on a lavish banquet as well. The parable is talking about God's attitude towards us in just the same way that Paul does: "God in Christ was reconciling the world to himself, not holding men's faults against them."

Application

There is a challenge here too, made clear when we reflect on our previous Lenten Sunday readings. The temptations of Christ prepare him for his radical ministry of reconciliation, while the transfiguration shows us the glory that is to be revealed in Christ. We too are at a crossroads: we can, like the elder son, stick with the tired old ways and reject the Father's offer of new life, just as Israel did time after time – or we can act with grace and humility in response to the Father's overwhelming generosity. What is it to be?

This tale is not just about individual choices, but also about how we live as a Church. Forgiving others is probably the hardest thing any of us will ever be called to do, yet without it we cannot live, either individually or corporately, as the new people of God, as images of Christ.

"Unbind him, let him go free."

Illustration

In the chapel of New College, part of Oxford University in England, there is a sculpture by Jacob Epstein. The sculpture is of Lazarus being raised from the dead. It is a powerful and moving work. The artist has perfectly caught both the stiffness of the bound, dead body, and the life slowly returning to the limbs. Some of the grave bandages seem just about to slip off, others look as if they are about to be burst apart. Lazarus looks as if he has just stretched his neck for the first time after days in the tomb. His face has a strange but serene expression: a traveller who has just returned from the furthest destination, death.

Standing in the middle of the chapel looking back, you can see that the statue, made of white stone, is framed by a great dark wooden door. It looks like a tomb from which Lazarus has just emerged. The light stone glows quietly against the dark background. The viewer is struck by the sheer physical presence of the statue. This is not a ghost or a spirit; it conjures up the fact of Lazarus' physical revival. Yet the figure also looks bound, fragile, still subject to death. It seems to sum up many of the themes from today's Gospel. Although raised from the dead, Lazarus is still bound by the laws of nature and death. He cannot even undo the grave clothes. Jesus has to give the order: "Unbind him, let him go free." Only Jesus has the authority and power to work this astonishing miracle.

Gospel Teaching

Jesus, as true God, has that power over life and death that belongs only to God. Last week we heard how he restored the sight of a man blind from birth. As the tension mounts among the enemies of Jesus, he does something even greater, and raises Lazarus from the dead. Jesus sums up this aspect of his identity in the saying: "I am the resurrection and the life." This saying has given countless Christians hope and comfort when confronted by the death of a loved one, or their own death.

However, the raising of Lazarus is only a temporary sign of Christ's power. Lazarus will die again, like us, to await the final resurrection. Like Lazarus, we will receive our bodies again, but bodies that are no longer subject to death and corruption. As Paul reminds the Romans, we will rise with our glorified bodies, the glory that comes from having died and risen with Christ. The reality of our physical resurrection is shown in the first reading, where God speaks through the prophet Ezekiel.

The Gospel shows us another very important aspect of Jesus' identity. He is genuinely sad and distressed, both at the death of Lazarus and at the grief of Martha and Mary. John tells us that Jesus loved them. When he sees their grief, he weeps too. This is one of only two mentions of Jesus weeping in the Gospels. As well as being fully divine, Jesus is fully human. If anything, Jesus sees more clearly and feels more keenly the evil of death; and here is death at work among his friends.

Jesus, we might say, is weeping for us also. Lazarus stands for all fallen humanity, subject to death and sin. Jesus' tears are also prayers, as he prepares to offer himself up as our ransom: to save us from those very powers of sin and death.

Application

Perhaps St Augustine best summed up the Christian response to the tears of Christ. He wrote that if Christ wept for us, we ought to weep for ourselves. Jesus wept to teach us to weep. We remember too that in the Beatitudes Jesus said, "Blessed are they who mourn; for they shall be comforted." Perhaps we could learn to weep for our own failings, and also for the way in which sin is still active in the world; but not by weeping in a morbid or self-pitying way. Weeping, by its nature, has a cleansing effect. If we take our failings to the sacrament of reconciliation, we can be spiritually cleansed and strengthened. Our tears will not be in vain. They will be joined to those of Jesus, and will be given a redemptive power.

Lent is a good time for renewing our sorrow for sin. Like Lazarus being loosed from his grave clothes, we are loosed from the bonds of sin. In this way we are united more closely to Jesus, his sacred humanity and divinity, as we draw nearer to the time of joy at Easter.

5th Sunday of Lent

B

"And when I am lifted up from the earth, I shall draw all men to myself."

Illustration

One of the things many of us fear the most is exposure. We can all recall a moment when we have ended up looking foolish before other people. Perhaps reciting something before the class at school; being forced by proud parents to sing in front of aunts and uncles; or being the only person in the group who doesn't get a joke. We can all remember moments when we have suddenly felt exposed and vulnerable. Preachers have nightmares about standing in front of a congregation with little or nothing useful to say. On another level, there may be parts of our personality, or things we have done or failed to do, that we do not want other people to know about.

Gospel Teaching

In today's Gospel reading, Jesus talks about being "lifted up". This refers to two things. First, it shows what sort of death he was to die. By being lifted up on the cross, Jesus was publicly exposed and died a shameful death. Part of the purpose of crucifixion was to humiliate the victim, who would have been naked. Crucifixion usually took place where lots of people would pass by, so the shame of the victim would be increased. As the psalmist says prophetically, "All who see me mock me; they curl their lips and sneer; they shake their heads at me."

Secondly, Jesus is lifted up by being glorified by the Father. In John's Gospel, the "hour" of Jesus is the time both of his passion and of his glorification. By his loving obedience to the Father, Jesus gives him glory. As Jesus says, his whole mission culminates in this hour of sacrificial self-giving. "What shall I say: Father, save me from this hour? But it was for this very reason that I have come to this hour. Father, glorify your name!" This glorification is completed in the resurrection and ascension of Jesus, when he is publicly vindicated by the Father.

However, unlike us, Jesus does not fear this most terrible of exposures, his death on the cross. There is nothing for Christ to be ashamed of, as he is sinless. Although his suffering and humiliation are real, Christ willingly chooses them out of love for us. As the letter to the Hebrews says, "he endured the cross, disregarding the shamefulness of it".

Jesus also includes us in this great act of prayer and sacrifice. As the second reading tells us, while on earth Jesus prayed for us aloud and with silent tears, offering us up with his own offering, so that he could become "for all who obey him the source of eternal salvation". To use another phrase from the Psalms, during his earthly life Jesus sowed in tears. He wept over Jerusalem, at the death of Lazarus and in the garden of Gethsemane. But Christ then sang when he reaped. He is the grain of wheat that fell into the ground, watered with his blood and tears. He is the great fruit of the resurrection, the harvest of God's field, the great harvest song of the Father's glory. "Those who are sowing in tears will sing when they reap."

Application

Two sides of discipleship are shown to us in the readings. First, the way of exposure. As Jesus was lifted up to give glory to the Father, so we can bear witness to God through our own lives. This does not need to be dramatic and public. A life of quietly living in prayer and the sacraments can be a powerful witness to the message of the Gospel. Others may be called to a more public "exposure", for example a life in religious vows, a life as a priest, or a life as a missionary. By this public witness to Christ, people make themselves vulnerable.

This vulnerability leads to the second side of discipleship, that of letting our seed fall into the ground to die. We are called to sow in tears, like Christ, in the hope and expectation of singing when we reap. By joining ourselves to Christ we are called to share in his death and resurrection. All these things come together in the Eucharist: the image of seed and wheat; the image of suffering and death; the image of resurrection. When the sacred host is raised during Mass, when the chalice of the precious blood is raised up to the Father, can we not see an image of Jesus' words in the Gospel today? "And I, when I am lifted up, will draw all people to myself."

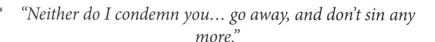

"Neither do I condemn you... go away, and don't sin any more."

Illustration

While preparing a group of young people to receive the sacrament of confirmation, the nun leading the group was teaching them about the sacrament of reconciliation. She had prepared a very thorough presentation, impressing upon the youngsters the importance of the sacrament and the theology surrounding it. At the end of the lesson she said, "I realise that has been a lot for you to take in, are there any questions?" One teenage boy raised his hand and said, "Sister, is it not really simple? Is it not the case that, in this sacrament, God is giving us as many chances as we need?" Sister was lost for words, as there was not much to add to the boy's insight; she had been catechised by him.

As we get older, and perhaps more knowledgeable, we tend to complicate things and lose sight of the simplicity at the heart of most things. Through their questioning, younger people, unencumbered by the layers of complication that age can bring, have a wonderful ability to cut through complex issues and get to the heart of the matter.

Gospel Teaching

This Gospel reading is full of questions: questions explicitly asked and questions that hover silently over the passage. If the woman was caught in the very act of committing adultery, where was the man? Why wasn't he captured? Did he run or did they let him go?

This situation makes the reader wonder if the adultery is really at the heart of the matter – or is the woman just an easy target for the plotting Pharisees? In her shame and naked vulnerability she is paraded through the streets and brought to Jesus. How will he react? This is the concern of the Pharisees, hoping to find something to use against him. However, Jesus' reaction is also of great concern to the woman in question and to the reader of the Gospel. Will he condemn, will he defuse the situation, with whom will he side? The suspense builds.

As is characteristic of Jesus, he turns the tables. The Pharisees have made the woman the focus of attention, but Jesus makes them the focal point of the trial. The heart of the matter is the hypocrisy of the men and not the sexual transgression of the woman. As she stands there in her shame, for all the world to see, it is notable that Jesus keeps his head down, writing in the sand. He doesn't want to add to her shame. Only when they are alone does he look at her.

In a brief conversation, made up of more questions, Jesus and the woman acknowledge that a sin has been committed and the law has been broken, but Jesus does not want the woman to be held hostage by it. "Neither do I condemn you… go away, and don't sin any more." Jesus' ministry brings liberty, not captivity.

Application

Can we readily identify with the woman? Have we known the experience of shame and vulnerability? Have we had people point the finger at us? If so, then the message of this Gospel, and the healing and forgiving words of Jesus, will have a special meaning for us.

At the beginning of every Mass we acknowledge that we are sinners in need of the Lord's mercy. But do we fully appreciate the enormous depth of God's forgiveness? Whether our sins are big or small, Jesus wants to restore our dignity and help us along the way. He is not in the business of keeping us trapped and stunting our growth. Jesus' approach is always of generous mercy in the hope that this will elicit a response: "Go, and sin no more."

Are there times when, if we're honest, we can also identify with the Pharisees? Have we been self-righteous at the expense of someone else's dignity? Have we, in our dealings with others, been hypocritical? If so, then the message of this Gospel and the teaching of Jesus will have a special significance for us.

The liturgy constantly reminds us that in the sight of God we are equal, and as such we are brothers and sisters. As a Christian community we have a duty of care for one another, and that care includes generous and wholehearted forgiveness. If we're quicker to judge than to forgive, we run the risk of being like the Pharisees. Jesus' response to sin is not to condemn but to be generous in mercy, in the hope that we will see the error of our ways and respond by going and sinning no more.

A

"He was humbler yet, even to accepting death, death on a cross."

Illustration

In churches up and down the land, Christian communities are holding Palm Sunday processions, waving palm crosses. But do we have a sense of the global celebration of Palm Sunday and how the suffering of Christ resonates with specific communities? This weekend, families in Jerusalem's Christian quarter will process down the Mount of Olives carrying palm branches; in a Nigerian parish a priest will ride a real donkey into church; in communities in the Dominican Republic everybody will dress up as characters in the Passion narrative and Roman soldiers will march down the streets!

Many interesting stories lie behind Palm Sunday celebrations around the world. Catholics in China have trouble getting hold of palms, so they use native plants such as sago, cypress or sweet basil. Shanghai Catholics buy these in because there aren't many trees in the city and people are not allowed simply to pull branches. In the cold and dry regions north of the Yangtze river, cypress is used. Evergreen cypress is one of the few plants available in early spring when other plants are just sprouting.

Thousands of miles away, in Ecuador, in 2007, many Ecuadorean Catholics waved corn stalks and reeds instead of traditional woven palm crosses. The change was part of a campaign to save Ecuador's endangered wax palm and two bird species which depend on the palm for nesting and refuge. Many Quito parishes asked their parishioners not to buy palm branches, saying that branches of any kind could be blessed on Palm Sunday.

For many communities, the symbols that confront us on Palm Sunday have special significance, especially the cross. For many years political prisoners in El Salvador made small crosses carved out of seeds and painted by the prisoners to raise money for their families. The "mothers of the disappeared" in the same country – the only country named after the Saviour – made little crosses out of black string, which they gave to visitors in memory of their tortured children.

Gospel Teaching

The Passion story from Matthew is bleak indeed. It starts with the betrayal by Judas and then Jesus accurately predicts that all his disciples will desert him, even Peter. No angel comes to minister to Jesus in Gethsemane, and give him strength, as happens in Luke's account. Jesus is spat at and "hit with fists" before the Sanhedrin. He is mocked right up to the point of death, and cries out, "My God, my God, why have you deserted me?" Note the cosmological dimension of the crucifixion – the sky turning dark, the earth quaking and rocks splitting. Those present must have been terrified.

The story grips us. It encompasses the best and worst of human nature. Can we empathise with the plight of Judas, who tries to undo a terrible mistake but finds that it is too late? Shall we blame the disciples for choosing sleep over prayer? Did the follower of Jesus who drew his sword and injured the high priest's servant act unreasonably? Apparently Jesus thought so. Being a man of peace, he ordered the man to put his sword away, "for all who draw the sword will die by the sword". Notice that it was the women following Jesus who stayed with him right up to the end, even though they were kept at a distance.

Elements of the story will resonate with all of us, for what they reflect about human nature. It was this very humanity that Jesus embraced. Jesus was betrayed by practically everybody, but he did not betray our humanity. That he could do this is the foundation of our ultimate hope, not only in God, but in humanity too.

Application

Let us go back to the international dimensions of Palm Sunday celebrations. In Ethiopia, decorated crosses are made out of beaten silver, but they have an unusual feature – a hinge. This hinge suggests that the cross is a door to spiritual reality. As humans we grow in likeness to God through our love, service and justice. Through the power of sacrificial love and forgiveness, we bear the beams of God's embracing love.

Where do we see ourselves on Palm Sunday? Do we recognise elements of ourselves in the cheering crowd, yelling for a messiah that might free them from oppressive overlords, but then turning against him; in the disciples who ran away when Jesus was arrested; in the Roman soldiers, given the dirty job of executing criminals; in the thieves who taunted a fellow sufferer? When we wave our crosses of palms, we recognise the cross mirrored in us, the universal family of the people of God.

B

"In truth this man was a son of God."

Illustration

Soap operas on television get their highest ratings when episodes are screened centring around two or more characters whose relationships are reaching a climax. The dialogue is generally very emotional and keeps us on the edge of our sofas. We are drawn into the story because it could easily be one that we have to live ourselves. Perhaps it is even one that we recognise.

As we watch the story unfold, we wonder how we ourselves would react in the same situations. What would we have said to that person? Mercifully, we don't have to cope with many of the things that soap-opera characters have to. However, they do make us wonder, don't they?

Gospel Teaching

It is not easy to understand all that is happening in today's Passion narrative, even with the benefit of hindsight and the experience of the Church. How much harder it must have been for the disciples, who found themselves in the very middle of the proceedings. They lurch from the intimacy and trust of the Last Supper to the pain and loneliness in the garden, then on to the confusion and fear of the trial. The fear leads to panic, so they flee, and finally they hear the news that their master is dead.

These are the same men who saw the many miracles worked by Jesus, who realised that he made a difference wherever he went. But on Good Friday they didn't understand what was going on and were afraid for their lives. Nonetheless, for all their lack of faith, courage and fidelity, this was not the end of their relationship with Jesus. Soon after the crucifixion, they realised the full significance of what had happened that day on Calvary, and their lives were changed for ever.

In Mark's Gospel, Jesus' identity is fully affirmed, not by one of his close disciples, but by one of his executioners. The centurion states, when Jesus dies: "In truth this man was a son of God." Here is a soldier who was not around Jesus during the glory days, witnessing miracles and conversions. But in the death of Jesus he finds something extraordinary, something out of this world. There was obviously something in the way Jesus died that moved the hearts of people who otherwise wouldn't have cared about him.

For the centurion, the penny drops at the very end. But it is still not too late. There is still an opportunity to follow Jesus. Death has not brought an end to this story; the best is yet to come.

Application

When, in our quieter moments, we sit confused, wondering about Jesus and our faith in him, it is all too easy to think, "If only I had been around two thousand years ago and had known Jesus in the flesh. If only I had been one of his disciples and had seen him cure and preach. If only… then my faith in Jesus would be stronger and my relationship with him would be more real." But the reality is that we just don't know how we would have reacted, had we been around all those years ago. We might well have fled, we might well have sided with the authorities, we might well have shouted: "Crucify him! Crucify him!" The fact that we were not with Jesus during his earthly ministry does not prevent us from coming to know and follow him now.

For many people it is during their days of suffering that they come to realise who this man Jesus is. In our darkness and pain, we can relate to the pain and passion of Jesus and begin to have some appreciation of what he has done for us. By dying, Jesus opened the way to the Father and to heaven – for us now, for the people who have gone before us and for those yet to come. His earthly life was limited to a specific period of history, but through his death and resurrection he is now outside time and accessible to us all. We can know Jesus today, because he is the same now as he was two thousand years ago.

As we make the journey with Jesus through this week, let us be sure to take time to deepen our appreciation of what he has done for us. Then, like the centurion, we will be able to proclaim that Jesus is truly the Son of God. It is never too late to meet him.

Passion (Palm) Sunday

C

"Christ… was humbler yet, even to accepting death, death on a cross. But God raised him high."

Illustration

In recent years devotion to the Sacred Heart has become much less popular than it was some years ago. Many of the pictures or statues of the past probably don't appeal to modern tastes. However, the images of the Sacred Heart provided a tangible reminder of the love of God, revealed in the love of Jesus for his friends. In an appalling scene of poverty in the film *Angela's Ashes*, based on Frank McCourt's memoir of life in the Ireland of the 1930s and 1940s, the family have only a few pieces of old furniture, their ground-floor room is submerged in water, but they have carried with them a picture of the Sacred Heart in whom they continue to trust.

Gospel Teaching

The Sacred Heart helped people to focus on the gentleness of Jesus and the love Jesus had for those who had strayed away from their faith, or who failed in the moral life or had committed serious sins. Compared with the infinite greatness of God's love, sin pales into insignificance. God remains faithful and gentle whilst people are often fickle and cruel. This focus on the gentleness of Jesus is also found in Luke's portrait of Jesus. By listening to his account, we can hear certain themes that are characteristic not only of his account of the passion but of his entire Gospel.

Luke paints a picture of the gentleness of Jesus and the way in which he reveals his forgiving love towards those around him. Jesus knows that Peter will be tempted by Satan and will betray him. Luke tells us that even in this act of betrayal Jesus will continue to pray for Peter. Once he has repented, he will be restored in his relationship with Christ and then have the task of strengthening the new and vulnerable Christians who are the Church. The love of Jesus, shown in his prayer for Peter, is steadfast and continuous. He wants him to be a disciple but knows that he will often be a weak disciple. However, Peter will ultimately give his life for the sake of his faith. Growth in discipleship is usually rather slow.

The gentleness of Jesus is also shown in the way that he heals the ear of one of the people who come to arrest him. Only in Luke's portrait of Jesus does this occur. Jesus' care for those who are troubled is shown when Luke describes the way in which Jesus gives the women of Jerusalem a warning about the suffering that will befall them in the future. It is better to be prepared than unprepared. The forgiving gentleness of Jesus is further presented by Jesus' forgiveness of the good thief. Jesus is ready to forgive him and welcome him into the kingdom. Finally Jesus surrenders to the Father and prays in trust, "Father, into your hands I commit my spirit."

These aspects of Luke's Passion narrative reveal the depth of God's love, which touches all those who seek God's help. God desires healing, forgiveness, trust and conversion. People are invited to trust in the gentleness of Christ. Many of the crowd who shouted praise to Jesus during his entry into Jerusalem will quickly turn their shouts to "crucify him" when the mood changes. They are fickle; true disciples are called to be faithful.

Application

Holy Week is the most sacred time of the Church's year, in which we remember the great events that reveal that God so loved the world that he sent his Son to be our saviour. Jesus offers healing to those who are sick and suffering. Jesus offers forgiveness to those who confess their sins. Jesus offers paradise to those who pray, "Jesus, remember me when you come into your kingdom."

The response is left to each one of us: we can either be stubborn and trust only in ourselves, or we can ask for the help of God, and be open to accept it, like the good thief on the cross. Jesus presents a portrait of how we are to live and build a community of disciples who are the Church. This life is characterised by healing words and actions, forgiveness and trusting in the good of other people.

Holy Week invites each of us to journey with Christ in the events of the Passion so that after Calvary we may come to live in the hope of resurrection. Only when we begin to recognise the depth of God's love, revealed in Christ, will we become faithful rather than fickle followers.

"I have given you an example."

Illustration

Our blood reveals a lot about us. It can disclose our history – our parentage and our geographical background. It also tells us about our current physical well-being. Blood tests give us information about the functioning of vital organs such as the liver and kidneys. They help in early diagnosis of conditions such as diabetes. They are essential for important times of life such as pregnancy. They are employed to test sportspeople for the use of illegal drugs. They are used at crime scenes to identify cause of death. And of course, without blood transfusions, many simple and routine operations would become life-threatening or simply impossible. Simply stated – our blood is our life; it is who we are.

Gospel Teaching

Blood lies at the heart of the events of Maundy Thursday and Good Friday. In preparation for their liberation from slavery in Egypt, the people of Israel are commanded by God to slaughter an animal – such as a lamb – and then eat it in a hurried meal, in preparation for their escape into freedom. They are to smear the lamb's blood around their doorposts and lintels, to identify their houses, so that the angel of death will pass over them and do them no harm. The blood of the lamb becomes a very powerful symbol of being saved from death and liberated from slavery.

Matthew, Mark and Luke all tell us that Jesus' last meal with his disciples was a Passover meal – eaten as a memorial of that escape into freedom. St John's Gospel offers us a different timescale. John tells us that Jesus' final meal takes place before the festival of the Passover. So in St John's Gospel, the moment that Jesus dies on the cross – spilling his blood for humanity – is the very moment when the priests are sacrificing the lambs in the Temple, in preparation for the Passover meal.

John's meaning is clear. Jesus is the true Lamb of God – the one whose blood truly sets his people free. This helps explain why, in St John's Gospel, we get no account of the Passover meal, with the breaking of bread and sharing of the cup. Instead, Jesus uses a different, powerful, symbolic action to explain the meaning of his sacrifice on the cross the next day. Jesus washes his disciples' feet – the act of a slave. Jesus shows that his death will be an act of service, for all people. He serves by pouring out his lifeblood – a supreme act of self-giving, selfless love, so that God's people might be set free.

St Paul describes this as a new covenant in the blood of Christ – the promise of a new beginning. This Eucharist is our new Passover. God has set us free from something greater than physical slavery and oppression. Here we celebrate our liberation even from the grip of sin and the power of death.

Application
If our own blood tells us much about ourselves, the blood of Christ tells us so much more. It tells us that we are immensely loved – loved without limit, without reserve, loved passionately. Jesus' blood seals a new relationship between God and us – a new covenant – in which God our liberator assures us that he will set us free from everything that chains, imprisons, frightens and threatens us. Death does not have the final word. The blood of the Son of God is poured out so that we might have life, life to the full. So tonight we celebrate the Eucharist – to remember and give thanks.

But as we celebrate the Eucharist together, the love that is at the heart of the Eucharist calls out to us and forms us. Christ's generous pouring out of himself – of his lifeblood – in service of others invites and empowers us to do likewise. Love calls forth love. The only way to true freedom is the way of foot-washing, the way of service, the way of costly love. Whether we serve as a parent, a carer, a friend, or a good neighbour, we try generously to pour out who we are, what we have, in lives of loving service, so that through us Christ may continue to wash the feet of all humanity. As we eat his body and drink his blood, he empowers us here and now with his life, enabling us to love with his love, serve with his compassion, so that others might be freed. May we do this each day of our lives, as a memorial of him.

"So you are a king then?"

Illustration

Pontius Pilate may have been born in Scotland, or Spain, or Germany. There are local legends that associate him with Fortingall in Scotland, with Tarragona in Spain, and with Forchheim in Germany. His manner and place of death are also the stuff of legend. Some reports say that he converted and became a Christian, together with his wife. Others say that he was recalled to Rome, and that he committed suicide. None of these stories can be confirmed, but some things are certain. Pontius Pilate was governor of Judaea from AD 26 to 36. He would normally reside at the seaside town of Caesarea. He would come to Jerusalem only on the occasion of great festivals, when the city would receive a large influx of visitors, and the likelihood of disturbance would be greater. To counteract this danger, Pilate would have at his command a garrison of around three thousand soldiers.

Pilate's responsibility was to preserve the peace, to prevent disturbance, to suppress agitation. As long as he kept Palestine quiet, he would be regarded as doing a good job. The Jewish people were notoriously difficult to handle, and the Roman authorities were happy to give them a certain degree of self-rule, provided that taxes were duly paid, and control duly exercised. Pilate was not popular, and his relations with the Jewish leaders were always somewhat difficult. The last thing he needed was a political agitator to unsettle the uneasy peace he presided over.

Gospel Teaching

When Jesus is brought to his court, Pilate is initially dismissive. "See to it yourselves!" he tells his visitors. Why disturb his morning? But when the visitors insist, Pilate goes indoors and talks to Jesus personally. "What is all this stuff about being a king?" That is political. When asked, Jesus is careful not to mislead the governor. "Mine is not a kingdom of this world." Pressed on the issue of kingship, Jesus replies "yes and no". No, not a political leader, but yes, a king of truth.

Now Pilate can see the lie of the land. Truth, justice, morality. He does not deal in such things. He deals in power, superior force and advantage, not in these wishy-washy virtues that "good" people like to talk about. This Jesus is no problem to him now. He's a joke. A good man, no doubt, and for that reason Pilate will try to save him, but a political threat? No!

Maybe if he dresses him up like a king, for a laugh, everyone will lighten up and let the thing drop. Go away and forget about it. But no. The sight of a scourged Jesus, with crown and purple robe, is the sign for a chant to begin. "Crucify him! Crucify him!" the mob begins to sing. Now Pilate is rocking. His plan has misfired and the noisy crowd is getting restless. They "up the ante" now, with accusations about being a Son of God, and of being a rival to Caesar. Pilate is now trapped. He has come to like this strange man who stands before him. Something has passed between them, and Pilate now sees how deeply good this man is. But it is too late. The call has been made. Jesus or Caesar? Who is it to be?

Pilate washes his hands to show that he disassociates himself from this judicial murder, but he cannot wash away responsibility for what he allows to happen next. He gives permission for execution. The governor of Judaea has shown us how weak a man he is. Political pressure, cleverly exerted, has made him a puppet in the hands of his subjects. Jesus is led away.

Application
There is one thing left for Pilate still to do. As governor it is his responsibility to post a notice above the executed person to tell the public the nature of the crime. So Pilate orders a notice to be made: "Jesus the Nazarene, King of the Jews". This notice is then copied into two other languages so that everyone will be left in no doubt about who this person is, and what this person has done.

The notice is written out, in Hebrew, Latin and Greek, and nailed, like the victim, to the cross. When the Jewish leaders complain about it, Pilate, for the one and only time, stands his ground. "What I have written, I have written." He will be pushed around no more this day. At some point in life a person must tell the truth. Pilate, that day, wrote the Gospel.

The Season
of Easter

"We have eaten and drunk with him after his resurrection from the dead."

Illustration

The legendary Greek poet Homer is credited with the epic story of Odysseus. The hero of the story, which dates from the eighth century before Christ, spent twenty years on a great adventure to the city of Troy and back. Odysseus encountered many trials and overcame many foes before he settled back at home to live happily ever after. The story is a great military drama, a folk tale recited from memory for many years before it was put into written form.

Many centuries later, the Irish writer James Joyce used the name of Odysseus, in its Latin form, Ulysses, to tell a similar tale of human endeavour. The amazing thing about Joyce's story is that the events all take place in the space of one day. A 900-page book devoted to the happenings of some ordinary Dubliners in the course of twenty-four hours. What is the point of that?

Joyce wanted to emphasise the value of ordinary things and ordinary people. He wanted to get away from the so-called glory of war and violence that he knew full well in the days of the First World War, and of the Irish rebellion. His telling of every minute detail of daily life, and of the thoughts that go through our heads all day long, is a celebration of what life is.

There is a deep strand in us that says that my personal life, with all its foibles and follies, is still immensely valuable and worthy of celebration. There is a stubborn something inside us that says that no matter how ugly and horrible life can be, it is still a supreme reality. My life is important, not just to me, and in itself it deserves to be.

Gospel Teaching

When Peter stood up to speak to the people in Jerusalem, he told them a story. Not a made-up story, but a true story. He referred to what everyone knew about. "You must have heard about the recent happenings in Judaea..." He went on to say how he and his friends were there to witness it all: the preaching, the teaching, the healing work, the arrest, the trial and the killing on a tree. Yes, everyone had heard that story.

But then Peter went on to tell an extraordinary part of the story, a part the people had not heard before: that Jesus was raised to life. And just as Peter had been a witness to the first part of the story, he was also a witness to this "unbelievable" part. And how was that witness demonstrated? Peter's answer is simple: "We have eaten and drunk with him after his resurrection from the dead." Ghosts do not eat and drink. Illusions do not take meals. Real people sit down to share food together, and that is what Peter is telling us. Peter sat with him at table and broke bread.

It was this simple act of feeding that was the proof for Peter. That is how he knew it was true. That is why he is a witness for us. He witnesses to what he has experienced. On this experience of the risen Christ, Peter will stake his life, and dedicate his life, and finally give his life. The foundation of our faith is on the witness of the apostles, and Peter is its foremost witness. Food and drink, these ordinary things, have given our faith its foundation.

Application

Now we know for sure that our life is worthwhile, worth living. It is a life, a journey, whose destination is in heaven, at God's right hand, where Jesus sits. For this reason we will live a heavenly life here on earth, and everything about this world has eternal value. Nothing about this life is useless or a waste of time, except selfishness and sin. Everything else is of immortal value, is what the Jesuit priest and poet Gerard Manley Hopkins called "immortal diamond".

We, the followers of Jesus, now know what "true life" is. The glory of it is hidden in Christ. This world's difficulty and darkness make it so. But it does not deter us. We know the tomb is empty, but our life is not void. It is filled with the glory of the risen Lord, Jesus Christ.

It was those ordinary things, bread and wine, that revealed the truth to Peter. So it is for us. The bread and wine of the Eucharist reveal the risen Lord. Partaking of this meal, we become new bread ourselves, enriching daily life with sincerity and truth. Let us celebrate the feast!

"You too will be revealed in all your glory with him."

Illustration

On a windswept hillside on a remote coastal peninsula a hillwalker came across human remains. They had been lying there for anything up to ten years. The police were called and an investigation was begun. There were two main lines of enquiry. The first was a forensic examination of the body and of the scene. The second was to examine the files in police records of missing persons in the area over the past ten years. There was also a third dimension to be considered. Many families in the area had a relative who had gone missing, and so many old wounds would be reopened; and the police were very sensitive to this fact.

Who was this person who had gone missing? How did he die? And why? Who are his family, his loved ones, and how have they coped all these years? Such discoveries remind us that there are many people all over the world who go missing and are never seen again. And there are many families who live with that loss and mourn for their loved and lost ones.

Gospel Teaching

On the first Easter morning Mary of Magdala came to the tomb to mourn and to anoint the body of Jesus. When she arrived at the tomb she found that there was no body to anoint. The tomb was empty. She was faced with a missing-person enquiry. Where was Jesus? Who had taken the body? And why? In her confusion and upset and panic, she came running back to the disciples and told them what she had seen. Or rather, what she had not seen.

Peter and John go to see for themselves. They find nothing – but they discover everything. They know that the body has not been stolen. Who would want to steal it? At this moment, as they look at an empty tomb, they begin to see the meaning of Christ's words to them when he spoke of rising from the dead. Death is so final; and so the words of Jesus were not making any sense. But now that death is done with, those words make all the sense in the world.

Now that Jesus is alive, it is not a dead body that the disciples seek, but a missing person. They do not have long to wait. Peter tells us the story himself. At the house of the Roman soldier Cornelius, he tells his listeners the whole story of Jesus. How they, the disciples, had been with Jesus for three years, and heard his teaching and witnessed his power of healing. How they had seen him die on a cross and how they had laid him to rest. And then came Easter morning. And now they had seen him and eaten and drunk with him after his resurrection. They are the witnesses to all this.

Hearing this story, Cornelius and all his household are overjoyed. This is the greatest story ever told. They have heard it from the mouth of Peter and they accept its truth. They receive baptism and become followers, not of a dead man, nor of a missing person, but of Jesus, the Lord of life.

Application

On this Easter Day, we gather to rejoice in the resurrection of the Lord and to proclaim to all the world, "Jesus Christ is risen from the dead." We speak to a world that is often anxious about death and worried about life. We speak to people who are touched by death every day in the violent arena of our planet. We speak to people who have lost loved ones in upsetting circumstances. We speak to people who live every day with the memory of dear ones who have disappeared. Perhaps we are those people too.

Today we are reminded that we have a ministry to perform for the love of this world and all the people in it. We have been ordered, like Peter, to proclaim the resurrection of Jesus to the whole of creation. We are to keep our minds and hearts fixed firmly on heavenly things and, in this faith, to comfort those in sorrow, to cheer those who weep, and to turn our eyes to behold the glory of Christ.

The Lord of life will not allow anyone to be lost, except the one who chooses to be lost. All the missing persons of this world Jesus Christ will care for. Jesus himself was the most abandoned in this world, and look – he is risen!

"He bent down and saw the linen cloths lying on the ground."

Illustration

The old man had been a soldier of the Second World War, and then a coalminer. When he died, his grave was a simple place, with a black headstone, bearing his name and the dates of his birth and death. The earth itself was simply grassed over. About a year after his death his daughter came over from Germany, accompanied by her German husband, and they brought with them a beautiful black lantern, which they placed on the grave. It is a familiar custom in Germany to adorn the graves of loved ones with lanterns, and to light candles within them on those special days in November when the dead are commemorated. How poignant, too, that a German son-in-law should place a lantern on the grave of an English soldier. Sadly they never got the chance to light the lantern on that grave, for, within a few months of it being placed there, the beautiful lantern was stolen.

This stealing from graves is nothing rare these days. "Is nothing sacred?" it might be asked. Apparently not. Yet it remains a most upsetting thing to have anything stolen from a grave. Our loved ones are precious to us, and their graves are sacred places. Though they are gone from us, we tend their graves and keep them neat and tidy, just as we hold their memory ever dear.

Gospel Teaching

On the morning of Easter Day, the women who went to the tomb were about to begin the process of tending the grave, by anointing the dead body of Jesus and then closing the tomb once again. How shocked they must have been to see the stone rolled away. How much more upsetting to discover that the body was not there. It must have been stolen! "Someone has taken it," Mary Magdalene cries. Going back to the disciples, the women bring the terrible news.

This news has to be verified, so Peter and John run to the garden where the tomb is located, and the evidence is lying there before them. Grave cloths on the ground. Head cloth rolled up in a place by itself. What does it mean? What has happened here? This is not the work of grave robbers. Why would they unwrap the body? No. Something stranger still than grave robbery has happened here. This is death robbery. Death has been robbed of its power – of its power to devastate and to destroy. Life has returned to this place, and to this world, and to our lives.

"Till this moment", the Gospel of John says, the disciples "had failed to understand the teaching of scripture, that he must rise from the dead." Some things are very hard for us to understand. Some things are outside of our experience, and some are beyond our wildest expectations. For many people some things are beyond the realms of possibility. Rising from the dead is one of those things. It just does not happen. All the evidence tells us that death is pretty final. It is the end of everything. It is our dissolution.

Acceptance of the fact of death is in many ways a mature attitude, a realistic response to the fact of our mortality. Yet there is another response, a rebellion against death, a protest that the poet Dylan Thomas so eloquently expressed when he told us to "rage, rage against the dying of the light". Is it not true that death in so many ways makes a mockery of life? It is almost an insult to all that life hoped to be, for to die is to lose life.

Application
Now, here, on this Easter Day, we have the great discovery, the great find. Life wins. Love wins. John, the beloved disciple, who was to write so eloquently of life and love, went into the tomb; and "he saw and he believed". What he saw was an empty tomb, but he also "saw" more deeply into the mystery of what the empty tomb means. It means that the Lord is risen, and in him the fullness of life has been restored to us.

So even the stealing of a lantern from a grave is not the end of the world. Christ is the light of the world, a light that darkness cannot overpower. St John saw that for himself on that first Easter morning. May that same Easter light shine on us today.

A

"Happy are those who have not seen and yet believe."

Illustration

"Look at Joan. She weighed 280 pounds and had tried every diet under the sun. But after only three months on our new sensible-eating plan she is down to an incredible 140 pounds. Joan says she is now full of confidence and her whole outlook on life has changed."

"Dave is only thirty and already his hair has turned grey. But thanks to our new formula hair colorant, Dave has not just regained his natural hair colour, but has found that women who used to ignore him now pay him a lot more attention."

A lot of advertisements we see these days use this "before and after" format to sell their products. Pictures don't lie, we tell ourselves, and there's nothing so convincing as having the evidence of dramatic change put before our eyes to make us believe the extravagant claims of the advertisers.

Gospel Teaching

The theme of today's readings could be described as being an early version of this type of "before and after" selling. In the Gospel, Thomas is the ultimate hard-bitten consumer, unwilling to believe anyone's claims, even his friends', unless he has the evidence in front of him. Jesus risen from the dead? He won't believe it unless he can see it with his own eyes, in fact unless he can feel the very wounds of the cross on Christ's body. And, of course, Jesus duly obliges: "Put your finger here… Give me your hand; put it into my side. Doubt no longer but believe." Faced with such overwhelming evidence, Thomas does indeed believe.

But there is another striking "before and after" image presented to us in today's readings. John tells us that "the doors were closed in the room where the disciples were, for fear of the Jews." But the picture of what happened after that, once Jesus had given the gift of the Holy Spirit, is totally different. The description of the early Christian community in the Acts of the Apostles is light years away from the frightened, disheartened, tiny group of disciples huddled together in that upper room. Once the Spirit is given, all fear is gone. The disciples preach openly, the community grows in numbers, they are full of praise and courage.

And the second reading goes even further. It also describes a "before" and an "after". The "before" is this present life of faith, which gives us joy and hope but is also tinged with trials and suffering. Peter promises that there will be an "after" – once this time of testing is over – when we can come into the inheritance promised to us, an eternal reward that can never be spoiled, the salvation of our souls.

Application

The readings today are not simply descriptions of past events, of what happened to Thomas and that early Christian community. They are paradigms, models of what God can do to us in our individual lives and in our parish and religious communities. The Lord takes away our fear and replaces it with his peace. He fills us with his Spirit so that we too can form a community that is faithful to the teaching of the apostles, centred on the breaking of bread and prayer, and where all members care for each other's needs. He sends us out, with a mission, his mission, and he promises to work with us – through "miracles and signs" – to confirm the message he gives. We are simply called to make that leap of faith, as Thomas did.

This is no fairy story or wishful thinking: this is the common experience of Christians throughout the centuries. The community Peter wrote to didn't live in some romantic Christian idyll. They knew real danger, real pain, even death for the sake of their faith in Christ. But he reminds them – and us – that, no matter what trials we face, real faith is possible: "You did not see him, yet you love him." In other words, as Jesus tells Thomas: "Happy are those who have not seen and yet believe."

We each face the trials of life and of faith in our own particular ways – perhaps we face rejection or hostility because of our faith; perhaps our faith has cost us in terms of career or friends; perhaps our cross is that of physical illness, mental anguish, grief, poverty or loneliness. Whatever our trials, Peter encourages us to take heart, to keep our faith alive, to remember the hope we now have, and to look forward to that glorious "after" which awaits all those who remain faithful.

"Doubt no longer but believe."

Illustration

Several years before he became Pope Benedict XVI, Joseph Ratzinger wrote a book on the Creed. In it he recounts a story, first told by the great Jewish philosopher Martin Buber, which shows us that doubt can afflict both the believer and the atheist. One day, a very clever atheist went to argue with a famous rabbi, to attempt to show him that his faith was groundless. But as he entered the room he saw the rabbi pacing up and down, engrossed in a book that he held in his hands. Then the rabbi looked up and said, "But perhaps it is true after all."

The atheist was shaken by these words, but the rabbi said to him, "My son, the great scholars with whom you have argued wasted their words on you; as you departed you laughed at them. They were unable to lay God and his kingdom on the table before you and nor can I. But think, my son, perhaps it is true." The atheist left the rabbi's presence with doubts in his own beliefs, or lack of them. In fact this powerful "perhaps" broke down his resistance and he eventually came to faith.

The future Pope points out in the same book that even the great saints like St Thérèse of Lisieux were assailed by doubts about their faith. Faith inevitably includes an element of doubt, whether you are a believer or an atheist.

Gospel Teaching

In the first part of St John's Gospel we are given several examples of how different people make the journey to faith in Jesus: Nicodemus, the Samaritan woman, the man born blind, Martha and Mary. Some achieve a deeper faith, but for all it is a gradual journey.

How do Jesus' close disciples come to faith in the resurrection? On Easter Sunday, the greatest day of the Christian year, perhaps it's easy to be dazzled by the message that Christ is risen. We may get carried away by the sheer joy of the good news that Christ has conquered death. How could you not believe?

Now today, a week later, on what is sometimes called Low Sunday, we come down to earth and see that faith in the resurrection may be more challenging than we thought. St John tells us that when Jesus came to the disciples they were locked in a room by fear. It was only once he had shown them that it really was him, that they were filled with joy. But we are told that Thomas was not present and would not accept their witness. He wanted proof and presence. He made his faith conditional on physical evidence. Unless I can see and touch Jesus' wounds, he said, I refuse to believe.

When Jesus does appear to Thomas, a week later, Jesus does not chide him; but he probes Thomas with the challenge to touch him. "Doubting" Thomas then makes the greatest profession of faith of all the disciples when he says to Jesus, "My Lord and my God!"

Thomas' doubt was removed by Jesus' presence, but Jesus speaks to the future generations of people like us who have not seen Jesus: "Happy are those who have not seen and yet believe."

Application

Is it easy to believe? For some who live in a Christian family or community, with the supports and signs of faith around them, then belief may come easily. But, for the majority of people in our world today, faith is an act made in the face of doubt and uncertainty. Joseph Ratzinger speaks of the "oppressive power of unbelief" in the contemporary world, which affects our own will to believe. There are many "Thomases" today who want empirical, scientific proof before they will risk breaking out of a room where they are locked in by their own suspicions.

There are some Christians who feel guilty about having doubts, feeling that they should have no difficulty in just accepting everything they are told in church. Today's Gospel is a reassurance and reminder that doubt was present right from the beginning of the Church, even in the apostles. They came by stages to faith, helped by Jesus and the Holy Spirit, the Spirit that St John calls "another witness" and "the truth". Faith will always involve a risk and an act of trust. Thomas expressed his doubts but ended with a profound faith. And the history of the Church shows how, down through the centuries, Christians have overcome their doubts, developed a strong faith in the risen Christ and are indeed blessed because "they have not seen and yet believe".

C

"Peace be with you."

Illustration

The Tate Modern is a fantastic showcase for contemporary art, on London's South Bank. The setting is amazing, right next to the River Thames; and here modern art is housed in a disused power station complete with a sky-scraping factory chimney. The entrance hall is the size of a cathedral and draws your eyes upwards in the same way.

One of the exhibits in the Tate Modern's collection is a sculpture called *Three Points*, by the British artist Henry Moore. It is cast in bronze and is not one of the huge outdoor pieces for which he is well known – it is small, and initially it has a round feeling to it. However, each end comes to a sharp point that doesn't quite touch the other. It has two end points, and one middle point that reaches up towards the other two but can't quite get there. Moore himself said, "This pointing has an emotional or physical action in it where things are just about to touch but don't… like the points in the sparking plug of a car… the spark has to jump across the gap."

The points seek to reach each other, but there is an empty space between them. It feels as though there is doubt in the chasm between the points – were we made to reach each other or to remain stretching into the void? There is no spark, like there would be in a car engine – these points never touch.

Gospel Teaching

In the locked room, the disciples are waiting, afraid. Jesus has been killed, and they fear they could be next. They are not really sure what they are supposed to do. Thomas, at least, is full of doubt and cannot bring himself to believe what some of the others have been saying about seeing a risen Christ. He needs proof. He is moving away from belief, towards unbelief. Yet when Christ appears Thomas seems ready, somehow, to believe. When Jesus says, "Peace be with you", Thomas is not just reassured, he is full of joy and awe. "My Lord and my God!" he says.

But to reach this point, to repeat Henry Moore's phrase, "the spark has to jump across the gap". Some commentators believe that Thomas had actually become rather cynical and almost didn't want to believe. Even faced with the testimony of people close to him, he rejected what he heard.

But surely, to move so quickly from a state of doubt to a profound belief in Jesus as God, Thomas must have been reaching out in some way, at least wanting to believe?

When he sees and experiences God's presence, when he hears the word "Peace", his anxieties and doubts are quelled, and he believes. He is ready to accept his mission and continue Christ's work. "Doubt no longer but believe," says Jesus; and Thomas is quick to accept the invitation.

Application

Most of us have experienced periods of doubt. Anxiety and fear can become blocks or barriers, as they were for the people who didn't dare to join the faithful in our first reading. We are afraid to believe – we cannot take that leap across what feels like empty space. Why are we so frightened? Is it because of the possible consequences? What might it mean to our comfortable lives if we really believed and accepted Christ's mission? Or is it a lack of trust? Unless we hear Jesus say to us, "Peace be with you", we are not convinced of his presence and we are not ready for our mission. We are like the points in Henry Moore's sculpture that can't quite touch – we reach out but, because we can't believe we can get there, we don't stretch ourselves enough and we remain limited.

We are called to move towards belief and towards trust. God is with us. But we can only really come to believe and trust in God if we are open to do so. The feeling of openness can be frightening, because, in our human experience, when we allow people to get close to us, we know we can be hurt. But God loves us. When Thomas expresses his doubt, Jesus does not appear in a blaze of anger and send Thomas away. He invites Thomas to come closer, to see and to touch his wounds.

Peace is God's action among us. God's presence brings joy, not fear. We can overcome our doubts, our fear and our anxiety as we move towards belief, towards trust. We stretch ourselves out towards God, who invites us to come closer.

"Their eyes were opened and they recognised him."

Illustration

Elie Wiesel survived the Holocaust of the Second World War. A Romanian-born Jew, he describes in his book *Night* how he was taken to a concentration camp in the spring of 1944 at the age of only fourteen. One of Wiesel's most horrifying memories of Auschwitz was when the guards first tortured and then hanged a young Jewish boy, "a sad-eyed angel". Just before the hanging, Elie heard someone behind him whisper, "Where is God? Where is he?" Thousands of prisoners were forced to watch the hanging – it took the boy half an hour to die – and then to march past, looking the corpse full in the face. Behind him Elie heard the same voice ask, "Where is God now?" Wiesel writes, "And I heard a voice within me answer him: Where is he? Here he is – he is hanging here on this gallows."

Gospel Teaching

Today's Gospel story starts with a journey of despondency. Where is Jesus? Where is he? You can imagine the conversation of the two crestfallen disciples. They are walking away from Jerusalem to the village of Emmaus. We know the name of only one of them, Cleopas. The two are journeying from a painful past to a hopeless future.

But then something unexpected happens. Suddenly a stranger joins them on the road. In fact, he wasn't a stranger at all, but why didn't they recognise him? Grief over the loss of someone dear can dull and blind us to life. Of course, nobody expects to encounter a dead person alive again and walking down the road. The two disciples had heard about some women going to the tomb and not finding the body of Jesus. It does not seem to have occurred to them that if the women's report about the empty tomb was true, their report that Jesus had risen from the dead might also be true. They had evidently decided that their part in the community of Jesus' disciples was over.

The story tells us that they were jolted into a new reality: first challenged about their despair, then receiving teaching about the scriptures, and finally recognising Jesus fully alive. Back they race to Jerusalem, hastening to tell the apostles they have met the risen Jesus who made their hearts burn within them.

Application

What can we learn from this story?

Being followers of Jesus gives our lives meaning and direction. We are often moving and busy but without a strong sense of purpose and meaning. Our hearts can burn within us too when we discover that Jesus is not just a historical character. He is living and ready to engage with us as we journey through life. Yet Jesus may walk beside us unrecognised.

The story also reminds us that an encounter with Jesus can lead us to take unexpected paths. The disciples envisaged the reign of God as a political triumph, and were disappointed when the crucifixion ended this expectation. Like the disciples of Emmaus, we, too, have our own ideas of Jesus Christ, his message and his Church. To see with the eyes of faith we are called to let go of our private and limited vision.

It is important too that the two disciples recognised Jesus in the act of breaking bread. This act reveals Jesus in a special way. Early in the Church's life, the term "the breaking of bread" came to mean the celebration of the Lord's Supper – a sacred experience of worship and communion. Additionally, it would be hypocritical to break bread at the Eucharist and fail to respond to the suffering of the world's poor who do not have bread broken with them, who are starving.

We also reflect that followers of Jesus are called to be people of hope. We can take great inspiration from today's first and second readings where Peter demonstrates to the earliest Christians his great faith and hope in the risen Lord and the activity of the Holy Spirit. Amidst the disappointments in everyday life or the violence in today's world we are called to look for the signs of hope and retain a positive vision. It is particularly important to face up to suffering rather than to be like the two disciples, wanting to take a road to avoid the pain. The stranger would not let these two run from the pain of dealing with the crucifixion.

"Where is Christ? Where is he?" Through the sufferings and joys in our lives and in the world, Christ is with us.

B

"Touch me and see for yourselves."

Illustration

A few years ago, a Chinese Catholic described to a group on retreat how she had copied out, by hand, the Gospels from an old Bible. She wanted to know them more deeply and to have a text to share with other Christians or people interested in Christianity.

The Bible had belonged to her grandmother, who had kept it hidden from the authorities for almost fifty years. At the time of the Cultural Revolution of the 1960s she was worried that it would be found and that she would be sent to a prison camp.

The story reminds us of the early monks like Eadfrith who copied out the Gospels in Britain during the Dark Ages. Particular letters were illuminated by paint and fine artwork was included. The wonderful Book of Kells, kept on display at Trinity College Library in Dublin, and the Lindisfarne Gospels, now in the British Library, show the work of the Celtic monks.

Like those monks, the Christians who have faced persecution in China witness that Christ is risen from the dead. They are part of the great river of people through the ages who have celebrated Easter. Three weeks ago the paschal candle was lit from the new fire at churches throughout the world. Among small groups of Christians gathering in China, at Masses in London or New York, at celebrations in small barrios in Latin America and at rich cathedrals in Europe the same message was proclaimed.

Gospel Teaching

It is perhaps difficult for us today to imagine the deep fear of the first disciples after the death of Jesus. They had fled from the cross; only the women had remained there in prayer. Then the disciples walking to Emmaus met a stranger who explained the meaning of the Gospel to them. As soon as they recognised him as Jesus, he vanished from their sight. All the disciples found it difficult to believe that Christ had risen from the dead. His appearance, described in today's Gospel, frightened them at first. Maybe it was just because in their hearts they still believed that Jesus was dead and that they were seeing a ghost. But perhaps it's true that a meeting with God always involves fear or awe.

By describing Jesus eating with his disciples, Luke shows his readers that he was not a ghost. Christ had been raised from the dead in his totality. The body of Jesus was transformed, but they could still recognise him. After this meeting, the apostles knew that they had to preach the good news of the resurrection, even if it led to persecution or martyrdom.

The disciples were transformed by the presence of the risen Christ. They became able to face opposition, to proclaim that Jesus had been raised from the dead. Peter was able to face crucifixion. Stephen was prepared to be stoned to death. Today, some Christians suffer imprisonment for their faith, and even in our society believers are often seen as a little odd. Nurses and doctors can suffer for asserting the value of human life. There are many ways in which loyalty to the faith can lead to suffering, from speaking out about an injustice at work to telling a truth that is painful.

Peter, in his preaching in Jerusalem, calls upon those who caused the death of Jesus to repent. We usually associate repentance with the season of Lent, but it is something that is needed at all times. The saints witness to the fact that as people grow in holiness, they become more aware of the need of God's mercy and forgiveness.

Application
Each and every Christian is called to be a witness to the resurrection. For some, this happens in daily life as they bring their faith to bear on the situations they meet. Telling the truth, being honest, standing up for those who are weak: all are ways of witnessing to the faith. Perhaps one of the greatest witnesses is joining the Christian community on Sunday to celebrate the Eucharist. This strengthens the faith of all present.

Some are called to witness in more dramatic ways. Let us not forget the Chinese Catholics, and others across the world whose faith has to be secret and may be the cause of persecution.

"Do you love me?"

Illustration

When William was diagnosed as having terminal cancer, his whole family went into shock. They found it difficult to face up to, let alone talk about. Even when William left hospital to go home to die, Annie, his wife, carried on as if nothing had changed. She still fussed about the cleaning, the cooking, the shopping, all the little details that go to make up life, but which you might expect to put on hold as you spent the last few days with your loved one.

The truth was, that was the only way that Annie – and her family – could cope with the situation. They were so shocked at the diagnosis that they simply couldn't accept it, and it was only after William's funeral that the reality began to hit home. Only gradually were they able to begin to accept that it had really happened, and that William had really died, so that the process of grieving and of inner healing could begin.

Gospel Teaching

Perhaps the disciples in today's Gospel were in a similar situation. They were in a state of shock after Jesus' death. And even though the risen Jesus had already shown himself to them, they were unable to take in these strange events. So they carried on with their lives as if nothing had happened. Like Annie with her cooking and cleaning, the apostles turned to what was familiar: they went fishing. They were in denial, avoiding facing up to what had happened; and, symbolically, they came back empty-handed – they had caught nothing. Avoidance and denial are not productive strategies for dealing with life's crises.

Then Jesus enters the scene. Significantly, the night is over and the dawn has broken. Light is always symbolic in John's Gospel, and although at first the disciples don't recognise him, the presence of Jesus signals the end of the darkness and the dawn of a new day for them. He helps them find what they have been looking for – not simply fish, but a way of moving forward out of their state of shock and grief, a way of moving from denial to acceptance, from disbelief to faith, from death to perceiving the truth of the resurrection. The penny drops – "It is the Lord" – and, typically, it is the impetuous Peter who plunges straight in to reach Jesus.

The scene that follows illustrates how Jesus helps Peter to move forward. He gently leads Peter to face up to his past. Perhaps the easiest thing would have been for Jesus to have glossed over Peter's threefold denial. But Jesus knows that if Peter is to move on, he needs to confront his past and grow from it. So, gathered around a charcoal fire, reminiscent of the charcoal fire by which Peter had stood the night he denied Christ, Jesus gently begins the healing process. He knows that Peter's denials have been eating away inside him, and so he gives Peter a chance to be redeemed, to make good the past. By his questioning, Jesus is actually helping Peter overcome the wound that he had inflicted on himself, pouring in his forgiveness and healing. This time Peter is able to make more than a merely impetuous profession of love: he makes a deep commitment. This is what Christ elicits from Peter – for Peter's sake – so that Peter will be able to face his future without running away again, without denying the Lord he loves.

Application

In our own lives, we meet situations that cause us shock, which we find hard to accept or deal with. There are things in the past of each one of us that are painful and in need of healing or forgiveness. If we try to avoid them and just focus on the superficialities of our daily lives, these wounds will eat away inside us. They will keep us in the tomb of denial, anger, despair, darkness. We will remain dead inside.

But if, like the beloved disciple, we can recognise the presence of the Lord, he will help us face our problems and heal our wounds, as he helped Peter. We find in Christ not condemnation and recrimination, but forgiveness and acceptance of who we are. He is the light that can dispel our inner darkness, the hope that drives away despair. And if, like Peter, we can commit ourselves in love to Christ, he will invite us to follow him and to exercise a loving, pastoral responsibility towards others: "Feed my sheep." This will undoubtedly lead us to the cross – but the future need hold no terror for us, for the cross always leads us to the light of the resurrection.

A

"The sheep follow because they know his voice."

Illustration

A priest in a rural parish had spent a glorious summer's morning on a local farm, after having been invited by the farmer to assist in gathering the sheep from the fell top. Until then his encounters with sheep had been limited mainly to rescuing the occasional errant lamb that found itself stuck in one of the fences near the church while reaching for the grass on the other side. But the morning's work had gone well: he had not sent the sheep the wrong way or lost any – or even lost himself on the fell.

Later that week he assisted the farmer in feeding the sheep. These pastoral experiences gave him a glow of inward satisfaction and he resolved that he would bring them into his homily at Mass the following Sunday. But when Sunday arrived, the rain was lashing down and the roads to the church were flooded. The congregation was consequently reduced to a handful and so he debated with himself as to whether, because of the small number of people, he should deliver the full homily or give only a brief summary.

He opted for the full homily – but then sensed that it hadn't gone down too well. Afterwards he said to the farmer, "Well, I thought of saying just a few words and then I thought of you feeding the sheep. If only a few come, you still feed them, don't you?" "That's as may be," replied the farmer. "But I don't give them the full bag of feed, do I?"

Gospel Teaching

The farmer, like any good shepherd, knew that to give his sheep too much was as bad as giving them too little. In the Old Testament the relationship of God with the people of Israel is compared to that between a shepherd and his sheep. Isaiah says that God is like "a shepherd feeding his flock, gathering lambs in his arms"; God says to Ezekiel, "I myself will pasture my sheep... I shall be a true shepherd to them."

The concept of God as shepherd is fulfilled in Jesus, who calls his sheep individually by name. The sheep follow him because they know his voice. He is also the "gate of the sheepfold" as through him the sheep are sure of finding pasture. It is through Christ that the people of God, called by name and responding to his voice, enter into the pastures of eternal life.

In the Roman catacombs there are numerous Christian symbols: the peacock representing immortality; the dove signifying reconciliation and peace; the fish as a sign of Christ. But the most frequently used image is that of the Good Shepherd. A beautiful wall fresco in the Catacomb of Domitilla shows a figure of a young Christ in a woodland glade with trees on either side of him. On his shoulders he carries a lamb, clasping its legs with his right hand; in his left hand he holds a staff. Two sheep gaze up at him; two feed near his feet.

On a Christian tombstone in the same catacomb is a similar pastoral image. A shepherd sits underneath a tree; in his left hand he holds a shepherd's crook, in his right he holds panpipes. A reclining sheep gazes up at him. This image is different in that it was pagan in origin, but the early Christians understood that, pagan or Christian, a shepherd has a unique relationship with his sheep. The pagan image became that of Christ, the shepherd in whom the sheep find pasture beneath the tree of life – the wood of the cross.

Application
Just as these early disciples gave a Christian meaning to a pagan symbol, so pagan festivals were superseded by Christian feasts, as in the case of Christmas and Easter. In the present age it sometimes seems that a reversal is in process and that the meaning of a Christian celebration is taken over by a kind of paganism that elevates secular things almost to the status of "gods".

What should be our response? As Christians, we are called to participate in the work of the Good Shepherd. We are called to have nothing of the "false shepherd" about us, and therefore nothing that prevents us from having at least something of that Spirit-filled courage that enabled Peter to stand up before the crowd and proclaim Jesus as Lord and Christ. Like the farmer who fed his sheep neither too much nor too little, we are to present our faith to others with integrity.

B

"I am the good shepherd: the good shepherd is one who lays down his life for his sheep."

Illustration

A simple wooden cross with its inscription, "No matarás", stands by the side of a road on the outskirts of Lima, in Peru. Emphasising the commandment "You shall not kill", it recalls a sister of the Missionary Society of St Columban who was killed at this spot alongside escaped prisoners in 1983.

Sister Joan Sawyer was aged fifty-one when she and eight prisoners died on the dusty road outside a squalid prison in Peru's capital city. Originally from Ireland, Sister Joan used to go to the Lurigancho Prison three or four days a week to visit prisoners. Conditions there were bad, and out of five thousand prisoners only one thousand had been sentenced. The rest were awaiting sentence and many were probably innocent. Sister Joan used to bring them relief – medicines for some, a kind word for others, news about how their legal papers were progressing in the Ministry for Justice. The majority came from the poor areas of Lima where they never had enough to eat, didn't finish school and couldn't find decent work.

On the morning of 14th December 1983 a group of prisoners tried to escape. Sister Joan was one of the hostages taken. After all-day negotiations with the prison authorities it was agreed that the prisoners and their hostages would be allowed to leave the prison in the evening in an ambulance. They were no sooner outside the prison gate than waiting police riddled the ambulance with bullets from all sides. Four bullets struck Joan and when she was removed from the ambulance she was dead.

During Joan's funeral, a large banner placed over the altar read: "There is no greater love than to lay down your life for your friends."

Gospel Teaching

All four Gospel writers use the metaphor of Jesus as shepherd. God is also described as a shepherd in Hebrew scripture. So John's use of the metaphor is nothing new. What is new is John's description of the relationship between the shepherd and the individual sheep.

John explains that the life and work of Jesus demonstrate God's love for every individual. Jesus the shepherd knows the name of each one of his sheep and each person has a one-to-one relationship with Jesus. It's a two-way relationship. Just as the sheep recognise the shepherd's voice, so we know the voice of Jesus when he calls us. This kind of love resembles the kind of love the Father has for Jesus. It is a love that binds us at once to the Father, to Jesus, and to each other.

Today's Gospel reading presents Jesus as the "good shepherd". The word "good" here means "good" in the sense of "noble" or "ideal", and not simply "good at" something. Unlike bad shepherds who let the sheep be eaten by wolves, Jesus is willing to lay down his life for the sheep. This relationship is the basis for the sacrifice that Jesus makes on behalf of the sheep. Note that it also extends to sheep "not of this fold" – this refers to future generations of believers and possibly the future entry of Gentiles into the fold of Christianity.

Application

The image of the good shepherd invites us today to reflect on those who have given dedicated service to the Church and its people – people like Sister Joan Sawyer and many others throughout our world, especially those who have worked for justice, peace and reconciliation. We are talking about laity, as well as clergy and religious, some well known and others less well known, who have followed the model of Jesus in being good shepherds. We may want to reflect on those places in our Church where we still need "good shepherding" or where the "shepherding" has left us in need. Some issues cry out for our Church's response, like the special needs of immigrants and refugees, the need to bring an end to violence and militarism, the trade policies that marginalise poorer nations.

Today's image of the good shepherd can also challenge us to apply the image to the wider world. Does not the good shepherd challenge our international institutions to show a special care for those in need – those who are poor and powerless, vulnerable children and minorities? Does it not challenge our nation and its institutions to a more sincere respect for human rights?

A world that makes real the loving care of the good shepherd must work to put an end to all kinds of abuse that God's people currently endure.

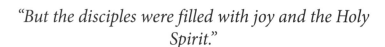

C

"But the disciples were filled with joy and the Holy Spirit."

Illustration

Richard Attenborough is someone who has done many different things, and achieved much in his long life. In his younger years he was an actor in the theatre and in film. Later on he became a film director and has produced some outstanding work. But, as he said himself, he never wanted to be a film director, he just wanted to direct one film. That film was *Gandhi*.

In 1962 he was handed a biography of the great Indian leader and, once he had read it, he knew he had to make the film. It took him another twenty years before he achieved his goal, but the result was well worth the wait.

The film tells the story of a man of peace who spent his life fighting against the injustice and violent tendencies of the world. In one scene, we see the Mahatma very weak from fasting in an attempt to curb the violence in his own land. From his sickbed he says, "All the lessons of history tell us that violence never succeeds. For a time it appears to win, but in the end it always fails. Always."

Gospel Teaching

Like Gandhi, the early Christian Church found itself faced with the constant threat of violence. At first its opponents offered argument, and verbal abuse, then it developed into threats and assaults, and eventually Christians found themselves facing arrest, imprisonment and even death. The apostle Paul experienced all these things, in an ascending order of hostility throughout the course of his missionary life. His visit to Antioch in Pisidia with Barnabas is welcomed by the local people, but resented by the Jewish community, his own people. Paul and Barnabas are expelled from the city.

The Christian community in Rome suffered terrible treatment at the hands of the emperor, Nero. They were made scapegoats for the fire that destroyed a great part of the city. They were most cruelly dealt with to distract the population from uncomfortable rumours about the emperor himself. The shock of this violence prompted John the apostle to write about them and to reassure the followers of Jesus that all would be well.

The people who went "through the great persecution", as John describes it in today's second reading, were the Christians of Rome, who suffered at the hands of Nero in AD 64. John tells us that God will wipe away all tears from their eyes. He wants us to persevere in our faith and in our love and not to yield to the temptation to turn to violence ourselves.

Our great example in all this is Jesus: the one who describes himself as a shepherd, who cares for his sheep, even to the point of laying down his life for them. In conversation with the Jewish religious leaders, Jesus speaks of his true followers as those who listen to his voice. That voice speaks of peace; it also speaks of justice and truth. It is a voice that will not be silenced. Violence cannot stop the force of truth.

Application

Today's generation, like every generation that has gone before, is plagued by violence. People suffer greatly through the anger, hostility and downright viciousness that occur every day around the globe. The evil that people do lives after them, spawning more evil in its turn, creating cycles of violence.

Looking at history, as Gandhi did, do we learn the lesson it teaches? Looking to Jesus, do we hear his voice? As the followers of Christ, are we true members of his flock, living peaceful lives? John, in his vision, sees a huge number of people, made up from every nation, race, tribe and language. They are people who have suffered, but who have come through suffering and are now victorious. That victory is not only over the violence of others, but also over the temptation to violence that we find in ourselves. This is the greater victory, the victory over ourselves.

Gandhi was inspired in his life by the teaching of Jesus in the Beatitudes: "Blessed are the peacemakers." In his turn, Gandhi inspired Martin Luther King, who led the great movement in America in the 1960s for justice and equality. Both these men, Gandhi and King, met with violent deaths. But they were not defeated. Their message, their voice, their example lives on.

In the face of evil, Jesus does not ask us to do nothing. He asks us to do everything that will lead people into the ways of peace.

A

"Lord, we do not know where you are going, so how can we know the way?"

Illustration

Have you ever been lost? It can be an alarming experience. In these days of satellite navigation systems, there are many technological aids to help us find our way to where we want to go. But sometimes a bit of human support and help, and maybe the experience of someone who personally knows the route, is what we'd rather have.

It doesn't always work like that. A story tells of a couple of tourists who were spending an idyllic few days on holiday in the country. They enjoyed walking the rural roads and byways. But one day they wandered so far that they had no idea how to find their way back to the hotel where they were staying. The daylight hours were nearing their end, and they were relieved suddenly to spot an old man sitting in the doorway of his cottage enjoying the evening sun. Explaining their predicament, and where they needed to get back to, they asked for directions. The old man thought for a few moments, shook his head slowly, and said, "Ah, I know the place you mean. The trouble is, if you want to get there, you wouldn't want to be starting from here."

Gospel Teaching

"You wouldn't want to be starting from here." In a way, that's what the disciples seem to be thinking in today's Gospel. Jesus has just told them that he is going away. Despite all his assurances, and his words of comfort to them, they are worried. When they'd committed themselves to Jesus, they'd imagined that he would remain with them in person, guiding their footsteps, helping them to make their way through life with him. But now here he is talking about leaving them, going on ahead of them. How will they ever manage to follow? Thomas sums up what they are all silently thinking: "Lord, we do not know where you are going, so how can we know the way?" This is most definitely not where they want to be starting from.

In response to the question, Jesus doesn't draw them a map. He doesn't give them a set of directions. "I am the Way," he says. And not only "the Way", but also "the Truth and the Life". It must have been hard for the disciples to comprehend those words at first, to understand the full depth of their meaning. Yet it would not be long before those same disciples were known as "followers of the Way".

The months and years they had spent with Jesus had been for a purpose. As they'd spent time with him, hearing his words, watching the things he did, sharing the life he lived, they had changed. Sometimes they'd been slow to understand. Sometimes they'd got things wrong, and they still would. But they'd learned, not only from Jesus' teaching but also from his example. They'd seen the way he related to people. They'd seen the way that he put the loving will of God his Father first. They'd seen the way he lived his life. And slowly but surely, though not always smoothly, they'd begun to know that way, and even to live it out themselves. They'd come to see it as the way of truth; they'd come to know it as the way to life. And so they became followers of the Way.

Application

How can we do the same? We too are called to follow Jesus' example; but we're not expected to do so alone. When Jesus told his disciples that he would no longer be physically present with them, he also gave them a promise. When he returned to his Father, he would send them the Spirit of truth, who would remain with them always. It's through that Spirit that they would, incredible though it may have seemed to them at the time, be able to perform even greater works than those they had seen Jesus perform himself. We see this happening in the amazing growth of the Church which we read about in the Acts of the Apostles through this Easter season.

That promise holds true for us today. We are the followers of the Way. We are not lost on the road; we are not abandoned to make our own way. We are, in Peter's words, "a chosen race, a royal priesthood, a consecrated nation". As we follow the Way, we can know that we have the promised Spirit with us, to guide us and to show us the way to our true and eternal home.

5th Sunday of Easter

"Remain in me."

Illustration

Many years ago a newly ordained priest arrived in an inner-city parish to which he had been assigned by his bishop. He was eager to begin work and the parish priest gave him the poorest area of the parish to visit systematically house by house. He had very little money and few possessions, but that didn't matter. He had never been happier in his life. His other duties included acting as chaplain to the parish school, saying daily Mass at the local convent and visiting those who were sick in the large city hospital.

The day came when he received an urgent call from the hospital to attend a dying man. The priest thought the nurse on the telephone had said the dying man was aged seventy. Imagine his shock, when, on pulling aside the curtains surrounding the patient's bed, he discovered that it was in fact a young man of seventeen. The young man was also an orphan and had no friends or family to comfort him as he lay dying.

Furthermore, the young man was in agony and could hardly breathe, let alone speak. Nevertheless, when the priest asked if he would like the sacrament of the sick and Holy Communion, such was the young man's faith that he nodded vigorously. As the priest anointed him and gave him Holy Communion, the young man became totally calm and serene. A few minutes later he died peacefully. He had clearly died in union with Christ. This was the first time the newly ordained priest had been present when someone died.

Gospel Teaching

Using a metaphor taken from the vineyard, a familiar sight to his listeners, Jesus describes himself to his disciples as the true vine and his Father as the vinedresser. He goes on to speak of them as branches and explains that, provided they remain part of the vine, they will bear much fruit. In other words, they will enable others to enter the kingdom of heaven. On the other hand, they will not bear fruit if they are cut off from Christ.

It is, in essence, a simple lesson that can be learnt from the vine, or from any other growing plant. To grow, to flourish, to bear fruit, it is necessary to remain part of the whole. A branch that is connected to the vine will continue to draw life and health from its roots. It will eventually bear the fruit that it was made to bear. A branch that is cut off, on the other hand, can only wither and fade; it will never bear fruit.

This teaching was something greatly appreciated by the dying young man. Even in the depths of his suffering, he knew how vital it was for him to remain one with Christ. The extent of his faith also had a deep influence on the newly ordained priest. Alone in the world, the dying man hugely valued his discipleship with Christ. This was something the priest never forgot. It thereafter influenced how he ministered to those in the parish who were sick or dying.

Jesus goes on to say that those disciples who do not remain in him are like branches that will be thrown away and destroyed, whilst those who remain in him may ask whatever they like and their prayers will be heard. Jesus concludes by pointing out that by bearing fruit they will bring glory to God the Father. Then they will truly be his disciples.

Application
For us, like the young man dying in hospital, there are times when our need for Christ is urgent. We may be sick, in pain, lonely or depressed. We may have problems that seem to overwhelm us or difficulties that appear to have no solution. We may be distressed by events around us or which we hear about on the news or see on television. Hopefully we may find comfort from others in our community, such as Saul, in the first reading, received from Barnabas, and eventually from the rest of the disciples.

Most of all, however, we can be reassured by the Gospel that, if we remain true to our belief in Jesus and remain as much a part of him as branches are part of a vine, then we shall ultimately have our prayers heard whatever our situation. Like the young man dying in hospital, we shall know what it is to be in Christ's presence.

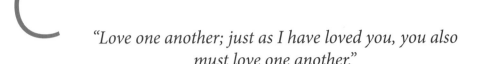

"Love one another; just as I have loved you, you also must love one another."

Illustration

In the summer months the seaside town becomes very busy. Its well-planned streets, with their brightly coloured shops and houses, are thronged with tourists and holidaymakers. The tree-lined street is filled with cars, and traffic brings noise and bustle to everyday life. On the high street itself stands the Catholic church, a tall grey building. Stepping in off the busy street, and through the porch, one enters a totally different world.

The interior of the building is an enclosed sacred space. The high walls and ceiling encircle a huge space, but not an empty space. This interior is full of silence, peace, light and shadow, colour and stillness. In this spot a person can sit and be still and let all the cares of life fall away.

In a side chapel beside the sanctuary, candles flicker and a few souls can be seen kneeling in prayer. On the altar the Blessed Sacrament is exposed. Yet that real presence of God is felt in every part of this church, it is so well designed. The words of the apostle John, in his vision of heaven, come flooding into the mind: "Here God lives among men."

The people of the town are rightly proud of their church. It is a holy place. Apart from Mass and other ceremonies, people call in to pray at all times of the day. The very air of the building is fragrant with prayer. "They shall be his people, and he will be their God."

Whatever credit must go to the architect – and he deserves much – perhaps the people must be given more. For it is prayerful contact with the living God that truly creates the atmosphere of a holy place.

Gospel Teaching

When Paul and Barnabas were making their missionary journeys through Asia, their first priority was to create communities of faith, places where God would dwell among his people. They had much success in their work and were able to appoint elders to oversee the communities when they moved on. Whenever they returned to visit these communities, it was like finding a home from home. They were greeted warmly and welcomed into the house of God.

When the missionary journey was completed, Paul and Barnabas arrived back safely in Antioch. They had come full circle, and now back in this community they were able to recount the story of their travels, and of the joys and difficulties they had experienced. In return, the community gave them welcome, recognition and rest.

These experiences of community all flow from the room of the Lord's Last Supper. There, as he broke bread with his disciples, Jesus gave them the great commandment, the new commandment: not just to love one another, but rather to love as Jesus had loved. This is a transforming love. It changes the one who loves and it changes the one who receives that love.

This powerful commandment Jesus gave to his friends at the very time that he was being betrayed. Judas had just gone out into the night to give his friend away. At that moment, back in the upper room, Jesus was telling his disciples that this moment of betrayal was also the moment when his glory as the Son of God was being revealed. To persevere in love when you are surrounded by chaos and cruelty, surely this is something glorious, something divine.

Application

All these experiences – of churches, of communities, of the Eucharist, of the Gospel – these belong to us as Christian people. We have tasted something of the divine, something of John's vision of heaven, in the course of our life. But for many people these things are unknown. They have never felt the nearness of God. But they do know about tears, and death, and mourning and sadness. This is the world they live in. A walk into a peaceful church may soothe but will not solve their problems. What will?

In talking with his disciples, Jesus says very clearly, "By this love you have for one another, everyone will know that you are my disciples." Our faith in Jesus Christ calls us to persevere in love, even in the face of hostility and hardships. As Paul and Barnabas remind us, "We all have to experience many hardships before we enter the kingdom of God."

By this love let us help to wipe away the tears from people's eyes. When they feel that they are loved, then they will know that the world is new.

A

"Always have your answer ready for people who ask you the reason for the hope that you all have."

Illustration

Ethiopia is a land that is familiar with hardship, with famines, droughts and wars that increase the suffering of the people. For the love of these people, Bishop Armido Gasparini, an Italian missionary, made Awasa, in southern Ethiopia, his home. He and his small band of Comboni missionaries showed the love of God through their tireless work in training lay catechists, establishing medical clinics in rural areas and providing schools.

From having one parish in the early 1960s, the Church in Awasa has grown to twenty parishes, with many more outstations. There are now hundreds of catechists and the Catholic population has increased enormously. Every day many hundreds of people are treated in the clinics, and thousands of children are receiving an education who would not otherwise have done so. When Bishop Gasparini retired in 1993, he explained how he could see the difference that Christ had made in the lives of the people.

Gospel Teaching

We cannot all be missionaries in distant countries, but we can take the love of Christ to the people around us. It has never been easy to evangelise, and persecution has been the response to many who have gone before us. When Philip the deacon first went to the Samaritan town he was by no means assured of a warm welcome. This was shortly after Stephen, another deacon, had been stoned to death, and Saul of Tarsus had begun his persecution of Christians. Philip had escaped to the northern province of the Samaritans, a people who expected the Messiah but were considered heretics by the Jews. Philip proclaimed the Good News of Christ and by his authentic witness won over the people there. The power he had drawn on to enable him to do his work was the Spirit of truth. This was promised by Jesus, in today's Gospel, to all who love him and who keep his commandments.

In Peter's first letter, written at a time of persecution, we are advised to be prepared to explain what our faith is about and why we continue to be people of hope. But whatever words we use, it is by the way we lead our lives that we are judged. If we keep Christ's commandments, we can keep a clear conscience and anyone who slanders us will be proved wrong. And, like Philip, we do not have to struggle alone. The promised Holy Spirit will come into our lives to give us strength and encouragement. As Bishop Gasparini observed, it is Christ through the Holy Spirit who makes a difference in our lives and in those of the people who accept him with joyful hearts.

Application

As Christians we have received the Holy Spirit in baptism – a power that is not of our own making. This power is the very same that sustained the martyrs in their gruelling punishments and executions; the same that encourages missionaries to endure hardships for the love of other people. It is the Spirit that enables us to find the words to use to describe why we are followers of Christ.

But the Spirit needs our cooperation too. Philip could not have converted the Samaritans if he had not gone to them, nor could Bishop Gasparini have established his schools and clinics if he had not settled in Ethiopia. To have the answer ready for anybody who wants to know about Christianity, we do have to give the matter some attention. We need to know about our faith in order to share it with others. It helps if we have access to courses, or books or other means of deepening our knowledge. Talking about it with our friends and family can help us put our thoughts into words. Studying scripture and spending time in prayer are also vital ways of preparing for the times we need to explain our beliefs to others.

Yet note how St Peter cautions that our words have to be given with courtesy and respect. How easy it is, when something so dear to us is discussed, to allow ourselves to become embroiled in arguments. Yet it is also in the way we conduct ourselves, and in what we do, that the message is most effectively conveyed. But we need not be discouraged, for even if we do not think we have said the right things or been great models of Christian living, it is the Spirit who will work in the hearts of the other people; and we know we can leave the results of our endeavours safely in the keeping of that same Holy Spirit.

B

"Love one another, as I have loved you."

Illustration

There's an old Jewish saying, from a wise rabbi, that goes: "Ten strong things have been created in the world. Rock is hard, but iron cleaves it. Iron is hard, but fire softens it. Fire is powerful, but water quenches it. Water is heavy, but clouds bear it. Clouds are thick, but wind scatters them. Wind is strong, but a body resists it. A body is strong, but fear crushes it. Fear is powerful, but wine banishes it. Wine is strong, but sleep works it off. Sleep is strong, but death is stronger. And yet love delivers from death."

There was a news story a while ago about a mother who pushed her baby's pram out of the way of an oncoming truck. The mother was killed; but her child lived. This was a split-second decision, yet one that demonstrates the power of love, and the willingness of true love to be self-giving and self-sacrificial. The mother would be remembered for this act; her child would grow up not knowing her mother, but knowing that her mother had loved her.

Gospel Teaching

We may have a problem today when we hear the word "love". Yet the problem lies in the way that we use the word itself. The world today tends not to use it in the same sense as the New Testament writers do. We trivialise it, talking about loving chocolate, or loving our favourite football team, pop group or TV programme. Popular music is filled with words about love, but usually the meaning is sentimental.

So when we read, in the first letter of John, that God is love; and then when our Gospel today begins by talking of the love the Father has for Jesus – "As the Father has loved me, so I have loved you" – we may wonder what this all means. The love within the inner relationships in the depths of the Trinity is, of course, beyond our understanding; but it's certainly not a trivial or sentimental love. In fact it is a love that is deep and self-sacrificial.

John's letter tells us that God the Father's sacrificial love is shown through the activity of the Son: "God's love for us when he sent his Son to be the sacrifice that takes our sins away". Jesus has often been called "the man for others"; and he showed that generous love for us supremely on the cross.

Accepting crucifixion was clearly not trivial or sentimental. It was a tough, brutal, self-giving act of love on the part of Jesus.

And Jesus calls us to make that standard of love our own. "Remain in my love," he says – that same love that is in the heart of the Trinity, that same love that is demonstrated in the life and death of Jesus. "Love one another, as I have loved you." Jesus is calling us to live that love for others: that love that we saw demonstrated a few short weeks ago when he washed the feet of his friends; and then supremely when he offered his life for us on the cross.

Application
This is the love in which we are called to remain all our lives. This is a love that reflects the true meaning of the word: not something that is trivial or sentimental, not just an emotion that is simply an internal response to some external stimulus. When we are called to Christian love, this is something different and has little to do with our emotions.

To remain in Jesus' love is not to sit back and enjoy peace of mind and a sublime state of equilibrium that is untroubled by all that passes by. It is not a self-indulgent sense of the certainty of our own salvation without reference to anyone else. Jesus calls us to love as he did. That means a love that does not concern itself with our own wants, our own desires, our own emotions: it means a love that is willing to give of ourselves, a love that does not count the cost, a love that is extended even to those we would not normally want to love. This is, truly, a love that is stronger than death.

If we can learn to show this love, then we too become people for others, just as Jesus was. So let us pray for a deeper commitment in our lives to that true Christian love that does not just inwardly desire but outwardly gives.

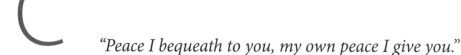

"Peace I bequeath to you, my own peace I give you."

Illustration

Anyone who has worked with people will know that success comes down to listening to each other. Those charged with helping others in a professional way would tell us that ninety per cent of their time is taken up in listening to what is said and, more importantly, in noting the underlying fears and anxieties. This is a special gift, as we humans tend to make things more complicated than they need to be.

An interesting way to test people's listening skills is to ask them to pass on one or two lines of information by simply whispering it to the person next to them. If this is done in a group, then, as the message is passed from person to person, people will mishear the message or add their own twist to the story, so that the final version may bear little resemblance to the original news.

Gospel Teaching

The writer of the Apocalypse tries to convey his vision of the heavenly city, the kingdom of light where all will be perfect and united around the Almighty. The Church on earth witnesses to this kingdom and in some ways is a forerunner of it, but that doesn't mean that we remain free from turmoil.

The history of the early Church is one of division. Sometimes traditions would collide, yet often communities stood firm, connected to Christ the cornerstone. The dispute at Antioch is a good example of the kind of struggle that occurs in every age. The visitors had come to command and condemn, not to listen; they wanted to impose the demands of race and culture on this fledgling Christian community. The question of circumcision disguised a bigger debate: whether it was the law that saved, or being baptised into Christ. It was also about who held the power in the Church, which was quickly becoming predominantly Gentile.

The disquiet of the locals is matched by the unspoken fears of these self-appointed teachers. Yet let's not be too quick to judge them. Acting out of arrogance and self-importance, it can be easy to justify certain positions, forgetting that it is the Spirit that gives us the gift of faith. In this particular debate it is the same Spirit that brings the peace of Christ to the community.

So what is this peace that is promised by Christ? It is a peace the world cannot give, because it is intimately connected with the kingdom. Jesus tells his followers of the Pentecost experience. He must return to the Father, so that the Advocate can be sent to be with them. The Spirit will be a helper and defender who will teach and hold them together through times of trial. They will be strengthened by the Spirit dwelling within them in Christ's name. The promise made to the covenant people is fulfilled. The peace of Christ is nothing less than a sharing in life eternal. It is something his followers can have now, if they are willing to keep his word and listen to the Advocate. That Spirit continues to dwell within our communities, casting out fear and binding us together.

Application

Peace is more than the absence of conflict and war. Christ asks us not to be afraid, reassuring us that he has left us a companion for the journey. Yet the Spirit of Pentecost usually indicates a time of testing to come. The Spirit is sent among us to quell our fears in the midst of the world. The presence of the Spirit certainly does not preclude debate within the Church – in fact this is the way the Church has developed through the years. It is possible to disagree and still love each other enough to try to listen and understand. It also helps to find time for prayer, that we might give ear to the Spirit within.

The disputes of the early Christians may seem a bit obscure and irrelevant to us. But one thing is clear, in their time and in ours: it is hard to be open to people and resist the temptation to place our burdens on them. It's more convenient to tell others we have everything worked out and that their role is simply to follow our way of doing things. Yet all the while Jesus makes it so simple: "If anyone loves me he will keep my word." Others might be able to cast a new light on that word for us. God's Spirit can work in amazing and unexpected ways, in us and in others – are our minds and hearts truly open to believe that?

A

"You will be my witnesses."

Illustration

"Nothing is permanent except change," the Greek philosopher Heraclitus wrote two and a half thousand years ago. To live is to change. And whenever there is an important change or a new beginning in the life of an individual or of a community, there are ceremonies and rites to mark those changes.

Psychologically, it's important to acknowledge the transition from the old to the new, from the past to the future, from what was to what is to be. We often use commissioning ceremonies to mark such new beginnings, especially if the changes are planned and intentional, if they're the result of careful planning, preparation or training. We hold commissioning services for everything from new hospitals and ships to new officers in the military. It's a way of showing that something – or someone – is now fit for purpose.

Gospel Teaching

Each of the Gospels ends with a commissioning of some sort, a way of marking the transition from the time when Jesus physically walked the earth with his disciples to the time after the ascension, when they learnt to recognise his presence among them in different ways. Today's readings provide us with the descriptions by both Matthew and Luke of that moment of transition and Christ's commissioning of the disciples for their new life.

Matthew tells us that Jesus gave his disciples some quite specific instructions: they are to make disciples of all nations, baptise them and teach them to observe all his commands. This "great commission", as it is known, shows that the disciples' task is simply to carry on the ministry of Jesus. They themselves have absorbed his teaching and spirit – made it their own – so that they in turn are now able to pass it on to others.

Now they are to call people into a life of discipleship, just as Jesus called them to be disciples; and they are to invite people to become members of the family of Christ, through baptism, just as Jesus himself had welcomed them into his family. Jesus assures the disciples that he will continue to be with them to the end of time. How? Through the very things he speaks of in commissioning them: through his words and teachings, through the sacramental life of his family, through a life of faithful discipleship in community.

In the first reading, Luke gives us a very dramatic description of that moment of transition and commissioning. Central to the whole of Jesus' life has been the proclamation of the kingdom of God, and the risen Jesus continues to speak about it to his disciples. So when the disciples ask a question about restoring the kingdom to Israel, he corrects their misunderstanding.

The kingdom that he proclaims is not about politics and territory, but rather is about the rule of God over minds and hearts – not just of the people of Israel, but of all the peoples of the world. And so the great commission he gives his disciples is to be his witnesses to the whole world. They are to carry on Jesus' work for the kingdom of God, by drawing all peoples into that kingdom. The same Spirit working in Jesus will continue to work for the kingdom through the disciples.

Application

In our liturgical life, this feast of the ascension marks a transition between the resurrection of Christ at Easter and the coming of the Holy Spirit at Pentecost – it's an opportune time for us to reflect on our own commissioning as disciples of the Lord, and to ask ourselves if we, and our community, remain fit for purpose.

We might look to the way we celebrate Christ's ongoing presence: What is the quality of our listening to his words and teaching in scripture, and how do we communicate the teaching and spirit of Christ to others? Are we open and welcoming to others – do we invite them to join the family of Christ? In our own personal discipleship, are we faithful to our commitment to follow Christ through our life of prayer and service of others?

We might ask whether our community is fit for that most fundamental purpose, the reason why we exist as a Christian family – to be witnesses to the risen Christ, to all people. This daunting task is the greatest of all commissions, but not one we need fear. For Jesus is with us always – in word and sacrament and community – and he sends us the Holy Spirit, to give us power and confidence for our mission.

"God goes up with shouts of joy."

Illustration

Travel by the great motorways is reckoned to be the safest form of travel for the average motorist. Accidents seldom happen. However, when they do, not only are the consequences likely to be serious; but often there is a further hazard, posed by what are popularly known as "rubberneckers". Rubberneckers are the motorists who take their eye off the road, or even slow down, in order to gaze across the carriageway and get a better view of what's happening at the site of the accident. A police officer on the scene will always signal such dangerous drivers to keep moving.

While this is a well-known phenomenon, a young teacher was more than a little surprised when she asked the children to describe what happened on the day of the ascension, and heard one reply: "Well, Miss, Jesus shot up into heaven and the apostles just stood there rubbernecking." It was a reply obviously sparked off by today's first reading, which tells how, as Jesus ascended into the heavens, his friends stood "staring into the sky"; that is, until two angelic figures appeared, rather like a couple of heavenly police officers gently moving them on. They have a job to do.

Gospel Teaching

It must have taken time for the apostles to come to terms with the marvel of the ascension; little wonder they stood for a while gazing into the clouds. For forty days since his resurrection Jesus had constantly been with them. Now they surely experienced mixed feelings. Their Master was leaving them; no longer would they enjoy his visible presence. This spelt sadness. Yet they knew that he was returning in his humanity to his beloved Father, completing the triumph begun by his resurrection. And they were sure, as the Gospel puts it, that the Lord would be "working with them" as they went out to preach and baptise; moreover, they had the assurance that this was no final goodbye: one day he would return. And so if they had sadness on the day of the ascension, above all they had great joy. The next we hear of them they are waiting expectantly for that coming of the Holy Spirit that would launch them, in Jesus' words, as "my witnesses… to the ends of the earth".

It is the joy of the occasion that is captured in today's liturgy, especially in the responsorial psalm. "God goes up with shouts of joy" was the response that we repeated over and over again; and the psalm urged: "All peoples, clap your hands." It seems that this psalm was originally part of an annual celebration at which the ark of the covenant, symbol of God's presence, was carried in procession up to the Temple amid crowds of rejoicing worshippers. There would be rhythmical hand-clapping, the blaring of the trumpet (fashioned from a ram's horn), and repeated cries of "Sing praise for God", "sing praise to our king" and "God is king of all the earth."

Application

On this day we are invited to raise our voices in praise of the Lord who has ascended to his heavenly throne as King of kings. Our presence at this Mass is itself a sign that we want to respond to the invitation; we want to praise our dear Lord for his personal triumph; we want to thank him too because of the hope that he has brought to us, the "rich glories" he promises us and the power, which Paul calls "infinitely great", that he exercises on our behalf.

And yet we dare not stop there. To do so might be described as a type of spiritual rubbernecking, being so fascinated with one aspect of today's great feast that we forget the other: we forget that the last words of the Lord at his ascension were that we should spread the Good News, that we should be his witnesses.

That's a task that we fulfil principally by the way we live our daily lives. The Gospel may speak of some of the marvels "associated with believers" in the early days of the Church, such as healings, and casting out of devils and speaking with tongues, but we too, in our own small, less dramatic way – by our patience, our little acts of kindness, our concern for others, our readiness to forgive, our joy, our humble living out of the Gospel – we too are bearing witness to our Lord's message, we too are living signs confirming that Jesus has risen, Jesus has ascended, Jesus is Lord.

"I am sending down to you what the Father has promised."

Illustration

A few years ago a remarkable soldier was asked to be part of a reconnaissance team removing landmines from a war-torn African country. During this undertaking he was badly injured and had most of his leg removed. He returned home, and like many others began the slow process of recovery.

Anyone who has sustained major injuries will tell you that, as you attempt to recover, there will be moments when you are prone to depression. Healing often depends on the attitude you adopt in a given situation. This man found that he was able to battle his way back to health, and with the aid of a prosthetic leg even took up long-distance running. In speaking of his ordeal, he said that he could have become very angry and bitter. He went on to say, "But who wants to live with someone like that?" He had discovered an important truth: that beyond our human frailties, our sufferings and our failure, we can find hope.

Gospel Teaching

Today we are presented with two versions of the ascension story, both written by Luke. In the Gospel, Luke explains that suffering is not the last word for any of us. Christ comes to his followers and offers them his blessing. Through his death, resurrection and ascension he restores to them a sense of hope and peace. This experience of faith will remain with them in the Spirit promised by the Father. A great sense of joy and enthusiasm comes through in these accounts. Sadness gives way to worship and praise.

This is also clear in the rest of the Acts of the Apostles. Throughout the book, Luke tells of the presence of Christ in the early Church, reminding us of the Lord's promise that we will never be alone. Yet he also reminds us that it is the events of Christ's passion and his rising from death that are the source of our hope. Both of today's accounts of Christ's ascension show us that the mission of the disciples is to share this good news with others, so that Christ's message of hope may be spread throughout the world. It is only when they accept the Spirit that they are enabled to do this.

The ascension experience is recounted in different ways but in essence it tells us that Christ has conquered all, and is now the ruler of all, past and present; he is ruler too of our joys, fears and regrets. He has now conquered everything and is with us to the end of time. He leaves behind the Advocate, that we might be people of the Spirit: people with a new dignity, who are reconciled with one another. His return to the Father in glory gives us new cause to celebrate our humanity. Through the power of the Spirit, we are offered the wonderful gift of awareness: to be able, in Paul's words, to "see what hope his call holds for us".

Application

Often we are not open to the new possibilities in Christ. We can lead our lives worrying about future plans, or regretting something that happened on our journey, which we cannot undo. These ascension stories are a reminder to us that Christ has overcome everything and has left us a Consoler who brings peace.

As we gather around his table, let us each ask the question: What is it that stops me celebrating my human dignity? One thing that often holds us back is our fear: fear of failure, fear of being alone, fear of being misunderstood, fear of death. The simple truth is, there is nothing in our lives that has not already been conquered by the Christ who shared the same body as us. He asks us to trust in him and let our fears go, entering into a prayer of praise in the Spirit that we might ascend to a new level of hope.

Christ asks that the primary message to be preached is one of forgiveness and change. That means offering reconciliation to those who have hurt us, but also forgiving ourselves for being weak. We are called to be people of hope. As people who believe in the redemption won by Christ's resurrection and ascension, we are compelled to look in trust beyond present realities, knowing that change is a possibility for all, even for ourselves.

A

"I have made your name known to the men you took from the world to give me."

Illustration

The story is told of a priest who had just been given his first parish. As something of an intellectual, he had spent many years working for the diocese in many different capacities, but had never worked full-time in a parish before. Understandably, he was rather nervous and unsure of himself. He decided his first job would be to visit the First Communion children at home. On arrival at the first home, he was greeted at the door by a little girl. He asked her name. She said it was Lucy. Uncertain what to do next, he said to her, "Do you know who I am?" The little girl promptly ran to her mother and said there was a man at the door who did not know who he was.

Names are important: they indicate who we are. Yet our true identity is only discovered when people are allowed to come close to us. In the Gospel, Jesus has shared his identity with his followers. Yet he has done much more. He has taught them the name of his Father, and shared his sonship with them.

Gospel Teaching

"The Word was made flesh, he lived among us, and we saw his glory." John opens his account of the story of Jesus with this revelation. As if he were writing a detective story, he gives us a vital piece of information, a key to unlock the mystery. Today we are in the privileged position of being able to hear the prayer of Jesus. Just as we pray for those things that are close to our hearts, so Jesus prays one of his final prayers for his trusted band of followers.

By dedicating himself to his Father, Jesus reveals his identity for us. The glory Jesus asks for is the cross. That symbol of brutality, used by the Romans to humiliate their opponents, was to most people a sign of failure. Yet this will be for Jesus a gateway to eternal life, proving that what the world sees as defeat is really a triumph. He has taught his disciples by a life of service and love, and they have learned how to follow him. As he prepares to leave them, he places them in the hands of the Father. Now they can share in the promised eternal life. We are told how to remain faithful to Jesus: it involves building a relationship with our loving Father.

Jesus has made known to us the name of the Father. He is not the distant figure some have imagined, but one who loved us into being and awaits our turning back to him; who listens, hoping we will call on him using words that his Son taught us. Jesus knows his followers are still in the world, but after the triumph of the cross they now walk in the light of the resurrection. In the prayer we hear today, we discover the identity of Christ our Lord, who dedicates us to the Father. We also see our own identity. Christ becomes our gateway to the Father. As we live in relationship with him and with each other, we become his adopted brothers and sisters.

Application

Some might say that these sentiments are fine for the disciples: they knew Jesus, they saw his glory. But let us remember that John was writing his account for the early Christian community long after the earthly life of Jesus. They were confused as to who they were. They were in a world that did not understand them or their faith. They were laughed at if they confessed their belief in the man from Galilee who died on a cross. The prayer of Jesus is spoken for followers like this.

We too live in a world that doesn't accept the Easter message. It is for us to proclaim to those around us that Christ is risen. We are given the strength to do this by the Spirit of Pentecost. But it is also encouraging to hear that we have been entrusted to our loving Father in a unique way. We belong to a community of faith, one that gathers to share the Eucharist and to celebrate its identity. Who we are is brought home to us when we come together as God's family. No matter what our weaknesses may be, we know that the Father is still close to us. Jesus offers us the chance of eternal life. All we have to do is call on the name he made known to us, praying in the words he taught us.

"Your word is truth."

Illustration

Today we are used to everything coming in an "instant" variety, whether it be our coffee, a political sound bite, or even a brand of quick-fix religion. We hope for instant cures for the ills that afflict us, for instant solutions to our problems. So, after dramatic incidents in our lives, the temptation may be to expect an instant return to normality.

This may be difficult if the drama involves a real encounter with the living God. You may have been on a pilgrimage to Lourdes, Rome, the Holy Land, or some other holy place. Afterwards it may have been hard to return to ordinary daily life. This should not surprise you. You may have been deeply touched and your emotions stirred. What you would normally do without thinking becomes a struggle. New questions arise: Should I be doing this? What does God really desire of me in this situation?

On the other hand, you may never have been on a grand pilgrimage to foreign parts but you may have experienced something similar after going on retreat or attending a parish mission. Whatever the experience, all of us may have asked questions like these: How do I carry this experience forward with me into my daily life? How can I let it change me?

Sometimes we may feel it would have been better if we had never had the experience at all because of the struggle it causes: a bit like the person waking up with a bad hangover and saying, "I'm never doing that again." At such times the temptation will be to act as though nothing had happened. But if we can summon up the courage to cooperate with these special times of grace we will notice that our thoughts and behaviour do change, even if only in small ways.

Gospel Teaching

In today's Gospel, Jesus is aware that, in the period after his ascension to the Father, the disciples are going to be asking the same kind of questions that we ask after dramatic events. How are they to make sense of the death and rising of Jesus? How are they going to let that truth change their lives? What are they to do with this new knowledge?

Jesus, during this last discourse, is concerned also with ensuring that his own ministry and mission are continued. This concern is seen also in our first reading, where the apostles are looking for one to take Judas' place so that the mission may develop.

Jesus prays to the Father. He prays that his disciples will be protected from evil and that they may experience the same unity in love among themselves as Jesus shares with his Father in heaven. This will be achieved by the disciples being consecrated in the truth. The truth, as Christ tells us, is the Father's word. This word of love is spoken in and through Christ and the scriptures. If the disciples are to continue the mission of Christ they must continue to hear this word of love, reflecting on the life and work of Christ and searching the scriptures for the Father's word of life.

Application

The apostles were going to find their mission a difficult and dangerous one in the midst of a hostile world. The same may be true of us. What are we to do? Will we simply live our lives as though we had not received Christ's message of love and the touch of his grace? Or will we strive, like the apostles, to proclaim the Good News?

We know that it is not enough to stay in the Holy Land, or away in some distant retreat centre, or revelling in the experience of a parish mission. We are called to return to normal life, yet to be transformed by the power of the experience. How do we do this? Simply by doing as the first disciples did after the ascension of the Lord: meditating on the life, works and words of the Lord Jesus, and searching the scriptures for the Father's word of life. This is not easy. There are no instant ways to become Jesus' true followers. There is only one way to be changed by the experience of grace – to ponder it in our hearts and let our hearts be transformed.

Only when we continue to dwell on Christ and the word of God will we be drawn nearer to the Father and one another. And only then will Christ's prayer be fully realised: "May they be one."

7th Sunday of Easter

"May they all be one."

Illustration

At the time of the Irish rebellion – Easter 1916 – people in Ireland were thrown into the turmoil of division. The War of Independence was to follow, and after that the tragedy of civil war. Two young men, Michael Collins and Harry Boland, fought side by side in the War of Independence. They were great friends, and were rivals in love for the same girl. When a political compromise secured a form of independence, these loyal friends found themselves on opposite sides as the bloodshed of civil war began. Their friendship was not broken, nor their faith in each other, but their politics drove them apart.

In the struggles that followed, Harry Boland was shot and killed by soldiers working for Collins. "The Big Fellow", as Collins was called, mourned deeply the loss of his friend. All too soon, Collins himself would be caught in the crossfire, and he too was killed. Since then, books and films have been made telling the story of this period, the tragedy of war, the waste of life and the heartbreaking tales of friendships destroyed. People who want the same thing go about getting it in different and conflicting ways, and find themselves destroying one another in the process.

As this particular story approaches its centenary in the coming years, its lessons are there for all to see. How easily we fall into hostilities with one another; how, without our wanting it, we can become enemies of those we love; how our good intentions and fervent desires can blind us to that greater good that we should love one another above all things.

Gospel Teaching

In the early days of the Church, two young men appear in the story as conflict and hostilities break out. Both are religious young men. Both are eager for the cause of God and the salvation of people. Both have been brought up to be fervent followers of their Jewish faith. In other circumstances they might even have become firm friends, but the events that brought them together were troublesome and violent.

The first young man is Stephen, who has become a Christian and is a superb preacher of the "new way". His success as a preacher brings him into conflict with the presiding authorities and with their version of religious truth. If Stephen will not desist from his preaching, the authorities will have to take steps. When Stephen becomes "intolerable" to his foes, he is taken out and killed. That is when we meet the second young man. His name is Saul.

Saul is an equally fervent young man. Concerned for the purity of the faith, he stands by as a witness to the execution of Stephen. He even approves of it. Soon his world will change and he will become a Christian, like Stephen. He will preach the same Gospel message, and one day he, too, will meet his death because he preached Jesus Christ.

Saul, who became Paul, never forgot his previous career as a persecutor of the Church. He confessed it many times. That day in Jerusalem, when Stephen prayed for his persecutors and "fell asleep in the Lord", must have remained with Paul his whole life long. He learned so many lessons from that experience. How foolish and stubborn religious people can be; how easily we can destroy the very good that we are trying to do; how vital it is that, in trying to change the world, we begin by changing ourselves.

Application

At the Last Supper, the great prayer that Jesus prays is for unity among his followers. It is an intensely strong bond of unity that Jesus prays for. With God in Jesus, and Jesus in us, the consequence is that God will be in us. Such a bond will resist all attempts to break it. In fact, if we are "completely" united, the world will wake up and realise the reality of God. When words fail, and gestures are refused, only the force of love can affect people for the better.

So many people see religion as the cause of all the trouble in the world, not as its cure. Arguments leave them unimpressed. Eloquence is lost on them. Actions can be misinterpreted. But love cannot. If our lives express the love of God for others, this can only do good. "Love is the one thing that cannot hurt your neighbour," St Paul said.

Like those young men, Stephen and Saul, another fervent young man, Gandhi, learned the lesson of life: "We must *be* the change that we want to see in the world."

A

"A variety of gifts but always the same Spirit."

Illustration

Like other artists of his time, the seventeenth-century Flemish painter Rubens had a group of apprentices working with him. They watched closely and strove to imitate him. He would sometimes pause for a moment, gazing at the rather hesitant creation of one of the would-be artists. Then, seizing the brush from the hands of the pupil, he would add the finishing touches. It was those touches that brought the painting to life. After alluding to this practice of Rubens, a modern scripture scholar notes that until the day of Pentecost the disciples, our Lord's "apprentices", had been clumsily trying to copy their Master; but on that day "the Spirit… finished the painting".

It is a neat way of summarising the effects of the first Pentecost. It explains why Pentecost is spoken of as the Church's birthday, the day when the Church truly sprang to life; the day when it was made ready for its mission of taking the Good News to the ends of the earth. The mighty wind, which shook the house where the disciples had gathered, soon grew still; the flames of fire, which hovered over their heads, soon disappeared. But the Holy Spirit, whose coming had been announced by wind and fire, had come to stay, had come to be with the Church until the end of time, to be its very soul, its life principle. And the Holy Spirit never grows old!

Gospel Teaching

Today's second reading is from a letter of Paul to his friends in Corinth. He explains that it is not even possible to acknowledge that Jesus is Lord without the assistance of the Spirit. To put the point positively, it is the active presence of the Spirit that enables us to accept the truth at the heart of Christianity – Jesus is risen, he is with us, he is Lord.

Paul goes on to say that the Spirit blesses the Church with a variety of gifts, or charisms. In ordinary speech a charism means an exceptional natural talent, but as used by Paul it means a special gift bestowed by the Holy Spirit. It is a grace given by God for the common good. Such gifts are allotted to the laity just as much as to the ordained. Some are dramatic, such as those of healing or of speaking in tongues; but many are less striking, such as those of teaching, of helping others, of administration. Indeed, every gift we have is a potential charism, something that can be put at the service of all.

Paul insists that the Holy Spirit who is responsible for the rich diversity of gifts in the Church is also responsible for the gift of unity. Many gifts, "but always the same Spirit"; "all sorts of service to be done, but always to the same Lord"; and "in all sorts of different ways in different people, it is the same God who is working in all". "Just as a human body," says Paul, "though it is made up of many parts", remains "a single unit", so, thanks to the Holy Spirit, the Church is one, though made up of many different members, each with their own unique gifts.

Application

An early Christian writer, speaking of the effects of Holy Communion, noted that anyone "who eats the bread [of the Eucharist] with faith, eats at the same time the fire of the Holy Spirit". On this Sunday we might consider our own parish community and ask to what extent the "fire of the Holy Spirit" is in evidence here. Is our parish alive? Are people devoting their time, their gifts, their energies to the building up of community? Are we open to new ways of doing things or firmly anchored in the past? Are we self-centred as a parish or do we look beyond our parochial bounds? Is our unity manifested in genuine friendliness to one another, in readiness to listen to and serve one another? Does our parish community live in harmony or is it riven by divisions?

Asking such questions can be valuable. But only if we are prepared to ask a supplementary question: If things are not as they should be, what can I do to improve the situation? If enough of us were ready to adopt that attitude, who knows what might happen? Might not the Holy Spirit put the finishing touches to our small efforts, bringing about a miniature Pentecost in our midst and so renewing the face of the earth right here?

B

"How does it happen that each of us hears them in his own native language?"

Illustration

In 1887 Dr Ludwig Lazarus Zamenhof published the idea of a new international language, known as Esperanto. Zamenhof was a Jew who was born and brought up in Byalistok, in what was, at that time, Russian Poland. As a young man in his native town he noticed that the various ethnic groups who lived there always kept to themselves and did not mix, because they could not understand one another. They spoke different languages: Russian, Yiddish, German or Polish. This separation of people often led to suspicion and animosity. It was then that the young Ludwig thought how good it would be if there was a common language that everyone could learn to speak. Not a language to replace their own native tongue, but a second language that could be a source of unity for all.

At first Ludwig thought that Latin might serve as the international language, but he quickly realised that it would be too difficult for many people to learn. So Ludwig conceived the idea of creating a new language.

The word "Esperanto" in the new language means "one who hopes"; and it was the good doctor's hope that this new tongue would be a means for promoting unity and understanding throughout the world. The success of Esperanto may have been limited, but the inspiration behind it was noble and honourable. Ludwig Zamenhof knew that if people could speak freely with each other, they would begin to understand one another and would grow in mutual respect.

Gospel Teaching

At the beginning of the Church's life, on this feast of Pentecost, we are also celebrating the birth of a new language, the language of the Holy Spirit of God, the language of the Gospel. Just as the apostles were emboldened to go out from the upper room and to teach all nations, so every generation of the Church's children is given the same grace and the same mandate: "Go out to the whole world, proclaim the Good News." There is no need to be afraid of the powers of this world. Let your lives be a witness to the love of God.

The new language of the Holy Spirit is also a force for unity among the peoples of the world. This force was clearly demonstrated on the day of Pentecost, when the crowds of people in Jerusalem heard the apostles speaking to them in every language. It was a miracle of understanding. Not only did they understand what the words meant, but they also understood the message for their own lives. For it is our daily life, our human behaviour, that is the most fundamental language of all. Our actions speak louder than our words, and everything we say and do is an act of communication. If our lives are guided by the Spirit, then we are speaking the new language of God, and that language will bring people to unity and peace.

St Paul was at pains to stress this teaching to his converts in Galatia. These new Christians had no familiarity with the Jewish law and they were floundering in their attempts to understand what freedom means. So Paul spells out the way of life that the Holy Spirit of God inspires. It is the life of virtue and it brings blessings on all. Virtue is an international language of unity and peace. Its opposite – vice and selfishness – is no language at all, for it does not embrace people, but rather offends them. Virtue is a language which we are called to learn and in which we are called to grow. There will be no peace in our world today if we are not virtuous people.

Application

When Ludwig Zamenhof died in 1917 the world was deep in darkness and bitter strife. Millions were dying in the First World War and in the Russian Revolution. And that was only the beginning of the troubles for the century that followed.

We live today in a world that is still not free from conflict and trouble. Every war represents a failure to communicate, a failure to understand, a failure to reach out in hope to one another. It could well be that we, too, are part of that failure. Am I able to speak to my brothers and sisters? Am I able to speak to my enemies? Am I able to let them speak to me? Come, Holy Spirit, and renew the face of the earth.

"Send forth your Spirit, O Lord, and renew the face of the earth."

Illustration

Everyone likes receiving gifts. But gifts can be deceptive. We all know that feeling we get when in the supermarket or at the petrol pump or in the newspaper we come across a notice that proclaims, in big letters, "free gift". The first reaction might well be one of interest (we all like to get something for nothing), but, as likely as not, the second will be one of caution (none of us likes to be duped). What's the catch, we wonder.

But there's one kind of gift that has no catches and which we're always ready to receive. It's the gift that expresses love – the gift of a child to its parents, of a friend to a friend, of a husband to his wife or vice versa. It might be argued that even here there are strings attached, but these are strings of the most delightful kind, strings that draw us closer to the one we love.

The reason we are celebrating today is precisely because it was at Pentecost that we received what one of our hymns calls the "best gift of God above" – the precious gift of the Holy Spirit. This is supremely a gift of love, for the Holy Spirit is the burning love that flows between Father and Son, and so to receive the Spirit is to have God's own love poured into our hearts, drawing us closer to God and closer to each other.

Gospel Teaching

Our Lord had promised his friends that they would receive the gift of the Spirit once he had ascended to his Father. And today the promise is fulfilled. The Holy Spirit is freely given, poured out unreservedly upon the disciples in the upper room who prepared for the great event by uniting in prayer. The results are spectacular – "a powerful wind", "tongues of fire", timid disciples turned into fearless heroes, speechless cowards publicly proclaiming to all who will listen "the marvels of God"; and, though the people who have gathered are from many different nations, they are all able to understand, as though the message was being delivered in their own native tongue.

However, as a rule, the Holy Spirit works in humbler ways: Paul reminds us, for example, that it's only through the empowering of the Spirit that we are able to recognise Jesus as Lord; and in today's second reading he insists that it is the power of the Spirit that enables us to call upon God as "Abba, Father".

Application

Perhaps it's because the Holy Spirit is a "free gift", costing us nothing, that we take the Spirit so much for granted. The presence of the Holy Spirit produces a whole variety of gifts, many of them so unspectacular that we hardly notice them: like the gift of being a good listener; the gift of being cheerful even when things are difficult; the gift of being a good and patient parent; the gift of being able to say "Jesus is Lord" when troubled by sickness or temptation.

When people open up their lives to the Holy Spirit, things begin to happen: their lives change, things that seemed impossible become possible. When Pope John XXIII said that he wanted the Second Vatican Council to be another Pentecost, he was professing his faith in the transforming power of the Spirit.

The story is told of a peasant who day after day visited the holy man in his village to ask how he could find God. For a while nothing happened, but finally the holy man led him to a nearby river and invited him in for a swim. Suddenly the holy man plunged him under the water, so that he came up fighting for breath. The two walked home in silence but, just before they parted, the holy man said: "When you know you need God as much as you need the air you breathe, only then will you find God."

Do we realise even now how much we need the Holy Spirit, that the Spirit is as basic as breathing to our Christian lives? In our response to the psalm we prayed: "Send forth your Spirit, O Lord, and renew the face of the earth." Do we believe that? Do we believe the Holy Spirit can renew even that dark, dry and, as it may seem, unpromising piece of earth which is ourselves? If so, then, especially on this day, the prayer "Send forth your Spirit" will echo and re-echo in our hearts.

Feasts of
the Lord
in
Ordinary Time

"God loved the world so much that he gave his only Son."

Illustration

In his novel *Monsignor Quixote*, the Catholic author Graham Greene tells a delightful story about friendship and faith. Set in Spain, sometime after the era of General Franco, the book explores the relationship between two key characters. One of them, the local parish priest, is a Christian; the other, the former communist mayor, is an atheist. They decide to leave behind their small village and familiar surroundings to set off together on a journey of discovery.

As they travel, the conversation often turns, perhaps inevitably, to the subject of religion. Early on in the book, we find the two figures seated on a hillside sharing some bottles of wine. Choosing his moment, the mayor addresses the priest with these words: "What puzzles me, friend, is how you can believe in so many incompatible ideas. For example, the Trinity. It's worse than higher mathematics. Can you explain the Trinity to me?"

The priest pauses to think and then replies. He explains that the wine they have been drinking has come from different bottles. The first bottle represents God the Father; the second bottle represents God the Son. Although in different bottles, the wine they contain is of the same substance, it was born at the same time. The third bottle, which brings what he calls the "extra spark of life", represents the Holy Spirit. So, the priest concludes, although from three different bottles, the wine in each is inseparable, it shares one and the same substance and is of the same vintage. Therefore, "Whoever partakes of one partakes of all three."

Gospel Teaching

Our celebration today calls us to contemplate the very essence of who God really is. By the power of our own intelligence we might well be able to recognise a creator behind our universe, a supreme being who is the cause of everything that exists. We might even have a sense of wonder at the beauty of creation and an awareness of the spiritual qualities that underpin our life. Yet there is more to God than this.

It is in the person of Jesus that we come to a full understanding of who God is. It is Jesus who reveals God to us as a heavenly Father, his Father and our Father. It is Jesus who shows himself to be the Son of that Father, and ourselves as his sisters and brothers. It is Jesus who promises to send the Holy Spirit as a gift from his Father and himself so that they might make their home within us. In word and action, Jesus teaches us the truth about God as Father, Son and Holy Spirit, something we could never fully grasp by reasoning alone.

When he spoke with Nicodemus, Jesus didn't use the language of philosophy to explain why he had been sent by the Father; he used the language of love. It is the loving Father who sends his beloved Son so that the way to eternal life might be opened up for all. The Father and Son exist in a relationship of love and the bond of love that binds them together is the Holy Spirit. The God of tenderness and compassion revealed to Moses is now shown completely as the God who is a community of three persons, Father, Son and Holy Spirit, existing as one in a relationship of perfect love.

Application

Monsignor Quixote's explanation doesn't answer every question about the Trinity. In fact, in the book, he comes unstuck by representing the Holy Spirit by a half bottle of wine instead of the full bottle used for God the Father and God the Son. He accuses himself of failing to teach that the Holy Spirit is equal in all respects to the Father and the Son.

We certainly do need an intellectual understanding of what we believe, and in this images and examples can help us. It was, after all, St Patrick who famously used the three-leafed shamrock to explain the unity of God in three persons. However, the so-called mystery of the Trinity is not a problem that needs to be solved. It is an experience of faith which we are called to encounter.

We do this by allowing ourselves to be loved by the God who is love. By opening our hearts to the living love of the Holy Spirit we are drawn into the loving relationship that exists between the Father and the Son. As we become partakers of the very life of the Trinity, so those we encounter will also partake of God.

The Most Holy Trinity

B

"Was there ever a word so majestic, from one end of heaven to the other?"

Illustration

Trinity College in Dublin is an old and famous university. One of its particular claims to fame is to be found in the Old Library building of the university, where an ancient book is reverently housed. The Book of Kells is an eighth-century manuscript of the four Gospels, written in Latin on vellum, and illuminated throughout with the most beautiful and colourful images and pictures. It is an exquisite masterpiece, each page a work of art in itself.

In the days before printing, it was the laborious work of copying by hand that produced the books, which held the knowledge that was passed down from generation to generation. In the monasteries of medieval times, the work of writing out the scriptures by hand was a labour of love, since all of life was dedicated to the service of the word of God. The Gospels, especially, would receive great care and reverent handling in their production; and, of all the scriptures that were copied, the pages that reproduced the Gospel story would be given every expression of art and beauty. Such a work is the Book of Kells.

This masterpiece of reverential beauty is a direct echo of the words spoken by Moses to his people on their way to the promised land. Was there ever a more beautiful message heard in the whole history of the world, from the days of Adam until now? What message could match the word of God that was given to the chosen people?

Gospel Teaching

The Jews hold their scriptures in great reverence. They are full of the stories of salvation and of the wisdom of God. How blessed are the people who hear the word of God and treasure it in their hearts. The fullness of that blessing has come to us in the person of Jesus Christ. When the apostles gathered with Jesus on the mountain after his resurrection, he told them to go and to share that blessing with the world – to teach the world "all the commands I gave you". This instruction was carried out first in the missionary journeys that the apostles made, in their preaching and founding of new churches. Then the time came to preserve and pass on the word of God to the next generation, and so the Gospels were put down in writing, the Gospels we have today.

But it is not only the written scrolls and printed books or beautiful manuscripts that pass on the word of God: it is the living body of believers, who, in every generation, make up the Church. That body of believers lives and breathes by the Holy Spirit that has been given to it. That Spirit makes our lives something beautiful, even a work of art. That Spirit enables us to say "Our Father" – and those who are able to pray like that do so because they have been given the grace to live as children of God, and so to treat others as brothers and sisters in the Lord.

Application

The work of making a manuscript, such as the Book of Kells, was a daily task. Each day the monks would sit at their writing desks in the scriptorium, the place set aside for writing, and would carefully copy the sacred words onto the new, blank page. The beautiful script would be adorned with colourful images that would draw the eye onto the page to ingest the sacred text.

In the same way Christian people are called each day to the task of writing a new page in their own lives as part of the great story of the world. Each day, like a blank, new page of vellum, waits to receive the mark and the imprint that we will put upon it. As children of God the Father, as disciples of Jesus, and with the Holy Spirit within us, we can write well. We may even be able to create something of beauty to adorn the pages of our lives, something that will draw the eye of the beholder to see in us a glimpse of the kindness and the love of God.

The Book of Kells has survived for a thousand years and more. Its creation not only gave joy to those who composed it, but has also given joy to millions ever since, who have seen it in Trinity College, or in reproduction copies. The same is true of a human life well lived. The message rings out loud and clear from a true disciple of Christ. We are God's work of art. God loves us.

"Everything the Father has is mine."

Illustration

One of the most popular songs of recent times has come from the animated film *The Lion King*. It's called "The Circle of Life". The song celebrates the fact that there is an interconnectedness between every aspect of life and creation. It also tells of how we will probably never be able fully to appreciate that: "From the day we arrive on the planet and, blinking, step into the sun, there's more to see than can ever be seen, more to do than can ever be done." In short, the song helps us appreciate that life and our being are a mystery that cannot be easily explained. There will always be more than we can see, touch or understand.

As a working definition, this would be a good one for the word "mystery". A mystery is not an unfathomable puzzle; rather it is a thing to be lived and experienced. The whole of life is therefore a mystery, a wonderful unfolding of things not immediately apparent or obvious. God, the creator of life, is certainly a wonderful mystery and that's what we celebrate today.

Gospel Teaching

Jesus has spent the past few years instructing the disciples. However, there have been times when they have been slow to learn and mistaken in their assumptions. Time is running out and Jesus knows he will not be with them much longer, but he knows that at this time they are not going to be able to take on board what he has yet to teach them. The time will come for them to learn more, and then it will be the job of the Spirit to teach them.

While the disciples may have realised that they were not the best of students, they would surely have been puzzled by Jesus' words in today's Gospel. Perhaps they feared the worst and were worried about the things that were to come, and wondered why Jesus didn't just say it out straight. Perhaps they were disappointed that Jesus didn't trust them enough to know the fullness of his message now. Or perhaps they were so used to Jesus' ways that they simply trusted that what he said would come to pass in due course.

Whatever the case, Jesus goes to great trouble to stress to the disciples that there is unity between himself and God. He spells out that God is his

Father and that they share everything, so much so that Jesus cannot claim anything as his own. He stresses that the Spirit will be continuing his work through the disciples. The Spirit will not come and initiate something new; rather the Spirit will bring to fulfilment all that Jesus started and brought into being.

It is clear that Jesus wants the disciples to understand that in, through and with God there is unity and harmony, and all this will be revealed in the fullness of time. Jesus knows that the disciples will probably struggle to comprehend this concept, but he knows that a relationship with God is not an intellectual pursuit but an experience. He knows that when the disciples experience the coming of the Spirit, they will understand the full wonder of God and proclaim it.

Application

"There is more to see than can ever be seen, more to do than can ever be done." Today the Church gives us this feast to consider the fact that God is present and at work in more ways than we can see or fully grasp.

This feast is not meant to tie us in theological knots; it is concerned more with the wonder of God's mysterious and loving presence. We are being asked to be inspired by and to imitate the unity of the Trinity, the love of the persons of the Trinity, the harmony that exists within the Trinity. The Trinity is a seamless unity of persons, a community of love. The Father is the one who loves, the Son is the one who is loved and the Spirit is the very act of loving. Therefore this reality, which we call mystery, teaches us three things: how to love, how to be loved and how to be love.

As we sign ourselves with the cross today, a simple action that many of us have been doing almost automatically since we were children, let us remember that we are signing ourselves in love and so let us live accordingly. We might not be able to help people understand the theological intricacies of this mystery, but we certainly can help them experience love.

A

"Anyone who eats this bread will live for ever."

Illustration

Westminster Abbey in London is the home of Poets' Corner, where many poets and writers are commemorated in stone. Just inside the main door of the abbey is the Tomb of the Unknown Warrior, whose memorial, erected after the First World War, is dedicated to all those who died serving their country. In 1996, just a few yards away, outside the main door of the abbey, a new, circular memorial was dedicated. There is no body beneath it, because it draws attention to a war that has not ended and seems to know no end: it is a memorial to Innocent Victims of Oppression, Violence and War.

Memorials are important, and never more so than when they are to human lives, lived and lost. Poets' Corner is a celebration of literary greats, serving to honour the work of men and women of letters. The Tomb of the Unknown Warrior represents so much more: it symbolises the supreme sacrifice made by thousands of men and women, many of whose bodies now rest in unmarked graves. It is a reminder of the immense human cost of war.

The memorial to Innocent Victims of Oppression, Violence and War goes a step further. It too honours human lives, lived and lost; it too serves as a reminder of the human cost of war. But it is also a call to action. The suffering and death to which it draws attention continue each and every day. This memorial symbolises the cry of suffering humanity for justice, reconciliation and peace.

Gospel Teaching

Today's readings are also about a memorial. It is not made of stone, but is nonetheless real: a memorial meal. The Eucharist which we celebrate today is the memorial instituted by Jesus. It draws attention to his life; it proclaims his death; and it celebrates his resurrection from the dead. Like the new memorial at Westminster Abbey, the Eucharist draws attention to issues that have not gone away, and do not go away: sacrifice, service, presence and redemptive love.

In today's first reading, Moses reminds the people of God's saving goodness, shown to them over many years. The remembering is important, because it keeps the people alive to the continuing saving presence of God. Similarly, Paul emphasises the importance of the Eucharist, this memorial that represents an intimate sharing in the life of Christ, which binds people together more surely than war can tear them apart.

Jesus draws on the familiar tradition of God's provision for the people in the desert and takes it much further. It is not manna which now feeds and nourishes. It is his own flesh, given for the life of the world. Here we have a memorial that draws on the past, takes place in the present and promises the future. It effects union with Christ, and so with the Father.

So this celebration works on many levels at once. We hear again of the sacrifice of Jesus, his self-giving, his offering of his own life that we might live. We are reminded that in the Eucharist we enjoy communion with Jesus, and so are drawn into his life with the Father. We are also drawn together in faith and become a community with Christ's self-giving at its centre. And we commit ourselves to Christ's kingdom of justice, reconciliation and peace.

Application
When we celebrate the Eucharist, we are caught up in a living memorial. We are challenged to deepen our commitment to each other as we reflect on the example of Jesus, who gives generously of himself, that we might live. His life of loving service inspires us and empowers us to serve as he does.

Our communion with Christ and with each other in the Eucharist is the beginning of eternal life. In Christ we are already in the tomb, and already risen and ascended to the Father. Eternal life has already begun for us. The eucharistic memorial is where we are reminded of this and taken up into it. Our communion is our salvation, tangible and very near.

Our great memorials commemorate lives lived and lost, and the Eucharist is no exception; but it is much more too. The life that was lived and lost was found again. Jesus died and was raised from the dead. And so too our lives are lived, will be lost and will be restored to us by God's grace. A memorial that can do this can only come from God.

The Body and Blood of Christ

"This is my body... This is my blood."

Illustration

Ross McGinnis was born in June 1987, and brought up in Knox, north of Pittsburgh, in the United States. He was a Boy Scout, loved playing sports and hoped to become a car mechanic. At the age of seventeen, he joined the army for the training to help him reach that goal, as well as to serve his country.

His unit, the 26th Infantry Regiment, went out to Iraq in August 2006. Ross served as a gunner in a military vehicle, a Humvee, patrolling a notoriously violent area outside Baghdad. On 4th December 2006, a grenade was thrown from a rooftop at the vehicle, and it fell into the hatch. Ross yelled, "Grenade", and was about to jump out, as he was supposed to do. However, he realised that his four colleagues did not have time to escape, so, making a split-second decision, he threw himself on top of the grenade. The explosion blew the doors off the Humvee, but, apart from Ross, there were no other casualties. In June 2008, Ross McGinnis was posthumously awarded the Medal of Honor, America's highest award for valour.

Gospel Teaching

When Ross McGinnis used his body as a shield to protect his friends, he was giving up his entire being, his life with all its potential. His was a true sacrifice of love, a holy – and truly human – action. Jesus Christ was the person in history most truly human, and what Ross did at that moment was a Christ-like act, and so a fundamentally human one.

When Jesus died on the cross, he too was using his body as the shield to save his friends – that includes us, and the whole of fallen creation. He put his body between us and everything that makes us inhuman, all that brings destruction to the world. It was not just his words that Jesus gave in service, not just the ability to heal, to perform miracles, to teach with authority. He also served through giving up his body, his being, his life, that we may receive his body, his being, his life. In his body he gave concrete expression to the love of God for us. And in the Eucharist he gives us himself as real food to build us into his body. This is why the Church, the body of Christ, today celebrates and delights in this feast of the Body and Blood of Christ.

Application

We are not a people who exist in a spiritual, other-worldly environment. We are human beings of flesh and blood, with our feet on the ground in this world. We do not live in and for ourselves, in some kind of abstract, interior, closed world. With our bodies, we relate to the world and to other people around us. And now, since the death and resurrection of Christ, we live in a new way in relation to the world and to other people.

We live as members of a eucharistic community, a people formed, grounded and fed by the Eucharist, a people in communion with God and with each other. We need food for our bodies, in the physical form of bread and wine, as well as in the spiritual form of the words of God spoken to us in scripture, in the liturgy and in private prayer. For we are a unity, body and soul, just as the eucharistic host is the body and blood, the soul and divinity of Christ, in which he is really, wholly and entirely present.

When we receive Christ in communion, it is the whole Christ we are receiving – the being, the life, the fullness. By taking his life into our own we are allowing him to take us into his life, the life of the most fully human person who has ever lived. That has consequences in the here and now.

Instead of using the expression "It's only human" for some lapse of standards, we can now pray to become more fully human. For only when we are conformed to the humanity of Jesus are we truly human. If we are fully conformed to Christ we cannot be petty, cruel, spiteful, malicious – or anything else that reduces the stature of that humanity. We may even be willing to give up our own lives for others. May we honour, revere and love the sacrament that builds up our humanity by conforming us more and more to the body of Christ.

The Body and Blood of Christ

"Give them something to eat yourselves."

Illustration

In 1987 Jean Vanier was awarded a special medal of honour for his work with people with learning disabilities. He was appointed a "Companion of the Order of Canada". On the back of the medal there is an inscription in Latin, which reads *Desiderantes Meliorem Patriam* – "they desire a better country". The medal reflects the great work and self-sacrifice of the recipient in spending their life in the service of others. The inscription is well crafted. Jean Vanier does desire a better country. He wants to make this world a better place.

Jean Vanier's early life involved him in the business of war. He was a trained navy officer. But he left the things of war and went in search of peace. That journey led him to a meeting with people with learning disabilities. That first meeting changed Vanier. He felt that he heard their scream, their desire for love. "Do you love me? Am I lovable? Have I any value? Why have I been abandoned?" Vanier bought a house and invited two people with learning disabilities to join him. This was the beginning of the organisation called "L'Arche".

In the course of living with people with disabilities, Vanier has grown in his own life and understanding. Instead of climbing up the ladder of success, Vanier discovered the way of going down the ladder to be with people who have often experienced brokenness and pain. In this meeting Vanier discovered his own brokenness and hardness of heart. In wanting to help others, Vanier was helped and healed himself. He is blessed and broken.

Reflecting on his whole experience, Vanier says that society can only be truly human when it is founded on welcome and respect for those who are weak and downtrodden. It is by the mutual gift of attention and love that we will make this world a better place.

Gospel Teaching

When the crowds follow Jesus into the hillsides of Galilee, they are hungry for a better place and a better life. Luke tells us that Jesus begins by welcoming them. This first kindness is followed by conversation about the kingdom of God, and by the healing of those who are sick. This is similar to our formula at Mass, where we are welcomed together, where we confess our brokenness, and where we are inspired by hearing the word of God.

Then, as the day grows late, Jesus feeds the crowd. His disciples have pointed out, in a telling phrase, the nature of this world. "This is a lonely place," they say. Not only the hills of Galilee, but the streets of our modern world are indeed a lonely place, and people go hungry for food, material and spiritual, every day. Jesus instructs his disciples to organise a dinner. With the little that they have, the disciples discover that they have fed the crowd, and that there are scraps left over. The food has been blessed and broken and shared. No one goes hungry.

This is the world that Jesus creates, a eucharistic world. He teaches us to give thanks to God for all we have. We break our bread and we share it with everyone, especially with the starving poor. We exclude no one. There is plenty for us all.

Application
The Christians in Corinth needed to learn that lesson, when they were excluding those who were poor, and enjoying comfortable meals themselves. Paul reminds them of what he had learned from the Lord about the meaning of the Eucharist. Every time we take part in the Eucharist, we are joining in the suffering and death of Jesus, the rich one who became poor for our sake. We are going down into the poverty and suffering of this world in order to be raised up together with the Lord.

This way of life is open to us all: to live the Eucharist, the life of thanksgiving love. This life involves us with those who suffer. You may be called to share your life with people who are sick and old, or with people out of work, or with people caught in the world of drugs. You may be with people who are terribly angry because of the hurt they suffered when they were young. There are so many hungry and suffering people, lost people. They say of life, "This is a lonely place." And in reply the Lord says to you, "Give them something to eat yourselves."

Sundays in Ordinary Time
Year A

A

"I will make you the light of the nations so that my salvation may reach to the ends of the earth."

Illustration

The Jews have always had mixed feelings about being God's chosen people. The psalms reveal the depth and variety of exchange that took place between them and God. Every human emotion is displayed. Is God on our side? Why doesn't God show himself more? Why doesn't God get off our backs? What a good God he is!

This flavour of intimacy and concern continues in modern Jewish writing, often in humour and wit. Two things remain clear in the Jewish vision down through the ages. One is that we cannot get away from God. The other is that God demands commitment. This is what being chosen by God means.

Our modern Western ideas of being chosen are wishy-washy by comparison. Advertising suggests it is a matter of luck or fate. "It could be you!" proclaimed the adverts for the national lottery when it was first introduced into Britain, and many companies send out unsolicited but ornate envelopes informing us that we have been specially chosen to receive a prize. Mind you, there is usually some condition attached that lurks in the small print. Being chosen is linked to the idea of reward rather than responsibility.

Unfortunately this expectation can affect even the most important choices in our lives. Partners may choose to marry for what they expect to receive rather than for what they might give. Or the commitment required to live with another person day after day, in sickness and health, proves too much of a demand, and they run away.

Gospel Teaching

God's choosing presents a much clearer picture. A special relationship is established with the chosen one, and it is that relationship which empowers the chosen to carry out the assignment that goes with the act of election. In Isaiah the nature of the relationship is defined first of all as that of a servant, but it is a special sort of servant. It is the servant who is honoured in the eyes of his Lord and who has God as his strength. Through the servant God is glorified, a theme explored at length in John's

Gospel during the farewell discourse of Jesus to his disciples at the Last Supper. Thus energised by God, the servant will not only reconcile the people of Israel but will be a light for all nations so that salvation may be offered to all.

Similarly, Paul, in the first line of his greeting to the church in Corinth, refers to the fact that he has been appointed by God to be an apostle. He too has been chosen, and his assignment is that of an apostle, to proclaim the Good News of Jesus Christ.

Again, John's account of the beginning of Jesus' public life puts the accent on his special election through the descent of the Spirit. Just as the Spirit hovered over the waters in the first creation, so the Spirit now comes down upon Jesus, the instrument of God's new creation. He will take away the sins of the world and in his turn will baptise with the Spirit, his assignment as the chosen one of God.

Application

We too are the chosen ones of God. In baptism the Holy Spirit descends on us and makes us sharers in God's own life. Our responsibility as chosen ones is to take up the assignments we have just heard of in the life of Jesus, in the life of Paul and in the life of the servant disciple. We are called to take away the sins of the world, to be apostles and to be the light of the nations, bringing salvation to the ends of the earth: all daunting tasks. We may be forgiven for trying to flee them or offload them on to those we consider to be especially trained for the purpose, the clergy and religious. But, through our baptism, we are each called to make unique contributions to these assignments.

It helps if we can see how in turn they have been communicated to us. As we have received, so shall we give. How have we been enlightened? What brings clear vision and understanding into our lives? What has our experience of forgiveness been? Have we really forgiven others or allowed ourselves to be truly forgiven? Finally, how have we received the Good News? What words or images moved or still move us? It is through our own experience of God that God will communicate his presence to others.

A

"The people that walked in darkness has seen a great light."

Illustration

In August 1999 there occurred a total eclipse of the sun. Its "flight path" crossed the globe from the north Atlantic to the Indian Ocean. In Britain, the eclipse was fully experienced in the south-west corner of England, in the county of Cornwall. Many people made their way down to that beautiful part of the world, and local hotels made good trade out of the great influx.

On the morning of the eclipse, a bright and sunny day, with clear skies overhead, thousands of people gathered on a Cornish beach and waited for the world to grow dark. Around eleven o'clock that morning, the shape of the moon could be seen to encroach on the blazing sun, and gradually the light of day was turned to darkest night. After a few minutes, the bright sunlight began to emerge again as the moon drifted past, and all the people were bathed in light once more. "The people that walked in darkness has seen a great light."

One observer, there in Cornwall, described the experience as "sacred" or "spiritual". Something very special, something out of the ordinary, a truly great wonder of nature had taken place and the watching crowd had felt united in sharing the experience together.

In this experience, it was the darkness that brought the feeling of closeness and unity to the people. It was the dying of the light that served to remind us how selfishly we abuse the light of day, misusing it for our own delight: how foolishly we forget our common inheritance as children of God. Sometimes we need the shock of the dark to bring us to our senses, to make us concentrate our attention on the unity of humankind, and on the unity of God. There is only one God, and we are all God's children.

Gospel Teaching

In the busy seaport of Corinth, Paul, the great apostle and preacher of Christ, came to plant the Christian faith. It was a tremendous place to come to: a thriving commercial centre, full of people, full of business, full of life and activity. Religions and philosophies vied with each other for pride of place in this great metropolis. Vice and immorality also found great space and scope for their activities. If the faith could be planted here, it could quickly spread to that whole area of southern Greece.

Paul established a strong community of believers, but it was not long before trouble broke out. It was hard enough to live the Christian life in an environment as complex as Corinth, but even harder when internal dissension broke out. Factions and infighting developed as people vied to be truer Christians than others. Dissension such as this casts a shadow over people's lives. Living with arguments and quarrels is like living in darkness and in the shadow of death. Paul has to write to the people and remind them to turn their gaze to the one person who really matters – Jesus Christ. It is this person, this name, this life that unites us. Let the darkness of our squabbling cease, and let us turn our eyes again to the source of our joy, the Lord himself.

On the day Christ died, a darkness covered the earth from the sixth hour until the ninth hour. The sun was blotted out, and the day became as black as night. But on Easter Day the Son of God rose from the dead, and light returned to this earth. As Paul tells us, no clever philosophy could explain this or understand it. It is God's doing, and we, who live together in the darkness of this world, have experienced the coming again of the light of life.

Application
Our world is dark enough. Everywhere on earth there is dissension, conflict and war. People turn against each other, shouting their slogans, waving their flags, and breathing death and destruction to the foe.

For the sake of justice and for the cause of peace, we cannot continue to live in the dark. Violence must not provoke us into wrongdoing or hostility against others. Paul tells us today what he told the Christians in Corinth: be united in your belief and in your practice. As the spiritual experience of eclipse and darkness might teach us: there is only one God, and we are all God's children.

"Theirs is the kingdom of heaven."

Illustration

Grandma had died. She left behind a large old house, full of a lifetime's collection of objects and memories. The family decided to sort through her possessions. They kept a few things of sentimental value, but most of her possessions were just ordinary, run-of-the-mill items – nothing of any great value. So they sold the contents of the house for a small sum to a firm who said they would dispose of everything. It was only months later that they discovered that the dusty old painting that had hung over Grandma's fireplace was in fact a minor masterpiece, worth more than all her other possessions put together. And they had let it go for next to nothing.

It is easy to be so familiar with something that you fail to see its true worth or beauty. We often need someone else, perhaps a visitor or a stranger, to point it out to us. The same can be true of our faith. Where is God in all the mess of our lives? Where do we find Jesus? Why doesn't God's kingdom come, why do we have to wait?

Gospel Teaching

Jesus' answer to us in today's Gospel is: open your eyes and look around you. The Beatitudes describe God's life in the world. They are signposts, indicating the presence and activity of God. They help us to recognise God.

Where do we find God? We find God whenever there are people with a real hunger and thirst for justice, where people actively work for what is right. God is there whenever we see someone treating others with gentleness, with respect, with compassion. God is there in the hearts of people who mourn, who grieve not just for their own loss but also for those who have lost dignity, faith and hope. God is experienced whenever mercy is shown, when the wife forgives her husband, or the victim his attacker. God is there in the single-minded dedication and commitment of the pure in heart, those who spend their lives in the service of their fellow men and women. God is there in the people who work to achieve peace – peace for the individual, peace between individuals, peace between communities and nations. God is there in those who are poor. The God of the Bible is always on the side of those who have no one else to defend them. God is on the side of those who are too weak and powerless to look after themselves.

God is on the side of the poor in spirit, those who recognise their own neediness, their own dependence on God, their inability to get by without the help of God.

The Beatitudes help us to recognise God in the world, indicating where we can expect to find God at work. They are also the best description we have of Jesus. In the Beatitudes, we have a real, in-depth description of what kind of person he is. He is the one who is totally poor in spirit, totally dependent on God. It is he who is gentle and meek, who mourns for those who are oppressed and hurt. It is he who works to bring about what is right, who shows mercy to the sinner, who is completely committed to doing the will of his Father. And, supremely, it is Jesus who brings us peace and reconciles us with God and with each other.

Application

If the Beatitudes tell us where we can find God at work and describe the kind of person Jesus is and what he stands for, then they also act as a guide to us, reminding us, his disciples, that the treasures of God's kingdom are close at hand.

The Beatitudes are a manifesto, outlining not just where God is to be found, but where we, God's people, should be found. We are called to be alongside those who are poor, those in need, working to protect and defend them because that is what God is doing. We are called to show gentleness to those who are bruised and neglected in our world. We are called to work with others who hunger and thirst for what is right, helping to bring about justice. We are called to be at the forefront of efforts to bring peace into people's lives, encouraging forgiveness and reconciliation. It is then that we will be able to recognise the presence of God in the world and to recognise the face of Jesus in the most unexpected people. And we will rejoice to find ourselves part of the kingdom of heaven.

"Your light must shine in the sight of men, so that, seeing your good works, they may give praise to your Father in heaven."

Illustration

Many years ago, a church was built on one of the highest mountains in Switzerland. It was a beautiful church that had been built with great care by the villagers who lived nearby. But there was one thing that the church didn't have. It didn't have any lights. The church had been built too far away from power supplies and the cost to install electricity would have been too much.

Every Sunday evening, the people who lived on the mountainside opposite the tiny church saw something wonderful happen. The church bell would ring and people would gradually walk up the mountainside towards the church. They would enter the church and then all of a sudden the church would light up brightly. The villagers had to bring lights with them as they walked. When they arrived at church they hung them around the church on pegs set in the walls, so the light would spread all around. If only a few people came to church, the light would be very dim. But when many came to church there would be plenty of light. After the service the villagers would take their lanterns home. It was then that those who watched from a distance would see a stream of light pour out of the church and over the mountainside. For many it was a sign that all was well. God's light was with them and inside them. The only time the little church lit up was when people were there. That's when it truly became a church.

So it is here today. We carry in us the light of God and we gather here in this church where God's light is seen. Jesus says that we are the light of the world. He asks us to show his love to everyone when we leave here so that his light will give hope to those who see us.

Gospel Teaching

Jesus says that we are the light of the world. He says that we are salt to the earth. What an incredible thought that is. What a wonderful gift God has given us. Think of the people who have affected your life and helped you to believe in God. They are people who have lit up your life with meaning. They will be people who brought change into your life because they cared for you.

We are here today because the light of God has come into our lives. The only question now is, what are we going to do with that light? God asks very little of us. All our Lord wants is that we become the people he has made us. He wants us to become light for other people, and salt to inspire others. All Christ wants is that we follow him and witness to what we believe.

God makes us the salt of the earth. Salt, however, does not exist for its own sake. No one sits down to eat salt and salt alone. Salt is a seasoning. It is meant to preserve and flavour the food that people eat. And in the same way light is not meant to be looked at, it is not meant to be covered and treasured like some precious object; it is given so that people might see what is around them and walk in safety – it is meant to penetrate and overcome darkness.

In other words, we are saved not just for ourselves, but to be tools and assistance for others: this is doing the work of God.

Application
When we do the work of God, we stand proudly for our faith. And we can also trust that our faith will help us. When we do this, we are living our lives as God wants us to live. When we believe and act in faith, then we will be full of light – we will be beacons in a dark place.

Christ tells us that we are made as light and as salt. These things give life and help our life with God. Let your light shine before others, so that they may see your good works, and give glory to our Father in heaven.

A

"Do not imagine that I have come to abolish the Law or the Prophets."

Illustration

Two Buddhist monks were travelling along a muddy road in torrential rain. Suddenly, by the side of the road, they came upon a beautiful girl who was unable to cross because of the mud. The first monk lifted the girl in his arms and carried her to the other side. Then the two monks continued on their way.

Neither spoke until they neared their destination. Then the second monk couldn't restrain himself any longer. "We monks don't go near women," he said, "why did you lift that girl over the mud?" "I left the girl back there on the road," replied the first monk, "but are you still carrying her?"

The story illustrates an important truth that Jesus is teaching in today's Gospel. We cannot base our morality on law alone. It is on the direction of the heart that we will ultimately be judged. If our heart is in the right place, then the law poses no real problem for us. If our heart is right we will not even contemplate calling our brother a fool – let alone killing him. If our heart is right we will never allow ourselves to look on another person lustfully, let alone commit adultery. Jesus, in short, came not to abolish the law, but to put new heart into it. In the words of today's Gospel, he came to "complete" it.

Gospel Teaching

In this statement of Jesus we have a most important element of the Gospel and of St Matthew's Gospel in particular. Matthew emphasises the continuity between the Old and the New Testament. This is not surprising: he was himself a Jew; he was writing for Jews. Their conversion was clearly close to his heart. The realisation of this helps us to appreciate much that we find in Matthew's Gospel. For example, he cites the Old Testament forty-one times, introducing the majority of his texts with a formula, "that it might be fulfilled". Mark's Gospel, written for a non-Jewish audience, does not use the phrase at all.

The relationship between the old Jewish religion and the new Christian faith was one of the greatest tensions within the early Church. This tension reflects the arguments between Jesus himself and the scribes and

Pharisees. On the one hand, he condemns their shallow virtue; on the other, he upholds the Law of Moses.

Such a tension reflects the fact that Jesus was himself a Jew whose first task was to preach to "the lost sheep of Israel"; but, in the end, he was rejected by them. Yet there was nothing in the Old Testament that Jesus contradicted. Matthew shows how the Old Testament prepared for Christ's coming – for the place and manner of his birth, for his work of curing and preaching, for his messianic progress into Jerusalem, and for the lowliness and humility of his person.

The fact that Jesus is so often pictured in controversy with the scribes and Pharisees inclines many Christians to the belief that they were totally incompatible. Yet in truth, there were many worthy leading Jews – Nicodemus and Joseph of Arimathea, for example – who clearly recognised some continuity between the Law of Moses and the teaching of Jesus.

Application

Today's Gospel brings home to us the truth that the principal failing of many religious people, of whatever faith, is an inclination to legalism. The greatest sin is self-justification: the temptation to say to God, "I have fulfilled the law and so have done all that is demanded of me." Such "virtue" is precisely what is condemned by Jesus, whose primary concern is not with the fulfilment of the law so much as with the direction of the heart.

One of the marks of self-justification, or self-righteousness, is the persecution of other religions or races. This has undoubtedly been a sin among Christians in the past. But in the teaching of the Second Vatican Council the Church declares: "Mindful of her common patrimony with the Jews, and motivated by the Gospel's spiritual love and by no political considerations, she deplores the hatred, persecutions and displays of anti-Semitism directed against the Jews at any time and from any source" (*Nostra Aetate*, 4).

How deep is our virtue? The question is easily answered. It is not according to whether or not we have observed the law. It is according to whether we have left our sinful and hateful feelings back there on the road, or whether we still carry them with us.

"Love your enemies and pray for those who persecute you."

Illustration

Our culture constantly encourages us to treat each other as adversaries. The word "enemy" is carefully avoided, but we are encouraged to be competitors, combatants, or challengers. Our legal and political systems, our sports and games, relations between employers and unions all involve treating the other as an adversary who has in some way to be overcome.

If we are feeling noble, we will speak of how much we respect our adversaries. Members of the British Parliament, for example, address each other as "Honourable Member". But when the blood is up, our language quickly changes and degenerates. We begin to use phrases like "going in for the kill", or speak of "destroying" the opposition or their arguments.

Television as a medium thrives on providing simple, stereotyped, antagonistic views rather than reasoned debate, and violent films and series have great popularity. Sports develop crowds of fans whose strong emotions can spill over from chants of hatred to physical violence. Yet, if we were asked, most of us would say that we did not have any enemies, just people who got on our nerves from time to time.

Gospel Teaching

Jesus offers us a very different message to the one given us in the patterns described above. He does recognise the underlying violence in human attitudes and behaviour. The *lex talionis* – the principle of "an eye for an eye" – was a definite advance on the law of the jungle, whereby the strongest imposed their will on the weak with no possibility of retribution. But Jesus offers a higher principle still. We are not to impose our will on others but to be generous to those who hurt us, and to pray for them. Jesus will go on to model in his own life and death this most demanding of Christian principles. And, as he dies, he will be heard to say: "Father, forgive them; they do not know what they are doing." His example will be followed by his disciples. In the Acts of the Apostles, Stephen makes a similar plea for his murderers as he is stoned to death. The message and the example meant a great deal to the early Christians as they found themselves under threat of persecution and death.

At the same time, it is clear that Jesus recognises the difficulty of his demand, for he associates the pursuit of this principle with being perfect as our heavenly Father is perfect. We often have strange ideas about what perfection means. It can mean everything from keeping the house spotlessly clean to being untouched by any worldly concern. For Jesus, however, being perfect consists in being filled with unconditional love, the love that God has shown to us. It means not being satisfied with love that is second best, love that is half-hearted or shallow. It means showing love to someone even though society might encourage us to be indifferent or intolerant towards them.

Application

Jesus challenges us to think inclusively rather than exclusively. In our present world, perhaps in any world, there is a temptation to look for security by homing in on a particular set of truths or beliefs, which we put forward as the touchstone of orthodoxy. Those who agree with our convictions are with us. Those who disagree are against us, and we consequently exclude them from our group and our friendship. It does not usually begin as enmity. It is more that some people think differently from us, dress differently, speak differently, are just unlike us. They may or may not be hostile. Sometimes they just reveal to us aspects of ourselves that we try to hide. The question is, do we close down the hatches and try to protect ourselves from this alien and potentially hostile world; or do we feel secure enough to explore the differences we experience, find out what they mean, allow ourselves to be challenged?

Jesus indicates that his is the way we grow towards perfection. We do not start with this ability. He is addressed at one point in the Gospels as "good master" and immediately rejects the title because God alone is good. Our way to goodness, our way to perfection, lies in allowing our prejudices and fears to be challenged, by refusing to close our minds and our hearts to the needs of others. It is not a comfortable way of living, but it is the way we break through into true relations of peace and justice rather than false assumptions of the same. It is the way we discover what perfection is really about.

7th Sunday in Ordinary Time

"No one can be the slave of two masters."

Illustration

Darren's parents gave him a beautiful model car for his birthday. He was thrilled with all the things he could do with it. He changed gears, twirled the steering wheel, and imagined he was a racing driver. All through the day he showed it off to everybody. Everybody, that is, except Pip. He wouldn't let his little brother go anywhere near it.

Pip, of course, was extremely jealous and got up early the following morning to have his own close look at the marvellous car. When Darren came downstairs he found Pip happily examining the inner workings of the machine which lay upside down on the carpet.

Darren was furious. "You just break everything," he said, and gave Pip a blow across the head. He was much bigger than Pip and soon had his young brother in tears. Mother hurried into the room to see what was going on. She managed to separate them but she couldn't make peace. Pip was duly penitent, but Darren remained in a bad temper all day. He resolved to have his revenge on Pip for messing about with his car. A couple of days passed and Darren was still mad at his brother. His mother challenged him: "Darren, you love that silly car more than you love your brother." And Darren said he did.

Gospel Teaching

We may smile at children for taking little things so seriously, but before we do we might examine our own conscience. Adults also become attached to silly things. It is very easy to become over-possessive. Perhaps we want a better house, a bigger car, or simply for so-and-so to get out of "our chair". We want something so badly that we are prepared to hurt another person to get it. We love the new house, the bigger car, "my chair" more than we love our neighbour. So we love them more than we love God too.

Jesus knows exactly what we are like. He pointed out that such attachment to material things is a form of paganism. It is the pagans who set their hearts on material things. If we turn money or possessions into our only goal, we turn them into a god and we fall into idolatry. Jesus says to us today: "Set your hearts on [God's] kingdom first, and on his righteousness, and all these other things will be given you as well." He wants us to get our priorities right: first things first.

It is foolish to set our hearts on material possessions, because they cannot last. We are seeking happiness in something that passes away. Such happiness dissolves as material things dissolve. It is hard to realise at the time, but we can learn the lesson from children's presents. Toys that were so precious at Christmas, or birthdays, may soon get discarded and forgotten. Darren did not remember the incident of the toy car when his next birthday came round. But we have to remember that it is not only children who get priorities wrong.

In our responsorial psalm today we repeated the line: "In God alone is my soul at rest." Those words set the scene for our Lord's warning: "do not worry about tomorrow". He is not suggesting we should be improvident and make no plans beyond today. But he wants us to put things in perspective, first things first. Where do we set our heart?

Application
There is no cause for despondency when we realise that the things we are specially attached to must pass away. Everything that exists is made by God and is simply a reflection of God's goodness. But there is one thing that will not pass away – and that is the love of God. Focus on that central truth: God's love is faithful and true. Even if a mother forgets the child of her womb, yet God will not forget you. The image in the words of Isaiah from today's first reading reminds us of the love of God that surpasses all human love. We can have the utmost confidence in that love.

Do not worry about tomorrow. Jesus wants us to be happy and we can only be happy now. The past is gone, the future has not yet come, the present moment is the only time we have for living and loving. It was awareness of this which prompted the great spiritual writer Jean-Pierre de Caussade to develop the profound awareness of "the sacrament of the present moment". Every moment is charged with God's grace.

A

"A sensible man who built his house on rock."

Illustration

In one of the sketches in the classic TV comedy series *Monty Python's Flying Circus*, a chartered accountant tells a careers adviser that he wants to become a lion tamer. Though life presents us with a large number of choices, many people do not have a real choice about what job they do: there are limited opportunities; we are all limited further by our qualifications and experience. The humour of the *Monty Python* sketch lay in the absurdity of a man with the qualifications and experience to be a chartered accountant thinking that he was suited for dealing with ferocious animals.

Our choices in life are important, but we do need to have a realistic grasp of the possible. One of the most important choices anyone has to make is the decision to try to live as a good and unselfish person. We know that following the path of goodness leads to happiness; and that to follow the other path will lead to unhappiness.

The first reading today sees the path of goodness as the following of the law given by God: "I set before you today a blessing and a curse: a blessing, if you obey the commandments of the Lord our God that I enjoin on you today; a curse, if you disobey the commandments of the Lord your God and leave the way I have marked out for you." That seems pretty clear, but in the second reading Paul tells us that "both Jew and pagan sinned and forfeited God's glory". None of us has the necessary qualifications and experience to be good. Maybe we are about as qualified for obeying God's law as the *Monty Python* chartered accountant was to become a lion tamer!

Gospel Teaching

Fortunately the good news is that serving God does not depend upon our qualifications and experience. The only qualification for being just in God's eyes is that God loves us and that Jesus died for us. Paul tells us that we are "justified through the free gift of his grace by being redeemed in Christ Jesus who was appointed by God to sacrifice his life so as to win reconciliation through faith". This does not mean that we are not called to change our lives, however. God loves me just the way I am; but God does not leave me the way I am. Being justified means being changed into a person whose life is based on the solid teaching given by Christ.

In today's Gospel Jesus insists on real change: "It is not those who say to me, 'Lord, Lord', who will enter the kingdom of heaven, but the person who does the will of my Father in heaven." We are called to build our lives on the firm foundation of his teaching if our lives are to be changed: "everyone who listens to these words of mine and acts on them will be like a sensible man who built his house on rock". Listening or not listening to the words of Jesus is a matter of choice, a matter of life and death.

Application
It is quite easy to love a mental image of Jesus, something based on a picture or a statue we have seen. That is not enough. Calling out, "Lord, Lord", is not enough. It is vital to be sure that we love the *real* Jesus. If we are going to love the real Jesus and not the Jesus of our own imagination, we will need to be made and remade through listening to his words and following his teaching.

If we try to apply this truth to our lives in a practical way, we might start by reading the Gospels seriously and thinking about how to live according to the teachings of Jesus that we find in them. If that is too difficult, we could simply try to set aside a few minutes each week to think about the Sunday Gospel and ask ourselves some key questions. We could ask whether we have really accepted the values that Jesus teaches. We could ask whether they influence the way we treat others, our choices about the use of our time or maybe our choice of career. We can ask whether his teaching really influences our political ideas and social attitudes. If they do, then we are like people whose house is built upon a rock. Nothing can shake us, because we know just whose disciples we are.

A

"I did not come to call the virtuous, but sinners."

Illustration

The phone rings. So often it's at the worst possible moment – you're in the garden, or eating a meal, or in the bath. The voice at the other end asks, "Is that Mr or Mrs So-and-so?" They proceed to tell you that you've been specially chosen to receive an unmissable deal on a mobile phone, or perhaps that you've won a holiday (in a competition you didn't know you'd entered), or they try to tempt you with some other hard-to-resist offer. If you enquire further, you invariably find that it's not quite as straightforward as it seems. There is usually a catch. As you put the phone down, you may find yourself wondering why they picked on you to call: "Why me?"

Gospel Teaching

"Why me?" is a question that must have been asked by many of the people we meet in the scriptures. Abraham must have asked it when the Lord called him to leave his comfortable life in Ur and journey to an unknown land. Then, much later in life, he must have asked the question again. Abraham was entitled to wonder why he had been chosen above many apparently more suitable people. For, as Paul tells us in today's second reading, this time it was a calling that was way beyond any human expectation: the aged Abraham and his ninety-year-old wife Sarah were to become parents. It's not surprising that for each of them their first reaction was to fall about laughing.

Yet Abraham is seen as a model of faith, and his faith as a "type", a foreshadowing of Christian faith. Abraham's faith is in essence the same as our faith: belief in God who can bring the dead to life. God brought new life into the barren lives of Abraham and Sarah by promising them the gift of a child. Their circumstances seemed impossible, and their calling highly unlikely, but Abraham did not let that prevent him from believing in God's promise and accepting his calling.

"Why me?" Matthew must have asked the question too. Although the Gospel tells us that he responded immediately to Jesus' call, he must have wondered why he had been chosen. For Matthew was a tax collector. Tax collectors were despised as traitors, collaborators with the Roman occupying forces. They were also seen as crooks, overcharging and stealing from their own people to line their own pockets. They may have been rich, but they were unpopular, ritually unclean, outcasts from their community. Why would Jesus think of calling someone like him? Matthew must have asked himself the question; the Pharisees certainly asked it. But Jesus saw through any doubts Matthew may have had, and the disapproval of the Pharisees, to offer healing and new life to the sinner.

When people respond to God's call, their lives change. They are called to put their faith into action. Abraham had already left his home and family to begin a new way of life in response to God's call. Now his life was to change again as he took on the responsibility not only of parenthood, but of becoming "the father of many nations". And from now on his life would be based on a covenant relationship with God, a relationship of love and justice. Matthew's life also changed as he responded to Jesus' call. He left the customs house, and with it a life focused on the acquisition of money, to follow Jesus. This meant leaving behind the material riches of his former life to take on the life of a disciple. His life would from now on be founded on Christ's commandment of love.

Application

We, like Abraham, like Matthew, and like so many others down through the ages, are called by God. It may not be a calling that we expect, or even think we want. We may wonder why he has chosen us. Surely there are so many better, more suitable, more faithful people than you or me? Why would God want to choose us?

Jesus said: "I did not come to call the virtuous, but sinners." He calls us to set aside our doubts and our fears and to set out in faith with him. As we do so he offers us the gift of new life, a life lived in relationship with him, a life founded on his commandment of love. He does this simply because he loves us, and he wants us to take that love out to the world. This is why he has called us.

A

"These are the names of the twelve apostles."

Illustration

Most of us have probably given way to a slight impatience when a friend has started to tell a long and rambling "funny story", which we have heard before. Perhaps we have even felt that we could tell it better ourselves. At such times, we may well have "switched off" our attention until the story has reached its bitter end.

As the names of the twelve apostles were listed in the Gospel that we have just heard, were we tempted, perhaps, to "switch off"? After all, their names are well known to us; the list is familiar. There seems to be very little that can be said about them. And, with a few notable exceptions like Peter, James and John, most of them seem to have disappeared from reliable history almost as soon as they were appointed.

Gospel Teaching

Yet these are the men Jesus chose to preach the kingdom of God. They were to form the foundation of his Church for ever. But what a strangely assorted group of men they were: fishermen, a tax collector, two brothers whom Jesus nicknamed "Boanerges" or "Sons of Thunder". And, perhaps most startling, Simon, who belonged to a revolutionary party of Zealots dedicated to the overthrow of Roman power. One wonders how he would have got on with Matthew, who had just retired from collecting taxes for the Roman government? Their importance is obviously such that we cannot be content simply to pass them over as names that belong to a long list.

Perhaps the reason that so little is known about most of the apostles after Christ's ascension is that as *individuals* they are not so important. Jesus established them as a *group* or *body* of men. Just as in the first reading God established Israel as a "kingdom of priests, a consecrated nation", so in the Gospel Jesus, after praying to the Father, established the Twelve as a new people. It was together, in communion with one another and with their Lord, that their strength lay. Simon Peter, of course, was the leader; but alone he was powerless, as we will come to know as we read through the rest of the Gospel. Only *together* did the apostles enjoy the life and power of Christ.

This is an important truth. For the assortment of men and women – and even priests and bishops – in the Church remains an odd one. As we look around any congregation, we may well be tempted to wonder at God's wisdom in choosing such people. They are, perhaps, not the kind of people *we* would choose. But they *are* the kind of people God chooses. Individually we are weak; but in communion with the Church we enjoy the strength of unity.

The group of twelve apostles, of course, shared the life of Christ in a unique way. They witnessed the earthly life of Jesus and were personally instructed by him. And so they were given the authority to tell the world about Christ and record his life in written form in a way that would form the foundation for the future building of the Church till the end of time.

Application

In today's Gospel we see the beginnings of this work as the apostles are "sent out" by Jesus to look after a dispirited multitude. They were to put new spirit into them. They were given the authority, quite literally, to impart God's Holy Spirit which they themselves received from Christ. And in due course the apostles would choose and commission others to continue the work entrusted to them. Their mission has been handed down and continued in the Church through their successors, the bishops. This is what we mean when we say that the Church is "apostolic".

The apostles and their successors, the bishops, continue the compassion of Christ, which is eternal. As we reflect on the lives of the apostles, it is vital not to let their names pass by unnoticed. We cannot afford, indeed, to "pass by" any person chosen by Christ. For every person is flesh and blood, filled with hopes and fears. Every person, at times at least, is "harassed and dejected". Yet Jesus chose them for what they were – and for what they could become – in the same way as he chooses each one of us.

A

"Do not be afraid of those who kill the body but cannot kill the soul."

Illustration

Fr Shay Cullen, an Irish Columban priest, has tirelessly worked for justice in Olongapo City in the Philippines since 1969. Olongapo City developed around the United States Naval Base in Subic Bay. The base was used by the navy as a rest and recreation stop for their servicemen, and a thriving sex industry developed. Despite the navy's withdrawal a number of years ago, Olongapo remains a draw for sex tourists, particularly foreign paedophile tourists.

Fr Shay has made it his life's work to make sure that children are not throwaway objects of the international sex tourism trade. Together with Merle and Alex Hermoso, a Filipino couple, he set up the Preda Foundation in 1974 to rescue abused children, and after many years the services offered by Preda were expanded to schools, colleges and community groups building basic Christian communities among the urban poor of Olongapo. Fr Shay was an invited delegate to the 1989 conference in Helsinki drafting the Convention on the Rights of the Child, and was nominated for the Nobel Peace Prize in 2001.

Although Fr Shay has saved many lives and immeasurably helped many more, his stand for those who are poor and exploited has made him extremely unpopular in the Philippines. He has received countless death threats and is under constant harassment. Attempts have been made to deport him because his publicity has been damaging to local officials, some of whom have been involved in the promotion of the sex industry. Fr Shay has not only stood up to the local authorities but has tackled foreign sex abusers, bringing evidence to international attention.

Gospel Teaching

Today's Gospel is preceded by Jesus' commission to the disciples to go out in his name and proclaim God's kingdom. But the reading is a bit mysterious. It is about things hidden now being revealed tomorrow, about light and dark, and about whispers and proclamations. Above all it is about not being afraid of people or authorities who might abuse, arrest, torture or even execute us when we preach the Good News, because they cannot kill our souls – only God has the power to do that.

Jesus promises that he will declare himself for us in the presence of the Father, if we declare ourselves for him in the presence of other people. But what does it mean to declare ourselves for Jesus? Does it mean telling as many people as possible that Jesus is our personal saviour? Jesus clearly expects actions as well as words. By declaring ourselves for Jesus, we are called also to work for justice and peace. Does it just mean going to Mass every Sunday and saying grace before meals? Elsewhere in Matthew's Gospel, Jesus condemns filling one's life with religious ritual alone. He condemns the Pharisees for their hollow, ostentatious practices. Jesus is suggesting that discipleship must include speaking out and acting to bring about God's kingdom here on earth, despite the persecution this could engender.

Application

We are to fear and love God above all things. So often, we Christians are in situations where we are called to speak words from the Lord's teachings to our government, our church, our family or our friends. Yet we are often afraid to do so because of possible rejection and persecution, or simply the fear of being made to feel foolish. So often we keep our mouths shut and hide in the safety of silence because we shy away from tensions. We do not have the courage to be truthful.

Just as Fr Shay Cullen and countless other Christians throughout the world are fearless in declaring themselves for Jesus and what he stands for, we too are urged to proclaim God's kingdom in words and actions. Some do this by speaking out against the arms trade and protesting outside arms factories, others involve themselves in rallies for trade justice and the cancellation of the developing world's debt. Some Christian churches address the issue of poverty in our own society and support campaigns for a decent living wage and the provision of more affordable housing. The Church's social teaching stands alongside scripture in urging Christians to be proactive in promoting Gospel values.

If we meet opposition when we proclaim the Good News of God's love for all people, and the justice and righteousness that the kingdom of God will bring, we have nothing to fear. For we know that we are under the loving protection of a God who cares for every sparrow that falls from the sky, and even knows exactly how many hairs there are on our head.

12th Sunday in Ordinary Time

A

"Anyone who welcomes you welcomes me."

Illustration

Opera is for the elite. Or at least we could be forgiven for thinking so. The rather esoteric culture surrounding the world's major opera houses, the high prices of tickets, and the strong perception that there is little in opera to appeal to the masses, all pose a problem to the management of opera companies. How can they ask for public subsidies for an art form that will benefit only the very few?

As long ago as 1728, an opera with a different thrust hit the English stage. Composed by John Gay, *The Beggar's Opera* deliberately challenged every received notion of what opera was and who it was for. Gay set the opera in London – not the London of high society, but back-street, low-life London. The beggars, criminals and prostitutes, excluded from regular opera, were the stars. And Gay's message was clear. The upper-class elite who would see his opera would be faced with the uncomfortable truth that their wealthy lifestyle was at least in part responsible for the squalor and deprivation of so many.

The religion of the scribes and the Pharisees was for the elite. The ritual requirements of the law were almost impossible to observe in full, and religious leaders exploited this fact to wield an authority way above what they deserved. Jesus was reclaiming religion for all, especially for the most excluded. Often it was the elite who were directly faced with his message, and challenged to respond.

Gospel Teaching

Jesus taught that discipleship was not a hobby for religious people. It was meant to be something wholehearted, and accessible to all. Discipleship is a priority, *the* priority, to the extent that Jesus can say that only those who lose their lives for his sake will find life.

The rich woman in today's first reading extended hospitality to a traveller, the prophet Elisha, and received the unlooked-for reward of a son. The second reading, from the letter to the Romans, prepares us to see how this story is relevant today. It shows the close identification of the believer with Christ. As in baptism we share his death, so also we share his resurrection. What happens to him also happens to those who follow him. So Jesus is able to say that if anyone performs even the lowliest service for a disciple of his, they will most emphatically not lose their reward. Their attention to a disciple is hospitality to the master, Jesus himself.

Jesus radically undermines the religion of the scribes and Pharisees and hands God back to the masses, who have been so long deprived of him. It is no wonder Jesus had such a following among the underclass, and that he was so resented by the powers that be. No longer do the pious need to give all their attention to the ritual of the Temple in Jerusalem; no longer do they seek to please God by paranoid adherence to the details of the law. God is much closer than that. God, in Jesus, is as close as his nearest disciple. And to serve the disciple is to serve him.

Application
As the wealthy woman offered hospitality to Elisha, so we are called to do the same to those we meet who are engaged in the Lord's service. Our hospitality may not be in the form of a meal or a bed for the night. It could be a simple greeting, an offer of help, a supportive word. We offer this service because it is good in itself, but also because we know that in serving them we serve Christ who sent them.

For Jesus, service of God is inextricably bound up with service of people. We cannot have a religion that is exclusively focused on rules and ritual. They have their place, but it is not at the heart of faith. We are not to become like the scribes and Pharisees. Rather we focus on Christ, serving him and honouring him wherever we meet him.

And then there is the call to commitment. Jesus is quite clear that our religion isn't a hobby or a minor interest. It is central to our identity as individuals and as a community; it offers the authentic interpretation of our life, and holds before us our final end: eternal life with God. We do not live our faith by being religious in what we wear or say. Rather, we live our faith in simple service of the Christ who, though Lord and Master, came to serve us.

A

"I bless you, Father, Lord of heaven and of earth, for hiding these things from the learned and the clever and revealing them to mere children."

Illustration

Childhood is, of course, a vital and complicated time. It can also be a time of contradiction. Children can be very kind, but they can also be very cruel. They can be very generous, but they can also be very selfish and greedy. Friendships started in childhood may fade away, or they can last for a whole lifetime.

There are, we might say, two aspects to being a child. One we might call being childish. The other we might call being childlike. The first we hope to grow out of, the second we hope will flourish into a mature and authentic way of adulthood, especially in our relationship with God. In her spiritual autobiography St Thérèse of Lisieux recalled the more childish aspects of her character: tears and tantrums, self-will, wanting her own way. Once, when presented with a basket of toys and asked to choose, she cried, "I choose it all!"

Sadly, our society seems to want to keep us in our childish ways. It promises instant gratification, rights without obligations, and makes an idol out of being a permanent adolescent. It is this sort of childishness that St Paul talks about when he says, "When I was a child, I used to talk like a child, and think like a child, and argue like a child, but now I am a man, all childish ways are put behind me."

Being childlike is different, and refers to the positive side of childhood where we learn to trust, to love, to make friends and to ask big questions. When playing with her brother Rodrigo when they were children, Teresa of Ávila used to wonder what God was like, and what eternity would be like. It is of this childlikeness that Jesus says, "I tell you solemnly, unless you change and become like little children you will never enter the kingdom of heaven."

Gospel Teaching

It is exactly this childlike quality, and also the gift of friendship, that Jesus is referring to in the Gospel reading. We are privileged to hear this prayer of Christ to the Father. During the prayer we even get a mention.

We, and the whole Church, are the ones to whom the saving truth of the Trinity has been revealed. This is because Christ has made us his friends. Elsewhere Jesus says, "I call you friends, because I have made known to you everything I have learnt from my Father." By the gift of the Spirit we are given the childlike attitude of trust and acceptance needed in order for us to be transformed by Christ's teaching. The love of the Father, Son and Spirit is opened up to us and we are invited to take part in it, to become part of it.

A key word in Jesus' prayer is "learn". He asks us to cooperate in being taught by him. This works at several levels. We are asked to listen and hear the teaching that Christ gives us: his teaching about the Father and the Spirit, his teaching about himself, his teaching about the sacraments, resurrection and eternal life. By this learning our minds are made holy.

We are also called to learn how to put these teachings into practice. St Paul talks about living in the Spirit, about the Holy Spirit dwelling within us.

Application

Jesus invites us to put his "yoke" on our shoulders. Normally being yoked may not seem an attractive option: it implies forced labour and servitude. But Christ's yoke is light because the gift of the Spirit moves us to enjoy carrying out the will of God, even though at times we fail.

"My yoke is easy and my burden light," Christ says to us. His commandments are not complicated and burdensome: Jesus asks us simply to love God, and to love our neighbour as ourselves. In doing this, we are following him, we are loving as Christ has loved us; and we can know that, as we do so, he himself will help us to shoulder the yoke. Compared to the complicated and constant requirements of the old law, Christ's yoke is very light.

As St Thomas Aquinas put it, the commandments of the new law are fewer and easier to carry out than those of the old! By his incarnation Christ teaches us all these things and allows us to begin, even in this life, to enjoy friendship with God which will blossom completely in eternity.

A

"The mysteries of the kingdom of heaven are revealed to you."

Illustration

For twelve-year-old Winston and his classmates from the inner city, their first night's camping on the farm was one of amazing new experiences. The very darkness was frightening, although they could see stars for the first time in their lives. The silence was another horror but, next morning, the sight of sheep and cows, the sound of birdsong and the smell of grass made up for it all. They learnt where their food came from, and the significance of the seasons. They forgot their MP3 players and computer games while they absorbed information about the fertility of nature, and the cycle of life and death in creation.

Gospel Teaching

Today's readings use nature to teach spiritual lessons, but also concern the whole of nature itself. For, as biblical scholar Raymond E. Brown once wrote, "In Jesus risen the earth shares our future." Because of that, he added, "We should take care of it." Jesus himself was fully aware of the natural world, growing up in the stony hill country around Galilee. There he would witness farmers sowing their crops by hand before ploughing in those seeds that had fallen in decent soil. There would be a great deal of waste, but the harvest that would result was worth the risk.

The sower is used as a type of evangelist, casting his message before all, and hoping that some of it will take root in people prepared to listen with open minds. Not everyone wants to give the Good News a hearing – it can seem irrelevant, or too challenging; or they are just too self-absorbed and busy even to listen. Those who are "poor in spirit" will listen, for they know that the kingdom of justice, peace, forgiveness and healing is not anything they pay for with money, nor can they bring it about by their own achievement.

Only God can bring in the kingdom, as only God can make crops grow or rain fall or the sun shine. For God is the source and cause of the whole creation – this creation which is damaged by human sin, and yearns, or, as Paul puts it in his letter to the Romans, groans like a woman in labour, for its transformation. That transformation will surely come, slowly and quietly, like the growth of plants. It has been promised and has begun already with the coming of Christ.

This transformation is, as Paul expresses again, freedom from "slavery to decadence" – decadence being decay, suffering, death, all the consequences of the Fall. It is a transforming freedom for the whole of creation, for everything on earth has been touched by both human sin and divine redemption. Our minds can scarcely take in the scope of this wonderful kingdom where the whole of nature is renewed and where there is no more decay, no pain, no death.

Application
We hear the Good News of this kingdom, but ask ourselves what sort of soil we are. Do we enable the message to take root and grow? Do we produce a harvest of good works, signs pointing towards the kingdom and helping to bring it about? We also ask ourselves what sort of seed we are. Do we die to ourselves that Jesus may live in us? For Jesus says elsewhere that a seed has to die to itself to be transformed into a plant.

Yet another question is: what sort of sower are we? Do we attend to the word of God, reading, studying, praying and knowing scripture so well that we can be confident in relaying the Good News to others? Or do we rely on the "professionals" to do the work of sowing the word, the office-holders in the Church, the priests and religious? Is it enough to have faith sufficient for ourselves, but to be unable to explain or express that faith to others who may be hungry for it? How can we expect a harvest if we keep the seed to ourselves?

Yet we are assured that the kingdom will come, that goodness and healing will prevail. God's purpose will not be frustrated, but, in his great freedom, the Lord has entrusted us with the responsibility of working with him to bring it about. God's power and life make the plants grow, but the farmer has to work preparing the land, acquiring and sowing the seed, cutting the crops at harvest and grinding the ears to become flour. The kingdom will come about; but what are we doing to help to make it so?

A

"Let them both grow till the harvest."

Illustration

In the 1950s, faced with the spread of Soviet and Chinese communism, the United States turned in on itself to root out the enemy within. Home-grown communists were believed to be everywhere – from Hollywood actors and directors, to lawyers, civil rights workers, teachers and trade unionists. J. Edgar Hoover's FBI spearheaded the efforts to weed out this internal threat. There was an atmosphere of mistrust and fear as friends and colleagues denounced each other, thousands of government workers were dismissed without just cause, while other people, such as the great Charlie Chaplin, abandoned the USA in search of greater freedom abroad. The very standards and values of democracy which the US government was so determined to defend were in fact being eroded by the corrupt methods used to identify the so-called "Reds under the bed".

Gospel Teaching

The desire to root out perceived evil is a universal temptation for humanity. Hitler's concentration camps, Stalin's purges, China's Cultural Revolution, the Spanish Inquisition and the witch-hunts of medieval Europe – humanity's history is littered with the bloody attempts to create by force a pure and uncontaminated society.

Religion is particularly prone to the desire to create a perfect community of the saved. After all, isn't that the point of faith – to strive for perfection and to root out sin? So it is striking to hear Jesus warn against such zeal. In response no doubt to questions about how the faithful should respond to the presence of evil in the world – and perhaps even within the community of believers – Jesus rejects the solution of the witch-hunt and inquisition: let both weed and wheat grow together, side by side, until the harvest.

Only God can judge the human heart, and if mere human beings set themselves up to be judge, jury and executioner, then the long dark history of persecutions, show trials and extermination camps provides ample evidence that the good are inevitably going to be destroyed along with the bad, the wheat will be pulled up with the darnel.

That is not the way with the kingdom of God. The other two parables go on to show that the kingdom is not to be imposed by force and violence.

It is a kingdom that grows gradually – even from small beginnings – like the mustard seed. Such growth needs time, it has a rhythm all of its own – God's rhythm. And the effect of the kingdom is that it gradually transforms people from within – like yeast which turns the dough into nourishing bread. There is no room for compulsion or imposition in the kingdom.

Human kingdoms and empires might grow by means of conquest or force, but the kingdom of God grows when people respond to it freely, when there is good soil – a receptive heart, which can bring forth a rich harvest of good works. The seed of the kingdom has the power to transform both individuals and the world. But never by force, and never in a hurry.

Application

Today's first reading provides the key to God's patience: God's delay in uprooting evil is to provide us with the hope and opportunity of repentance. Just as every community is composed of good and bad, so it is with every individual. Our lives are a mixture of wheat and darnel. The Lord is patient in order to allow us to respond to his love, so that our wheat may ripen, the seed of God's word may grow within us and our true selves may flourish.

God gives us the time to show by our lives that our fundamental choice is for the values of the kingdom – that we choose to be life-giving wheat rather than life-choking weeds. And if we accept this time as a moment of grace, then we will learn from God to be equally patient and compassionate towards our brothers and sisters, as the book of Wisdom tells us.

The way of the people of the kingdom is not to do violence to ourselves or to others, but to allow God's gentle and persistent love to bring forth a harvest of good works within us. If we focus on the good in our lives and our world – if we allow God's kingdom to grow within us and transform our lives – then we need not be concerned with the darnel. God can deal with that in God's good time. Today we rejoice that the Lord is patient and mild in judgement – and gives us all time to grow into kingdom people.

A

"He goes and sells everything he owns and buys it."

Illustration

When St Thérèse of Lisieux was a little girl in the 1870s, she was desperate to enter the religious life. At the age of nine, Thérèse privately informed the prioress of the local Carmelite convent of her desire to become a nun, but the prioress informed her that the minimum age was sixteen. For the next six years Thérèse persisted in her desire, encountering a series of obstacles along the way. Thérèse was certain that her vocation was the method by which she would obtain the kingdom of heaven.

So strong was this conviction that, as time went by, she determined to seek a dispensation to enter the convent earlier than was usual. The superior of the Carmelite convent, however, was adamant in her refusal to consider Thérèse's entry, as were the prioress and the convent's spiritual director. In her disappointment Thérèse persuaded her father to accompany her to put her case before the bishop and his vicar-general. Again, however, she experienced disappointment. The bishop and his assistant talked of waiting and how she ought to continue living with her father a little longer.

Four days later, Thérèse, her father and one of her sisters went on a diocesan pilgrimage to Rome. It was Thérèse's intention to ask the Pope personally for permission to enter the convent. When she knelt before him and when he held out his hand to her she said, "Most Holy Father, in honour of your Jubilee, let me enter Carmel at fifteen." She went on, "Holy Father, if you said yes, everyone else would be willing." To this the Pope replied, "Well… well… you will enter if it is God's will." Meanwhile officials intervened and literally dragged the tearful Thérèse out of the room.

On her return home Thérèse once again wrote to her local bishop and this time received his permission to enter the convent at Lisieux. She did so on 9th April 1888, aged fifteen. Her struggle and determination were finally rewarded. She was on her way to obtaining the kingdom of heaven, as well as sanctity en route. Her story illustrates the truth contained in the first two parables of today's Gospel – how a disciple must joyfully abandon all attachments in order to follow Jesus.

Gospel Teaching

Both parables, of the man who finds treasure hidden in a field and the merchant who discovers a pearl of great value, make the same point: the man and the merchant sell all that they have in order to purchase what they have found. This is the situation of disciples of Jesus. They also have found treasure – the kingdom of heaven – and they are to leave everything to possess it. This same teaching of Jesus occurs later on in the Gospel when Jesus tells a young man, "Sell what you own and give the money to the poor, and you will have treasure in heaven; then come, follow me." There can be no half measures.

The third parable in today's Gospel reading, that of the dragnet, is told by Jesus to illustrate how, here on earth, saints and sinners live side by side. These will be separated by the angels on the last day, just as fishermen separate good and bad fish.

Jesus concludes this section of teaching in Matthew's Gospel by comparing a scribe, who becomes a disciple, to a householder bringing out of his storeroom things both old and new. Jesus here is probably referring to the teaching that his disciples already have – the Jewish law and the prophets – as things old, and his own instruction to them as things new.

Application

True disciples of Jesus are prepared to put him and the kingdom of heaven first in their lives. On our part this may involve surrendering some of the things to which we are most attached, either in the material sense or in the sense of ideas and ambitions we hold dear. We are encouraged to see this, however, as something that will bring us joy, just as the man who found a treasure in a field went off happily to sell everything he owned, in order to purchase the field.

In our case, becoming disciples of Jesus will bring us similar fulfilment, but it requires courage along the way, just as Thérèse of Lisieux needed it in her quest. In this way we shall then become, as today's second reading, from St Paul's letter to the Romans, says, true images of Jesus.

A

"Listen, listen to me and you will have good things to eat and rich food to enjoy."

Illustration

We are all too familiar these days with those heart-rending television pictures that show people in the developing world, often tiny children, ravaged by the effects of hunger and thirst. They are a potent reminder that food and drink are among our most basic necessities; without them, we suffer intensely and ultimately we die.

In our first reading today the Lord, through the prophet Isaiah, assures his people that their exile will soon be over: the happy future that then awaits them is symbolised by a plentiful supply of food and drink – an abundance of corn, wine and milk – and all free of charge.

Gospel Teaching

The Gospel reading takes the theme of providing food a stage further. Having heard the tragic news that John the Baptist has been murdered, and no doubt wondering what his own fate might be, Jesus decides to slip across the Lake of Galilee and spend a few quiet hours with his friends. But the huge crowds that have been following him have other ideas. They hurry round the lake on foot so that, as his little boat comes to shore, there they are awaiting him, like a mammoth welcoming committee. The moment he sees them, all thought of solitude vanishes. At once he is at their disposal, eager to help them and to offer those who are sick his healing touch.

By the time evening falls the disciples are at a loss – and, it must be said, in something of a panic – as to how they are going to feed five thousand and more unexpected guests with nothing more than a few loaves and fishes. Jesus seems to brush aside their anxieties as he takes hold of the loaves and fishes and prays over them. Incredibly, as the disciples distribute them to the people, now sitting on the green grass, not only does everyone eat to their heart's desire, but at the end there are enough scraps left over to fill a dozen baskets. There could scarcely be a more startling proof that God is concerned for those who are hungry; and that for God numbers – five or five thousand – do not matter.

However, there is more than that to the miracle. We can take note not merely of *what* Jesus does, but of *how* he does it. He makes the very gestures that one day will be used in the institution of the Eucharist, gestures that we still see at Mass today. Jesus took the bread and, raising his eyes to heaven, blessed it, broke it and then gave it to the disciples to distribute. In the early Church "the breaking of bread" was another name for the Mass. It is as if Jesus were saying: "This material food, I know, is vital for you – that is why I provide it – but it can never satisfy your deepest hungers. However, there will come a day when I will provide for those needs also."

Application
In 1984, on returning from a visit to an Ethiopia devastated by famine, Cardinal Basil Hume told of a memorable meeting he had had with a little Ethiopian boy. The child, an orphan, clutched the cardinal's hand and was reluctant to let go. After a while he pointed towards his open mouth; there was no need for an interpreter to explain that the child wanted food. Then he gently rubbed his cheek against the cardinal's hand, again a self-explanatory sign of his desire for affection. The cardinal commented that the youngster was expressing the needs of every man, woman and child – the need for nourishment and the need for love. Without food there is no life; without love there is no life worth having. In the Eucharist we receive the bread of eternal life and the most powerful pledge of boundless love. After all, the sacrifice of the Mass – the body given for us, the blood shed for us – cost Jesus his life.

Today we are being invited to recognise, with joy and gratitude, that in this Mass, as in every Mass, God is offering us food from heaven: food free of charge; food that satisfies our deepest needs; food that is proof of Christ's overwhelming love, of his desire to accompany us on our journey through life; food that assures us, in the words of St Paul, that no power, no adversity, absolutely nothing, not even death itself, can separate us from the love of God made visible in Christ Jesus our Lord.

18th Sunday in Ordinary Time

A

"Lord! Save me!"

Illustration

To mark the Millennium, a new footbridge was built in the centre of London, right in the heart of the city's financial district. It looked beautiful and linked St Paul's Cathedral with the new Tate Modern art gallery, housed in an old power station. However, when it first opened to the public the bridge wobbled; and it was closed for over a year while engineers restructured it so it wouldn't wobble any more. Today many pedestrians still tread gingerly, hoping they won't start the wobble.

In Israel they have built a bridge across part of the Sea of Galilee. An important thing about this bridge is that it is transparent and is at the same level as the water. It's designed for the pilgrims, to let people see what it's like to walk on water, to walk where Jesus walked.

Today's Gospel is one of the most graphic stories we have of Jesus' life. But it is more about Peter walking on the water than about Jesus. What did Peter really think he was doing, climbing out of the boat and walking towards what he at first thought was a ghost?

Gospel Teaching

Some people think that, if you have enough faith, life will be all plain sailing. But at some time or other we all face difficult and trying circumstances and situations in our lives. Faith does not shield us from the harsh knocks of life. At those times it is as if the Lord is asking us to walk on water. But at the same time he stretches out his hand and holds us up. Elijah in the first reading was a great man of faith. He was being persecuted and threatened with death and he sought refuge and protection in a cave. A beaten and broken man, he just wanted to die. However, in the cave he experienced the presence of God and was strengthened by that experience to carry on.

To live by faith means to trust God and to rely on God's power. God won't carry us but will hold us up if we let go. We are called to take the risk; only then can God help us.

Peter knew that whatever Jesus commanded was possible. It was really a way of testing faith. They had all just seen him cure people, teach them, feed five thousand people with a little bread and fish. Peter has no doubt that what Jesus commands will happen. But the command needs a response, and we learn that the success of the response depends on his faith. Peter had no choice but to leave the boat and risk his life to learn perhaps the most valuable lesson: the realisation of both his own weakness and the power of Jesus. If Peter had stayed in the boat, his faith would have been worthless and never tested.

Application

Peter is the model of a very human journey of faith. He seeks, he steps, he fails, he is saved, he praises – and it all repeats again. If we say we are Christians and never make a step like Peter, trusting our faith and trusting Christ, then how do we know we really do believe? Every time Peter tried to show his faith, he failed: he betrayed Jesus verbally, he ran away, he took the side of Satan; and in today's story he took his eyes off Jesus and began to sink. But every time he fell and his faith failed, he rose up again and became closer to Christ. He had the good sense at least to call out for help. In the moments of his weakness he knew enough to reach out to Christ. The failures of Peter only made him love Christ more – only made him rely on Christ more.

The sea is often used as a metaphor for life. Perhaps the Gospel is saying that no matter how dark life might be, and no matter how high the waves are or how rough the sea, Jesus is still able to reach us and is still able to lift us out of life's trauma, if only we trust him totally and keep our eyes fixed on him. God does not necessarily work by way of miracles in our lives. God probably doesn't want us walking on water. The Lord simply assures us he will be with us always. And when our faith is weak or when it fails completely, we can still be like Peter and call out: "Lord! Save me!"

A

"God has imprisoned all… in their own disobedience only to show mercy to all."

Illustration

In 2007 Pope Benedict XVI published a book entitled *Jesus of Nazareth*. In the later years of his life, and after so many years of theological study and teaching, the Holy Father wanted to write a simple and straightforward story of Jesus. As he said in the foreword of the book, it "is solely an expression of my personal search 'for the face of the Lord'".

In the book Pope Benedict asked the question, "What did Jesus bring to the world?" He did not bring world peace. He did not bring prosperity. So what has he brought to us? The answer is very simple, Pope Benedict said. Jesus has brought God to the world. He has told us about God, whom he calls "the Father". He has shown us that in looking upon Jesus we are looking upon God in human form. As he said to the apostle Philip, "To have seen me is to have seen the Father."

The one, true God, the Lord who revealed himself to Abraham and Moses, who made Israel his special people, this God now comes among us in Jesus of Nazareth. In particular, he comes first to his own Jewish people. His mission is to the Jews. "I was sent only to the lost sheep of the House of Israel," he tells the Canaanite woman in today's Gospel. Yet in this encounter there is the beginning of Jesus' universal mission to the world.

Gospel Teaching

Jesus escapes from the pressures of confrontation in Galilee, and seeks peace and quiet in the border region of pagan territory. But even here demands are made upon him. An anxious mother, concerned for her tormented daughter, beseeches Jesus for help and healing. The conversation that follows is a verbal jousting match, a battle of wits between the tormented mother and the tired-out preacher. Jesus tries silence, then defence, then a put-down, to try to shake off the attention. But this is one determined woman, and she will not be put down or put off. It appears that she overcomes Jesus in the battle of wits; but Jesus is happy to admit defeat.

Yes, he is tired. Yes, his mission is to his own people. Yes, there are limits to what any person can reasonably be expected to do. But this woman needs help and she is pleading for it. "Woman, you have great faith," Jesus says to her. Indeed she has. God's mercy does not recognise boundaries. It has no limits. God's loving kindness is for everyone.

In telling this story, Matthew shows us how Jesus' life and ministry were centred on his own people in the first place. But it was a ministry intended for the salvation of the whole world. This "border" story shows us how the boundary between Jew and Gentile is soon to be broken. The mission of Jesus to "the lost sheep of the House of Israel" will soon become a mission to gather into one the scattered children of God throughout the world.

Application

At the end of Matthew's Gospel we find the disciples of Jesus gathered with the risen Lord on a mountain. There, Jesus gives the command to go out to the whole world and "make disciples of all the nations". This scene is reminiscent of Isaiah's vision, where the prophet sees foreigners coming to join the chosen people: "these I will bring to my holy mountain".

St Paul was given the express mandate of being the "apostle of the Gentiles". Although he is happy to take on this commission, his sorrow over losing his own Jewish people never leaves him. He hopes that, one day, his own people and his adopted people will share the same joy of being united in Christ. For no matter how disobedient we may be, God's mercy is greater still.

And it is the practice of mercy that reveals the face of God to the world. Loving kindness removes all barriers and heals all wounds. It includes justice, and it includes integrity, and it brings salvation to all people. As Matthew's Gospel tells us, Jesus did not come to destroy the Jewish faith, but to fulfil it. Faith in Jesus Christ now calls us to remove all barriers in our minds, and to show love and mercy to one and all.

A

"It was not flesh and blood that revealed this to you but my Father in heaven."

Illustration

Bob travelled to work every day on the train. He had his usual seat. For as long as he could remember, the man sitting opposite him had made the same daily journey. Over time, Bob had got to know a bit about his fellow commuter. He guessed from the way he dressed that he probably worked in an office in the city. He observed that he liked to read detective novels. In cold weather he wore what looked like an old college scarf. Bob could tell when the man was running late, because he brought a cereal bar for his breakfast. And he assumed he had a family, because he carried a picture of what Bob thought must be his wife and two children in his wallet. But although the two travellers had nodded to each other, they had never spoken.

Then one day the train ground to a halt. Bob listened to the dreaded announcement, something about a blockage on the line. They were in for a long delay. His neighbour sighed. Then he leaned over from his seat and reached out his hand towards Bob. "Hi," he said, "I'm Jim."

At that moment, their relationship changed. Bob had known a certain amount about Jim, but until then he could never have said that he knew him. Now, as they chatted, he began to get to know him. But if Jim hadn't taken the initiative, they would have remained strangers.

Gospel Teaching

In a way, the same sort of thing happened to Peter. He'd been with Jesus for some time. He knew a lot about him: where he came from, his family background. He'd travelled with him. He'd heard his teaching. He'd seen the things that Jesus had done, the way he treated those who were sick, those who were poor, those who were outcasts. But did he really know him? Who was this man?

Peter wasn't alone in wondering. People had all sorts of theories about Jesus, who he might be, what his mission was. They talked about it among themselves. But nobody could truly claim to know. When Jesus finally asked his disciples the question, a lot of different answers came gushing out. "But you," he said, "who do you say I am?"

Peter wasn't sure where the words came from. But suddenly he knew. Suddenly he realised who Jesus was, what his teaching was about. It was as though the sun had dawned, bringing light into the darkness. "You are the Christ, the Son of the living God."

What had happened? How did Peter know this? He'd known about as much as anyone could know about a person. He'd followed him, seen all that he did and hung upon his every word. But now he'd taken a decisive step further. He'd moved beyond simply knowing about Jesus and begun truly to know him. Jesus himself recognised what had happened. This wasn't a step that Peter, or anyone else, could take alone. It could only be taken with God's help. It was nothing less than a gift of God.

Application

There are many ways, many opportunities, to learn about God. We can read books, watch TV programmes or videos, listen to tapes. We can go and listen to skilful teachers and inspiring preachers. But if all that happens is that we learn facts and listen to opinions, then it may be the case that we know *about* God – but do we really *know* God?

"How rich are the depths of God – how deep his wisdom and knowledge – and how impossible to penetrate his motives or understand his methods!" Paul's exclamation of wonder and praise may make us wonder what is the point of trying to learn the ways of God. Paul, like Peter, came to know that this is not something that we can do on our own. Paul, a highly educated and extremely religious Pharisee, thought that he knew all there was to know about God. But it was only after God had taken the initiative on the road to Damascus that Paul truly came to know God. Peter thought he knew as much about Jesus as anyone could. But it was only when the Father revealed the truth to Peter that he truly began to know him.

Can we take that step further? Can we progress from knowing about God to knowing God? It's something we can only do with God's help. God has shown us the way in Jesus. Are we willing to journey with him, not as strangers but as friends?

A

"The way you think is not God's way."

Illustration

A teacher is talking to a class of children. "Look around you," she says. "See how many things you can see in the classroom that are coloured red." For a minute or two, the children look around intently, trying to find as many red objects as they can.

"OK," says the teacher, "now tell me what you have noticed." Straight away the answers come flooding out: books on the shelves; the red marker pen on the teacher's desk; the fire alarm bell; Jo's sweater. Each of the children is keen to find something new.

After a few minutes, the list seems to be exhausted. "Now", says the teacher, "I want you to close your eyes." The children do so, waiting for their memories to be tested. There is a pause. "Now", says the teacher, "keep your eyes closed. And tell me the things that are coloured *green*." This time there is silence. The children have been concentrating so much on things that are red that it's hard to think of anything different.

Gospel Teaching

Last Sunday, we heard how Peter finally recognised Jesus as "the Christ, the Son of the living God". At last the longed-for Messiah had come. The Jewish people had been waiting for centuries for the Lord's anointed to come and deliver them. The popular expectation was that he would be a great political leader, who would subdue the enemies of Israel and guide the nation to an era of peace and prosperity. Jesus' response to Peter's insight was to call him blessed, to call him the "rock", and to talk about the keys of the kingdom.

We can only imagine how Peter must have felt. The Messiah's kingdom was coming, and he, Peter, the fisherman, was to have an important role in it. What would this mean? His mind must have been filled with many things as he contemplated the future in the light of this revelation.

But the Jewish people, especially the religious leaders, failed to recognise Jesus as the Christ. He was not the Messiah they were looking for. Their expectations were filled with the image of the political leader, the royal figure of power and might. They thought they knew what the Messiah would be like; and they couldn't see him in this poor son of a carpenter from Nazareth.

In a sense Peter fell into the same trap. He could accept Jesus as the Christ. But once he had done so, his mind was filled with all the usual preconceptions of what the Messiah would be like, what he would do, how he would be the powerful leader of Israel. And so, when Jesus began to speak about the need for him to suffer and to die, it simply did not fit in with the way Peter was thinking. The popular image of the Messiah had filled his mind, and he found it impossible to think of him in a different way. Jesus had to begin to teach his disciples a new way of looking at things. It would take Peter a long time to realise the truth of his teaching.

Application
As we live in the world today, our minds are filled with many things. As we grow and develop in faith, some of our attitudes and perceptions can change. But it's still true that many of our views are swayed by the prevailing beliefs of the society in which we live. And so we tend to see happiness and fulfilment in terms of material success, wealth, and worldly status or influence. It's hard to accept that there is another way.

This is a truth that Paul recognises. He calls us to use our minds, our intellects, to live as "thinking beings". But he teaches us too not to be conformed to the world around us, not to be bound and restricted by the world's thinking. We are to allow the Gospel to free our minds to "discover the will of God and know what is good, what it is that God wants, what is the perfect thing to do".

Jesus had to show his disciples that the way of God is different from the way of the world. The Christ, the chosen one of God, would face suffering and death as he followed God's way. It may be hard at times for us to see that the way of the cross is the better way. But if we want to follow Christ, we have to be willing to walk that way.

A

"Love… cannot hurt your neighbour."

Illustration

There's a huge growth industry in mediation services. Perhaps we see it most often in the field of marriage, when couples facing difficulties in their relationship go to a third party – a counsellor or person trained in conciliation skills – in order to get help in dealing with the underlying issues that are causing problems in their marriage.

But couples are not the only people who avail themselves of such services: sometimes it is parents and children who need help, or professional assistance is needed to resolve disputes between employers and employees or their unions; sometimes an outside agency is brought in to settle disagreements between neighbours. We all understand the need for third-party intervention and assistance in our lives – for the help of someone who is objective, dispassionate and skilled in dealing with conflict management.

Gospel Teaching

Today's Gospel comes from chapter 18 in Matthew's Gospel, sometimes called the "Community Rule Book". It gives instructions on how people within the family of the Church should relate to one another. In our passage today we hear Jesus' instructions on how to deal with conflict within the community.

The basic principle is: do everything you possibly can to reach a reconciliation, to keep the lines of communication open. Today, we would call that arbitration or mediation. First try to deal with the issue informally, just between the two of you. Then – presumably because the issue is serious enough – get some witnesses. This brings the issue into the public arena, but it is also a way of ensuring clarity. In other words, check out your facts and your thinking, to ensure that this isn't just a case of both sides being unreasonable, or blinded by anger or resentment. It's about caring enough to point out a painful truth to your neighbour, your "brother". It is not by chance that this passage follows on from the teaching about the shepherd who goes out in search of the lost sheep. Finally, you bring the matter to the whole Church – to the wider community. If people persist in wrongdoing in the face of a clear rejection of their action by the whole community, then they are in fact separating themselves from the

Church, cutting themselves off. And this needs to be acknowledged. Not to punish – but to bring the perpetrators back to the path of right.

Such an attitude might seem a little harsh, but the purpose is reconciliation, not vengeance. The prophet Ezekiel has the same mentality when he stresses the importance of speaking the truth – "Wicked wretch, you are to die." Better to speak the truth even though it is painful, than to keep the peace and thereby allow someone to die in their sin.

We often hear phrases such as "tough love" and "speak the truth in love". Though these may have become somewhat clichéd, they do reflect an important truth: that being a Christian is not the same as being nice. Peace is not the highest value that there is. Injustice and wrongdoing have to be actively named and opposed, not simply ignored or wished away. That is why justice and peace are always linked together – because without justice there can be no real peace, only appeasement and compromise, which are simply ways of allowing evil to triumph.

Application

Christians have a duty to be people of love. "Love is the one thing that cannot hurt your neighbour; that is why it is the answer to every one of the commandments," as Paul tells us. That sounds simple and clear-cut, but it isn't. Love cuts both ways. It is relatively easy to love when that means being generous, caring and compassionate. But the deeper love is one that cares enough to confront, challenge and, if need be, oppose.

Genuine love of neighbour refuses to collude with wrongdoing through silence or inaction. Such love requires real courage, because it is liable to be misunderstood and can easily lead to hostility and rejection. But as a Church we are called to bind and to loose: to bind the forces of evil that enslave people, to loosen the bonds of oppression that prevent people from living the fullness of life of God's kingdom. Whether that means opposing individuals or governments, a society's values or sinful economic structures, the challenge of the Gospel means Christians need to love enough to speak uncomfortable truths – in humility, but with courage. And when we do that, we know that Christ promises to be there with us.

"Peter went up to Jesus and said: 'Lord, how often must I forgive?'"

Illustration

In his book *The Railway Man*, Eric Lomax tells the true account of his imprisonment during the Second World War. He was one of thousands of soldiers forced to work on the infamous Burma–Siam railway. Labouring virtually as slaves, the half-starved men suffered in the burning heat, while living under conditions of exhaustion and malnutrition. Even worse than this, some, like Lomax, were tortured: he was choked with water, endlessly beaten and mercilessly interrogated. He came close to death on many occasions.

When the war ended, Eric Lomax returned to England, but his life was never the same. Tormenting pictures that came as nightmares, together with the physical and mental scars his experience left behind, meant his quality of life was severely diminished. However, the story doesn't stop here. A strange sequence of events eventually led Lomax to return to Japan some fifty years later to meet face to face with one of his tormentors, someone whose life had equally been devastated by the war. The description of their encounter is heart-rending in its honesty. It reaches a climax when the two men finally decide to put the past to rest. Lomax tells his former interrogator that while the memory of what happened in that prison back in 1943 would always remain with him, he can be sure of his total forgiveness. Given all that had happened, what an incredible statement: he offered total forgiveness, an act pardoning more wrongs than it was possible to remember.

The book finishes in Thailand, with the author and his wife gazing over a war cemetery: "For a moment," he writes, "we both knew we should be there. Then I said: 'Sometime the hating has to stop.'"

Gospel Teaching

When Peter asked Jesus how often he must forgive the person who wronged him, he probably thought he was being generous in suggesting seven times as a possible answer. Perhaps he even expected praise; at last Jesus would recognise that Peter was on the right track. He had finally grasped that God's ways are more abundant than human ways, that God wants us to go that bit further, forgiving more than just once or twice. If we could go back and see Peter's expression as he heard Jesus' reply, it would probably have been a combination of shock and horror. Not forgiveness seven times, but seventy-seven – in other words, as often as required: in effect, always.

To explore the significance of forgiveness more fully, Jesus added the story we know as the parable of the unforgiving servant. A master, who mercifully cancels a great debt to his servant, later learns that the same servant has been cruelly unforgiving in cancelling a much smaller debt owed to him. The master's anger is so great that he recalls his servant, withdraws his generosity and imprisons him until the debt is paid.

In telling the parable, Jesus didn't just want to illustrate his answer to Peter's question. He wanted to explain not merely *how often* we must forgive, but also *why* we should forgive a brother or sister when they wrong us. Our reason for showing mercy time and time again is because that is how God forgives us. If we can be forgiven much, and we certainly can through God's love and compassion, then, in gratitude and imitation of God's way, we too should forgive much in return. Ecclesiasticus puts it another way: "If someone nurses anger against another, can they demand compassion from the Lord?" St Paul helps deepen this understanding: because we belong to the Lord and live under Christ's reign, his forgiveness and reconciliation will have an impact in our lives, and, through us, on the lives of other people.

Application

Eric Lomax concluded his book with the words: "Sometime the hating has to stop." Hate is a strong word, but to a greater or lesser degree we all know it in our hearts. We face conflict with those around us: family, friends and even strangers. We carry our prejudices and judgements, we cling to the hurts and offences caused by others.

Whatever its form, however trivial, however serious, there is a time for hating to stop in every life, in all our relationships, and throughout our world. This may not always be easy; it might not come quickly, but we are called to recapture the fact that we live for the Lord, not merely for ourselves. Hating will only stop when forgiveness begins. How often must we forgive? Always. Why? Because God has forgiven us in Christ.

A

"You go to my vineyard too and I will give you a fair wage."

Illustration

A March 2007 report on workers who cleaned streets and collected rubbish in a city in northern England found that those directly employed by the city council received a decent wage, sick pay, and had job security. Others, who were employed on a day-to-day basis, earned between £2 and £2.50 an hour less than their directly employed counterparts – and for the same work.

Some of these people were asked to turn up at between five and six in the morning to find out whether they would have work for the day. In another city in the same region, casual labourers were brought in from Poland by distribution centres for big retailers, to work alongside permanent staff. Recruited through agencies, they were typically doing the same work for £2 an hour less.

The discrepancies in pay led to tensions between local workers and the new arrivals. All were desperate for an income and there was little bargaining power over wages. It is no wonder, then, that feelings often ran high between employers and their workers and between the employees themselves.

Gospel Teaching

In first-century Palestine, too, casual labour was at the mercy of rich employers and landowners. Plenty of them were unscrupulous, paying as little as possible for a day's work. However, the landowner in today's parable is a decent man. He goes out again and again searching for those who are unemployed, understanding their hardships, for unemployment is not only an economic problem but also a spiritual problem that demoralises people.

The labourers who have done "a heavy day's work in all the heat" complain because others have received the same wages for working only one hour. It seems to be so unfair, particularly when the last in are paid first. Yet one denarius is a just wage for a day's work and that is what they had agreed upon. The employer has been moved with compassion for the unemployed people he found in the marketplace. Out of genuine concern for them and their families he pays them a wage that is not proportionate to the work done but proportionate to their needs.

But the employer's actions do not go down well with everyone. The parable focuses on two attitudes – jealousy and generosity. Jealousy is shown by the first workers in the vineyard. However understandable their sense of grievance, their feelings of injustice do not take into account the needs of the workers who came later in the day to feed themselves and their families. Their envy of the good fortune of others is disappointing, and contrasts with the generosity of the landowner. His actions are intended to demonstrate God's compassion and munificence towards all.

In the kingdom of God there are surprises. Those who worked the whole day got a full day's wage, but those who worked only for one hour also received a full day's wage. This is the righteousness of the kingdom.

Application
Jesus tells the story about the vineyard labourers in order to teach us something about God's kingdom. It also teaches us something about ourselves and the society we live in. Can we recognise ourselves in this parable, where the attitudes of jealousy and generosity are contrasted? Would we be complaining like the labourers employed in the morning, or deeply grateful like the labourers employed towards the end of the day? Would we appreciate a generous employer, even if others seem to be reaping more benefit?

In the society in which we live, those who have a good start in life, those who are influential and well educated, get more. Those who are strong often exploit those who are weak. This is the righteousness of the world. In the perspective of the kingdom, those who are powerful and influential will not get more. God's arithmetic is different. We are being told that the kingdom of heaven is about God's abundance and God's indiscriminate generosity.

Experiencing God's benevolence transforms who we are and the way we see our lives. We can recognise the blessings given to us. We can take joy in our homes, our daily bread, our schools, our jobs, the people who care for us, and even the blessings in the challenges we face. Too often we complain: "I should be earning more than him"; "Why are other people more gifted than me?"; "Why are others healthy, while I have a chronic illness?" In fact, everything is a gift from God. We are called to be thankful for what we have, and not complain about what we have not been given.

"Which of the two did the Father's will?"

Illustration

How often are we misled by talk or appearances? We have many proverbs that caution us against such susceptibility. "The proof of the pudding is in the eating." "Handsome is as handsome does." Nevertheless, we are still easily hoodwinked by glossy presentation or weasel words.

Sometimes the position of a person impresses us. Perhaps it is the need in us to be reassured, that uncertainty which naively asks the professionals for honest advice when their main concern may be selling us something. There will always be someone only too willing to take advantage of our vulnerability, in any field. The difficulty today is that the skills of advertising have leapt from the marketplace to nearly every aspect of life. We are all asked to sell ourselves in some way. By which is usually meant that we are required to spend our energies more on the appearance of what we are offering than on its real content.

Too often there is a gap between the glossy presentation and the reality within. As we spend so much time on the appearance of what we are offering, we can lose sight of the actual content. We have a lovely brochure saying what sort of school, church, community we are. We even convince ourselves of the truth of what we say. But the detached observer sees only too easily that the emperor is not wearing any clothes.

Gospel Teaching

It is this sort of contradiction between word and action that Jesus identifies in the leaders of the people. After arriving in Jerusalem he enters into altercation with them about the genuine fulfilment of the Law and the Prophets. There is always a temptation for leaders to believe too much in their own authority. They tend to think that because they have such an important position in society, then what they say must be true.

Jesus challenges such an assumption. There must always be a coherence between what we preach to others and what we do ourselves. John the Baptist had come, a pattern of righteousness, but the people who listened to him and accepted his message, changing their lives accordingly, had been the public sinners in society. The leaders and supposedly righteous had refused to believe him, just as now they refused to believe Jesus and his message.

St Paul in his letter to the Philippians is aware of the same temptation. He tells his listeners that they must not be drawn into competition or conceit, for such attitudes breed dissent and disunity. Rather we are called to put other people's interests first. Our pattern is that of Christ Jesus, who cast off his equality with God and chose rather to assume the condition of a slave.

This is a total reversal of the power game, but it is because of his self-emptying that Jesus is raised on high and given a name above all other names to the glory of God the Father.

Application

How do we prevent ourselves being drawn into a world of false appearances? How do we ensure that we always practise what we preach? It is easy to start out with the best of intentions, but, as we have noted, the nature of our world is so shot through with the idea of selling ourselves that it can be difficult to pursue an alternative path.

It is as though Jesus recognises this difficulty by being so uncompromising in his own words and practice. His way of ensuring an integrity of word and deed is to empty himself of any claim to power or position. Elsewhere he will address the question of fancy titles. The only title he uses for himself is that of "Son of Man", and the only way of life he follows is that of a wandering preacher, with nowhere to lay his head. If we examine our own positions in life (and are honest in that examination) we will acknowledge just how much we are tempted to say one thing and do another, to use our power or that of others to achieve our ends.

When we empty ourselves of such trappings of power, we have no means of pretence any more. And, perhaps ironically, we now have a greater freedom to adhere to the truth, for we are no longer bound by that complex world of expectations that comes from the world of propaganda. We are free to do what we say we will do.

"The kingdom of God will be... given to a people who will produce its fruit."

Illustration

Speakers' Corner in London is a place where anyone can exercise the right to freedom of speech, no matter how outrageous their beliefs. Each Sunday, people gather to listen to the many speakers who loudly express their views about everything from current wars and conflicts to race relations and matters of sexual equality.

The majority speak about religion. There are usually representatives from Christianity, Islam, Judaism, atheism and more. Most speakers mount a soapbox and harangue passers-by with their particular message. It's as if they think that if only they can shout loud enough, they will convince people of the truth of their brand of religion.

But one man just stands there, saying nothing, his simple message written on a placard, paraphrasing the prophet Amos: "God says this: 'Stuff religion. Do justice.'" Amid all the competing noisy claims about God at Speakers' Corner, this man's silent witness speaks eloquently.

Gospel Teaching

His message is borne out by today's readings. God often spoke of the chosen people as a vineyard, which God had planted and cares for. The psalm tells of how God prepared a land for this vine, this people Israel, and cared for them so that they would flourish. But the prophet Isaiah laments that this vineyard, which the Lord loves so much, has not produced the goods. The privilege of being the chosen people of God brings the responsibility of living as God requires, of producing the fruit the Lord expects from his people: the choice wine of justice and integrity. Instead, the people have produced the sour wine of bloodshed and distress, injustice and oppression.

And so the psalm tells how the Lord seems to have abandoned them, though in fact it is they who have turned away from God. The vineyard has ceased to be a vineyard; it no longer yields good wine – the people have stopped acting as God's chosen people. And so in the psalm the people promise to return to the Lord, they ask God to save them and promise never to leave him again.

Jesus uses this image to speak of himself and his mission. He has come to call the people back to their true selves, to enable them to produce this fruit of justice which God expects. He speaks a damning parable to the religious leaders, to those entrusted with ensuring that the life of the people is according to God's expectations. He tells them that they have abused their responsibility, that they persistently reject the word of God, thinking only of their own profit and interests, not those of God. They have focused on religion at the expense of justice; they have stressed the importance of external piety and religious rules while stifling the message of the prophets, that justice and integrity constitute the true worship that God wants. They are encouraging people to practise "religion" rather than to practise "justice". The man at Speakers' Corner is echoing the message of Jesus to us all. Religion without justice and integrity is a vineyard without wine, a waste of time and space.

Application
When people ask us what it means to be Catholic, perhaps the natural thing is to speak in terms of religious faith and practice: prayer, Mass, the sacraments. But underpinning this has to be something more. Beneath these religious expressions must be a desire for justice, which simply means living as God expects, doing as God wants. It means welcoming God's unsettling message, not seeking to silence God's messengers. It means looking not just at the quality of our religious practices, but at how these are reflected in our lifestyles. It means allowing the word of God – in scripture, in homilies, in the witness of other Christians – to confront our lives, to influence our choices, to challenge our attitudes and prejudices, to expose our selfishness, to question our commitments and relationships. If we desire to belong to God's kingdom, our lives should be characterised by justice and integrity.

Is a passion for justice a hallmark of our lives, as individuals and as communities? Do we seek the integrity that ensures that our Sunday beliefs are translated into weekday reality? If we follow Paul's advice, and focus on those things that are true, noble, pure and good, and especially if we seek to do those things, as he did, then justice and integrity will be the fruits of our lives, and we too will know the God of peace. Because when we do justice, then we have found true religion.

"The wedding hall was filled with guests."

Illustration

Scientists in London have reconstructed the face of an Egyptian priestess who died three thousand years ago. Using state-of-the-art scanning and imaging techniques on the mummified remains of the woman, her weight, size, height and even appearance can be estimated – an astonishing feat, considering the age of the mummy. Her name, spelled out in hieroglyphics on her tomb in Luxor, was Tjentmuntengebtin.

This Egyptian woman from long ago achieved, after a fashion, what she hoped for – immortality. Buried with food to nourish her on her journey to the afterlife, and with plentiful treasure so that she might lack nothing as she journeyed, she was laid to rest for millennia.

We all live with the hope of immortality. We may not have the material resources available to this Egyptian priestess – indeed our beliefs would make such elaborate material preparations irrelevant – but we do hope to live for ever with the Lord. How do we attain this immortality? How do we respond to God's invitation to us?

Gospel Teaching

Isaiah's vision of God's kingdom is of abundance, joy and peace, gifts of the Lord. The prophet describes the reign of God using familiar, tangible images, and we can easily grasp what he describes. It is an immortality that immediately appeals. But Isaiah does not simply describe: he teaches. On the day when we attain the kingdom, we will recognise the Lord's goodness and truly rejoice. For Isaiah, the good things that make up the kingdom are inseparable from the presence of the Lord: "for the hand of the Lord rests on this mountain".

Paul takes a similar approach. For him, the presence of God is everything – strength, life and salvation. And, like Isaiah, his vision of God's kingdom, a gift of the generous God, leads him to give glory to God. Is the vision of Isaiah and Paul the same as that of Jesus?

Today's Gospel is admonitory. Jesus describes our invitation to God's kingdom, while warning of the dangers of taking it for granted. The kingdom is like a wedding feast, an image of the kingdom used frequently by Jesus. But here the emphasis is not on abundance or on celebration. It is on accepting the invitation so generously extended by God. And here is the warning: immortality, or at least a blissful immortality, is by no means guaranteed. "Many are called," he says, "but few are chosen."

Let's look more closely at this parable. Firstly, it is told to the chief priests and elders, those who perhaps would be most complacent about their own inclusion in God's kingdom. Complacency, to Jesus, is a true enemy of the soul. The first response of those who are invited is to ignore the invitation. The repeated invitation is unambiguous: those invited are compelled to respond this time, and their response is to seize, maltreat and finally kill the servants of the king. The message of Jesus is clear: to refuse the invitation of God can put us in the position of enemies of the kingdom.

In the final part of the parable, we see that the invitation of the king is then extended more widely than before, because the original guests refused to attend. But those who do attend are careful to make preparations. Again, complacency is intolerable. The person who turns up at the feast underdressed, unprepared, is cast out into the darkness. Many are called, some respond, and, of those who do respond, not all take seriously the nature of the feast.

Application

We cannot afford to take lightly our destiny, in this world or the next. To do so is to neglect the whole purpose of our life. Complacency is truly the enemy of our soul, because we are treating lightly what should be treated most seriously of all: our eternal happiness. If there is a hell for us or for anyone else, it is a hell of isolation that we have constructed for ourselves and for each other. And God's constant invitation is an ever-present lifeline to a world of peace and joy.

There are three possibilities for us in this parable. Are we the invited guests who choose not to attend? Are we those who do not prepare for the feast? Are we those who accept eagerly, prepare, and enjoy the feast? With these possibilities clearly before us, and with God's help, how could we choose ill? Three thousand years ago, the Egyptians were taking seriously the business of the afterlife with painstaking care. We can do no less for ourselves, in Christ.

A

"Give back to Caesar what belongs to Caesar – and to God what belongs to God."

Illustration

On 6th July 1535, Thomas More, one of the most illustrious Englishmen of his day, stood at the foot of the scaffold on Tower Hill in London. He had been condemned to death for refusing to take the Oath of Supremacy, which would have been to acknowledge King Henry VIII as "only supreme head of the Church of England". More was a scholar, the author of many learned books; a devoted public servant, chosen by Henry himself to be his Chancellor; a much-loved family man, deeply attached to wife and children, and anxious that his daughters should be educated far beyond the level usually available to women in those days: he was, as C.S. Lewis wrote of him, "a man before whom the best of us must stand uncovered".

He had told the judges who condemned him that he prayed that he and they would "all meet merrily in heaven"; and even as he was mounting the rickety ladder to the scaffold, he retained his customary wit. "I pray, Lord Lieutenant," he jested, "see me safe up, and for my coming down let me shift for myself." Then, after a few words of encouragement to the assembled crowd, he declared that he was about to die as "the king's good servant but God's first".

Gospel Teaching

"The king's good servant but God's first": those words might serve as a commentary on what our Lord says in today's Gospel. Let's recall the situation. Jesus has come up to Jerusalem for the last time; he has already been involved in controversy with the religious leaders. Finally the Pharisees decide to try to entrap him. They begin with honeyed words, intended no doubt to put him off his guard. In fact the Pharisees don't come themselves but send some intermediaries, so it's these intermediaries who use the honeyed words: "Master, we know that you are an honest man… and that you are not afraid of anyone."

But after the compliments comes the barbed question, aimed to put Jesus in a no-win situation. "Tell us," they enquire, "is it permissible to pay taxes to Caesar or not?" The tax involved, a kind of poll tax, was detested by the Jews on two counts: first because it was a painful reminder that they were a subject people; and second because the coinage in which it was paid bore the head of the Roman emperor and an inscription that proclaimed him to be divine. And so if Jesus were to say that the tax should be paid, he would at once lose all credibility with the people; on the other hand, if he were to say it should not, he could then be accused of fomenting disobedience, even rebellion, against Rome, and that could have – literally – fatal consequences.

You can imagine the tension in the crowd as Jesus calmly holds up one of the well-known silver coins used for paying the tax and asks, "Whose head is this? Whose name?" Well, everyone knows the answer to those questions: the head and the name are of course "Caesar's" (the Roman emperor's). "Very well," says Jesus, "give back to Caesar what belongs to Caesar – and to God what belongs to God." By having such coinage in their possession, they were at least implicitly acknowledging Caesar's right to tax them.

Application

However, Jesus' answer is more than an ingenious way of slipping out of a trap. By adding that what belongs to God ought to go back to God, he's making a further point: that our overriding commitment has to be to God. Of course we must accept lawful civil authority; indeed as Christians we are called to be the best of citizens. Being good, responsible citizens, working for the common good of the community, these are our Christian duty – in that sense, already part of our giving to God what belongs to God. At the same time we do not look to the State as our moral guide: the law may countenance abortion, for example, or the sale of arms to oppressive regimes; but the fact that such activities are legal does not make them morally right. And if ever there were a genuine clash between our duties to the State and our duties to God, there is no doubt where our Christian duty lies. It is God's law, not the State's, that has the last word.

Today, let us remember in our prayers all who face this stark choice: that they may courageously follow conscience, no matter what price they have to pay.

"On these two commandments hang the whole Law, and the Prophets also."

30th Sunday in Ordinary Time

Illustration

In 1976 Muhammad Yunus was a young economics professor at Chittagong University in Bangladesh. Realising that the people in the nearby village of Jobra were struggling to recover from poverty in the aftermath of the terrible 1974 famine, Yunus made a group of forty-two women a small loan of $27.

Up until then, their only course of action had been to borrow money from loan sharks so they could buy bamboo to make furniture, and hope to claw their way out of destitution. Of course only a lucky few made it that way.

Yunus' loan was the first transaction of what would become the Grameen Bank, or "Bank of the Villages". Today, the bank still specialises in microcredit – providing affordable loans of very modest sums to some of the world's poorest people – and it is estimated that over half of Grameen's fifty million Bangladeshi borrowers have risen out of acute poverty thanks to their loans. In 2006 Yunus and the bank were jointly awarded the Nobel Peace Prize, "for their efforts to create economic and social development from below".

Gospel Teaching

Today's reading from the book of Exodus is part of a long speech the Lord delivers to Moses to pass on to the Israelites. There were great disparities in wealth and power in Israelite society, and incomers, widows and orphans were among the most economically vulnerable, which is why God commands that they should be treated with fairness and respect.

Had we started reading the chapter from the first verse, we would have heard numerous detailed laws with specific examples concerning animal theft, compensation and the violation of women. When we come to this section, however, we are not so much looking at the letter of the law as the spirit of the law. It is as though we had "zoomed out" from the minute detail, of who does what to whom and how they are to be punished, to a more general moral guideline. If we, like many people, consider the first five books of the Old Testament largely irrelevant to modern life, we can look again. We will find we often come across real pearls of wisdom like these – often every bit as relevant as they ever were.

When we look at the Gospel reading, we find that Jesus has "zoomed out" again to take an even greater overview. Indeed, every law, every guideline, every commandment has become distilled into these two great commandments, which sum up the new covenant – the Good News that Jesus came to earth to proclaim. While the letter of the law might change depending on the age and cultural context in which we live, the spirit of the law does not. We can be sure that these two great commandments have never changed, and will never change.

Application
It is clear that there are commandments within commandments: that if we follow the spirit of the two great commandments, the smaller ones will take care of themselves. For who, with love in their heart, could mistreat an orphan or a woman who had lost her husband?

So, you might ask, if we have these overarching commandments, what's the point of the detail? Well, as the saying goes: "When you are up to your neck in alligators, it is difficult to remind yourself your initial objective was to drain the swamp!"

Day-to-day reality means it's easy to lose the bigger picture, and at times we need specific guidance to help us deal with the interferences and negotiate the obstacles that life puts in our way. The details can function as stepping stones so that we can haul ourselves up onto them and gradually work our way back out of the swamp to see the bigger picture again. Muhammad Yunus was able to help the women of Jobra most effectively by taking the smallest of steps, enabling them to work up to bigger things. Indeed, the Grameen Bank now has over two thousand branches in Bangladesh and continues to expand.

We could perhaps distil Jesus' two great commandments even further into the single word "love". As The Beatles sang, it's all you need. But the problem is that it becomes something so rarefied, such a huge concept, that it's overwhelming, impossible to apply to everyday life. If, on the other hand, we start with small steps, by treating each other with basic fairness and respect, as the Israelites were commanded, we will get glimpses of the love that Jesus tells us about.

"You must therefore do what they tell you... but do not be guided by what they do."

Illustration

At first hearing, today's Gospel seems like a perfect description of many religious leaders; perhaps especially the Catholic clergy. Many of them wear special clothes; they have prominent places in church when we celebrate the Eucharist. They teach the strict rules of the Church, like those on divorce and remarriage, and contraception. In our Lord's words, "They tie up heavy burdens and lay them on men's shoulders; but will they lift a finger to move them? Not they!" Traditionally, priests have even been called "Father". The Pope is often referred to as "the Holy Father", which seems to be directly against the teaching of the Lord as we hear it in today's Gospel. This is certainly the way the clergy are seen by many people, both inside and outside the Church.

There are, however, at least two major flaws in this approach. The first is the historical point that the majority of scribes and Pharisees were not members of the clergy at the time of Jesus. Certainly some of them were Temple clergy, but the majority of them were what we would today call "laity".

The second point has to do with language. We can mean something in an absolute sense, or in a relative sense. Here Jesus is warning against using language like "father", "teacher" and "master" in an absolute sense, about a creature. These terms should only be used in an absolute sense about God. In many of his parables, Jesus himself quite happily makes his characters use the words "father" and "master" in a relative sense. The fourth commandment tells us to "honour your father and mother". Here the terms are clearly being used in a very natural and relative way.

Gospel Teaching

The whole of Jesus' teaching is about getting things the right way round. "Set your hearts on God's kingdom first... and all these other things will be given you." What does this mean? Perhaps it means that if we see that everything comes from God and returns to God, then the rest will fall into place. If we try to usurp the place of God, or start to think that God's kingdom and teaching belong to us, then we have got things the wrong way round.

If we think we own God's justice and teaching, we set ourselves up as experts in the life of faith. Because all fallen humans are fallible, such claims to expertise start to look ugly and ridiculous. This is what hypocrisy is. All of us, whatever our place in the Church, have sinned and fallen short of the glory of God. This is why we all begin the Mass by asking for God's and each other's forgiveness.

This does not mean we give up on the quest for holiness. Whatever our own faults or the faults of our pastors, we still have the objective justice of the kingdom, and the core teaching of Christ through the Church. These never change. That is why our Lord advises people to do what the scribes say, but not to follow their example if it is a bad one.

This brings us back to the Lord's words about words. Only God is absolutely our Father. Only Christ, true man and true God, is absolutely our Master and our Teacher. St Paul puts it beautifully when he writes, "For this reason I bow my knees before the Father, from whom every family in heaven and on earth takes its name." Everything comes from and returns to God, and God the Father sent his only Son into the world to be the way, the truth and the life.

Application
Living the life of faith within the Church brings us up against both the hard realities of our human weakness, and the glories of our human lives transformed by grace. On the one hand, we may be tempted to give up altogether. On the other, we might be tempted into being like one of the hard-hearted Pharisees, deluded about our own goodness.

Jesus knows how we are tempted, and gave us the sacraments to help us with temptations. The sacrament of penance helps us face up to our faults without despairing. The sacrament of the Eucharist nourishes us with grace. It joins us more completely to the passion, death and resurrection of Christ. This opens our hearts more to a life formed by love and the desire to forgive: to forgive others and sometimes ourselves, just as Christ forgives us.

"We believe that Jesus died and rose again."

Illustration

One Sunday morning in the west of Ireland a parish priest was saying his farewells to the congregation assembled at Mass. In his opening remarks he made the following statement: "There are some people who think that the parish priest walks on water. There are others who think that he hasn't enough sense to come in out of the rain. But most people don't mind what he is like as long as he doesn't keep them too long on a Sunday morning."

A good and a popular priest, with a lightness of touch and a sense of humour, he was a wise man and would be much missed. His comical remarks, including self-mockery, put the people at their ease and set the tone for an affectionate farewell. In those opening lines there can be discerned the qualities of wisdom.

The one who "walks on water", a clear reference to Jesus, reminds us of the mystical quality of wisdom. If wisdom works wonders, it does so through the power of prayer, in the secret of silence and in the far reaches of reflection. Having "enough sense to come in out of the rain" is a pointed emphasis on the need for practical know-how in the business of daily living: being sensitive to circumstance and responsive to prevailing conditions. Not keeping people "too long on a Sunday morning" is an example of the need for human awareness and consideration. It is no use being wise, if nobody else ever feels the benefit of your wisdom.

Here then are three qualities of wisdom, comically laid out for us in that parish priest's remarks, and repeated for us today in the readings of the liturgy.

Gospel Teaching

Wisdom is described, in our first reading today, as a bright and precious gift that wants to share herself with all humankind. Wisdom makes life bright and enriches all who possess her. She is to be found in the very young as well as in the very old. But the old, especially, through long experience of life, should possess wisdom in great measure. "There is no fool like an old fool."

In the tradition of the Church, and especially in the monasteries and convents of Christianity, the practice of meditation, made together as a community, has been a constant feature of daily life. In the stillness and silence of those gathered communities, the Holy Spirit of God is present and moving in the souls of those at prayer. Down ordinary streets and in quiet houses the practice of prayer goes on, an unseen communing with the Spirit of God. Down one such street one day, a priest, out visiting, came upon an old man, living alone, sitting by his fireside. "I don't go to Mass, Father," the old man said. "But I never forget my prayers." Then he reached down beside his chair and brought out an old, well-thumbed prayer book. There, in that quiet, unfrequented house, wisdom had found a home.

The thoughtful and reflective quality of wisdom will often express itself in down-to-earth, no-nonsense teaching. When Paul writes to the Thessalonians, he wants them to avoid idle speculation about the next world and the afterlife. He speaks plainly, and is not afraid to tell them that there are things we do not know. He says that Jesus died and rose again, and by this we know that when we die, we will go into eternal life with God. As for speculation about the end of the world, we do not know when that will be, so we are not to waste our time with foolish notions.

Application
The mystery of our religion is very deep. What we know is wonderful. What God has revealed to us is not simply information about the next world, but an inspiration for living our lives in this world. It is a call to live as wise people and not as fools. Live in the Lord's presence now, and then we shall live with him for ever.

"With such thoughts as these you should comfort one another." These words of Paul are often spoken at Requiem Masses and funerals. They tell a listening world about the life to come. They bring comfort to the sorrowful and bright hope to everyone. So may the Lord bless us with wisdom: the reflective kind that walks on water; the practical kind that knows when to come in out of the rain; and the considerate kind that knows how to care for people… and not keep them too long.

32nd Sunday in Ordinary Time

"Well done, good and faithful servant."

Illustration

Michael Ramsey, Archbishop of Canterbury from 1961 to 1974, was a round and cuddly man, in the Pope John XXIII mould, warm and welcoming, a kindly, grandfatherly figure. He was easily recognised, too, by his amazing eyebrows that seemed to have a life of their own, and careered off in various directions. On one occasion this lovely man was accused by an interviewer of being wise.

"Am I?" he asked. "I don't think so really. I think it is just the impression given by the fecundity of my eyebrows." "Well, Your Grace," the interviewer persisted, "how would you define wisdom?" "Wisdom?" Ramsey thought for a while. "Oh, I should say wisdom is the ability to cope."

On first hearing, this definition sounds rather disappointing, and nothing like the lofty quality usually associated with this special word. We tend to think of a wise person being deep in meditation, abstracted from the world, sitting on a high mountain top, with far-seeing eyes. But on closer inspection we begin to see the wisdom of the definition.

The ability to cope with life involves the qualities of reflection and silence, and the practical ability to deal with people and events in the everyday world. Silence inspires our actions, and involvement feeds our reflection.

Gospel Teaching

The book of Proverbs deals entirely with the issues of wisdom and foolishness. It gives pride of place to the quality of "the fear of the Lord". This means a reverential respect for God and for all that God has made. It is the quality of our approach and our attitude to every living thing.

Today's excerpt from Proverbs draws a picture of wisdom as a perfect wife. This wise woman is the heart of her household. She cares for all and oversees all. Her ways are kindness and tenderness. She attends to every human need and practical requirement. She has a care for those outside her household, too, helping those who are poor. She is trustworthy, diligent and generous to all. In spiritual attitude and in practical concerns, this woman is the embodiment of wisdom.

In our reading from his first letter to the Thessalonians, St Paul challenges us to realise the wisdom that we have been given. Because of Christ, we are sons and daughters of the day, not of the night. We live in the light and not in the darkness. We may not know when the end of the world is to be, but we do know that the light has come, in Jesus Christ.

In today's Gospel, often known as the parable of the talents, Jesus teaches us how to be wise. If we understand our life as gift, we will live generous lives. If we do not appreciate life as a gift of God, there is every danger that we might become miserly and negative. The sheer negativity of the wicked servant is there for all to see, and he is rightly called a "good-for-nothing".

Application
Life, of course, begins as a mystery, something greater than we can fathom. It always remains a mystery, something greater than we can grasp. We often describe life as a journey, and this is a good image, for every day we travel into new territory, gain new experiences and grow older. But tomorrow is always "beyond our ken", and the future remains unknown. And yet, despite what we do not know, there is so much that we do know, because of Jesus Christ.

This is the Gospel message today. Jesus Christ is our wisdom. His teaching, his life story, his death and resurrection, have become for us the light of life. Jesus is the wisdom of God, and the Son of God, and the Son of Man. In him we understand ourselves, and the meaning of our life. We place our hope in the ultimate goodness of life, which is in itself a gift of God. We receive our life as gift, and we are faithful in little things, everyday things, because they matter. Christ not only taught us the truth of this, but showed us in the way he lived his earthly life.

Human beings are the summit of God's creation, and every person matters. So, St Paul says, I will happily spend myself and be spent for others. Such an attitude is foolishness in the eyes of many people, but it is true wisdom. "So we should not go on sleeping, as everybody else does, but stay wide awake and sober."

A

"Come, you whom my Father has blessed."

Illustration

At Monasterboice in County Louth, Ireland, an ancient Celtic cross depicts the story of the Last Judgement in graphic terms. Christ is weighing souls in a pair of scales. Those who are found worthy are seated on the right side of Christ with faces towards him, whilst those who are found unworthy are being prodded away by little devils with pitchforks, their faces aghast and facing away from Christ. The stone, which has survived the weather of more than ten centuries, was an early means of teaching the Gospel to a people who were illiterate. Only the monks and priests had access to handwritten texts of the Gospel. If the cross could speak of the people who had gathered there, name those who had prayed there, witness to the history written in the fields and villages, the history of Christian people in that place would be told.

The story told would be of the deeds and acts of love that were done without thinking, often unrecognised and unacknowledged. The heroes of the story would be the unknown of the history books: a woman who nursed a dying neighbour; a man who gave a stranger food and drink one cold November evening; perhaps a woman who hid a priest on the run for being a Catholic in penal times. These moments in history were sudden and quickly passed; but they are moments when the Gospel was lived out.

Gospel Teaching

The Gospel highlights the paradox of the Christian life. Christ is met in the most unusual and unknown circumstances of life, often in the most unlikely and unexpected people. In a world in which style and presentation are very important in advertising, and images of rich and beautiful people abound, the Gospel reminds us of the *anawim*, "the poor", those who can rely only on God because they have nothing and are considered by most others as nothing. They are the people whose history is not written in the history books and whose tombstones, if they could afford a tombstone, are the only reminders of their lives.

Perhaps it is difficult to reconcile the story of the Last Judgement with the mercy and love of God, which is often the focus of preaching today. The feast of Christ the King celebrates God's love and justice. In the first reading, God is presented as a shepherd who cares for each of his sheep. The shepherd seeks each out, knows each by name, strengthens, heals and bandages the wounded. Christ the good shepherd deepens this understanding in the story of the shepherd who seeks out the one lost sheep of the hundred in the fold. He carries it home on his shoulders. To this story of God's love, we are called to respond and follow in discipleship. The story of the Last Judgement is a reminder that we are called to take responsibility for our lives and that the commandment of love is the invitation to be followed. God does not reject us, but in freedom we have the possibility of rejecting God and God's invitation to love. Through our actions, we determine how God will judge us.

Christ the King presents an image of humble love and service of others. God knows our weakness and need for healing but invites us out of our brokenness to be close to those who are weakest in society. It is important to recognise one's Achilles heel in order to be compassionate to others.

Application
At the end of the Church's year and as we prepare for Advent, we are invited to take stock of our lives and recognise the action of God's grace in shepherding us throughout the last year. Can I see the times of darkness or the times when God has healed me? Are there times when God's love, through love of those around me, rescued me from darkness and despair? Do I thank God for this love?

If I stood before the cross at Monasterboice, what would it say to me? How have I responded to the invitations with which I have been presented in those who are poor and weak? With gratitude let us thank God for the way we have responded. Perhaps there is also need for repentance for moments of selfishness and carelessness: God who heals can forgive and show mercy, which can restore us to new life.

The feast of Christ the King is a celebration of God's love, which extends to the ends of the earth. To recognise God's love is a call to praise and gratitude.

Our Lord Jesus Christ, Universal King

Sundays in
Ordinary Time
Year B

"Where do you live?"

Illustration

At 12.30 p.m. on 22nd November 1963, shots rang out in Dallas, Texas, and the world was stunned to learn of the assassination of John F. Kennedy, the thirty-fifth President of the United States. Whatever historians subsequently unearthed about the man's alleged shortcomings, there was a palpable sense of tragedy, of a promising bright future being brought abruptly and cruelly to an end.

People who were alive at the time will almost invariably be able to tell you where they were, what they were doing and whom they were with, when they learned the shocking news of Kennedy's death. It was a decisive moment of history, an event that literally changed the course of world events. Things would never be the same again.

Gospel Teaching

There is the same sense of a momentous event in today's Gospel. We are told the exact time when those two disciples of John the Baptist first met Jesus: the tenth hour, about four o'clock in the afternoon. An unimportant, trivial fact perhaps, but an indication of just how important, how life-changing that first encounter was for Andrew and the other disciple. Their lives changed so much that they can tell us exactly when and where it happened.

Tantalisingly, the evangelist doesn't tell us the content of that encounter. He doesn't tell us what Jesus said to Andrew and the other unnamed disciple, nor what questions they asked. He doesn't describe Jesus or where he was living. John simply says that they accepted his invitation to come and see, and that they stayed with him for the rest of the day. Perhaps the conversation was too personal to be recorded, or perhaps a written account would not be able to convey its effect or the power of the presence of Jesus. Certainly the Lord had a profound effect: the two disciples left John the Baptist to become followers of Jesus, and Andrew wasted no time in telling his brother Simon Peter, "We have found the Messiah."

Perhaps, too, the Gospel writer realises that an encounter with the Lord must be a unique event, something that each potential follower has to experience personally. It's not something that can happen at second hand;

it cannot be experienced vicariously. The Lord issues an invitation, but it is up to each of us to respond. We have to be in a state of readiness, open to hear the Lord's call. Samuel in our first reading was already living in the Lord's sanctuary – in the right place to hear the call. And the two disciples were already followers of John the Baptist – predisposed to the coming of the Messiah. When the call came, they responded without hesitation.

Application

As Christians, we believe that we have been called, and that we are following the Lord, however falteringly or hesitantly. But we are called to a real personal meeting with the Lord, and not simply to go by what others have told us about him. Whether or not we can pinpoint an exact moment when we first encountered him, we are called to allow our relationship with Christ to change our lives irrevocably. By spending time in his presence, we learn to see as he sees, judge as he judges, act and speak as he does.

The call to follow, the invitation to spend time with the Lord, is never a once-and-for-all experience. It is a daily happening. As we grow in discipleship, as we learn to recognise his voice and walk in his ways, we learn that he speaks in many ways: not just through the authentic teaching of the Pope and bishops who, like Eli and John the Baptist, are able to point us in the right direction. Christ is also able to speak to us through everyday events and people. Peter, remember, was brought to the Lord by his brother Andrew.

As Samuel shows us, recognising the Lord's voice and presence can be a gradual affair, just as discipleship is a lifelong commitment, not a one-off decision. Perhaps today the Lord is calling to us most persistently in the faces of those in need: in the faces of those who are poor; those who are homeless; the victims of war, violence or oppression; those who are sick and dying; those who are lonely and unloved. When we can see and serve the Lord in these people, we can know that we really have become his disciples.

B

"Repent, and believe the Good News."

Illustration

"What do you want to be when you grow up?" As soon as the teacher asked the question, a forest of hands shot up. The children were keen to answer. "A vet, because I like animals." "A nurse, because I want to help people." "A farmer." "A shopkeeper." "A teacher."

When it came to John's turn, he was very definite. He wanted to be a zookeeper. Outings to the zoo with his parents had made him think it was the best job in the world. More than that, he knew that what he really wanted to do was to look after the monkeys. They were funny, friendly and lovable. He couldn't think of anything better than to spend his time being with them and caring for them.

Thirty years later, when John found himself as a parish priest, he often looked back on his childhood dream with a certain amusement.

Gospel Teaching

"Expect the unexpected" would be good advice for many of the characters we meet in the scriptures. Take, for example, Jonah. Jonah was living an unremarkable and presumably happy life until the word of the Lord came to him, asking him to go and preach repentance to the people of Nineveh. It was not a calling that Jonah wanted. It wasn't just that he didn't want the disruption to his life that the call to be a prophet would undoubtedly cause. It also disturbed and challenged his comfortable prejudices. He thought of Nineveh as nothing more than a notoriously wicked pagan city. The people didn't merit the chance to hear the word of the Lord. Why should they be given the chance to repent and find salvation when, as far as Jonah was concerned, all they deserved was to be punished for their sins? So Jonah's first reaction was to resist the Lord's call and to run away. It was only after a series of adventures, culminating in the episode with the great fish, that the reluctant prophet accepted his calling and took God's message to Nineveh.

Then there was Simon. From his earliest days, Simon had known what he wanted to do. He wanted to be a fisherman. He had been brought up with the life, living in a lakeside community. He had learned well, and was good at his job. He had married, and settled down to provide for his family. And he enjoyed working with his brother Andrew. It was a hard life, but it was a good life. This, he assumed, would be his future. But the Lord had other plans for Simon and his brother. They met Jesus, this new, different preacher, who seemed to speak with an authority they'd never heard before. And when he called them to be his disciples, everything changed. In contrast to Jonah, there was no attempt to resist the call or to run away. On the contrary, "at once they left their nets and followed him". Somehow they knew that it was the only thing to do. Even though it meant that their lives would never be the same again.

Application

Are we open to hearing God's call? And how do we respond when it comes? We all have our own plans, our own dreams, our hopes for the future. But sometimes these can become set in stone. It becomes hard to conceive of different ways of thinking. Yet all of us will face times of change in our lives. When things don't turn out the way we expect, can we perceive the hand of God in this?

Paul's advice is clear. He calls us to set our eyes on God. Paul expected the second coming of Christ to be very soon, and he exhorted his congregations to live in constant expectation of it. But his counsel not to become engrossed in the ways of the world is still as valid as ever. We are called to have a different perspective, and to be open to the word of God whenever and however it comes.

Both Jonah and Jesus preached repentance. Repentance may not be a popular word nowadays. But the word "repent" means to "change one's mind". And so the call to repentance is a call to look at the direction of our lives. We are called to have minds that are open to hear God's word to us. And if that word calls us to change direction, to change the way our lives are heading, to change the way we think and act, then our calling is to respond to it as the first disciples did.

B

"And the unclean spirit... went out of him."

Illustration

Counselling has been called the world's new religion. In Britain, there are hundreds of training courses, with many thousands of students learning how to counsel. It has been estimated that over two million people in Britain practise some kind of counselling as therapy, and the numbers continue to grow. What prompts people to seek counselling? What do counsellors have to offer?

People look for counselling for a variety of reasons. Some are seeking a way out of depression, or are trying to deal with stress, trying to make a difficult decision or looking for something more from their life. Other people are seeking to escape their demons, those dark passions that cause so much suffering to so many. It is clear that just as talking can hurt people, so too it can heal. Talking to someone can be a constructive way of talking to oneself, nurturing a desire to live.

Just as there are good counsellors, however, there are also those whose skills and practice leave something to be desired. And discerning the good from the bad is no easy task. In the time of Jesus, there were healers and there were charlatans. How were the people to tell the difference? If they went to someone who claimed to be a healer, would they in fact be healed or harmed?

Gospel Teaching

In today's first reading, Moses announces to the people that God is going to raise up a prophet from among them, and they must listen to his words. The prophet will speak only what the Lord commands, and in this way will be an instrument of life and health. Many years later, John the Baptist will announce his coming; Jesus is anointed by the Spirit to speak to the people. When they hear him, they are hearing God, and hearing the truth.

It was immediately obvious to the people in the synagogue at Capernaum that Jesus was different from the scribes. They were used to religious teachers explaining the scriptures; they were used to being told about the law; they were used to being harangued about how to live. But with Jesus, they realised they were in the presence of someone different. They could not describe exactly what that difference was. But he spoke with authority. There was an integrity about his words that led them to believe he was genuine. And as if their own surmising was not enough, Jesus demonstrated dramatically his power.

The unclean spirit had no problem recognising Jesus; like the congregation in the synagogue, it heard his words and recognised his authority. It fled, and the man was set free. No wonder the word spread throughout the countryside. Here indeed was something entirely different. The power of God's word, spoken directly, was plain for all to see. We know that not all who heard Jesus were convinced by his words; the human heart sometimes hears only what it wants to hear. Jesus never shouts or demands to be heard. He lets those who have ears hear.

Application

We know that words, as well as harming, can heal. The well-chosen word can comfort, bring forgiveness, show love, set free. The inspired word can teach and spur to goodness. Responding to bad news, words can bring good news, Gospel news. So talking can be therapeutic. But as Christians we believe more. We believe that when we talk in the spirit of Christ, obedient to God, we can work miracles. Just as Jesus spoke with authority, people of faith can speak with authority too. Not like the scribes who seemed to use their positions as teachers to rule and control; but like our Lord, who used words to encourage and inspire.

If we meet unclean spirits, in the darkness in our own souls or the souls of others, we need not be afraid. Christ is Lord of all, even of places that seem dark and impenetrable to us. His word of authority can overcome all. And his word can be our word too. When it is one of integrity and truth, when it is spoken humbly and in love, then it has the authority of Christ. It is a healing word, a word wounded people in a hurting world so desperately need.

"Let us go… to the neighbouring country towns, so that I can preach there too."

Illustration

The film *The Scarlet and the Black* is set in 1943, during the Second World War and the German occupation of Rome. It tells the true story of the relationship between Monsignor Hugh O'Flaherty, a priest working in the Vatican, and Colonel Herbert Kappler, Rome's brutal chief Gestapo officer. In helping Allied prisoners of war to escape home, the priest falls foul of the German colonel. Consequently, the order is given that the priest be killed should he set foot outside Vatican territory. However, nothing seems to be able to stop the priest continuing his work. He even disguises himself as a nun to protect his identity.

With the German army facing increasing setbacks, the decision is taken to pull out from Rome. Kappler knows his own life is in danger but, more importantly, he fears for the lives of his wife and children. Secretly, he arranges a meeting with the priest and asks him to secure safe passage out of Italy for his family. The priest is furious that someone responsible for so many deaths should now want assistance to enable his family to live. Kappler leaves disheartened, shouting that everything the priest stands for, everything he believes, in the end, counts for nothing.

Only after the war, while in prison for his crimes, did Kappler learn that his family were in fact helped to escape and were safe. Throughout many years of his long imprisonment, the only visitor Kappler received was O'Flaherty, month in, month out. And, in an incredible twist, Kappler was eventually baptised by the priest whose death he had once ordered. The story bears witness to the truth that preaching the Gospel, in words and actions, can change people's lives and bring them to Christ.

Gospel Teaching

Preaching is very much at the heart of the New Testament readings that we heard today. Jesus sums up his whole mission by explaining that he came to preach, and we know that his message was the Good News of God's love. However, we would be mistaken if we thought Jesus' preaching was like a sermon delivered from a pulpit. We know that the Gospels are not merely records of what Jesus said: they also include what he did, the actions that proclaimed who Jesus was and is, and what he was and is

B

about. In the same way, Jesus' preaching doesn't just mean what he said: it also embraces everything he did.

In the first reading we find Job completely despondent in the face of human suffering. While Jesus doesn't explain suffering or necessarily remove it, his words and actions do offer a way through it. Mark tells of how Jesus healed Simon Peter's mother-in-law and how he cured those suffering sickness and disease. By physically reaching out to those who are suffering and rejected, Jesus preaches a powerful message about caring and valuing people who are less able and more vulnerable than most.

Paul learnt all these lessons. Although he had his own difficulties and knew his weaknesses, his only boast was in Christ crucified. He was so convinced of the truth of Christ's message that he could do nothing other than dedicate his whole life to preaching it. And for this he wanted no reward; it was enough to be able to freely and simply tell people of the marvellous wonders of Jesus Christ. Paul did this by meeting people where they were, speaking as openly and widely as he could, being all things to all people for a chance to share the blessings of the Gospel.

Application

Jesus identifies preaching as the very purpose of his coming. In the same way that we cannot separate words and actions in his preaching, neither should these be separated in our discipleship. We know that people who say one thing and do another are false and unattractive. Isn't it the very integrity of Jesus that draws us to him? What he said and what he did hold together as true.

Paul speaks of the great responsibility of being able to offer people the Good News. As Christians, we too share that same responsibility. Many people don't think of themselves as preachers, but perhaps we all should. In whatever ways we can, no matter how small, let's be encouraged to continue trying to witness in our lives to the faith we speak with our lips. When we do this we are preaching; we are giving testimony with our whole life to the fact that the Gospel can be lived and shared with integrity.

"Feeling sorry for him, Jesus stretched out his hand and touched him."

Illustration

One October morning in 2006, in China, a bus driver had been hired to take elderly passengers to a medical clinic. Yet, when he saw his passengers, he put his foot on the accelerator and sped away. The passengers were not surprised. The group, many of them missing hands or fingers, were used to the stigma of leprosy. Even though they had long been cured of infection, they remained living in an isolated leper colony in China's Sichuan province, where they had been since the 1950s. "I never want to live outside the village, because people are so afraid of us," said one of the group. "When we approach them, they run off."

Patches on the skin are an early sign of leprosy, a biblical disease that continues today to affect millions of people in poor countries. Leprosy destroys nerves controlling feeling and movement. With no feeling, sufferers can hurt or cut themselves; parts of the body become dry, which makes skin more liable to crack, allowing infection to set in.

For close to three thousand years, the disease has carried a stigma. Despite there having been a cure for more than six decades, the historical tradition of discrimination and social exclusion is still present even today. Lepers around the world are still shunned because others are afraid of catching the disease from them and find their deformities distressing.

Gospel Teaching

The book of Leviticus tells us that lepers had to cry out to warn others of their presence – "Unclean, unclean" – and dwell apart from the rest of society. After contracting leprosy a person had to leave family, friends, livelihood and way of life. It was, in a sense, the death of all familiar bonds and intimacy. The leper in today's Gospel was not supposed to approach Jesus, let alone speak to him. Yet he does, and he makes his desperate plea for healing, recognising that Jesus has the power to make a leper clean. "If you want to," he says, "you can cure me"; and Jesus does indeed touch and heal him.

Both Jesus and the leper break with biblical rules and tradition by crossing social and ritual boundaries. Jesus had already broken a few boundaries – for example, by healing on the sabbath day.

The compassion of Jesus causes him to do extraordinary things. Perhaps the only thing more startling than an unclean person publicly and intentionally approaching a clean person is for that clean person then deliberately to reach out and touch the unclean person. Ironically, the one who was once unclean can now enter normal society, while Jesus is forced to remain outside in deserted places, at least for the time being. According to the laws regarding leprosy in Leviticus, those who come into contact with the unclean will become unclean themselves. Just as the leper has begun his journey back into society, Jesus is alienated from it. Yet people are still attracted to him and seek him out.

Application

To bring help to outcasts, Jesus himself had to become an outcast and, according to the Gospel, "stay outside in places where nobody lived". Which of our "rules" might Jesus break if he were walking around today? Which of our practices might we need to challenge in order to get close to Jesus? Who are the outcasts in our own society? How does our church congregation relate to HIV/Aids sufferers, or people with mental illness, or those who are homeless, for example? Are there people whom we wouldn't want to touch? Or do we ever feel like this leper? Have we ever experienced Jesus in the way he did? How has Jesus healed and restored us to wholeness?

Like the leper, we are called to be faithful witnesses to God's healing power – not just with words, but by actions too. We follow Jesus every time we reach out and cross boundaries to contact people who are ostracised and in need of healing. Jesus sees the person behind the illness or stigma, and sees the potential for wholeness that exists. He is deeply moved by the leper and acts immediately: he stretches out his hand and touches him. Jesus decides to perform a radical act and touches the leper: the kingdom of God is realised.

Let us seek out ways to reach outside of our comfortable worshipping communities to people who feel themselves to be socially excluded. In doing this, we too will be building the kingdom of God.

"We have never seen anything like this."

Illustration

The Marian shrine of Lourdes in France continues to attract pilgrims from all over the world. It is a holy and special place where those who are sick and suffering are given priority. Thousands upon thousands of people travel to Lourdes in faith to seek healing and hope in the midst of their illnesses.

One of the most poignant and moving images in Lourdes is of sick and frail people being carried and wheeled by helpers, friends and family members. Many helpers, often frail themselves, are willing to put themselves out for those in their care. As one young disabled boy remarked, "Lourdes is a place where no one stares at us." Lourdes is indeed a Gospel place where the world's usual priorities and assumptions, about who and what are important, are challenged and turned upside down. Often the external pilgrimage results in an internal change.

Gospel Teaching

Making room for those who are sick, frightened and estranged lies at the heart of the ministry of Jesus. Confronting structures and religious practices that put people at a distance from God and keep them paralysed is a major driving force for Jesus. In today's Gospel, word is out that he is in the neighbourhood and the people flock to see and hear him. In the midst of the crowds gathered in a local house, some scribes, guardians of the law, have come to see what this man Jesus is all about.

A paralysed man is carried by friends to see Jesus, but the crowd is in the way. The man's resourceful friends, undeterred by the obstacles, seek a new way of getting to Jesus. As they break an opening in the roof and lower the man to the ground, a new possibility is created.

For the Jewish people of biblical times, sin and sickness were linked. Since sickness was thought to be the result of sin, then any cure from sickness required the forgiveness of sin. This is the dynamic at the heart of this episode. Jesus not only demonstrates God's power to forgive sin and therefore heal but also seeks to break the link between sin and sickness. In this he is signing his own death warrant in the presence of the legal experts of his day. For Jesus, the problem is not with God's forgiveness but with our own.

In Jesus, God's power to forgive was made manifest. But that was not all. In this moment and throughout the Gospel, Jesus challenges people to forgive one another as God forgives. This extension of God's forgiveness transforms the human situation. From now on every act of love, every word and gesture of forgiveness, is divine. The scribes could not make this leap of imagination or of faith. As the paralysed man got to his feet and found freedom, they remained paralysed and limited.

Application

Through our scripture today we hear a voice of hope reminding us that with and in God our past does not need to be our prison. So many of us suffer tremendous resentment, anger, shame and fear as we contemplate our mistakes, our refusals and our limitations. Yet today we are reminded that our past does not have to be our present or our future. By trusting in God's ability to forgive us, by practising the forgiveness of others, we can find new freedom and hope. We can move on. God looks forward and beyond to new beginnings and always calls us to new life.

By trusting in God we are enabled to let go of whatever holds us back and to begin our journey into the future without being dragged down by all that has gone before. In this way, what once seemed impossible becomes possible, what once seemed far off looms closer. Faith, in this light, is about finding new solutions to old problems. This can mean seeking a different approach to whatever has baffled us in the past. It may also require letting go of control and developing a new attitude of trust in the goodness of life and of God.

Sometimes we can carry others into life; and sometimes we may need to be carried ourselves. Sometimes we will have the strength to help others; and sometimes we may have to recognise our own helplessness and vulnerability. Wherever we are currently on the journey of life, we can find encouragement from those clever pilgrim helpers whose faith knew no obstacles and whose imagination and resourcefulness enabled a paralysed man to begin his own pilgrimage to freedom.

B

"I will betroth you to myself... with tenderness and love."

Illustration

Boy meets girl. They fall madly in love. They marry. But then the husband discovers that his young wife has been unfaithful. His first thought is to get rid of her. But his heart won't let him; he loves her still. And so instead of suing for a divorce, he woos and wins her back.

This isn't a made-up story. It's a fairly accurate description of what happened to Hosea, one of Israel's great prophets. Of course Hosea isn't the first man to have had an unfaithful wife, nor even the first to have pardoned such a wife. But he is the first, so far as we know, to have come through such a bitter experience with a new and clearer vision of God's goodness and love.

In fact the central theme of the book of Hosea is the story of how God rescued the Israelites from slavery in Egypt, led them through the desert, and there made them into a people, God's very own people. We might say, using the prophet's imagery, that God wedded them to himself, they became his beloved bride and were showered with every blessing. But once they reached the promised land, they proved unfaithful: they rushed off to the pagan shrines, made new gods for themselves of dumb idols.

What is God going to do now? Cast them off? No, says Hosea. Drawing upon his own experience, he knows what God will do. God will lure the people back, lead them into the wilderness and speak to their hearts. It was in the desert that God had first taken them to himself, and now the courtship days are to be renewed in the hope that the people will respond and return to the Lord.

Gospel Teaching

What a magnificent and heartening picture of God – the ever-faithful, ever-forgiving, ever-loving One! And what light it throws on today's Gospel. In the course of a controversy over fasting, Jesus suggests that this is a unique situation. Why? Because "the bridegroom" is here. Jesus' presence makes it wedding time! At such a time, fasting would be as inappropriate as sewing a piece of unshrunk cloth onto an old garment or putting new wine into brittle old wineskins. That would leave a torn cloak or burst wine containers. The clear implication is that Jesus is presenting himself as "the bridegroom". He even speaks of the bridegroom one day being "taken away", an allusion to his death.

If in Hosea we heard about God's love and mercy and faithfulness, in the Gospel we see that love, mercy and faithfulness in action. God, in his dear Son Jesus, pursues us, becomes one of us, lives among us, and in the end lays down his life for us. However, just as the fidelity and love of a husband for a wayward wife are not of themselves enough to bring about reconciliation – she must respond to her husband's initiative – so the same is true of reconciliation with God: there is nothing, absolutely nothing, God will not do to bring it about, but in the end the response, or lack of it, is down to us.

Application

Against that backcloth our Sunday Mass takes on a fresh significance. We gather here because, to use the words of Hosea, God has lured us and led us "into the wilderness" – away from the bustle and activity of daily life. For a short time, as the scriptures are read, we are invited to be still, to allow God to speak to our hearts. Then in communion, again in the astonishing words of Hosea, the Lord will "betroth" us to himself "with tenderness and love". We are all sinners, unfaithful in big matters or small. But the Mass is the assurance of the Lord's willingness and eagerness to forgive, his longing to restore us to friendship.

In a homily, which was intended to be delivered in Easter week 2005, just before his death, Pope John Paul II wrote: "Our resurrected Lord gives us this love which forgives, reconciles and reopens the soul to hope." It's the thought of that love which fills us with the desire to respond. It is the thought of that love which gives us hope, enabling us to step out into a new week with a spring in our step. It is that love which fills us with confidence that we have been forgiven, even more wonderfully than Hosea's wife, and have been drawn close to our loving Lord.

B

"The Son of Man is master even of the sabbath."

Illustration

The Old Testament tells how the Lord gave his people the sabbath as a gift. As today's first reading explains, this was to enable them to take a much-needed rest from their labours and to give them an opportunity to praise God together with their families, servants and visitors. To take a break, to relax. But like many traditions that grow from a local, tribal or social human need, by Jesus' time the law given by God to Moses had developed into a religious observance so rigid that human need was forgotten. God's precious gift had become a requirement and the essence of its meaning was lost. The sabbath observance became an end in itself; it was being worshipped rather than the God who gave it.

Gospel Teaching

Today's Gospel reading contains many oddities and raises several curious questions. Why was Jesus out walking in the fields on the sabbath? And why were the Pharisees also there, oblivious to their own breaking of the law? Why did Jesus refer to King David when there was no comparison between David's need so long ago and the disciples' offence on this day? Perhaps the answer to all these questions is simply that it was necessary – necessary that Jesus began to raise in everyone's mind the one, big question: Who was he? It is a question he directly asks the disciples later in Mark's Gospel: "Who do people say that I am?" He then follows it up with a more personal question: "Who do *you* say that I am?"

Jesus engaged in an activity that challenged the Pharisees and confronted them with their legalistic interpretation of the meaning of the sabbath. In comparing himself with King David, Jesus set the stage for proving his credentials, not only by his family lineage, but in the depth of his personal relationship with almighty God. Jesus showed them his power in declaring the truth of God's gift, given for humanity – that the sabbath was made for us. That God's gift should never become a weapon with which to catch people out, to beat them with or to make them feel guilty. Human beings go too far when they seek to control others by such means. The Son of Man is "master even of the sabbath", and we abuse or ignore that knowledge at our peril.

And, so that there should be no doubt in anyone's mind, Jesus cured the withered hand of the man in the synagogue. People may spread guilt and commit evil on the sabbath, but nothing will prevent the Lord from liberating and doing good if he so chooses.

Application

In Jesus' teaching there is always the offer of a new life, a real sympathy with our weakness, and a warning. Today he gives us back the sabbath for its rightful purpose. He heals our weakness as he did the withered hand. Then he warns us against confusing ourselves with God, of the danger of overstepping our responsibilities and claiming a power that we do not possess, and of the sin in using that power against others to control them.

So who *do* we say that he is? Who is the Lord of the sabbath for us? When we acknowledge Jesus as Son of the living God, we have no problem with his taking charge of each and every day. We have no problem with God being in charge because we know that, when God is in charge of our days and of our lives, therein lies our perfect freedom and our present and eternal happiness. When we allow other human beings to determine our relationship with God, we suffer their fears and their misunderstandings and misinterpretations.

When God in Christ rules the sabbath, we can joyfully accept this precious gift and use it fully to praise him in all manner of ways. We can go to church, visit those who are sick, welcome family and stranger or have a party, without guilt and with joy. God's generosity is praised in all good and wholesome deeds, just so long as God underpins the day. When God is the foundation and God's presence in our lives is acknowledged and praised, then, with the burden of legalistic restrictions lifted, we can experience the greatest possible liberation. If God is in charge, we can live fully and abundantly and without fear. Blessed be God for ever!

B

"Anyone who does the will of God... is my brother and sister and mother."

Illustration

How many of us have, at some moment of acute exasperation in our lives, heard ourselves say: "What on earth possessed me to do that?" We imply that we were taken over by something outside ourselves and that we are not therefore completely to blame for our actions.

We have all kinds of responsibility-shifting expressions: "You drive me to drink"; "It's in the genes"; "But everybody else does it." It began in Eden, didn't it? "The woman made me eat," said Adam; and then Eve shifted the blame further down: "The serpent told me to do it." In today's climate we blame so many others for failure. We can blame the government for a great many of our ills, our parents for some, the weather for a few more, and when all else fails there is always God. Of course, there may be good reason for apportioning blame, but all too easily we can shed responsibility for our contribution.

Gospel Teaching

The first reading today challenges us to move out of this particular way of shifting blame away from ourselves. Of course, it is true, Adam and Eve had not planted that desirable tree in the garden. God had, and God in his wisdom knew it would harm them; and in the same way that we forbid our children to eat what is poisonous, so God forbade Adam and Eve to take its fruit.

Events do happen outside our control: accidents occur, lightning does strike. Of these things we can say: "But it is not my fault." What is our choice is how we receive them – whether we grumble and become embittered, or whether we use them to keep close to God, trusting in God's care of us.

In the second reading Paul gives us a clue to this way of seeing God's design for us. His challenge is that we keep an awareness of the inner life of the spirit. What Paul saw was not only what was visible in the world around him, but what was invisible, the other reality, the world of the spirit, of God dwelling in God's creatures.

And in today's Gospel we find more excuses and more blaming. The family of Jesus could not understand him, so decided he was out of his mind. The religious leaders declared him to be in league with the devil and in so doing excused themselves from accepting his teaching. The miracles could not be denied, and the scribes feared their effect on the people who thronged about this challenging man. To say that Jesus worked by the power of God was to demand that they recognise him as a man of God; and where then would their authority be? So in an extraordinary poverty of argument they accused him of casting out devils by the power of Satan. They are saying, in effect, "We need not believe him because all his seemingly good works are evil."

No wonder Christ demolished their reasoning in a few succinct sentences. For Satan to cast out devils was self-destruction. Christ, like the strong man in the parable, can bind Satan because his is the greater power. That first binding had taken place in the desert, before the start of his public ministry, when he had refused all Satan's easy options, and with them Satan's power over him.

And then, as if all this were not enough, there was the family of Jesus asking for him, wanting to save him from himself, not understanding his mission – perhaps a little ashamed of him and worried lest he stir up trouble for himself and them. His mother, too, concerned surely more for his safety than his sanity, was included in the family trying to reach him through the crowd.

Jesus' response is wonderful. It becomes an invitation to all of us. If we do the will of God, we are his family. We are his brothers and his sisters and his mother. We call God our Father, and, as Mary did, we bring him and his love into our world.

Application

There are times for all of us when we want to shift the blame onto something or someone else. Times when we want to make excuses for not heeding the words of Christ. Times when we want to run away from being responsible. But if we can remember that we have the Spirit of God in us, we can dare all things, and in doing Christ's will can become his family.

B

*"Once it is sown it grows into the
biggest shrub of them all."*

Illustration

In 1973 E.F. Schumacher published his famous book called *Small is Beautiful*, with the subtitle *Economics as if People Mattered*, in which he examined the economic structure of the Western world. The book became highly popular and sold over 700,000 copies. Its title became a catchphrase and was applied to all sorts of things besides economics. The phrase was also used to imply that, because something was small, it didn't mean that it was either unimportant or without influence – quite the contrary.

It is certainly a phrase that could be used in relation to the shepherd boy David in the Bible and especially in the famous story of his defeat of the giant Goliath. Down the centuries countless painters have shown the small but sturdy David, armed only with a sling and five smooth stones, going out to meet the Philistine Goliath. Many have shown the wounded Goliath, felled by a stone to the forehead, lying on the ground, and the boy David drawing Goliath's own sword to cut off his head. Others have portrayed David either holding up Goliath's head or carrying it to Jerusalem in triumph. From the outset, however, David himself made it clear that it was God who gave him the victory.

Small may not always be beautiful, but it is frequently either impressive or effective. This is often the case with people who are small of stature. It could be said to be true not only of David, but also for example of Mother Teresa or St Paul, whose very name in Greek, Paulos, means "small". St Paul may have been small, but the effectiveness of his preaching and writing was enormous. It largely accounts, in the beginning, for the spread of the Gospel throughout the Roman empire.

Gospel Teaching

In today's Gospel Jesus first speaks of how the kingdom of God grows through the activity of providence, like seed scattered on the land. Although people may sow and scatter the seed, it is not they who enable the seed to grow in the earth, but God. Jesus goes on to compare the kingdom of heaven to a mustard seed, which, though he calls it "the smallest of all the seeds on earth", grows into the largest shrub that exists. In other words,

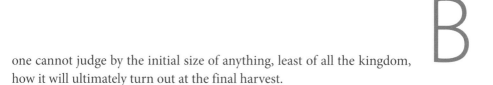

one cannot judge by the initial size of anything, least of all the kingdom, how it will ultimately turn out at the final harvest.

Just as the physical size of a person does not bear any relation to that person's quality, or influence on the world, so the kingdom of God is not dependent on such things. Jesus says that the kingdom of God is like the small mustard seed, which, once it has grown to maturity, will have "the birds of the air" coming to find shelter in its shade. So the nations of the world will be gathered together into the kingdom.

St Mark tells us that, whereas Jesus spoke to the crowds who came to hear him only in parables, he was careful to explain their meaning to his disciples when they were alone. Teaching and explanation have always been vital if we are to comprehend the full meaning of the parables.

Application
There are times when we might feel discouraged by the slow growth or even apparent decline of the kingdom of God throughout the world. In the West, for example, there are whole areas that have become completely secular in outlook. If we despair about this, however, we have forgotten that the growth of God's kingdom does not depend on us. It is God who is the sower; and it is God's providence, not our efforts alone, that enables the kingdom to grow.

On our own it's easy for us to feel dispirited, disillusioned, or simply confused. The Gospels reveal that the disciples in Jesus' day often felt the same. They needed the teaching of Jesus to help them begin to understand the kingdom. It is one of the tasks of the Church today to help interpret the parables of Jesus to us, just as he once explained them to his disciples.

Even if the kingdom may have the appearance of being small and insignificant, Jesus tells us that like the mustard seed it will eventually become large and will contain people from all the nations of the world. We are called to be a people of hope and to trust in the providence of God.

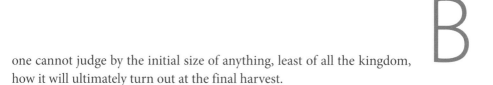

11th Sunday in Ordinary Time

B

"Who can this be? Even the wind and the sea obey him."

Illustration

We underestimate the sea at our peril. One day it can be so calm and flat that we are convinced we can cross its immensity in a rowing boat. The next day it can be whipped up to such boiling fury that even taking a step near its breakers may have us swept away and drowned. Down through the ages we have fought it, befriended it, feared it, even loved it. Island nations appreciate the security it offers them, but it still needs to be kept in check as it gnaws away at cliffs and beaches.

We have learnt to understand its ways through long experience, and tried to contain its storms and tantrums. But we are human. We forget, and we allow our hopes of material gain or economy to undermine the wisdom of the past. In some of the great flood disasters of recent years, for example the tsunami in eastern Asia and the hurricanes on the American Atlantic seaboard, the coastal defences had been weakened. The mango swamps had been removed to enable tourist beaches to be built. The ramparts protecting the land below sea level had not been soundly maintained. But the sea does not forget and it takes advantage of every weakness, whether of land or shipping. It just awaits its moment, perhaps encouraged by global warming or perhaps just following the natural rhythms of the tides and seasons. We ignore its immense powers and resources at our peril.

Gospel Teaching

There is not much love for the sea in the Old Testament. It is its unruly nature that is uppermost in the awareness of the writers. At the very beginning of Genesis the sea is identified with the formless void of the deep, and it is only through the action of the creator God that the heavens and earth are formed and the deep is held in check. The same theme is taken up by the book of Job. When the Lord wishes to answer Job's questions about his suffering, he begins by contrasting Job's finite lot with God's own superhuman powers. The Lord's first illustration is of how he has put bounds on the sea and controlled it. The message is quite clearly that only God can control the sea, as had been shown in the parting of the Red Sea as the Israelites made their way to the promised land.

But in the Gospel story Jesus controls the sea. The language of the story reflects that of the book of Job. The sea is told to be quiet and calm, and its accomplice the wind is rebuked and drops its force in obedience to the command. But Jesus is a human being. How can it be that he has such powers? Once again the question on the lips of both the disciples and others is: "Who can this be?" What sort of man is this who by his own power does what only God can do? This is the scandalous question that runs through this part of Mark's Gospel. What are we to make of such a man?

Application

A big question for any sailor is: "Do you trust your skipper?" If you don't, you should not be entrusting your life to this person. Sometimes it can seem that we have no choice. On the whole, we don't choose our employers. They choose us. In the old days sailors were press-ganged into employment, and we may still feel the same has happened to us. Trying to survive bad management is no easy matter.

In addition to whatever skills we can bring to bear on changing such situations, we are also asked to find the deeper centre in ourselves. In the midst of our sense of being overwhelmed by the depths of life's problems, Christ offers us a way forward. We put our trust in him. Elsewhere he will offer his disciples the inner peace that the world cannot give, and here we are asked to let go of our fears and accept that same gift. It does not mean that we will not experience life's storms and challenges. It does mean that we will be able to ride such encounters like a good sailor, accumulating the wisdom that centres us on what matters, what is true. Even when Jesus seems asleep in the boat, our trust in him can bring about the quietening of the wind and the calming of the sea. We need not be afraid.

"Do not be afraid; only have faith."

Illustration

In August 2005 Pope Benedict XVI made a special visit to Germany on the occasion of the World Youth Day, held in Cologne. In a scene reminiscent of Jesus at the Sea of Galilee, the Holy Father spoke to the throng of young people from a boat, moored beside the banks of the River Rhine. On the following day he spoke to them again at the Sunday Mass at Marienfeld. On that occasion he spoke about the power of Jesus to change the world.

A crowd of around one million young people had gathered for that Mass, and they listened willingly as the Pope addressed their concerns for a renewed and better world. While nation fights against nation, and while terror threatens to engulf us all, Pope Benedict pointed to the love of Jesus and to a different way of being in the world.

At the Last Supper Jesus faced the hour of his own death, and transformed that violent deed into his own act of love. By giving himself to us in bread and wine Jesus makes his death into our life. He makes his suffering into our joy. As the Holy Father put it, "Death as such is already conquered from within, the resurrection is already present in it. Death is, so to speak, mortally wounded, so that it can no longer have the last word."

As Pope Benedict said on an earlier occasion, in the first days of his pontificate, "The world is redeemed by the crucified, not by those who crucify."

Gospel Teaching

When Jesus crossed the Sea of Galilee and came to its western shore, he found a great crowd of people there to welcome him. They, too, were a willing crowd, eager to listen to the young preacher of Nazareth. But very quickly the demands of life make themselves felt. A desperate father, eager for the welfare of his daughter, comes and begs for help. An equally desperate woman, weary of medical interventions and failures, seeks out the healer of Galilee. They are looking for someone to change their worlds, from sickness to health, from death to life. They recognise in Jesus someone who has the power to change the world.

Jesus responds to these requests, no questions asked. It is God's will that everyone should be saved, that all should be well. The years of weariness that the woman has endured are brought to an end. Her suffering is over. Her story is an inspiration for all who struggle over time with personal sorrow. Seek out the Lord of life, and pray to be well. "If I can touch even his clothes…"

When Jesus turns to help the desperate father, he is met with news of death, the death of the little girl and the death of hope. To the grief-stricken father he gives words of life: "Do not be afraid; only have faith." What Jesus does then transforms a world of darkness into glorious light. "Little girl, I tell you to get up."

The people at the bedside are overcome with astonishment. Jesus has restored a girl to life, yes, but something more is happening here. Jesus is showing us something of his own identity. He is Lord of life. He is also showing us something of the mystery of the world to come: that death is not the end. There is something greater, something stronger than death, and it is here in the person of this preacher of Galilee.

Application

When Jesus was nailed to the cross, people taunted him with the comment, "He saved others, but he cannot save himself." When death came to Jesus, and violent death at that, he was not saved from its torment. But he was saved from its seeming power. God raised him high, and gave him the name of "the Lord of life".

Let us then approach this Lord of life. In the midst of the crowd, like that woman of long ago, let us humbly ask to be free of our afflictions. When the death of a loved one comes close to us, let us not be afraid. Look to the Lord of life, and have faith. And like the crowd that welcomed Jesus to the shore, let us set ourselves to listen to the Lord, and to follow him.

When darkness threatens to engulf us, hear the voice of the Lord, saying, "The world is not dead, but asleep." Let us set ourselves to wake the world to the love of God.

"He was amazed at their lack of faith."

Illustration

Who are the people that we tend to ignore or pass by? Many of us find it difficult to deal with beggars. It is easier to pretend not to see them and pass by. Some people tend to ignore people in wheelchairs, especially if they have somebody wheeling them or standing by. The conversation takes place with the person assumed to be the carer; wheelchair occupants are often treated as people who cannot speak for themselves.

People who serve us in shops or get us tickets for transport or leisure activities, they too can somehow disappear off our radar as human beings. We only really notice them when they are inefficient or all too human in their responses, perhaps a little like ourselves. Then we may ignore those who are closest to us in the household. As the saying goes, "Familiarity breeds contempt", and we can too easily take our nearest and dearest for granted, not really noticing who they are any more or what is concerning them.

There is an argument that we would become overloaded if we tried to take on board the full humanity of all the people we meet. Yet if we let go of that recognition of the other as an important human being, our equal and equally worthy of respect, we can lose sight of our own humanity. And if we lose sight of our own humanity, we lose sight of Christ.

Gospel Teaching

Jesus has just been consolidating the early days of his mission with miracles of healing, the casting out of unclean spirits, the healing of the woman with the haemorrhage and the raising of the daughter of Jairus. In each case the faith of the recipient has been highlighted. Now he returns to his own home town of Nazareth to find that he is not acknowledged in either his wisdom or his power to do miracles. The reason for the people's disbelief is quite simple. They know who he is. They have known him from his childhood, and they know all the members of his family. This knowledge creates a prejudice within them that cannot accept that Jesus may have an extraordinary message or extraordinary powers. He himself is said to be amazed at their lack of faith.

In his comments on this reaction of his neighbours Jesus aligns himself with the prophets who have gone before him. He has taken on their mantle, and like them he is rejected. As a result of this he will begin the journey that will take him to his own suffering and death. He will also be found living on the outskirts of the towns, in the wilderness or in foreign territories. The message of faith does not find its roots where we might expect, in the centres of traditional belief; instead it is heard on the margins of society. Jesus becomes the outsider who will inspire belief in those whose natural habitat is on the margins, ignored or kept at a distance by those who are powerful and successful.

Application

We still find Jesus where we least expect to encounter him. The gift of faith enables us to stay open to this possibility. Our assumption may be that we will find him in our churches, in holy, devout and respectable people. That is where we tend to look for him; and, if we become set in our ways, we forget that he appears in the very ordinariness of our humanity.

The incarnation reveals Jesus as the one who takes our humanity in its fullness and makes it divine. This mystery of salvation does not mean that our ordinariness is taken away. Rather it is our very ordinariness that becomes the instrument of transformation. On the one hand we see more clearly the miracle that we are. On the other hand this miraculous nature reveals itself to our new vision of faith. And it happens where and when we least expect it, in the casual exchange with a beggar on the streets, in the smiles of understanding offered at the checkout, in the little acts of kindness shared between family and friends.

That is why it is so important not to ignore each other or pass each other by. We miss the many-splendoured thing and become lost and sightless, thinking we see but only being aware of the outer semblance. Perhaps, too, we need to look in the mirror more carefully, at least from time to time, to remind ourselves of our own humanity and that Christ is present in us too.

B

"And he instructed them to take nothing for the journey."

Illustration

The Corsican adventurer and sometime emperor of France, Napoleon Bonaparte, once said that "an army marches on its stomach". He wasn't just talking about the need to feed the soldiers. The French army under Napoleon was expected to live off the land, as it went along. This enabled the army to move quickly, while other armies were held back by long and slow supply trains. This helped Napoleon win a series of unexpected victories. Not weighed down with baggage, his army could move fast, and react more quickly to a changing situation. This had some disadvantages too, especially for those who lived in the path of the army. And if the land they marched through was barren, the troops could starve, as on the famous retreat from Moscow. The strategy could bring great success, but was also very risky.

Long before, in the thirteenth century, the Church had tried a similar tactic in her fight against disbelief. Members of the Orders of St Francis and St Dominic often took to the road, lived off what people would give them, and responded quickly to requests for help from local bishops. In the campaigns of these friars, Francis and Dominic showed the way by example – often sleeping rough, begging for food and drink, eating whatever was put before them. Unburdened by property, they could move quickly. Friars like St Anthony of Padua or St Thomas Aquinas travelled thousands of miles, all over Europe, throughout their lives.

Gospel Teaching

Napoleon, of course, served his own ends all his life, and the soldiers who trusted in him were often let down and abandoned. The friars, following the example of Christ and the apostles, despite their high-risk strategy, were never let down. As they served the high king of heaven, the supplies of grace and providence that kept them on the road – on campaign, as it were – never dried up.

What Jesus is doing in today's Gospel is part of a larger strategy. In fact, as St Paul tells us, the strategy was laid down by God, "from the beginning", as a "predetermined plan". Jesus' choosing of twelve apostles is a deliberate way of showing that his aim is to refound the people of God, as once the twelve tribes of Israel were called by God.

The apostles are to move quickly, unburdened by anything except the message of repentance and healing. Where their preaching is not welcome, they are to move on swiftly. In another military image, it is what is known as a tactic of "fire and manoeuvre". The apostles are not to lay siege to anywhere that resists, but to move on. This creates a sense of the urgency of Christ's message. The kingdom of heaven is close at hand; the time is now. Even before the resurrection, we see the two main weapons that Christ gives the Church – the word of God and the sacraments. The apostles are to preach, and anoint with oil to heal those who are sick.

Application

Obviously Christ's strategy in the Gospel reading is not meant for all. The apostles are chosen for this task at this particular time. Most of us have quite different lives, with responsibilities that we can't just drop. However, we can all take something from this message.

Firstly, all of us carry around certain personal baggage that can hold us back, and make us less fruitful: perhaps an old grudge, a certain envy or resentment of someone else. We may find something difficult to forgive, we might be unreasonably fearful of something. We may be held back by an unworthy attachment to something. All such things can both frustrate our own development and prevent us from contributing all that we could. Part of the Gospel message of repentance is trying to put aside this negative baggage, to travel more lightly and be freer to serve.

Secondly, Christ has given us a means to get rid of this sort of baggage. Through the sacraments we can both leave behind what hinders us, and move forward in the service of Christ. We have each been chosen from all eternity, to be co-workers in God's plan of redemption; we have "been stamped with the seal of the Holy Spirit", enlisted in God's service, like the apostles. We "have heard the message of the truth and the good news of salvation, and have believed it". It took great faith and courage for the apostles to do what Christ told them, and we too can ask for that faith and courage.

"He took pity on them because they were like sheep without a shepherd."

Illustration

The catacombs in Rome are an amazing sight to see. They are burial places unlike the ones we're generally used to. Lying just outside the old Roman city walls, they consist of vast labyrinths of underground passageways, lined on either side by many tiers of burial places, like enormous dormitories of multilayered bunk beds. There are many miles of them. The early Christians in Rome buried their dead like this because they were not a wealthy community and they could not afford to buy all the land they would have needed to bury their dead in open-air cemeteries. It also gave them a place to worship when the Roman authorities were persecuting Christians, and it allowed these early Christian communities to bury their dead together, following Christian beliefs about death and the afterlife.

One tomb in the catacombs belongs to an eight-month-old baby boy, called Aurelius Castus. His mother, Antonia, had the tomb made for him when he died in the third century and she had both their names carved on the marble slab covering the opening of the tomb. But she didn't just have their names carved, she also had an image carved onto the marble slab. This image was of a man carrying a sheep across his shoulders with two more sheep at his feet. It is the image of the good shepherd.

Gospel Teaching

This image was not meant to be a portrait of Christ: it was meant as a symbol, like the Christian images we are more familiar with today, images of fish, or a dove, or the cross. It was a particularly apt symbol for burials as it called to mind the words of today's psalm, "The Lord is my shepherd", with its comforting message that we shall live in the Lord's house for ever. Images of shepherds crop up in many places in the Bible. In today's readings we have examples from both the Old and New Testaments with the prophet Jeremiah, the psalmist and Mark the evangelist all using the image of the shepherd to great effect.

In today's Gospel we hear about Jesus and his apostles, worn out from their ministry, seeking a bit of peace and quiet to recuperate. But, like the mother of a newborn baby, exhausted from sleepless nights but still able to comfort her child, Jesus still finds a bit more to give to the people who come to him. Mark describes the people as being "like sheep without a shepherd" and it seems Jesus cannot let them stay in this state. Jesus is the good shepherd for everyone. We only get half the story in today's reading, as the following verses in the Bible tell how these same people are fed in the famous miracle of the feeding of the five thousand. Jesus does not just look after their spiritual needs, he provides for their physical needs too. He really is a good shepherd.

Application

The image of the good shepherd can show us a few things about Jesus. Jesus as shepherd echoes the image of King David in the Old Testament, working as a shepherd before he became king. Jesus comes from the line of David as was prophesied in today's first reading. The genealogy of Jesus is detailed at the beginning of Matthew's Gospel to prove his relationship with King David. But Jesus truly is a shepherd king, ready to care for his flock rather than to take on the grandeur of power.

Picturing Jesus as our shepherd also emphasises God's kindness to us. Jesus takes on the role of caring for all our needs and guiding us through life if we will follow him. As he takes on this lowly role of shepherd, we can see that God isn't distant or unapproachable. In Jesus, God is physically present and is ready to meet all our needs.

The image of the good shepherd also highlights our weakness and folly. Compared with God's greatness we are as helpless as sheep. We may rather not think of this, preferring to be proud of our achievements and status, but it is good for us to be reminded that we are all dependent upon God's grace. Fortunately for us, through God's grace we are given the great gift of Jesus to be our shepherd, and we can be confident that if we follow him we are in the very best of care.

*"A large crowd followed him, impressed by
the signs he gave."*

Illustration

Fr Werenfried van Straaten was born in the Netherlands in 1913. He entered religious life as a Norbertine at the Abbey of Tongerlo in Belgium. His life coincided with the brutal conflicts that ran through much of twentieth-century history. In the deprivation and displacement of post-war Europe, it quickly became clear to him that millions of people, many of them Catholic, were suffering as refugees. More than this, behind the so-called Iron Curtain, clergy, religious and laity were being persecuted viciously on account of their faith in what he referred to as the "Church of Silence".

In response, on Christmas Day 1947, Fr Werenfried established the Catholic pastoral charity Aid to the Church in Need. Working initially in Eastern Europe, its mission expanded to support the struggling Church in Latin America, in Africa and in Asia. It now manages thousands of projects all over the world, from Siberia to China. It assists with the training of seminarians and offers support to religious brothers and sisters. It enables communities to build or rebuild their churches and chapels, often after warfare and persecution. It provides religious programming on radio and television, and prints Bibles. Faithful to the spirit of its founder, Aid to the Church in Need has a special concern for the needs of refugees.

In the light of his faith and his many experiences, some of which were incredibly tough, one of Fr Werenfried's simple yet profound comments was this: "God is better than we think."

Gospel Teaching

St John's Gospel doesn't speak of Jesus performing miracles. Instead, it describes the miraculous things Jesus did as signs. A sign either points us somewhere or tells us something and this is true of the signs Jesus gave us.

The feeding of a five-thousand-strong crowd was such an impressive sign that those who were fed by Jesus literally wanted to crown him as their king. But this sign operates on many different levels. It points, first of all, to the wonderful compassion of Jesus, who was so concerned for the human needs of those around him. This tells us that Jesus is interested in the details of our life, our worries and our fears.

Secondly, the feeding of the crowd points us to the faith of the disciples. Philip was unsure when Jesus asked him where enough bread could be bought to feed everyone. Andrew did a little better. He took a hesitant step in faith and pushed forward the small boy with five loaves and two fish. At the command of Jesus, however, the disciples trustingly did exactly what he asked. This tells us that living by faith can sometimes be shaky and unclear, but that the word of Jesus can be relied upon.

Finally, this sign points us to God's generous provision for our needs. We can often be tempted to doubt that God can supply the things that are essential. By miraculously feeding the impossibly large with the incredibly small, Jesus reminds us that God is better than we might think, that God always wants to nourish us, both humanly and spiritually. The supreme sign of this is the Eucharist, when we receive the food and drink that point us towards heaven and tell us we are loved.

Application

Fr Werenfried van Straaten staked his life on the truth Jesus teaches through this sign in the Gospel. He believed that God is generous, that God desires to give open-handedly. But Fr Werenfried also knew another truth. He knew that God uses people, mostly ordinary people, to meet the needs of others. The whole event of the feeding of the five thousand was founded on the generosity of a child who was willing to place what he had into the hands of Jesus, to put it at God's disposal.

The full version of the quotation from Fr Werenfried is actually this: "People are better than you think; God too is better than you think." Some people will only experience God's generosity through our willingness to give of what we have and, in faith, to allow God to multiply the graces and benefits that will flow from it.

In this Eucharist we present to God the smallness of our lives and the ordinariness of bread and wine. As we give thanks, in memory of Christ, these gifts are changed and we are made holy by the food of eternal life. May the power of God's love strengthen us to trust more deeply in God's care and to show that care to others by sharing what is ours.

"He who believes in me will never thirst."

Illustration

In an ancient parish church in Cyprus, an old woman was praying before an icon, a picture of a saint. As she prayed, she became convinced that there was something special about the icon. But when she spoke to others of this, they thought her a little foolish. There was nothing about the painting that marked it out as special or in any way different from the many other icons in the little church.

Yet the woman persisted in her belief, and so the parish priest had the icon examined. Lo and behold, beneath the surface of that very ordinary icon lay hidden a much older and immensely more valuable painting of the Mother of God. Somehow, the woman in her prayer had been able to perceive something that was not visible to the naked eye. Literally a treasure had been discovered.

Gospel Teaching

In our first reading, the Israelites were given a treasure. In their hunger, God gave them the gift of manna – bread from heaven, food for their journey to the promised land. But it was a treasure they did not understand or recognise. They needed Moses to explain it to them.

However, they had been given an even greater treasure, which they also failed to recognise: the treasure of their freedom. God had liberated them from their slavery in Egypt. And now, at the first hurdle, they bemoaned their fate and longed for the well-fed days of their slavery. At that moment, their God-given freedom was an unopened treasure, an unappreciated gift, which they had not yet discovered. They would gladly have exchanged their freedom for a loaf of bread.

In the Gospel, the crowds following Jesus similarly did not recognise the treasure they had found in him. They were following him for superficial reasons – because they had witnessed the miraculous feeding of the five thousand, when Jesus repeated that earlier miracle of the manna in the desert. They were following Jesus because he had fed their stomachs. They failed to appreciate the true meaning of the miracle, unable to see beyond the surface. They were like children who are more captivated by the wrapping paper than by the gift inside.

Jesus explains that he can give more than physical food for the body: he himself is the bread of life, in whom humanity's deepest hungers are satisfied. Not simply bread that satisfies physical hunger, but bread of life – bread for life. Jesus is able to answer the human heart's infinite longing for love, our fundamental thirst for meaning and for life itself. Like Moses before him, he explains to the people the treasure that God is offering: the food that leads to eternal life. All they need to do is respond by believing in him.

Application

These readings speak to our lives today. Jesus continues to invite us to recognise the treasures that God in his love is offering, but which we so often overlook or fail to appreciate. When we look at the situation of our own lives, or of our Church and world, perhaps our initial reaction is to do what the Israelites did: we moan and grumble about our lot. The Lord's response is always to send us his blessings and his love, just as he showered down bread in answer to the Israelites' hunger. The challenge for us is to listen to the voice of those who – like Moses – call us to recognise the goodness of God, the freedom God brings us, the promised land to which God is leading us.

Jesus makes the same appeal to us as he made to the crowd: "believe in me". Look beyond the surface and respond to the invitation God is making. The belief Jesus calls for is not mere intellectual assent. It involves much more than that. It is belief that involves commitment. In John's Gospel, to believe in Jesus means quite simply being committed to his way of love: "Love one another as I have loved you." This is what Paul, in the second reading, calls "the way you have learnt from Christ". It is only in being committed to Christ-like love that our deepest hungers and thirsts are satisfied, as Christ himself promised: anyone who comes to me will never hunger; anyone who believes in me will never thirst. That is the treasure which Jesus sets before us this day. We recognise this – we are able to discover this treasure and really own it – when we commit ourselves to belief in him, to following his way of love.

"Everybody who believes has eternal life."

Illustration

On 11th July 1942 Irène Némirovsky went for a walk in the pine forest. She often did this. In the quiet of the forest, away from the noise and trouble of occupied France, away from the disturbing news about the German occupation, Irène wrote her stories. Irène was a published writer, and very well received. Since the Germans had occupied Paris in June 1940, Irène, with her husband and two children, had moved to the countryside to be safe. But it became increasingly clear that nowhere in France was safe, if you were a Jew.

This was not the first persecution that Irène had known. Born in Kiev, in Ukraine, and brought up in Russia, Irène had to escape to Finland with her family during the October Revolution of 1917. From Finland they went to Sweden, and from Sweden finally to France, where they felt safe. Growing up happily in Paris, marrying and having children, Irène was safe until war broke out again, and Jews were persecuted again.

Now, sitting in the pine forest, Irène knew that her time was short. Writing a letter to her editor, Irène said, "My dear friend, think of me sometimes. I have done a lot of writing. I suppose they will be posthumous works, but it helps to pass the time." Two days later Irène was arrested. Two months later, in Auschwitz, she died. Sixty-two years later, in 2004, her manuscript, rescued by her daughter, was published. Her beautiful words are heard at last.

Gospel Teaching

The great prophet Elijah was also a man of great words, and a man familiar with persecution. His preaching of the true worship of God came into conflict with the pagan rites of Baal, and he found himself in the middle of great conflict. Threatened with death by Queen Jezebel, Elijah goes away into the wilderness. There he loses heart and wants to die. But he finds himself urged to eat, and to gather his strength again. He is reminded that he is on a journey, and the food will nourish him and help him to travel. Rejuvenated by that food, Elijah journeys on and comes to his destination, Horeb, the mountain of God.

The journey of our own life can often be very difficult. Problems and persecutions come in many shapes and guises. War and the threat of death affect many people. Tragedies strike down the lives of others. We are no strangers to sickness and sorrow. The will to live, the strength to carry on, can be drained out of the best of us. It is then that we need spiritual strength to revive us and to help us on life's journey. We need reminding that life is good, and that the Lord is drawing us to himself.

That is why Jesus says today, in no uncertain terms, "I am the bread of life." He is the living bread come down from heaven, so that we may eat and not die. His word gives life to the world. His self-sacrifice on the cross will set us free. Risen from the dead, he will raise us up on the last day. The victory of Jesus over death is the guarantee of victory for all who live and die in faithfulness. As Jesus says, "They will live for ever."

Application

This everlasting life is part of who we are now. We are believers even in the face of sorrow and persecution. Our faith in Jesus and in his resurrection finds expression in ordinary, everyday things. St Paul spells it out: "Do not grieve the Holy Spirit of God." Do not hold grudges, do not lose your temper, do not raise your voice, do not call each other names, do not be spiteful. Instead be friends, be kind, be forgiving, be loving. It is when life goes against us that we will see how great is the faith we have been given.

In the stories of Irène Némirovsky we see our humanity in all its frailty. Sometimes people can be very brave. Sometimes people can be very selfish. In times of chaos, such as war and displacement, we are very helpless creatures. It is frightening to see how poor we can be, but it is also instructive.

We do well to realise our humble state and to find our strength in God and God's goodness. Without God's grace we are nothing. In God's grace we may find the power to love one another.

"Come and eat my bread, drink the wine I have prepared!"

Illustration

It's sometimes said that the advertisements in between television programmes are often more entertaining than the actual programmes themselves. In what is such a short space of time, the adverts can awaken our interest, capture our imagination, or tug at our emotions. Some of the most memorable ones are those clever enough to make us laugh, especially if it's at ourselves, or at the eccentricities of day-to-day living.

A few years ago an advert appeared on screen for a small, stylish city car. It took an unusual angle by leading the viewer to think one thing and then have to realise another. A number of images were played out in sequence. One showed a seasoned fisherman going out to sea on a trawler. He then held up a sign that said, "I feel seasick." The next image showed a tough-looking bouncer standing menacingly outside a nightclub. He then held up a sign saying "sensitive". A third image showed a baby fastened in the back seat of a car scribbling on a notepad. The notepad was then reversed to reveal a line of complex mathematical equations. Finally, the advert moved to a picture of the car being marketed. Underneath was the caption: "Sometimes what you see isn't all you get." The point being that just as there was much more to each of the three images than could be seen at first glance, so there was much more to the car being advertised than might at first have been thought.

Gospel Teaching

Writing to the Church at Ephesus, St Paul urged the Christian community to focus on the deeper meaning of their discipleship. They were to be careful about the kinds of lives they were leading. They shouldn't be known for superficial or thoughtless qualities. In word and deed they should convey a deeper sense of God's Spirit. They ought to be people of profound thankfulness, such that their gratitude might overflow into praise and worship of the Father. Like an advertisement for the Gospel, people should be able to look at them and see something more, see something of Christ's own life. This same sentiment is echoed in the book of Proverbs. Exterior foolishness is to be left behind, so that the truly wise person will be seen as the one who walks closely with God along the path of understanding. Both the first and second readings invite us to look beyond first impressions, to search deeper into the inner significance of our lives of faith.

Over the past few Sundays, we have heard Jesus describing himself as the bread that gives life to the world. Today's Gospel follows directly from this and, again, Jesus is the living bread that has come down from heaven. Such repetition is an indication of the importance of this phrase as a way for us to understand more about the significance of who Jesus is. That he is "bread" reveals him as the fundamental source of nourishment for our spiritual journey. He is the staple food that satisfies the hunger of our yearning for God. That Jesus is "living bread" reminds us that this is food for growth, the fuel of a continuous and intensifying process that reaches into eternity.

Application

Jesus' proclamation that whoever eats his flesh and drinks his blood will have eternal life is like an advertisement for every Mass. It would be impossible to hear Jesus' words and not think of the Last Supper. There Jesus took the bread, blessed, broke and gave it to his friends. There he took the cup, blessed it and shared it with them. Since that event, the Eucharist has been the place for us to taste and see that the Lord is good.

In words attributed to St Thomas Aquinas, the Eucharist is God with us here in hiding. It's an encounter where our senses – our seeing, touching and tasting – are all deceived. For the bread we eat is no mere bread, and the wine we drink is no mere wine – it has a deeper meaning. This is the real nourishment of Christ's body and blood, the source of everlasting life. The Eucharist is the reminder of Christ crucified and risen, the living bread where God is revealed as food and drink for life, as food and drink for love.

"Sometimes what you see isn't all you get." In the Eucharist we see bread and wine; what we encounter and receive is Jesus himself, the life of the world.

B

"Choose today whom you wish to serve."

Illustration

Oscar Williams (not his real name) was a foreign news correspondent for a major TV channel. He loved the buzz of excitement every time he ventured into a dangerous war zone. He enjoyed travelling to countries where tourists rarely ventured and sampling the real lives of the people who lived there, often sharing their meals and sleeping places. In short, nothing could separate him from this job of his dreams, for which he had studied and worked hard for years.

That is, until he met Sophie. She was not his first girlfriend, but she meant something to him in a way that no other girlfriend ever had. He was deeply in love, and wanted to marry her. Sophie felt pretty much the same way about him, but did not want to hold back his career. For Oscar's was a job never given to married people, only to single people with no dependants. He had known that from the beginning, but it had not bothered him before.

One day Oscar was called to the office of his programme producer and given a new assignment. Decision time. He decided to give his life over to Sophie, told the boss, and was offered a safe desk job. That was several years ago. He has never regretted the decision he made. His wife and family mean more to him than anything.

Gospel Teaching

In today's first reading, the Israelites are also summoned to decision time. As they enter the promised land after slavery in Egypt and then years of wandering the desert, they are presented with the choice of serving the one God, or pagan gods. Based on their experience of God, they make their emphatic choice, one that will set them at odds with all the peoples among whom they will live.

In the Gospel today the disciples are also at decision time. Until this point they had been learning about Jesus; now they must decide whether to follow him or not. Many choose not to – and Jesus allows them their free choice. The passage comes immediately after the discourse on the Eucharist, where Jesus talks of giving his flesh to eat and blood to drink. In his reply to those disciples who are scandalised by the talk of eating his flesh and drinking his blood, Jesus asks them, with deep irony, what they would make of his ascension to heaven.

John's Gospel treats Jesus' being raised up on the cross as a raising up in glory, as if it were his ascension. Whenever the Eucharist is spoken of in the early Church, it is always associated with the death of Jesus, the life-giving death for the world. When Jesus now talks of the flesh having nothing to offer, he means that our ordinary human powers can comprehend nothing without the Spirit of God, the giver of life. It is by the Spirit – not through human reason – that understanding dawns of who Jesus really is, and of the life he has come to bring.

Application

When Oscar made his choice, he was not merely contemplating Sophie's qualities – her generosity and kindness, her good humour and ready smile, and so on. He did not just put her at the head of a list of likeable girlfriends. He wanted to commit his life to her, to share good times and bad with her. In short, to love her, as Christ, as today's second reading reminds us, loves the Church, loves all of us.

When Peter, speaking for the twelve apostles, affirms his belief in Jesus, it is in terms of staying with him, following him, committing himself to him completely. So often the word "belief" can mean just accepting statements or doctrines as true, a mere matter of opinion. Yet what today's Gospel tells us about belief is that it is about travelling along with Christ, following him no matter where, being committed to listening to his words and to acting upon them.

As in a marriage both partners are called to sustain each other and depend upon each other trustfully, disciples of Christ, all of us, are called to enter into that sort of relationship with him. It will never be straightforward. The first flush of romantic love, or the enthusiasm of the new convert, will be tried, will pass and, please God, will be replaced with a deeper, more mature love. That love has no end – it is eternal. You, Lord, have the message of eternal life.

B

"Such a man will stand firm for ever."

Illustration

The musical *Fiddler on the Roof* opens with a striking scene: a lone man balances precariously on the top of a roof, playing his violin. This is a symbol of the life of the Jewish people living in Tsarist Russia – with all its dangers, hardships and problems. Tevye, the main character, equates their life with being a "fiddler on the roof" – they are trying to scratch out a cheery little tune without falling and breaking their neck.

"How do we keep our balance?" he asks. "That I can tell you in one word: Tradition! Every one of us knows who he is and what God expects him to do." There is a tradition for every activity, from what to wear to how to sleep. Following tradition is what enables the people to keep their balance – to survive and even have joy in their difficult lives. Tevye knows: "Without our traditions, our lives would be as shaky as a fiddler on the roof!"

Gospel Teaching

The Jewish people of Jesus' day were also living in perilous times. And they too clung to their religious tradition to help them survive. That tradition was, after all, given to them by God through Moses, as our first reading clearly indicates. And yet often, in the Gospels, Jesus was accused of rejecting that God-given tradition. But for Jesus it was the religious leaders who had got the balance wrong. They were focusing so much on the minute rules (the "human traditions"), which had gradually been added over the centuries to explain the Law of God, that they had lost sight of what the Law was for.

The Law had become an end in itself. People had lost sight of its original purpose: to help the people to live as God intended them to live. In that beautiful phrase, Moses said: "Observe [the laws]… that you may have life." That is what God wants – that we should have life, and have it to the full. The laws are given to help people to live fully, to live humanly, so that we can reach our full potential. They aim to prevent us settling for less, to stop us being less than human, less than God's children, in the way we conduct our lives.

Jesus didn't reject tradition. In fact, he was steeped in the Jewish tradition, as we see when he quotes the prophet Isaiah: "This people honours me only with lip-service, while their hearts are far from me." The kind of tradition that Jesus says is good and healthy is when people worship God with sincerity, in their hearts and in the way they live, not just with their prayers and external religious rituals. Prayer and worship are worthless if they are disconnected from the rest of life. What the Pharisees were upholding wasn't living tradition but dead traditionalism: doing things for the sake of doing them, because they've always been done that way; making laws more important than people; judging people by the externals; reducing religion to rule-keeping – worshipping God in the right way, saying the right prayers, mixing with the right people, eating the right food. These, as Jesus indicated, don't of themselves make you a good person, a holy person. True religion is about how you show your love and respect for God through your love and concern for your neighbour. That is the healthy balance – authentic tradition. Or, as St James put it: "Pure unspoilt religion… is this: coming to the help of orphans and widows… and keeping oneself uncontaminated by the world."

Application

What is it that contaminates us, makes us unclean, not truly religious? Jesus mentions a whole list of what he calls "evil intentions": "fornication, theft, murder, adultery, avarice, malice, deceit, indecency, envy, slander, pride, folly". These are all sins against our neighbour, ways of manipulating, using, deceiving or harming others. Simply keeping religious rules like worshipping in the right church, observing holy days and fasts, will not give us life or make us pure in God's eyes. What puts us into a healthy, life-giving relationship with God is when we treat our fellow men and women with kindness, consideration, respect, compassion and love. It is when we marry our inner convictions, the values we cherish, with our actions.

The heart of true religion is never mere external observance, and never simply other-worldly. Life-giving religion is grounded in daily reality and looks outwards to our neighbour. That is the tradition which gives life and leads to the promised land of God's kingdom.

B

"He has done all things well."

Illustration

James was nine, the eldest of seven children who lived in a one-bedroom flat on a poor housing estate. His mother was alcoholic and his father, who came and went, was violent. James was "closed". At school he would not take off his coat and he wore his hood over his head. He would not speak and when he communicated it was by kicking, spitting or punching. Though it was often difficult and frustrating, James' teacher refused to give up on the possibility that James could be different. She believed that though she could do nothing about his home life, school could become a safe place where there was a real possibility of growth and hope.

There are many such children in our world who suffer not only from physical poverty but from a lack of emotional well-being and care. The media tell us so many stories of people who are suffering or in trouble that we can succumb to a degree of indifference; we shut our eyes and close our ears to their pain because we feel helpless to do anything about it.

Gospel Teaching

Isaiah proclaims with confidence that God is coming and, when that time comes, "the eyes of the blind shall be opened, the ears of the deaf unsealed". In our Gospel today that time has come. It begins with Mark describing the strange and circuitous route that Jesus has made to reach the place where he heals the man who has a double affliction with his hearing and his speech.

The reason for recording this unusual route, through pagan territories, is perhaps as an indicator of the length of time it would take for the disciples to be open to the message of Christ's teaching. Jesus was not travelling alone. The disciples were walking with him, listening to him, watching and observing his behaviour as he gradually revealed his message to them. The message of Jesus was radically different from anything they had ever experienced, and so the ability to absorb all he shared with them was never going to happen overnight.

When they reach their destination, word has already spread and people are waiting for Jesus with a man whose condition symbolises the inability of many to make sense of the world around them. When Christ takes him away from the crowd he demonstrates a profound respect for the man's dignity as a person; and then through Christ's prayer and touch the man can at last hear and speak. The one who is healed discovers the link between what life has been and what life can be.

Application

With James it took many weeks and months before his healing took place. As his teacher worked kindly and patiently with him, the barriers that James had built around himself started to fall away. Slowly James began to trust. His coat came off, he stopped grunting and he began to hear the teacher's gentle words of encouragement. As he allowed himself to relax, so his confidence began to grow. He started to smile and eventually his kicking and punching diminished. Within a year James' aggression had melted and he seemed to find hope and joy in living once more.

There is no one on this planet who is not in need of some healing. For some it will be physical healing, but for many it will be the healing that we need when we have been hurt by life. Sometimes we will be aware of what it is, but for some there will simply be something they find it hard to identify that causes a general feeling of distress or unhappiness. It may be a worry or an anxiety about the future or about a family member or friend. It may be because there are unresolved issues or conflicts that are gnawing away inside.

A question for us to reflect on in the coming week might be: "What is stopping me from being fully able to sing and leap with joy?" as Isaiah tells us will happen when people are released from what imprisons them. The story of Jesus healing the man who could not speak or hear is also a story for us. Can we allow ourselves to be healed of our impairment and become instruments of that healing love in our families and community? Let us pray that in the coming week the love that God has for us will be revealed and God will heal us in our need. Then we will be able to rejoice and say, "He has done all things well."

B

"He began to teach them that the Son of Man was destined to suffer grievously."

Illustration

Joe greeted his mother as she arrived home. "Mum, I've got two bits of good news, and only one bit of bad news," he said. "The first bit of good news is that I checked the lottery results, and your numbers have won the jackpot! And the other bit of good news is that I gave that bag of old clothes to the charity collection, like you said." "That's great," said Joe's mother. "But what's the bad news?" "Well," said Joe, "the bad news is that I think your lottery ticket was in the pocket of that old pair of trousers you wanted to get rid of."

Gospel Teaching

In today's Gospel there's a good news/bad news story, but it's certainly no joke. Throughout the first half of Mark's Gospel everyone seems to be trying to discover who Jesus is. They've heard his powerful words, witnessed his mighty deeds, and they keep asking: "Who then is this?" The religious leaders say he's in the power of Beelzebul, prince of devils. Many of the people suspect he might be a prophet. As for the disciples, they're bewildered, now reacting with wonder and complete confidence in him, now questioning and unsure.

So the scene is set for the episode in Caesarea Philippi, way up in the north of the country. Jesus, alone with his closest friends, asks them who people think he is. They tell him the current views and then he asks: "Who do you say I am?" This is the beginning of the good news/bad news story. The good news is summed up in Peter's dramatic reply: "You are the Christ." At long last they've discovered the truth about Jesus: he is the long-awaited Messiah.

But immediately Jesus responds: "Say nothing of this to anyone." Peter may have got the good news about Jesus but he's not ready for the bad news; and it must have sounded like very bad news indeed. The disciples had discovered Jesus' identity; now they are to discover his destiny, for "he began to teach them that the Son of Man was destined to suffer grievously, to be rejected by the elders and the chief priests and the scribes, and to be put to death".

They'd always thought of the Messiah as a powerful, victorious figure. But a Messiah destined to suffer, to be rejected, to be put to death? A defeated Messiah, a humiliated Messiah, a dead Messiah? Peter's immediate reaction is to take Jesus aside and argue with him. Jesus' response is to rebuke Peter in words that must have shaken him to the core: "Get behind me, Satan!" Peter is playing the devil's game, trying to dissuade Jesus from the path he must tread – a path that, humanly speaking, he would much rather avoid. Yet he goes forward boldly towards Jerusalem and certain death.

Alexander the Great, one of the greatest military leaders of all time, once made an eleven-day forced march with his troops. They were exhausted and almost dying of thirst. Some of the soldiers managed to collect water from a stream in a helmet and took it to their leader. After a moment's hesitation, Alexander handed the helmet back, its contents untouched. He wouldn't ask his men to do anything he wouldn't do himself. His action had an electrifying effect: with a leader like this, the soldiers could overcome weariness and thirst. Indeed, says the writer who recorded this incident, they looked upon themselves "as little less than immortal".

Application

Today Jesus is putting the question to us: Who do you say I am? Do you accept me as your leader? I tell you the truth: being my true followers means you must deny yourselves, take up your cross and follow me, though I assure you I will never ask you to do anything that I am not prepared to do. I know that following me can sometimes seem like a kind of dying. But through my death and resurrection, which you are celebrating at this Mass, I assure you that victory is yours.

Alexander's soldiers may have thought they were immortal; but if we are faithful followers of Jesus Christ we are immortal. Though we must die in this world, we are destined for a heavenly life of a richness and fullness we've never known before, life never marred by tears or sorrows, but a life of perfect joy and one that lasts for ever. This is no good news/bad news story. This is sheer good news – the best news the world has ever heard.

"If anyone wants to be first, he must make himself last of all and servant of all."

Illustration

The fourteenth century was a time of frequent wars and bloodshed in the city states of Italy. It was so bad that a nobleman, Bernardo Tolomei, withdrew to an isolated mountain, Monte Oliveto, together with other like-minded men, to found a monastery. There, the community spent its time in prayer and religious life, far removed from the violence and evils of the world.

However, in 1348, the plague swept through the nearby city of Siena, and the community faced a choice of whether to stay in the security of their religious life or to come down from their mountain sanctuary. They decided they could not stand by, watching people suffer and die, without attempting in some way to alleviate their suffering. They came down from their monastery and, despite the risks to themselves, spent their time ministering to the sick and dying. More than eighty monks from the community were killed by the plague – a danger they had been only too aware of.

Gospel Teaching

There is always a cost involved in service. There is always a need for us to come down from our "spiritual mountain". On the mountain that Jesus' disciples had just left, some of them had seen Jesus transfigured – they had glimpsed his divinity as God's Son. They had wanted to remain there on the mountain – to build three tents, three shrines to prolong that marvellous religious experience. But they had to come down – to leave that experience behind. Jesus wanted to explain to his disciples the nature of his mission, and that this would inevitably lead to him paying the cost of his life.

But the disciples are slow to understand, even though Jesus specifically takes them away from the crowds to teach them. And they are afraid to ask what he means. Perhaps they dare not ask because of the last time Jesus spoke of his impending death: Peter had protested that this must not happen, and, for his pains, Jesus had called him "Satan", accusing him of thinking as human beings think, not as God thinks. But perhaps the disciples simply prefer not to know what Jesus is talking about. He keeps referring to suffering and death, whereas they are obviously more interested in who is the greatest. They wonder which of them will get the important jobs, the key positions, in the kingdom, which they are sure Jesus, as the Messiah, is about to establish in Jerusalem.

The penny hasn't dropped about the true nature of discipleship. They think it is about glory, prestige and power. Jesus speaks simply in terms of service – and of the cost of service. It is as if the disciples are still up there on their religious mountain, refusing to come down to face the consequences – and the cost – of their faith in Christ.

Application
What does Jesus' teaching about the need to be "servant of all" and to welcome little children mean for us today? In the society of Jesus' day, a child was someone of no legal status – in a sense, an unimportant person. And so anything done to or for a child was done simply for the sake of the child, without hope of reward or advantage. This was an opportunity to show genuine, disinterested love, unfeigned respect.

This is to be the hallmark of Christ's disciples: that we will love without hope of profit or reward; that we will respect the intrinsic dignity and worth of others, no matter what their position, power or wealth. God loves unconditionally. When we love like that, then we are not just loving like God, we are loving God. In welcoming those who are lowest and least important, we are – in a very real way – welcoming and worshipping God. We are coming down from our religious mountain and putting our faith into practice.

There is always a price to be paid for true service. Love is not cost-free, even though that is an illusion that we – like the disciples – like to maintain. But Christ's teaching about the need to be prepared to suffer and die also contains the promise that this road leads to the glory of the resurrection. Like the monks of Oliveto, we have to decide if we want the illusion of pure, unsullied religion, or whether we are ready to get our hands dirty in serving real people in real situations, no matter what the cost. That is the only way to offer real love to God, and the only way to enter real, eternal life.

B

"No one who works a miracle in my name is likely to speak evil of me."

Illustration

Where can we find good role models in our modern world? Whose words do we admire for their wisdom and hope? Whose actions impress us with their compassion?

These questions were asked of a group of young Catholics attending a retreat. Their replies surprised their teachers, who had been expecting them to focus on Catholic role models. Mother Teresa's name was mentioned and her inspirational work in India caring for poor people in the Calcutta slums; also Pope John Paul II, who had faith that young people could play a positive role in Church and society. But many of the names were people who were not Catholic, indeed not even Christian.

For example, they talked of Martin Luther King, the African American Baptist leader prominent in the American civil rights movement. In 1964 he became the youngest person to receive the Nobel Peace Prize for his commitment to end racial segregation without using violence. They mentioned Mahatma Gandhi, an Indian Hindu who believed in political change through non-violence; and the Dalai Lama, a Buddhist spiritual leader who promotes peace internationally. Pop stars and actors who support justice campaigns on cancelling international debt, fair trade and climate change also struck a chord with the young people.

Is it a matter of concern that young people look up to figures who, in Catholic terms, are not one of us, some of whom may even have little time for organised religion?

Gospel Teaching

In today's Gospel one phrase is repeated twice: "not one of us". The apostle John is indignant that a man outside of their circle is casting out devils. "Because he was not one of us we tried to stop him," John tells Jesus. But Jesus stuns the disciples by telling them that they have no monopoly on the healing power of Jesus. "Anyone who is not against us is for us," he says. Shortly before this incident, the apostles themselves had been unsuccessful in trying to exorcise an unclean spirit from a young man. Now they were upset to see someone outside their circle being more successful.

From John's words, it appears that the apostles are trying to restrict Jesus' influence to their own small circle. They feel that the healing work of Jesus should be confined to them. They want something others don't have – perhaps to be honoured for it and to exercise power over others. Jesus makes clear that he does not support restricting God's power for good. Wherever evil is eradicated, the work has God's blessing.

This same message is given by Moses in today's Old Testament reading. Joshua contends that the Lord's spirit of prophecy can only enter those individuals who were "in the gathering" when that spirit was bestowed. Moses teaches that prophetic ministry can be exercised by anyone.

Application
The mission of healing and saving humanity and the world is not the sole responsibility of the disciples, or, in today's world, of clergy, or of Catholics. It is a mission that is entrusted to everyone. Jesus does not want to close the circle around him. As long as healing and reconciliation are taking place, Jesus does not draw boundaries. His followers are called to cooperate with all those in the world who are promoting human dignity, assisting those who are vulnerable and taking responsibility for building a more just world.

This is why Christian agencies have worked with Muslim relief agencies in Pakistan to bring humanitarian aid to earthquake victims; why Pope John Paul II met with pop stars Bob Geldof and Bono in 1999 to support the campaign for the debts of poor countries to be cancelled; why Christian campaigners against nuclear weapons rub shoulders with secular anti-nuclear organisations. In many local areas, churches link with secular bodies and other faiths in soup runs and schemes for befriending vulnerable people.

Jesus asks a lot of us here. Be easy on others, give them the benefit of the doubt, assume that God is working in them. Do not seek the prestige of wealth, possessions and power for yourself, and refuse to exploit others. Instead, demand simplicity, honesty and repentance as you push towards spiritual growth. God's Spirit is within our family and neighbours, and perhaps we can learn to recognise the prophets among us and listen to them.

Perhaps too we can begin to recognise the prophet deep inside our own selves that cautions us to be kind and gracious, not to support the waging of war and not to hurt or diminish the least among us.

B

"This is why a man leaves his father and mother and joins himself to his wife, and they become one body."

Illustration

Julia was excited at the prospect of her new job, teaching fifteen- and sixteen-year-olds a variety of subjects, including religion. She had passed her own exams at college with flying colours. She was young and attractive and was familiar with the culture of the day. She was looking forward to the challenge of helping other young people fulfil their dreams and she was especially excited at the prospect of trying to share her faith with them, when it seemed that so many others saw the teaching of religion as an impossible burden.

Nevertheless, nothing could have prepared her for what she was actually to encounter. The young people did indeed find her attractive and soon began to confide in her. There was Maria, the tormented soul who sat at the back, her face etched with frustration and anger: it transpired she had been appallingly abused by a close member of her family from early childhood. There was Stephen, a sullen and disruptive student, who countered his innate shyness by asserting himself whenever the opportunity arose. There was Brian, a confused young man with a chip on his shoulder, who had all the answers. She calculated that almost 50 per cent of her pupils were living either with a single parent or with a step-parent. Among the many subjects to be covered in that first term was Christian marriage. How on earth could she broach the subject with this group of people, many of whom were already scarred for life because of the unhappy marriages of their parents?

Gospel Teaching

Thank God, Julia was bright and capable. She quickly realised that before she looked at Jesus' teaching on marriage, she would need to convince these young people of his unconditional love for each of them and their families in all the mess that surrounded them and the society in which they were all struggling to cope and, hopefully, one day to make their mark. They looked at how Jesus dealt with people who came to him with different afflictions – physical, mental and spiritual – and they noted how he responded to them with love and compassion. What Julia may not have realised was that the person of Jesus was having a real influence on these youngsters, not so much because of what they learnt about him, but because of the love and compassion they realised she had for them.

When the time came for her to talk to them about Jesus' teaching on marriage, she was able to put it into context. Jesus was not going to be caught out by the Pharisees, but neither was he going to short-change his listeners. He stood by the teaching of the ancient scripture in Genesis that men and women were made for each other: they are called to be united as one body. But this would not be something that they could or would achieve by themselves. Such unity comes when we are also united with Christ and can treat each other with his love and compassion. As today's reading from the letter to the Hebrews reminds us, this was why Jesus lived among us: to share our sufferings so that we might become holy and share his glory.

Application

Although many in her class told Julia that they would never get married, saying that in their experience it was a recipe for disaster, deep down some of them were promising themselves that they would not make the same mistakes as their parents. In reality they dreamt of finding someone who would make them happy and with whom they could share their life and their love.

In this community gathered for Mass today, there are a thousand untold stories. We rejoice with those of you enjoying the ups and downs of life in stable and happy marriages, and pray that the Lord will continue to strengthen you and bless your homes and families. For those of you who are struggling to cope with the aftermath of divorce or separation, or who find yourselves in far-from-perfect circumstances of one kind or another, we hope and pray that you discover in this community the understanding and compassionate face of Christ. For him, no situation is beyond redemption.

Perhaps we might usefully spend a few quiet moments reflecting on how we as individuals and as a community could better support the families of our parish. Likewise we might ask whether we could be doing more to help those who are trying to rebuild their lives and families after the breakdown of their marriages.

B

"Everything is possible for God."

Illustration

A young student was talking to a group from the West about his experiences behind the Iron Curtain in Eastern Europe when the Church was still very much underground. He shared with them how the community took great risks to meet in quiet places to celebrate the Eucharist. If they had been found out, life would have been very difficult, if not impossible. Yet somehow they had come through it and supported each other.

A listener suggested that things must have changed now that the churches have been given back and people are free to meet. The young man agreed he was thankful that the old totalitarian regimes had gone. But he added that in a strange sort of way they had also lost something: the something that comes when we don't carry any extra baggage, when following Jesus means simply that we share our lives with others in his name.

Gospel Teaching

The man who seeks out Jesus in today's Gospel obviously makes an impression on the disciples. What is it that makes him so memorable? He's wealthy and also a man of some standing. If he were to join their number it might bring them a degree of security and respectability. He is genuinely seeking the truth about himself and about life, and approaches Jesus with a confidence that could be taken for arrogance. He is an observant and practising Jew, but hungers after something more.

He is looking for an insight into Jesus and the kingdom, but is offered much more than he bargained for. With a look of love, Jesus shows him how to be free. A whole life is reflected in those eyes. For the would-be disciple, wealth is tied up with belonging to the right family, being entitled to some precious land and, perhaps more importantly, being accepted in society as someone of worth. He is offered both a challenge and a question.

The challenge is to drop the false image that he hides behind, move beyond himself and enter into a new and personal relationship with Christ. The challenge is to step away from the easy certainties that come with status and privilege; to let go of the things that define his life, moving from the mere practice of religion into a new and vibrant faith where God can make all things possible for him. The challenge is to share his life with others.

The question is whether he is willing to accept that he is vulnerable; whether he can acknowledge that he can't find all the answers on his own; whether he can enter into a time of searching, depending on others to help rebuild his life in this kingdom, where everything is turned around and made new.

What makes this meeting unique is that he departs from the gaze of Jesus sad. There are many reactions towards Jesus, but people don't usually leave dejected. The man cannot find it within him to openly admit that he is weak. He returns to his possessions and status, the false image that now imprisons him, the baggage that holds him back.

Application

We don't know how his story ends, but perhaps we should not be worried about one whom Christ loved so much. We do know that the Word of God, who is Jesus, helped the enquirer to meet his real self just as he can help us to see ourselves in the clear light of day. The true knowledge, sought after by the author of the book of Wisdom, comes in the encounter with the Word of God. This is not always a comfortable experience. Getting close to Jesus means getting close to others, examining our own motives. This can change us. As we gather around God's table together, let's drop our pretences and bring our true selves to God.

It is difficult for us to give up what holds us back, but that is what we are called to do in this new kingdom. We are called from fear and isolation, into community; from conformity and simple observance into a new life together. Just like Mark's young, persecuted Church, the young student from the East found true community and strength even in the face of hostility. Let's remember that it is not the splendour of our buildings, nor the accuracy of our doctrines, that makes us powerful: it's our reliance on God's word and on each other, helping to build the kingdom out of our weakness and God's strength. For nothing is impossible to God.

B

"The cup that I must drink you shall drink, and with the baptism with which I must be baptised you shall be baptised."

Illustration

An old folk tale, found in many languages, tells the story of a poor woodman who was poised to chop down a tree when he heard the voice of a woodland spirit calling to him. "Please do not destroy this tree, for it is my home," said the spirit. "If you spare the tree, I will grant you three wishes." The woodman lowered his axe and the tree was saved.

That night, back in their humble cottage, the woodman told his wife what had happened. The wife was excited to hear of the three wishes. "So what will you wish for?" she asked. The woodman was hungry. "I wish that there was a sausage on my plate," he declared. And in a flash there appeared on his empty plate a delicious-looking sausage.

His wife, however, was furious. "You fool!" she said. "You could have used your precious wish to ask for riches or treasure, instead of this stupid sausage. I wish the sausage was on your nose!" Immediately there was a flash of light, and the sausage was no longer on the plate but stuck fast to the woodman's nose. And of course they had to use their third and final wish to have the sausage removed.

This of course is just a story, but the point is a good one. We should be careful what we wish for. Sometimes in getting what we want we can hurt others, disappoint ourselves and realise that we wanted something else all along.

Gospel Teaching

In today's Gospel, James and John are unwise in what they wish for. Jesus gives them every chance to get themselves out of trouble and tells them directly, "You do not know what you are asking." James and John imagine a kingdom of earthly power where they will be rulers. Even when Jesus asks them if they can drink his cup and share his baptism they rashly claim that they can. We might be reminded of St Peter declaring absolutely that he will never desert Jesus, not long before he denies him three times.

Here James and John reveal their ambition. But it seems they want "the bonus without the onus", as the saying goes. Jesus grants them their wish, but not in the way they expect. They will share the cup, the cup of his sufferings. They will share in his baptism, the baptism of his death, and no earthly reward will be theirs.

True discipleship, then, will involve suffering and even dying for Christ, and only then will there be a share in glory. Not the glory of this world, but that of eternal life with God. Jesus also teaches that as well as suffering, service is the hallmark of discipleship. Unlike the "so-called" rulers of the pagans, the apostles will live lives of service: service of God and service of neighbour. It is Christ himself who gives us this pattern, as, fulfilling the prophecy of Isaiah, he gives his life as a ransom for humanity, in loving obedience to the will of the Father.

Application
Our journey of faith is leading us to eternal life with God. On the way we are given the opportunity to build up God's kingdom and serve our neighbours. So first of all we are called to get our desires sorted out. If we go after the wrong things, or think that something or someone in this world will make us totally happy, we are sadly deceived.

Through the incarnation, God has shown us the way to eternal life. Christ our high priest has opened that way for us. He also knows the ways in which we are tempted, and how we can choose lesser goods over what is really true and good. Yet Christ still loves us, and continues to give himself to us in the sacraments. By living a sacramental life in the Church, we become conformed to Christ, and grow in his love. Through the gift of the Spirit, and the sacrament of confirmation, we are given the gifts of wisdom, understanding and knowledge. These can help lead us in the right direction on our journey of faith.

Like James and John, we sometimes fail to want the right thing, and, like them, the Lord teaches us and makes us his disciples, even despite ourselves. Through the sacraments we are renewed in heart and mind; and, in the words of one of the prayers in the Missal, are helped to love the things of heaven, and judge wisely the things of earth.

B

"What do you want me to do for you?"

Illustration

One of the most loved spiritual classics of the Russian Orthodox Church is called *The Way of a Pilgrim*. It purports to be the spiritual autobiography of a Russian peasant who lived in the middle of the nineteenth century. The author is not so much a pilgrim journeying to holy places as a wanderer over the face of the earth.

In Russian spirituality such a mixture of wandering and simplicity of life is revered because it reflects the early Christian ideals of spiritual freedom and detachment from the world. The choice of such a simple figure as the Pilgrim was intended to speak to all that was important to the Russian soul. He meets all sorts of characters on his journey, and his tale contrasts the Gospel life lived by these different members of society with the surrounding scenes of cruelty and violence, which are unsparingly portrayed as well. The Pilgrim's avowed aim is to expound the "Jesus Prayer" – "Lord Jesus Christ, Son of God, have mercy on me, a sinner" – as the source of spirituality for lay people as they go about their lives. His story also reveals the reverence with which he, the wandering peasant, is received by the true believers. The one who seems to have nothing is recognised as the one who is closest to the truths of Christian life and discipleship.

Gospel Teaching

During the Gospel readings of recent Sundays we have seen the disciples of Jesus failing to understand the true nature of discipleship. First the disciples could not comprehend Jesus' prophecy of his passion; then there was the young man who could not let go of his possessions; then the sons of Zebedee were eager to claim positions of power at Jesus' right hand.

After this catalogue of misunderstandings, Mark gives us an outstanding example of true discipleship. It is Bartimaeus, the blind beggar. Bartimaeus recognises Jesus for who he is, the Son of David, and, despite the crowd's attempts to put him off, he shouts out to him for mercy. Jesus stops and calls him to him. Bartimaeus throws off his beggar's cloak, his means of livelihood, the only thing he has in the world, and jumps up to go to Jesus. Jesus asks him the same question he has just asked James and John: "What do you want me to do for you?" The sons of Zebedee had asked him for positions of power. Bartimaeus asks for the restoration of his sight. The true disciple asks to see clearly and knows that he needs the power of the master to be able to do this.

Jesus acknowledges this plea as the sign of Bartimaeus' faith, the faith he has been preaching as the essential prerequisite for healing and insight into the truth. With his sight restored, Bartimaeus completes the pattern of discipleship. He follows Jesus along the road to Jerusalem. In other words, he takes up the way of life revealed by Jesus, which will lead to suffering and death. The chapter ends, and in the first line of the next chapter Jesus begins his approach to Jerusalem.

Application

One of the errors the Church has always resisted is that of Gnosticism, the claim that closeness to Christ depends on being a member of an elite group with special knowledge. The first step in discipleship is that of not knowing, the simplicity expressed by Bartimaeus the blind beggar, or the homelessness of the wanderer. True disciples lay no claim to being special. But something special happens to them through their encounter with Jesus.

The next step is that we place ourselves under his healing power. Sometimes, like Bartimaeus, we have to fling off even the little we have, our cloaks, our means of livelihood, what offers us fame and fortune in the world. But, in the act of healing, the great gift we receive is that of freedom. We are no longer bound by the burden of worldly expectations. Rather we are freed to follow Jesus in his dance along the road, a road of constant challenges.

The question Jesus continues to ask on the journey is the one he put to Bartimaeus: "What do you want me to do for you?" At times we can persecute ourselves with guilt or anxiety because we feel we are not doing enough for Jesus. Once again we have it the wrong way round. Jesus wants to know what he can do for us. As we answer the question, we hopefully make the same response as Bartimaeus and ask that we too may see.

B

"There is no commandment greater than these."

Illustration

In Oxford, England, there is a Catholic Worker House, part of the international Catholic Worker movement. It is a Christian community in which love of God and love of neighbour are at the heart of everything.

Every morning, the three people who live at the Oxford house spend time in prayer and reflection. They do this to keep in close touch with the life and teachings of Jesus as recorded in the Gospels. They also believe that the Spirit of God is within every person, and so time is spent quietly discerning God's will in guiding their lives.

As for love of neighbour, the community offers hospitality to people in need. A couple of spare bedrooms are given over to destitute asylum seekers. The house is also an open-door home where people who are lonely, needy or just looking for some company can enjoy a cup of tea and a warm welcome. The community also believes that living an environmentally sustainable lifestyle and working for peace are an important service to neighbours in the wider community. Members grow their own vegetables on an allotment, borrow or buy things second-hand and travel without a car. The community also involves itself in peace activities, particularly vigils and protests against the expansion of nuclear weapons establishments in the Oxford area.

Gospel Teaching

In today's Gospel, Jesus is asked by a scribe to settle what was at that time a regular dispute among rabbis: which commandment is the greatest? Jewish law contained over six hundred different regulations, and it was common for scholars to try to distil them into fewer, more fundamental principles. How does Jesus respond? "Love the Lord your God with all your heart, with all your soul, with all your mind and with all your strength." He then says that the second great commandment is to "love your neighbour as yourself". He tells the scribe that he is close to the kingdom of God because he realises that love of God and of neighbour is more important than the religious observances at the Temple.

Yet how do we express our love for God and neighbour? Despite so many of our songs and hymns and sermons being devoted to the subject of loving God, how do we actually do it in practical terms? Jesus does the best job of explaining what loving God means in the second of his great commands: "love your neighbour as yourself". Loving our neighbours is something we can tangibly do on a daily basis. And it seems that by loving our neighbours as ourselves, we are also loving God. The two commandments are linked. Jesus clearly had a broad understanding of who exactly the neighbour is; for him it included people in need, strangers and even enemies. It simply does not make sense to say you love God and are following Jesus, and not to love and live for others.

Application

There is a clear challenge here for the priorities in our individual lives, and indeed in our churches. Though false gods and idolatry may seem a thing of the past, let us reflect on how we spend our resources and our time. This will reveal where we place our faith. Perhaps we idolise things other than God – money, personal property, celebrities. It is easy for our faith to wither amidst selfishness and materialism. This is why the first reading too, from Deuteronomy, asks us to hold tight to loving God.

What do our bank balances and diaries reveal? Do we spend our time and money on life-giving things for ourselves, or for others? Do we worship the living God with living works – such as reaching out to the homeless, or lobbying for justice – or are our hearts set on things that are merely material or even destructive? These are just a few of the barometers by which our false gods are revealed, and clearly the temptation to idolatry is just as strong now as it was at the time of Jesus. We will only be able to love as Jesus loves if we are free from idols.

We are also called as a church community to reflect upon our priorities. How do we communicate our church's priorities to members and to the surrounding community? How far do we regard those suffering in other parts of the world as our neighbours – in need of more than occasional charity? If we feel we have a relationship with the whole of humanity, then work for global justice and peace may become a more significant part of church outreach.

B

"Rain on the face of the earth."

Illustration

It was a country road in Ireland fifty years ago. Sheep were being loaded into a lorry for market. In the glen an old woman stood at her farmhouse door, watching the operation. It was strange to her. She turned to her son and asked him what was happening. "They are loading sheep for market," he told her. "Well, I have seen everything now," the old woman replied. "It is no wonder that the young people will not walk a few miles to Mass on Sunday, when even the sheep are getting a lift into town!"

The old woman had walked everywhere during her long life. She walked her land to see to her cattle. She walked the road to Mass. She walked across bogland, eight miles to visit her relations by the sea. She was married for twenty years, and a widow for forty years. In that time she had struggled to bring up a family, in the days when Ireland was poor, and there was no social assistance to help. But she managed it.

She was a woman of great courage. Hardship and poverty had shaped her life. She was a strong character, and her voice was full of authority. Her family loved her – children, grandchildren and great-grandchildren. She was, to them, a great example of goodness, kindness and faith in God. When she died, they said of her, "Nan – she was mighty!"

Gospel Teaching

Sitting beside the Temple treasury today, Jesus catches sight of a widow. At the time Jesus is indulging in a spot of "people-watching". It can be quite fascinating to see the variety of human beings passing by, and their differing styles. Religious officials in long robes make an impressive sight. People bow and make way for them. They are important people. Then the widow comes along. Nobody takes any notice of her. In fact, Jesus has to call the attention of his disciples to this nobody, dropping a few copper coins into the collection box. There is something he wants to say about this sight.

What Jesus says is quite startling. This woman has given more than anyone. It is a paradox. It is the very opposite of what appears to be happening. Jesus is telling us, "Look carefully at what is really going on here." Well-to-do people are giving very generous donations to keep the system of religion going. This poor woman is placing her entire trust in God, because she has no one else to rely on. It is not the same activity at all.

The widow is teaching us a lesson from life. What money she has is very little, but she knows that money alone will not save her, or bring her comfort. Her life is in God's hands. She knows this. The disposition of her heart is to be generous. She trusts that God will not fail her. She prays for God's kingdom to come. She prays for daily bread. She prays for the grace to live in peace with others, and to be delivered from all evil.

Application
One day when Jesus was preaching to the people, a woman in the crowd was so impressed with him that she shouted out, "Blessed is the womb that bore you!" It was an early shout of praise for Mary, the mother of Jesus: Mary, the young girl of Nazareth, who also became a widow. It was a tribute to her womanly heart, and her motherly guidance of this eloquent preacher from Galilee.

In response to this cry, Jesus took the occasion to say, "Blessed are those who hear the word of God and keep it!" Our spiritual kinship with Jesus is even more important than the flesh-and-blood ties of earthly life. The Lord is reminding us that every day, as long as this today lasts, is a day to listen to what the Lord is saying to us. It is not for us to presume that we know everything there is to know. Each day is a day to grow in our knowledge and service of the Lord.

In times of hardship, in sad and sorrowful times, it is tempting to forget about the Lord. That is when we may need to listen to widows, those brave women who have known loss, and who have persevered in the love of God. "Jar of meal shall not be spent, jug of oil shall not be emptied, before the day when the Lord sends rain on the face of the earth."

"Take the fig tree as a parable."

Illustration

Throughout human history the art of storytelling has developed in many cultures as a way of keeping the past alive and comforting the people when the future looked bleak. Every country has its heroes and heroic stories.

An example of this can be found in the stories surrounding William Wallace, an early Scottish leader, who managed to unite the clans in their self-identity and rouse them to fight off the forces occupying his country. His short-lived rebellion was ultimately put down, yet even today his name continues to inspire a passion in his country, and the myths surrounding his achievements have grown with the centuries. A 1995 film, *Braveheart*, captures something of this, as Wallace rallies his small band of followers before a battle in which many of them will undoubtedly die. He convinces them that, in spite of the fate awaiting them, no one can take away their inner freedom.

Gospel Teaching

On some occasions a people or nation is called upon to stand up for the values it holds dear. This may cause hardship or even lead to wars in defence of human rights and religious freedoms. This was the position the Jewish people found themselves in when the book of Daniel was written. The writer sought to unite his people and offer them some solace. The faithful were under pressure from a military force, but also in a more insidious way, from the temptation to renounce their faith and blend into the crowd. Belief in the God of the Jews, and its corresponding way of life, did not seem politically correct in a world where expediency had replaced commitment. In every generation, the danger is that values remain valid only as long as those who shape public opinion deem them to be viable.

It is against this ever-changing landscape that Daniel proclaims the true destination of all our human longings. It is the Lord who has formed each of us for fullness of life with him.

Jesus of Nazareth would have been familiar with the imagery and comforting message of a bright new future, contained in the stories of his people and expressed in the book of Daniel, written about 150 years before his birth. He too lived in restless times under occupation. Yet, in a world much more connected to the earth and the changing of the seasons, Jesus talked about the signs of spring as an indication of our liberation. The words of today's Gospel were written to reassure a Christian people suffering persecution that the end would come soon, heralded by great cosmic signs. The truth is that, as Jesus himself says, no one knows for sure when these things may occur, not even the Son of Man himself.

What is certain is that through one sure and final redemptive act, we are for ever set free from our burden of sin, and are offered the possibility of eternal life. The only price for people of faith is that they trust in the saving power of a God who calls them by name, and for the moment play their part in the divine author's plan for humanity.

Application

As we act out the human story of our time, can we discern similar attitudes to those faced by the Jews in the book of Daniel? On the whole our Western society seems unsure of itself. Some seem to be turning to superficial forms of spirituality that offer easy answers with no commitment. We have a choice: accept the prevailing culture and its attendant confusion, or be a people of vision, a people who attempt to discern the signs of the times for ourselves and the world around us. Christ offers us a chance to be truly free, to glimpse the future possibilities and present reality of his kingdom working in our world.

As a community of faith, we are called to go beyond the superficial, and be alert to our world in the light of Christ, knowing that he is already saving the world. As the Church, that does not mean always rushing to condemn those around us. Nor does it mean simply waiting for the end times. Perhaps we are called in some way to be the signs of his life and freedom here and now, even if that means swimming against the tide. Discerning his presence means highlighting and supporting the good that we detect in our world. And, with his help, planting the seeds of hope around us that they might flower into the presence of God in our midst.

"Jesus… made us a line of kings, priests to serve his God and Father."

Illustration

There is a mid-fourteenth-century English poem called *The Pearl* in which a man's only daughter dies before she is two years old. He wanders about in the garden where she is buried, unable to control his grief. Then he has a vision where he sees a river, and, beyond it, a beautiful flowery garden in which a young woman is seated. This is his daughter, now grown to maturity. She chides him for missing her, for she is enjoying the delights of heaven. She explains that she is now a heavenly queen. "How can that be?" he asks. The Virgin Mary, she explains, is the Queen of courtesy, while she is queen by the courtesy of God, like all the blessed in heaven: all are kings and queens.

This idea is reflected in one of the traditions of the Orthodox Church. In their weddings, the bride and groom have crowns, or *stefana*, held above their heads, signifying the glory and honour with which God crowns them. In another example, at the end of the Narnia Chronicles by C.S. Lewis, generally recognised as Christian allegory, the central characters, the children, are given crowns.

Gospel Teaching

The image of the king and monarchy is a powerful one. In biblical times, monarchs in the countries around Israel were held to represent gods on earth, or at least to be intermediaries between the people and their gods. Many, such as the Pharaohs in Egypt, were despotic tyrants. God wanted the chosen people to govern themselves differently and, in the Old Testament, we see that God was at first reluctant to let the Israelite people have kings. However, they were allowed first Saul, and after him David, then Solomon. Following Solomon, the country divided, and kingship began to diminish in importance until it was eventually replaced. Temple priests and the people as a whole became the intermediaries, inheriting the promises God had made to the kings. The hope was kept alive, however, that one day a priestly king would arise who could lead his people back to the true faith in God.

Christ was recognised by his faithful as that special king, but human categories are never enough to describe the workings of God. What

Christ inaugurated was no simple earthly monarchy, but the messianic age itself. This age, this kingdom, will one day be fully and completely brought about by Christ's second coming. Often during Mass we make the acclamation "Christ has died" – using the past tense as an event in history; "Christ is risen" – as an ever-present event; and "Christ will come again" – a hope for the future. But it is not an entirely future experience. Because Christ came into the world, as a baby in Bethlehem, and because he rose from death at the first Easter, that kingdom is a reality in our world, and elements of it are discernible even now. All truth, all genuine love and all sincere compassion are signs of that kingdom in the here and now. This feast today, on the last Sunday in the Church's year, is a bridge between the two greatest celebrations in the calendar – Easter and Christmas – drawing them together with a reminder of Christ the King, bringer-in of the kingdom where all will be given crowns.

Application

The first reading today describes the people in the kingdom as being servants of God. The second, like the medieval poem, depicts them as kings. But there is really no difference between the two images. The servant-king is the most apt description of Christ, the "first fruits" of all who enter the kingdom. To be a servant-king is what inspires the Christian life. What are the characteristics of a servant-king? Well, in the play *Macbeth*, Shakespeare makes a list of qualities of kingship, or "king-becoming graces" as he calls them: "justice, verity, temperance, stableness, bounty, perseverance, mercy, lowliness, devotion, patience, courage, fortitude". Quite a standard to live up to – but nothing that should be beyond the capacity of each and every Christian who aspires to wear the heavenly crown.

This sort of kingship helps to describe how our dominion, or kingly rule, is to be exercised over creation. We are told at the beginning of Genesis that we have been given dominion, or kingly rule, over all other creatures. To be tyrants like Pharaoh? No. To be servants, like Christ. This is the challenge with which we are presented. The kingdom of which Christ is king seeks only the genuine happiness of others.

Sundays in Ordinary Time Year C

"There was a wedding."

Illustration

For most people, their wedding is the most important and life-changing event they experience, so important that they go to a huge amount of effort and expense to make sure that the day is an unforgettable experience. It has been calculated that the average wedding takes more than 250 hours to plan, and the average cost of an American wedding has been estimated at between $16,000 and $19,000, though the most expensive wedding is reckoned to have cost $44.5 million, and the biggest wedding had 150,000 guests present.

We splash out on weddings as a way of making a statement about who we are, and what we hope for the future life of the couple. The circle of the gold wedding band symbolises never-ending love; the confetti expresses a desire for fertility and an abundance of good fortune. Weddings speak of who we are, of our ideals, our hopes for the future, especially our desire for love, security, and a full and happy life.

Gospel Teaching

Many of those themes come together in our readings today. The image of a wedding is frequently used in the Old Testament to describe the relationship of the Lord and his people – God is Israel's husband, as Isaiah tells us, though often Israel is an unfaithful bride, who breaks her vows to her husband, worshipping false gods. And time and again God forgives her, turning her sadness into joy, as in today's first reading.

In the time of Jesus, the people's longing for the coming of the Messiah was often expressed in terms of a wedding: the days of the Messiah would be a time of great rejoicing, a wedding feast, with an abundance of wine and celebration. That is the context of today's Gospel. The abundance of wine at a wedding tells us that the days of the Messiah have arrived. The Lord's blessings are once again being poured out on his people, because the real groom – Jesus – has arrived to marry his bride, Israel.

Despite this rejoicing, the event is tinged with the shadow of the cross. Like all Jesus' signs, it points towards to the greatest of all signs: the glory of Jesus on the cross, saving the world through his perfect obedience to the Father, since this is how the Lord's relationship with his people is restored.

This is how the new covenant – the new marriage between God and God's people – is brought about. There are many hints of the cross in this story. Jesus speaks of his "hour" having not yet come, which is a reference to his death, when his glory would be fully revealed. Significantly, Jesus' mother is involved here in Cana, addressed by Jesus with the honorific title "woman". The only other time this happens is at the foot of the cross. The cross is the ultimate blessing the Lord can give his people: it is the source of eternal life to all who believe. So the 180 gallons of wine are indicative of the inexhaustible riches God the Father pours out on those who believe in the Son he has sent. This first sign does indeed produce faith: the disciples see his glory and believe in him.

Application

Just as a wedding is a sign of who we are and what we hope for in life – love, security, abundance of good things – so Cana is a sign of what the Lord offers us, his people who put our faith in him. Through the death of his Son, he offers us more than we could ever dream of – not simply the gifts of the Spirit Paul mentions, to help us in our daily lives, but the very fullness of life and love.

What the Lord asks of us is that we believe, as the disciples did, in Jesus' power to change our lives and to lead us to God. It is through faith in God that the water of our daily life can be transformed into something far superior. Our lives gain a new depth and meaning, a new quality, if we enter into this covenant, this marriage with God, which Jesus makes possible. Mary, as the first disciple, shows us how to do this: by doing whatever he tells us. And in John's Gospel that simply boils down to believing in Jesus and loving as he has loved us. Faith and love – all that is needed for a good marriage; all that God requires of us to have the fullness of life.

C

*"Jesus, with the power of the Spirit in him,
returned to Galilee."*

Illustration

In 1943 Pope Pius XII issued an encyclical letter about the Church. It was called *Mystici Corporis Christi*, "The Mystical Body of Christ". This letter reflected the teaching of St Paul that we hear today. Jesus is the head of the body and we are its members. The Pope spoke about the love of Christ for every member of his Church, and of the love by which we are called to esteem and value one another. This beautiful teaching was being given at a time when the whole world was locked into the most brutal and bloodthirsty war in the history of humankind. Beginning in Europe, but quickly spreading all over the globe, the Second World War trapped people in a frightening grip of mutual destructiveness. If ever there was an ironic contrast between theory and practice, it was this letter and that war.

In Germany itself, in the very centre of that dreadful conflict, the Catholic Bishop of Münster faithfully tended his flock. His name was Clemens von Galen. A bishop since 1933, he had spoken out against Hitler's Nazis on many occasions. As the bombing of German cities increased, von Galen, like so many others, lost everything except the clothes on his back. At the war's end, he was summoned to Rome to be made a cardinal. He returned to Münster in March 1946, and there, amidst the shattered ruins of his city and cathedral, 50,000 people gathered to welcome him and to listen to his words.

As the people faced the future and began to rebuild their devastated country, Cardinal von Galen thanked them for their constancy and for recognising his duty to speak clearly and plainly to them about the evil that was being done in their name by the Nazi leaders. Von Galen's motto, as a bishop, was "Neither with praise nor fear". He would not allow fear or favour to influence him in his duty to God and to God's people. He died shortly after returning to his city, faithful to that motto.

Gospel Teaching

When Jesus returns to Nazareth, his home town, in the early days of his preaching ministry, he, too, will not be influenced by fear or favour. St Luke tells us that Jesus came "with the power of the Spirit in him". What he had to say, and what he would do, would be done in a confident manner: not timid, not boastful, but with a gentle assuredness. This inner confidence, this gentle strength, will be needed as, first, he is warmly welcomed and his words enthusiastically received; then, as he is doubted and defied and in the end almost destroyed.

Today we hear about the welcome and the warm reception. Jesus stands up among his own people, who "know him so well", and he makes an astounding statement. He is the one, sent by God, to bring good news to all people. As the people live in expectation of deliverance and freedom, Jesus tells them, "Here, now, in your hearing, I am the fulfilment of that hope." It is an amazing thing to say. It is an amazing thing to hear. A carpenter from Nazareth is the fulfilment of this world's dreams of peace and happiness – how can that be?

Application

It has been the role of each generation since to ask that question and to try to discover the answer. Jesus, in his own body, in his life and death and resurrection, is the witness to the truth of what he says. His behaviour in life, his encounters with people, his wonderful teaching, his humble suffering, his patient endurance, his rising in glory: all bear witness to the truth of those words he spoke one quiet sabbath morning in Nazareth long ago.

Every Sunday Eucharist re-enacts that sabbath day in Nazareth. In this world the Church is now the mystical body of Christ, and every member of it is a witness to the Lord. This is a cause for great joy. As the priest Ezra told the people of Jerusalem, this is a day to rejoice. In the midst of this world's turmoil and trouble, here is a cause for confidence. The Lord is here among us, and we belong in him.

Each generation looks to the future for salvation and an escape from sin. Here, among us today, in this Eucharist, stands the Lord of life, as in Nazareth long ago. Isaiah's text is read again, and is being fulfilled even as we listen.

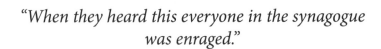

C

"When they heard this everyone in the synagogue was enraged."

4th Sunday in Ordinary Time

Illustration

On the night of 26th March 1996, Muslim gunmen attacked a Trappist monastery situated in the Atlas Mountains of Algeria, North Africa. They kidnapped its seven French Trappist monks. Two months later, all seven monks were found murdered with their throats slit. Catholics had been killed before by Islamic fundamentalists in this staunchly Muslim country, but these particular deaths came to international attention because of a letter written by one of the monks shortly before his abduction. It was opened after his death.

Dom Christian de Chergé knew that he was likely to die violently, but he wanted to forgive, as he wrote, "with all my heart the one who would strike me down". In fact, he called his killer his "last-minute friend", knowing that person would be the final face he would see in this life. Dom Christian loved Algeria and had great respect for Muslim believers. He had dedicated his life to dialogue between Muslims and Christians, and believed that in his brother and sister Muslims he discovered a part of the total face of Christ. The French monks of the Tibhirine monastery were thought strange by many Catholics in their home country, who wondered why they lived out their ministry in a country where Islam is the state religion and where there are few Catholics.

But the monks believed their mission was to cross boundaries, to work outside the Christian community, even though this bemused many French Catholics and antagonised Algerian Muslim fundamentalists. They risked abuse and danger in order to move outside their comfortable faith circle and build bridges with others. They were certainly loved by neighbouring villagers with whom they shared their garden.

Gospel Teaching

In today's Gospel, Jesus has just been enthusiastically acclaimed in the synagogue at Nazareth for announcing the promised Jubilee, which he called "the Lord's year of favour". Yet the whole mood suddenly changes. The listeners become so set against him that he is in mortal danger. But what was it that happened to make the crowd turn on him so quickly?

They were upset because Jesus had been working all kinds of miracles and healings in Capernaum and other places, only now returning to his home town of Nazareth. Jesus does not apologise. In fact, he antagonises them further by telling them that his mission and "the Lord's year of favour" will not be restricted to them, but will even extend to non-Jews and pagans. He reminds them of two non-Jews blessed by God in their scriptures. The listeners have felt a sense of privilege that comes from having one of the kids who grew up locally revealed as a miracle worker.

Yet they want to keep the best things in life – that is, God and God's favours – within their own closed little circle and the Jewish community. The sense of privilege, of having some special status with Jesus, quickly evaporates as it dawns on them that they are going to get no special treatment. What should have been joy at the prospect of many being helped by Jesus turns to rage that he would so freely bestow "the Lord's favour". Jesus' fellow villagers display their lack of openness to his message by pushing him out of the synagogue. In fact, they are about to hurl him over a cliff when he manages to slip away and continue his work elsewhere.

Application

God's love isn't just for Christians. It is for everybody. And how wonderful that love is. In the first reading, the Lord says: "Before I formed you in the womb I knew you." In the second reading, Paul talks about a love that "takes no pleasure in other people's sins but delights in the truth". This reading is perhaps heard most often at weddings, but the love it highlights goes beyond love of a partner. It is a love that is a way of life, extending to the whole human family.

Jesus calls on us to be open and loving outside our own community. He urges us not to be suspicious of other people just because they come from different cultural, religious or social backgrounds. We are asked not to settle into security, but to embrace newness and take risks for the sake of the kingdom. A true embrace of this mission will call us out of our comfort zones and challenge us to be witnesses of love in a divided world.

"Here I am, send me."

Illustration

The Keys of the Kingdom is a novel by the Scottish author A.J. Cronin. It tells the story of a young Scottish priest, Fr Francis Chisholm, who spends his life as a Christian missionary in China during the first part of the twentieth century. The film of the book, made in 1944, stars Gregory Peck as a handsome and dashing Fr Chisholm. Francis' best friend is Willie Tulloch. They grow up together, Francis becoming a priest, Willie a doctor. They are great friends, despite the fact that Willie is an atheist. He does not believe in God.

At one point in the novel, Willie comes out to visit Fr Francis in China. While he is there, a terrible plague breaks out in the town. Francis and Willie do wonderful work in containing the disease, but tragically Willie falls ill himself. There is a very moving scene when Willie is dying and his old friend Francis is with him. Francis knows Willie does not believe in God, and so is not administering the last rites or indeed saying any prayers. Francis is just sitting quietly with Willie, keeping his dear friend company.

Near the end, Willie looks up at Francis and says: "Francis, you have been a wonderful friend and I have always loved you. But I have never loved you as much as I do now, because you are not trying to force me into heaven. Francis, even now, I do not believe, I cannot believe." And Fr Francis, with tears in his eyes, looks at his old friend and replies: "Willie, it does not matter that you do not believe in God. Because, you see, Willie, God believes in you, God believes in you!"

Gospel Teaching

God believes in Isaiah, Paul and Simon Peter. These three men of faith have much in common. All of them have profound experiences of God. Isaiah in the Temple has a vision of the holiness of God. Paul has his Damascus-road experience. Simon Peter has witnessed remarkable things in the short time that he has known Jesus. Jesus has healed Peter's mother-in-law and for his previously luckless crew has brought about a huge catch of fish.

These three men react in the same way to their encounter with God. Each of them is overwhelmed with a feeling of unworthiness. Isaiah says: "What a wretched state I am in! I am lost, for I am a man of unclean lips." Paul knows he is unworthy; he has zealously persecuted Christians. Simon Peter realises that he is standing in the company of God and so sinks to his knees and exclaims: "Leave me, Lord; I am a sinful man." God's response is something like this: "Isaiah, Paul, Simon Peter, I believe in you. Stop looking at your limitations, your fears, your inadequacies. Concentrate on my love, my mercy, my strength, and you can be my apostles: together we can do great things."

And so, Isaiah, Paul and Simon Peter are invited to accept God's belief or faith in them. They are beggars who recognise their poverty before God but understand that God can fill that poverty with love, mercy and strength. With God working in and through them, they can do great things. Without the help of Jesus, Simon Peter will labour in vain. With the help of Jesus, anything is possible. Even a huge catch of fish, where before there were empty nets.

Application
Just as God believes in Isaiah, Paul and Simon Peter, God believes in you and me. God is not interested in our limitations. Rather, God is interested in our potential. The Lord asks us to concentrate on his love, mercy and strength working in and through us. Together with him, we can be God's apostles, God's messengers. Together with God, we can do great things.

St Francis of Assisi summed it all up centuries ago: "Lord, make me an instrument of your peace." This simple prayer describes the vocations of Isaiah, Paul and Simon Peter. This simple prayer describes our vocation. To be an apostle or a messenger of Jesus, we are called to let him do the work. We are called to be humble instruments or channels who allow God's love, peace and mercy to flow in and through us. God believes that we, along with Isaiah, Paul and Simon Peter, can be instruments of God's peace in the world. God believes in us.

With that recommendation ringing in our ears, we can be sure that we can do great things with and for God.

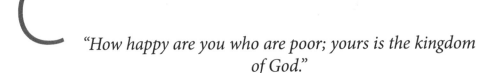

"How happy are you who are poor; yours is the kingdom of God."

Illustration

The year 1649 was a turbulent one in English history. The Parliamentary forces under the leadership of Oliver Cromwell had emerged victorious after a long and bloody Civil War. The defeated king, Charles I, was tried and executed. A time of social unrest and upheaval followed, as the country tried to come to terms with the changed situation, and the new rulers attempted to devise an acceptable form of government.

In those troubled times, it's not surprising that groups of dissenters arose. One such group alarmed the authorities when they began to plant vegetables on common land at St George's Hill in Surrey, and encouraged others to join them. Because of their activities, they became known as the Diggers. They were inspired by the vision of the early Christian community in the Acts of the Apostles, where "everything they owned was held in common". They had little time for the authorities of Church and State. Inevitably, it was not long before those same authorities felt threatened and clamped down on them, dispersing and putting an end to the Digger colony.

In the 1980s, the English songwriter Leon Rosselson composed a song based on these events, which was later recorded by the singer Billy Bragg. Its title was "The World Turned Upside Down".

Gospel Teaching

Jesus' words in today's Gospel, the beginning of what is known as Luke's sermon on the plain, describe a world turned upside down. That, at least, is how it must have seemed to the people who first heard them. Jesus pronounces a series of "beatitudes", followed by a contrasting set of "woes". Who are the blessed, the happy, in this vision of God's kingdom? It is those who are poor, those who are hungry, those who weep, those who are despised and rejected by the world. In contrast, says Jesus, "Alas" for the rich, for those who have their fill, for those who laugh, for those of whom the world speaks well.

It appears to turn the accepted world order on its head. And it certainly would have been against the expectations of those who heard it. Much conventional religious teaching contained the message that people's situation in the world reflected whether or not they had found favour with God: those who were rich and powerful, those who lived lives of plenty, knew God's favour. They were being rewarded. And therefore those who suffered, those who had nothing, were out of favour with God, and were being punished. So it's easy to see why Jesus' teaching would have been regarded by the religious authorities as subversive; and why they would eventually seek to put an end to him.

But is Jesus describing a world turned upside down? Or is he depicting the way in which an upside-down world is turned the right side up? This is an important theme in Luke's Gospel. Luke begins the ministry of Jesus with the sermon in the synagogue at Nazareth, in which Jesus announces that he has come "to bring the good news to the poor... to set the downtrodden free". Even before that, Mary's Magnificat proclaims that the Lord has filled the hungry with good things, and sent the rich away empty. And Jesus' birth is announced not to the rich and powerful, but to shepherds, among the outcasts of society.

Application

All this sets Jesus' proclamation of the Good News in the context of a world in which God had always intended that the lowly, those disregarded by the world, should have a valued place in God's kingdom. The Old Testament covenant with Israel had set out the duty of care for the poor, and established the principle of the Jubilee, in which people are set free from debt and oppression. The prophets had spoken out for those who were poor, calling for justice and compassion for them; and they had often been persecuted as a result.

So Jesus is speaking of a kingdom in which God's intentions for the world are restored. Things are put back as God means them to be, not so much overturned as put back the right way up. Jesus calls us not to sit back and wait for this to happen sometime in the future. He calls us to work for it now. God's kingdom will come in its fullness; but every time we pray "thy kingdom come" we are committing ourselves to be part of building up that kingdom in the world today. And justice, compassion and care for those who are poor are at the very heart of that kingdom.

"The Lord is compassion and love."

Illustration

The Bishop of Digne is troubled in the early morning by a loud disturbance outside his house and by the sound of knocking at his door. When he opens the door of his humble house he sees, held by the strong arms of three policemen, the wretched figure of a man. The man has been arrested for stealing silver plates from the table of the bishop. He was caught while running away from the small town. The silver plates and two silver candlesticks were the only items of value in the bishop's possession.

The captive is an ex-convict, who had been treated with disdain and contempt as he journeyed from village to village. He was refused food and board at the local inns and eventually found himself at the house of the bishop. The kind old man gladly fed him and gave him a bed for the night. However, in the middle of the night the ex-convict's old ways overtook him and he fled into the early morning light with the bishop's silver plates.

Now, as he stands before the bishop, the captive sees the madness of his act but also the inevitability of life again as a prisoner. The bishop smiles, looks straight at the man and says, "But you forgot the candlesticks I gave to you also." The police are taken aback and the man is staggered by this turn of events. Going to the mantelpiece, the bishop gets the candlesticks and hands them to the unbelieving man. The police are dismissed and the ex-convict, Jean Valjean, is left with the bishop. The bishop speaks to Jean Valjean, telling him that with this silver he has bought his soul for God, and urging him to use the treasure to become an honest man.

Gospel Teaching

Many people may recognise this story from the French author Victor Hugo's novel *Les Misérables*, also immortalised in the musical of the same name. The Bishop of Digne represents the very tenderness and compassion of God. This saintly man is not preoccupied with the trappings of power or spectacle; rather, his focus is upon those who are needy and poor, and his energy is consumed in serving them. His life exhibits the characteristics of the compassion that Jesus calls us all to live out in our daily lives: "Be compassionate as your Father is compassionate." In other places in the Gospels we hear that we are called to be as perfect as God, or as holy as

God. Is it possible that true perfection, holiness and compassion are the same thing?

As human beings we glimpse the nature of God in the life of Jesus Christ who comes with compassion, mercy and forgiveness for those who have sinned. In him are made visible the values of God's kingdom. His power does not dominate but liberates. He does not react to the taunts of his opponents but responds with the proclamation of God's love. He nurtures those who have been bruised and broken and raises up those who have been laid low by sickness or isolation. Each person is granted the dignity of the sons and daughters of God and called by Jesus to live that truth to the full.

Compassion is not simply the putting of pious words together into meaningful prayers for those who suffer. It is not simply a feeling of concern. It is, above all, taking action on behalf of people living in poverty, those suffering through ill health and those needing emotional support.

Application
Today's liturgy calls each one of us to examine anew our understanding of perfection and holiness. Does the search for perfection mean striving after some ideal moral state of innocence, or is it reaching out in all circumstances to those who are in need? Is holiness a solitary endeavour concerned with my own purity and salvation, or is it generous enough to embrace those who are despised and rejected in an embrace of love? In short, are we compassionate as our heavenly Father is compassionate?

Victor Hugo's novel poses the question of where the saintly bishop learned to be so different from the people around him. The only answer is from the Gospel. Let us pray that we also may learn how to be compassionate by reflecting upon and living out the Good News of Jesus Christ.

C

"Every tree can be told by its own fruit."

Illustration

Young Sarah was at a very impressionable age, so her parents tried their best to be most careful about their words and actions in front of her. They were anxious that she should grow up to be a kind and gentle person with a strong sense of justice and responsibility. One morning, as usual just before breakfast, Sarah's mother suggested that they say a prayer together. "I want to say daddy's favourite morning prayer," Sarah said. Pleased with her enthusiasm, Sarah's parents allowed her to say the prayer. Her expression changed to one of gloom and depression, then, closing her eyes, Sarah said in a grumpy voice, "Oh God, I wish it was Friday!" Sarah opened her eyes to be greeted with a look of absolute horror on her parents' faces.

Gospel Teaching

Children often copy what they see. They are impressed by actions rather than words, by what people do rather than what they say. Today's Gospel encourages us to look at our lives and consider how our actions may influence the lives of others. We are called to live in the way of the Gospel and to reach out to share the Good News with others; and the most effective way to show others the truth and the power of the Gospel is by example, rather than words.

In today's Gospel reading, Jesus tells his followers that they are called to put their own house in order before they can begin to tell others how to live and behave. In saying this, Jesus presents us, his followers today, with quite a considerable challenge. We may think that it is easy to see where others are going wrong – the splinters in other people's eyes are often very obvious to us. However, if we are blinded by the plank in our own eyes we will not be able to see where we are going wrong ourselves.

To live the Gospel, it is necessary to accept it first in our hearts. Jesus tells us that a good person "draws what is good from the store of goodness in his [or her] heart". The goodness that stems from belief in Jesus will influence all areas of our lives, affecting the way we treat our families, colleagues and friends. Their lives, in turn, will be helped by our example. If we live our own lives according to the Gospel, we may at the same time be helping others to live theirs, for in doing so we set an example that others can follow and we avoid the temptation to preach a hollow message. If we express our faith through all that we say and in all that we do, then we will be living teachers and living bearers of the Gospel message.

Application

Quite often it may not be necessary to tell people in so many words that we are Christians. Through our words and deeds our faith should be clear already. It's the small actions, not the grand gestures, which can reveal our true identity and which can also teach a great deal. For example, our morning greeting to our family, to our colleagues and to our friends can make a big difference to the beginning of the day, for us and for them. It's the small, gentle actions that touch the lives of others.

As we seek to grow in faith, then every day we can aim to change just a little – striving gradually to put our own house in order. If we truly want to change our lives and the lives of those around us, then it is best to be positive rather than critical and negative. We are called to challenge unkindness with kindness and love. If we honestly live the Gospel we will inspire others so that they, too, will want to have their lives shaped and moulded by the goodness of that message.

C

"I tell you, not even in Israel have I found faith like this."

Illustration

In May 2009 Pope Benedict XVI went on pilgrimage to the Holy Land. While there, the Holy Father made a visit to Yad Vashem, Israel's official memorial site to the Jewish victims of the Holocaust. There, in silence, he stood before the names of all those who had lost their lives. Their names will never be forgotten, the Pope said, and their story will never be allowed to fade from human memory.

The memorial site of Yad Vashem was set up in 1953, and great work has gone into collecting the names and the stories of the people remembered there. In addition, a second place of remembrance was set up, a garden dedicated to non-Jewish people who, at great peril to their own lives, gave help and assistance to the persecuted people of Israel. This garden is dedicated to "the Righteous among the Nations".

One of the new names to appear on this memorial was placed there only a few months before Pope Benedict's visit. In February 2009 the name of Wilhelm Hosenfeld was given honour and a place among the "Righteous of the Nations". Hosenfeld was a German army officer, stationed in Poland, who gave assistance to Poles and Jews. Captured by Soviet troops at the end of the war, he died in captivity, probably as a result of torture. He was a decent man, trying to act with humanity in a world of violent hatred. Now he is remembered as a righteous person, whose decency was not limited by human division.

Gospel Teaching

It is the issue of "human division" that captures our attention today. In every generation and in every place the issue of what divides human beings from one another presents enormous challenges. We differ from one another in matters of race, religion, colour and gender. These differences very often become matters of divisiveness and excuses for great injustice. What we do not know, we do not trust. Very easily we can find ourselves guilty of tribalism and prejudice. We can live in narrow worlds and miss out on the beautiful complexity of human life.

The prayer attributed to King Solomon that we heard in our first reading today was composed after the Jewish people had returned from exile. That very experience of other people and other places inspired the thought of making a prayer for the foreigner. It was a prayer which now realised that God is a God of *all* people, and not just of some. If we all come to know God's name, then we shall live in peace with one another.

In today's Gospel Jesus is asked by a foreigner, a Roman centurion, to heal a servant who is sick. In order to cross the racial and religious divide that separates them, the Roman asks some of his Jewish acquaintances to speak on his behalf. They put in a good word for him. He is not one of us, they effectively say, but he is a very good person. So good, in fact, that he built their synagogue. While Jesus absorbs this information a second message arrives from the centurion: "Please do not trouble yourself, just give the order and my servant will be cured." Jesus is amazed. "Not even in Israel", he says, "have I found faith like this."

Application

Jesus, a Jew, born into God's chosen people, of the line of David, is sent as saviour of the whole world, not just of his own race. This Gospel truth dawned on St Peter, when, at the house of the Roman centurion Cornelius, he said, "The truth I have now come to realise is that God does not have favourites." This same truth hit St Paul between the eyes, when, on the Damascus road, he heard a voice saying, "I am Jesus, and you are persecuting me."

The holiness of life that Jesus preached he found, alive and flourishing, in a pagan soldier. This man lived in peace with his Jewish neighbours. He spent his own money on building their place of worship. He treated his servants well and cared deeply for them. He asked the Lord for help with great humility: "I am not worthy to have you under my roof." He practised a faith in God that Jesus had not found even among God's chosen people, those who shared his own religion.

This Roman soldier truly deserved the title of "Righteous among the Nations". Like him may we come to know God's name, and to revere it, in relation to every human being.

"Young man, I tell you to get up."

Illustration

Today's Gospel begins with the dramatic spectacle of two large crowds approaching from different directions. The effect of the miracle that subsequently took place must have been even more dramatic. Following Jewish custom, the funeral procession would have included official mourners. Led by the distraught mother, it would have been a woeful group, grieving aloud. Jesus' followers, on the other hand, had just come from the cure of the centurion's son and their exuberance would still have been evident in noisiness of a different kind. In a very real way, the event was a clash between death and life.

The first effect of the clash, surely, was to reduce everyone to silence. As Jesus approached the bier, no one quite knew where to put themselves. Luke tells us simply that "the bearers stood still". Then Jesus' words broke the silence: "Young man, I tell you to get up." The authority of Jesus' calm command broke the tension. The young man was raised up to a new life.

Every person faces that same moment: the clash between death and life. On the one hand there is death, which seems so final, so absolute. And like the widows in today's first reading and Gospel, we may feel inconsolable grief. On the other hand, the creator of life is drawing us to himself, tearing us away from the familiar human existence that we know and love so well. The moment of the final clash, when Jesus approaches us to place his hand upon us, is the moment of total silence and stillness. But then, we believe, Jesus addresses us with the words: "I tell you to get up." That is the moment of new life, of resurrection.

Gospel Teaching

We cannot avoid death, although most of us try to avoid thinking about it. Our ability to accept it rests squarely on our willingness to face it in our daily life. For, as Christians, we begin to die, not on the deathbed or in the car accident, but at baptism. Christ described his own death as a "baptism", and in our baptism we share in Christ's death and resurrection. Christ transformed death, in other words, into a means of reaching the new life. He overcame death in his own life and he overcomes death in our life if we unite ourselves with him in the sacraments and daily prayer.

Nor is it only physical death over which God has control. As St Paul reminds us in today's second reading, God in Christ has power also over the death that comes from estrangement from him. Before he was touched by God, Paul himself had no experience of being alive to the truth. Indeed, he spent his life, as he tells us, in persecuting the Christian Church and trying to suppress the name of Christ. But the Lord brought him, so to speak, back from death and gave him a share in his new risen life. From that day forward, Paul was a new man.

Application

The new life that the Lord offers us in eternity is the same as the life that he offers us in the sacraments. Granted, here on earth we do not possess it to the full. But death does not put an end to one "type" of divine life in order to start another "type" in heaven. Rather, it perfects and completes the divine life we have already acquired here on earth. This work of "perfecting" has already begun. And again, as at baptism, it is done through daily death.

None of us, then, merely passes away quietly in our sleep or meets an unexpected sudden end in an accident. Whatever the circumstances, even if we are unconscious beforehand, our death is a real *act*. We are *doing* something. We are going out to meet death.

For the Christian who has understood the lesson of "dying" throughout life, this final death becomes a magnificent act of obedient surrender into the merciful hands of the Father. It is an act of faith in darkness, an act of hope when all seems lost, a supreme act of love for the one who seems to come only to judge. As Christ Jesus approaches us to touch us for the last time in this life, the horror of death is changed into a glorious "into your hands, O Lord, I commend my spirit".

"Go in peace."

Illustration

A woman named Jennifer was speaking on the radio. She told the story of how she had gone to university, got her degree and given up the practice of her faith; she had married, but, to her regret, had no children; she had worked abroad and lost her husband to another woman, though she had loved him dearly at the time, and still did now; she'd been very ill, "at death's door", they'd said, and then had miraculously pulled through. The interview was unhurried and she was given time to reflect. In the course of the conversation, she suddenly said: "You know, I haven't really lost my faith, well not completely anyway. I don't know how to explain it. I do believe there's a God and all that sort of thing. It's just that somehow I can't believe that God really loves me and you, that he cares about us, is even interested in us."

There are many Jennifers in this world, people who wouldn't deny God's existence but find it hard to believe that God can have any personal interest in the likes of them, particularly if over the years they know they've drifted away from God and above all if they know that they have not lived as they should.

Gospel Teaching

Yet at the very heart of the good news that Jesus Christ has brought is the amazing truth that God does love us, does care for every single individual as though we were the only person in the world, no matter who we are and no matter what we may have done or failed to do. Nor has this good news been presented simply by word of mouth. It's been proclaimed most convincingly by the Lord's own life, his wonderful deeds. We've had a small but telling example of it in today's Gospel.

Simon, one of the local religious leaders, has invited Jesus to his home for a meal. While they are together at table an incredible thing happens. In through the open door comes a woman who has "a bad name in the town". You can imagine the men nodding knowingly to each other as she approaches, but they can hardly have anticipated what's about to happen. Simon for his part has been coldly correct in welcoming Jesus. In contrast to that stinginess of attitude stands this woman's uninhibited generosity. She comes armed with a bottle of sweet-smelling ointment, intending to anoint Jesus. She drops to her knees, begins weeping so that the tears fall over his feet and then, without more ado, she lets down her long hair – a thing no self-respecting woman of those days would ever have done – and uses them to wipe his feet.

Simon and his fellow guests are appalled. What an exhibition! "This Jesus is supposed to be some kind of prophet, isn't he?" muses Simon. "Doesn't he know what kind of woman she is?" Yes, Simon, indeed he does. It's you who don't, though you think you do; you see her only as a good-time girl, a sinner, a little nobody, flaunting herself in public. But Jesus sees so much more: he sees her as a sinner, of course, but as a forgiven sinner and beyond that as a potential saint; she matters to him. Many sins have been forgiven her and that is why she has learned to be so generous in her return of love.

Application

In Jesus, we see God as perfectly as it's possible for us to do on this earth. Today's Gospel shows something more than Jesus', and therefore God's, readiness to forgive. It speaks also of God's personal interest in an individual: not only a high and mighty individual, like King David whom we heard about in the first reading; but also a small, insignificant individual, like the woman in the Gospel or, for that matter, like you and me. God's interest is full of concern, alive not only to our failures but still more to our goodness, and is allied with a love that is unconditional.

I suspect we all have our Jennifer moments, times when we wonder whether God has lost interest in us, whether God does really care about us any more. On such occasions confidence might be restored if we were to reflect on today's Gospel, for then we would see that nothing could be further from the mark than the crazy notion that God could ever lose interest in us; quite simply, we are far too dear to God for that.

C

"Who do you say I am?"

Illustration

What's in a name? More than we sometimes think. It can be very embarrassing to forget someone's name. When it happens, we try various subterfuges to disguise our predicament. The commonest is to say "Hi" or "Hello" in a massively cheerful way as though our smile will somehow cover up our memory loss. But why is it so important to remember other people's names or have our own remembered? Names reveal our identity. When you tell me your name you are admitting me into your world and agreeing to a certain level of familiarity.

Names, and particularly first names in Western culture, do not merely identify us. They carry power. Think of what it feels like to hear your name spoken by someone you love. Your spirits soar and your heart beats faster. At the other extreme, parents know only too well the effect of using a child's full name when they want to bring their offspring to order: there is a world of difference between an affectionate "Jo" or "Josie" and a stern "Josephine!"

Gospel Teaching

Jesus has been teaching his disciples by both his words and his deeds. Now he wants to check how far they have understood him. As in all cases in Luke's Gospel where he is making a big decision or taking a big step forward, he first of all prays – alone and yet in his disciples' presence. Then he approaches the matter indirectly. It is as though he first needs to clear the ground of false understandings.

The question is about his own identity. Who do the crowds say he is? A variety of answers are put forward by his disciples. There are names from the past, attempts to identify him with important characters in the story of Israel. Jesus is then able to ask the crucial question. Who do they, his disciples, say he is? Peter leaps in with the most accurate of responses. He is the one who is awaited, the Christ of God, the Messiah. Jesus accepts Peter's answer but immediately counsels his disciples not to make the truth known. Why? Because what the people expected from that title and what Jesus meant by it were very different. The people were expecting a king, who would bring in the reign of God. In the political context of the time such an act of salvation would, to them, be inextricably bound up with liberation from the yoke of Roman occupation. The crowds would misread his identity and misunderstand his mission.

Using the title he prefers when speaking of his mission, Jesus goes on to say that the "Son of Man" will not be a military warrior. Instead he will suffer and be rejected and be put to death, to rise again on the third day. The title "Son of Man" carries with it the sense of one who brings together and symbolises the people, and through it Jesus is able to take his disciples' understanding a step further. Those who follow him will have to accept a similar pattern of suffering. What is asked of Jesus will also be asked of his disciples.

Application

Our own mission depends on how we answer Christ's question. Who do we say he is? Put another way, what is our image of Christ? What is our image of God?

My image of God can be of a distant, punishing God who is always waiting to catch me out and rebuke me. Or it can be an abstract concept, the unmoved mover. God can also be a close friend, loving and uplifting, particularly when I am low. But does my God challenge me, asking me to live out the same pattern that we see in Jesus? And when the Lord makes this challenge, does he leave me on my own or is he my companion on the journey, not asking me to do anything except what he himself has already undertaken?

These are not always easy questions for us to answer, but we are called to answer as honestly as possible because in doing so we are not just making a statement about God's identity; we are also making one about our own. We are allowing God to ask us the question: Who are you?

Just as Jesus explores the question about his identity through his life and death, so do we. It is answered in how we live out each moment until that instant at the end of our life on earth when we join ourselves to Christ completely.

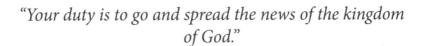

"Your duty is to go and spread the news of the kingdom of God."

Illustration

No one who lived through the Cuban missile crisis of 1962 will forget the tension and gloom that overshadowed those days. People were well aware that at any moment the brinkmanship between the United States and the Soviet Union could erupt into worldwide nuclear war. By all accounts it was a close call, but eventually the world breathed a huge sigh of relief. One story has it that an American general advised President Kennedy to go ahead anyway and order a nuclear strike, arguing that the West would never be as prepared in the future to face the Soviet threat. Fortunately, his advice was rejected.

Gospel Teaching

It's easy for us, like that general, to get caught up in the heat of the moment, as today's readings show. But often what is needed is not enthusiasm and passion, but a cool head and clear thinking. Elijah is sent by God to anoint Elisha as his successor, as God's prophet. Elijah goes, but he knows from his own bitter experience what a costly vocation this can be. After he has called Elisha, in obedience to God, you can almost hear the anguish in his voice as he says: "Go, go back; for have I done anything to you?" Elijah seems frightened by Elisha's naive enthusiasm. It's as if Elijah is disclaiming any responsibility for what might follow. Nevertheless, Elisha says his goodbyes and follows Elijah.

The Gospel too speaks of discipleship, of the cost of following the Lord. Here too we see rashness and impetuosity. The Lord has been refused admission to a Samaritan village, and James and John are so caught up in the heat of the moment that in their fury they want to destroy it; it's reminiscent of the American general wanting to initiate nuclear warfare, simply because his side was ready for it. Jesus, however, isn't into the dramatic gesture or the instant response: he calmly walks on to the next village. Common sense prevails.

The various would-be disciples that Luke then introduces also show a certain impetuosity, a lack of preparedness. To the first, Jesus points out the hardships that any disciple might have to face: no security, no place to call your own. To the next, who wishes first to discharge his sacred family responsibilities, Jesus starkly warns that being a disciple means placing God's kingdom before all other calls and commitments. To a third, who is still attached to his family, Jesus warns of the absolute primacy of his call above all other relationships. Nothing, not even natural affections, can come between the true disciple and his master.

The implied message in all these examples seems to be this: don't act on impulse. Don't choose rashly. Think seriously before you decide to be a follower of Christ. It involves hardship, commitment, self-sacrifice, courage and stamina. If you are half-hearted, if your loyalties are divided, if you don't think you can last the distance, then it is better not to begin the task at all.

Application

Where is the good news in this? Perhaps the key lies in the words of St Paul: "When Christ freed us, he meant us to remain free." The only true liberty lies in obedience to Christ, the Lord of life. It is the freedom to serve others, as Paul tells us, the freedom to love your neighbour as yourself. To some, such a "law" will be nothing but a restriction, a straitjacket to personal freedom. But to the Christian, true freedom lies not in personal licence, but in perfect obedience to the one who calls us, leads us and gives us eternal life.

Discipleship means following, following where someone else leads, where someone else has gone before. We follow a crucified Lord, one who resolutely set out for Jerusalem and the cross. The cross, the road to Jerusalem, is unavoidable in the life of every true disciple because there is no other way to find the freedom of the resurrection.

Today's Gospel warns us: don't be impetuous. Weigh up the cost of being the Lord's disciple. Are you prepared to pay it? If the Lord leads you by difficult or painful paths, will you follow? If he asks you to put him before family and friends, will you do it? If he asks you to act in his time, not yours, will you respond? Jesus isn't into dramatic gestures: he wants only our good, our freedom, our happiness. He will surely lead us onto the path of life, the fullness of joy in God's presence. Are you ready to follow where he leads?

C

"Peace to this house!"

Illustration

A rabbi asked his students how they could tell that night was over and a new day had begun. The answers came thick and fast. Some thought that it was when you saw a tree and could recognise that it was a fig tree rather than a lemon tree. Others said it was when you saw an animal in the garden and could see that it was a cat and not a fox. And so it went on. "You are all mistaken," the rabbi said. "You know a new day has begun when you see people in the street and recognise that they are your brothers and sisters. Until then it will always be night."

Gospel Teaching

Jesus was good at recognising people, not just by their appearance but by what was going on inside them. He could read their hearts. People felt comfortable in his presence. They felt understood, as if they had something in common with him. When he was with them they felt as if they were his brothers and sisters.

He was like this because there was no pretence in him. He had little time for questions of personal status. He was free to be himself. When you read the Gospels you get the impression that nothing got in his way. He was able to get close to people because his life was not cluttered by things that did not matter.

And when he sent his followers out, he wanted them to be like him. "Carry no purse, no haversack, no sandals," he said. "Let your first words be, 'Peace to this house!'" His disciples were to be recognised not by what they were wearing or carrying, but by who they were. Their presence was their message. They were bringers of peace and healing. And the kingdom of God would be very near because they were there.

Jesus speaks of peace. It was a situation of great need. The harvest was great and the labourers were few. But Jesus was not driven to panic measures. The greatest resource he had was the witness of his disciples, and they would only be effective if they took with them the simplicity, trust and peace they had seen in Jesus. So they went out, not to conquer the world, but to bring healing to those who were sick and peace to all who longed for it. And they came back rejoicing. Wonderful things happened when they went out in his name.

Application

St Seraphim of Sarov, a great Russian monk and mystic, used to say to his followers, "Have peace in your soul and all around you hundreds will be converted." Peace is the most powerful weapon in the world. Peacemakers are a force to be reckoned with; Jesus calls them children of God. Powerful people may rule the world, but people who are at peace with themselves may touch more lives.

If we are to be Jesus' disciples we are called to bring healing and peace to people, as he did. We are to be ministers of his presence and his peace. But this peace needs to be cultivated. It does not take root in our appearance or possessions, or even in our gifts and talents. It goes deeper than that. Jesus spoke of a place that was like a private room where we meet our Father in prayer. This is the heart, our sanctuary, where the peace of Christ can live and grow. And with this peace in their hearts his disciples needed little in the way of luggage. They had more than enough if they carried with them the spirit of their master and the simplicity and trust he had shared with them.

When the seventy-two disciples returned after their successful mission, they were delighted with all that they had been able to do, and Jesus celebrated with them. Amazing things had indeed happened in people's lives. Everything now seemed possible. Jesus knew what lay behind all this, and he went on to remind them that the greatest reason they had for rejoicing was that their names were written in heaven. They belonged in God's kingdom. They had a place in the mind and heart of God, and that would never change. They could rest in peace. Since we too are disciples of Christ, we can learn to rejoice and trust in him, sharing that peace with others.

"And who is my neighbour?"

Illustration

In June 2001, a Palestinian family made an unusual gesture of goodwill in the midst of the bloody violence and deep mistrust between Arabs and Israelis. The Djulani family donated vital organs of their dead son – including his heart – to four Israelis for life-saving transplants. Mazen Djulani was only thirty-four years old when he died after being shot in the head in east Jerusalem. The dead man's father said he wanted to save lives and to live in peace with the Israelis.

David Cohen, the father of one of the recipients of an organ, said he was "very surprised" by the gesture. "It is really touching, especially in these days when relations are so tense," he said. "This noble family comes and teaches us that it is possible to do things in a different way."

Gospel Teaching

When Jesus tells a lawyer that to inherit eternal life he must love God and love his neighbour as well as he loves himself, the question immediately follows, "And who is my neighbour?" Jesus does not define who the lawyer's neighbour might be, but tells him a story instead – the famous story of the Good Samaritan. The priest and the Levite in the story ignore the beaten stranger by the roadside, even though he is a fellow Jew; in contrast, the Samaritan, who is from a different and despised people, shows the injured man love and care.

Jewish ears would have been shocked to hear Jesus say that a Samaritan stopped to aid the victim. Samaritans were regarded as enemies, and yet here a Samaritan is the good guy. If Jesus had merely wanted to teach about neighbourly love, the third person could have been another Jew, or the victim might have been a Samaritan assisted by a Jew. In selecting a Samaritan as the hero, Jesus was turning the social world upside down and challenging deep-seated suppositions. It was the Samaritan who behaved like a loving neighbour even though he was under no obligation to do so. The priest and Levite, who were supposed to be examples of piety, rejected the opportunity to show love and to be good neighbours.

Jesus intended the story to demonstrate the nature of love in God's kingdom. The response to "Who is my neighbour?" is that everyone, including my enemy, is my neighbour. The Samaritan's compassion was costly. It involved making himself vulnerable to attack by robbers because he was walking instead of riding after giving the beaten man his mount. He also made a financial payment to an innkeeper to look after the victim without any expectation of being repaid. Another aspect is that he might have been ostracised by his own people for assisting a Jew. Jesus directly asks the lawyer which of the three travellers was a neighbour to the injured man. "The one who took pity on him," he replies. To underline the message still further, Jesus instructs the lawyer to "Go, and do the same yourself."

Application

Jesus asks that we care about our neighbours with the same intensity that we care about ourselves. We are to love as he loved us, and even an enemy is redefined as a neighbour. This love is more than simply smiling at strangers and trying to develop positive attitudes towards people we don't particularly like. The command to love our neighbour is placed immediately after the command to love our God, and it demands a serious effort to elevate the neighbour's need to the same level as our own. The norm of reciprocity is abandoned. We don't just serve those who serve us, or return favours because we have received them; we are called to love beyond the usual expectations of making special efforts only for family and friends.

Active involvement with those who are downtrodden and oppressed is a key feature of loving outreach in God's kingdom. It might mean taking initiatives to reach out to vulnerable and destitute people in our community who can never repay our favours. It might mean taking up campaigns for justice and peace which try to tackle the causes of suffering at home and overseas. Working to highlight root causes of violence and war where whole groups of people are demonised as "enemies" will almost certainly draw criticism since this goes against the prevailing culture, but it is what God expects of us. God's love and peace teach us that it is possible to go beyond the boundaries human society has constructed and to do things in a different and revolutionary way.

C

"Mary... sat down at the Lord's feet."

Illustration

It's Wednesday, so it must be Paris! We may smile at the mentality of tourists who "do Europe" in a week. They might travel halfway round the world, only to spend hours on tourist coaches being ferried around one capital city or another, in order to catch a glimpse of the Houses of Parliament, the Eiffel Tower, the Colosseum.

Such whirlwind tourists never get to encounter the real culture or people of a country – they get a potted, sanitised, cliché-ridden version of a place, which bears little resemblance to the reality of life in that country. And even when they visit the great landmarks of a city, some tourists hardly get to see the buildings for themselves – they remain firmly behind the camera or the video. They're so intent on "catching" the moment for the folks back home that they fail to experience it at first hand for themselves.

Gospel Teaching

In today's Gospel, Martha is so intent on doing everything that any real personal experience is missed. Our sympathies may lie with her as she runs around trying to make sure that the sacred duty of hospitality is fulfilled. So why is Martha criticised, while the apparently selfish, even lazy Mary is praised by Jesus? Surely Martha is doing the same as Abraham and Sarah in hurrying around to prepare food and drink for the guests? They received a blessing as their reward, and yet the Lord criticises Martha.

When Abraham's guests visit him, he acts as a servant, bowing to the ground in greeting. And rather than join them in the meal, he remains standing nearby – as a servant would – ready to see to their needs. In that way, it is Mary, rather than Martha, who is following Abraham's example. What are Jesus' needs? To be waited on, to be served? Far from it – Jesus himself came not to be served but to serve. And part of his mission was to make disciples, who would learn from him and spread his Gospel. In sitting at the Lord's feet, Mary is in fact serving the Lord. She is doing precisely what he wants – listening to his message, letting it sink into her heart. She is assuming – literally and figuratively – the position of a disciple. Martha, on the other hand, is too busy with her own ideas, her desire to be the perfect hostess – and she puts this first.

This story follows the parable of the Good Samaritan, and in fact acts as a kind of commentary on it. The priest and the Levite, like Martha, were too busy with their own projects to be able to see what was really asked of them. Like the Samaritan, who put aside his own plans to help the injured man, Mary was able to see what was essential, what the moment demanded. In so doing, she welcomed the Lord and was obedient – she sat and listened. Martha never heard. She was so preoccupied with what she thought was important, that she missed out on the experience herself of sitting at the Lord's feet, of being a disciple.

Application

It is easy for us to berate ourselves for being busy Marthas rather than contemplative Marys. That would be a simplistic misunderstanding of the readings. Superficially, what Martha did was exactly what Abraham did. The difference between them is not what they did, but their underlying intention. Martha was unable to set aside her own plans and ideas. Mary, on the other hand, was able to resist society's expectations of her role as a woman (serving, carrying, fetching), as well as Martha's complaints, because she was able to see that this was a moment of grace.

Whether our lives are superficially more like Martha's or Mary's, what is important is our inner attitude. Jesus calls us to learn to detach ourselves from our own preconceived ideas, our own plans and intentions – and the expectations of those around us too – in order to be free to do what the Lord wants. The heart of this story is obedience – meaning listening. We are called to have an open heart, which is able to make space and time to hear the Lord – all the more so if this challenges us or goes against what we expect. It is that openness, that ability to listen, for which Mary is praised. She comes out from behind the camera, so to speak, and encounters the Lord at first hand. It is a real, personal relationship. It is a lesson for us all.

C

"Lord, teach us to pray."

Illustration

The priest visited Richard, an elderly parishioner, on Christmas Eve and they got to talking about Christmases past. Richard pointed to a black-and-white photo of a young girl, and said: "Christmas is the day she died. We had all her toys for her wrapped up, but she never got to see them. She wasn't even three. Then they told us we couldn't have any more children. My faith went a bit dodgy after that. Sister Monica came to see us and we talked about it. She said: I'm going to pray for you every day until you have another baby. And she did. Thirteen years later, we went back to the maternity hospital and my wife Annie gave birth to a baby girl. We gave her the toys we'd kept for our first daughter. You see, Father, miracles do happen."

Gospel Teaching

The readings today speak to us of the power of intercessory prayer, the kind of prayer Sister Monica made for Richard and Annie. Abraham prays for the sinful people of Sodom, asking God not to destroy the just along with the unjust. Beneath the colourful description – more reminiscent of market haggling than prayer – lies the deep conviction of the power of prayer to change things.

It is a conviction that Jesus shared. When his disciples asked him to teach them to pray, Jesus taught them the "Our Father", which is simply a prayer made up of five petitions, two concerning God and three for the disciples' own needs. The reason why Jesus has confidence in the power of intercessory prayer is found quite simply in the opening word: in the language Jesus spoke it is "Abba", "daddy". God is his Father – not a remote figure but one who is intimately close to him. A person who regards God as "daddy" is someone who has complete confidence that God will act on his or her behalf. Prayer has power to change things when we have that intimate, trusting relationship with God who is Abba.

Prayer, for Jesus, is never simply about asking for things; it is about having that intimate relationship with God. The disciples ask Jesus to teach them to pray precisely because they see him doing it, so often and with such intensity. They perceive the depth of his relationship with God, and this is what they wish to have also.

Jesus didn't simply teach the disciples a prayer; he taught them a whole attitude, a way of relating to God. Jesus stresses the importance of persisting in prayer, even if at times God seems to be like the reluctant friend who is slow to answer. Jesus tells us we need to persevere. Sister Monica's prayer was only answered after thirteen years. And prayer is not like magic, coercing God to do what we want. If we have an intimate relationship with God, then as well as persevering in prayer, we will also trust God when things do not work out precisely as we would want. God is a loving Father and we can rely on his goodness. If sinful or weak human beings know how to be kind to their children, how much more is this true of God.

The ultimate proof that God the Father wants only good things for his children is in his gift of his very own life, the Holy Spirit. There is nothing more that God can give than to allow us to share in his Spirit, his life. This is pure self-giving.

Application
St Luke's community was composed largely of Gentile Christians who had none of the Jewish familiarity with prayer which other early Christian communities had. It is only in Luke's Gospel that the disciples ask Jesus to teach them to pray. This reflects Luke's concern simply to encourage his people to do it.

It is a timely message for us today. So much is written and spoken about prayer, but there is no substitute for the actual practice of it. And Jesus' teaching is not complicated. The basis of all prayer is a relationship of trust and intimacy with God. Jesus calls us to develop a childlike dependence on the Father, which quite simply expects God to act in answer to our prayers and to give us what we need. Jesus tells us to persevere in prayer and to count on God's kindness. The ultimate proof of God's overflowing generosity is the gift of the Holy Spirit. This is the answer to our deepest longings and our most heartfelt prayer. It is a gift worth asking for.

"A man's life is not made secure by what he owns."

Illustration

On 14th April 1912, at 11.40 p.m., the RMS *Titanic* struck an iceberg in the north Atlantic. Within four hours, this "practically unsinkable" ship lay on the seabed some 12,600 feet below. Of the 2,228 people on board, only 705 survived.

Originally, the *Titanic* had been designed to have forty-eight lifeboats on board (enough for all the passengers and crew if needed). However, so great was the confidence of the ship's designers that they reduced this to just twenty lifeboats, apparently in order to prevent the decks from appearing too cluttered. This was enough for about half the people on board.

The designers had got their priorities tragically wrong. They had placed appearance before safety, elegance before lives. Even as the ship began to sink, passengers were reluctant to leave the apparent security of the liner to take their chances on the open sea in small lifeboats. This meant that many of the first lifeboats to be lowered were less than half full – a further example of misplaced confidence and wrong priorities.

Gospel Teaching

When the man in the crowd asks Jesus to settle a financial dispute with his brother, Jesus refuses to get involved. He knows that the man's underlying problem isn't this particular squabble over money, but lies in his fundamentally covetous mentality. Jesus warns of the dangers of greed, which can lead us to misplace our trust. We can look to wealth and riches for security, but Jesus warns that they will not only let us down but will also lead us to get our priorities all wrong.

In the parable of the rich farmer, Jesus depicts a man who thinks that life is all about riches. Once he has more than enough, he thinks that his life is complete, that he has nothing more to worry about. He places his trust in wealth to make him happy and fulfilled. Jesus does not accuse the man of being wicked or sinful; the rich man is simply wrong. His wealth leads him to think that life is nothing more than eating and drinking and being comfortable. He is the ultimate materialist, and in this he sells himself

18th Sunday in Ordinary Time

short. It is as if the man is only worth the sum of his possessions. He is what he owns.

And he is also blind in thinking that this life is all there is; he cannot see beyond the horizon of his own comfort now. His wealth has made him forget his responsibilities to his neighbour and to God; he is totally self-centred. His thoughts are all "I", "me" and "my". He has no one to celebrate his good fortune with, and no one he wants to share it with either. His wealth has isolated him completely.

Application

The rich man's materialist philosophy – which is so prevalent today – insists that life is all about possessions, money and status. It makes us poor in those very areas of life that in fact should make life worth living: love, relationships, neighbourliness and hope for a future beyond death. It also robs us of our true worth as human beings. It tells us that our value is to be measured only by the size of our bank accounts.

If we live like that – if our jobs, our status, our money are more important to us than our family, our friends, our own spirit – then we have got our priorities totally wrong. We work to live, not the other way round. We need money for the essentials – but making money is not the essence of life. Life is far richer than that. As the parable illustrates, money cannot save us. St Paul tells us that greed is in fact the same as idolatry: it is God alone, not money, that provides us with ultimate security and purpose in life.

Like the designers of the *Titanic*, it is easy for us to get our priorities wrong – to think in terms of what looks good, what appears attractive on the surface. And like those passengers who were reluctant to get into the lifeboats, we can be afraid to let go of what we have been told provides security. Greed blinds us to what is essential. It blinds us to our duty to God, to the needs of others and, ironically, to our own needs too. It isolates us from our community. Security is not to be found in possessions. We are truly rich when we put on a new self – the life of Christ. He is the only security we need.

C

"It was for faith that our ancestors were commended."

Illustration

On 17th April 1928 Francis Xavier Nguyen Van Thuan was born into a prestigious Catholic family in Hué, the capital of Vietnam. As he grew up, he developed a deep love for Jesus in the Eucharist and eventually realised that God was calling him to the priesthood. He was ordained a priest in 1953 and, following further studies in Rome, returned to Vietnam to work in the seminary, training future priests. In 1967 Pope Paul VI nominated Fr Van Thuan to be the bishop of a diocese north of Saigon. Despite the horrors of the Vietnam War, Bishop Van Thuan worked to spread the Second Vatican Council's teaching that every member of the Church is called to holiness of life.

In April 1974 Bishop Van Thuan was named as successor to the Archbishop of Saigon. He was a clear choice and a popular pastor, but the appointment didn't please everyone. The Communist authorities interpreted the move as opposition and in August 1975 Archbishop Van Thuan was placed under house arrest. Religious persecution in Vietnam became worse and the archbishop was sent to a "re-education camp". He remained there for the next thirteen years, nine of which were spent in solitary confinement. Thanks to the pressure of various international groups, Archbishop Van Thuan was released in November 1988, although he was later expelled from his native country. Until his death in 2002, he spent the last years of his life, eventually as a cardinal, working in Rome at the Pontifical Council for Justice and Peace.

During his time in prison, Archbishop Van Thuan was desperate to encourage his people not to be afraid and not to lose heart. He began to send them short but inspiring messages of faith, one thousand and one in total. These were smuggled out of his cell and collected into a book. Despite having had everything taken away from him, Archbishop Van Thuan knew his captors couldn't steal his faith. This was his strength and his joy. Profound yet simple faith in Jesus Christ offered a light in the darkness. It was sure and certain guidance along the road of hope.

Gospel Teaching

Although we might sometimes take our faith for granted, the scriptures that are set before us today ask us to think more deeply about how and what we believe. This is at the heart of what it means to be a disciple.

For the people of Israel, a sense of faith is rooted in the experience of God who freed them from slavery in Egypt. They put their trust in God's promises and God was faithful. More than this, God continued to be faithful even when the Israelites doubted or were rebellious. In fact, one of the reasons for the book of Wisdom recalling the events of God's liberation of Israel from Egypt was to give an encouragement to faith in the face of later troubles and disappointments.

Reflecting then on the importance of faith, the figures of Abraham and Sarah give us further examples of what it means to live according to God's will. Their faith was so genuine and sincere that they could leave the security of their home for a land God would show them. Although Sarah was beyond the age of having children, they had faith in God's pledge that she would give birth to a child, and she did. Abraham was even prepared to sacrifice his son as a test of his faith. According to the letter to the Hebrews, he was confident that God could raise the dead so that the promise of descendants would be fulfilled.

With the coming of Jesus among us, faith takes on a new dimension. Jesus reveals God to us in and through the flesh and blood of a living person. We don't have an abstract or distant faith, but a personal relationship with God's Son. His words to us are important because they help us realise that everything we are and everything we do is bound up with the life of heaven. When Jesus tells his disciples to be ready, to keep awake, he's calling us to live each day in faithfulness, attentive to his promise to return in glory.

Application

In one of his spiritual messages Archbishop Van Thuan wrote that Christian faith is essentially about an unconditional acceptance of Jesus Christ as Lord, combined with a real determination to live and die with hope in him. This is what a personal and living faith really means.

C

"Do you suppose that I am here to bring peace on earth?"

Illustration

During the 1930s Winston Churchill experienced what are called his "wilderness years". He was out of government, out of office and out of style. His day was over and done with, his influence on British public life seemingly in decline. Churchill retired to his country home in Kent, south of London, tended his garden, built brick walls and brooded.

In particular, he brooded about Hitler and the rise of Fascism and Nazism in Europe. Alarmed at what he heard about the rearmament of Germany, Churchill began to make speeches in the House of Commons, calling on the government of the day to be vigilant and to rearm the country against the threat of German might.

In reply, Members of Parliament denounced Churchill as a warmonger. After the horror of the First World War, nobody wanted to contemplate the possibility of another conflict. Peace was the order of the day, and any talk of arms and fighting would only serve to depress people and to dishearten them. It was madness to talk of war, and only a madman would contemplate such a thing. Churchill was ignored. But Churchill was right. The sad truth came all too quickly, to blight another generation and to send millions to the grave.

Gospel Teaching

In Jerusalem long ago, the prophet Jeremiah found himself in a similar situation. For many years he had warned his own people about the coming disaster. Now the enemy was at the gate, and no amount of fighting would save the city from ruin. But this sad truth was not welcome. No one wanted to hear such a message. So Jeremiah was removed from the scene. He was not killed outright, but put in a well, where no one could see him or hear him or be influenced by him. There it was the intention that he should slowly rot, and starve to death. It was a cruel form of "shoot the messenger".

Jeremiah had found himself in an impossible position. He felt compelled to tell people the truth: that they should turn to God and rely on God rather than on human strength for their protection. At the same time

Jeremiah knew that people would not be able to accept what he said, because the situation was so desperate. He would merely be branded a coward, a traitor and a deserter. So, at the price of suffering and perhaps losing his life, Jeremiah was faithful to God and delivered the message.

As Jesus makes his way to Jerusalem and to his own date with destiny, he finds himself caught in this same dilemma. He is burning with zeal for his heavenly Father, and for the mission of love that he brings to the world. And yet the price he will have to pay for his efforts is frightening. The shadow of the cross looms large, and Jesus knows that his enemies will show him no mercy. The prospect of pain looms so large that Jesus yearns for the ordeal to be over and finished.

And as for talk of peace, Jesus knows that, for all his words about love and mercy and patience and perseverance, he will know no peace in this world. He is attacked and tormented at every turn by those who feel themselves threatened by his goodness. Holiness has enemies and they know how to torture their victims. Even families will find themselves at odds over Jesus and his Gospel.

Application

Today Jesus describes our lives quite simply in terms of trouble. The conflict that marked the life of Jesus marks our lives too. The Gospel of love, the Gospel of the resurrection, is signed with the cross; and if we are followers of Jesus then we too will be signed with that cross. We are urged today to keep our eyes firmly fixed on Our Lord, and not to lose sight of him. And we are encouraged in our struggles by the example and the spiritual company of all God's faithful people, who, together, walk this road of Calvary and Easter.

Many years ago, as a young theologian, Pope Benedict XVI described the life of a Christian in the world. Our first task, he said, is to preach the Gospel of Jesus. Our second task is to bring the fire of God's love to the world. Our final task is to suffer for the sake of others, as Our Lord did himself. This is the basic law for all disciples of Christ. This is the way we are called to follow.

C

"Yes, there are those now last who will be first, and those now first who will be last."

Illustration

The Russian author Dostoevsky once recalled how he found himself one Easter as a political prisoner in Siberia. He was so disgusted at the violence and drunkenness of his fellow prisoners that he retreated to his bunk to blot them out. There he suddenly remembered an incident from his childhood. While wandering alone one day in a meadow, he thought he heard a wolf coming. He ran in terror to the only other figure around, the family serf Marei, who was ploughing the field. Marei comforted him in his distress and asked him to make the sign of the cross. When Dostoevsky was unable to cross himself to take away his fear, Marei gently smiled at him and touched his lips.

Dostoevsky twenty years later recalled how Marei could not have looked at him with more serene love, had he been his own son. Yet Marei was a peasant serf, and Dostoevsky a nobleman's son. No one would know of his action and no one would reward him. Only God could know what a profound and human feeling, what delicate tenderness, may fill the heart of a rough Russian peasant serf. Dostoevsky got down from his bunk and found he was looking at his fellow prisoners with completely different eyes. Suddenly, as though by some miracle, all the hatred and anger had vanished from his heart.

Gospel Teaching

Luke reminds us again that Jesus is on his way to Jerusalem. He does not take us on a geographical journey. Rather it is a journey through the characteristics of discipleship, and Jesus illustrates in both words and deeds what following him means.

When the question of salvation is broached, who is to be saved and who not, Jesus avoids any statistical approach. His concern is rather to create an earnest desire in his listeners to pursue salvation with every ounce of their being. His teaching fits with today's reading from the letter to the Hebrews, which talks of how the Lord trains those he loves. A sense of intense concentration and commitment is required if we are to be true disciples.

In the first example Jesus gives us, he speaks of endeavouring to enter by the narrow door. In his next example the door is locked, and we cannot assume that we will gain entry just because we have vaguely associated with the right people. At the same time there will be many that we might think to be outsiders, not worthy either of our or of God's consideration, who will take their places at the feast in the kingdom. Luke combines his deep awareness that there is a universal call to salvation with his appreciation that, once we have heard that call, we are to respond with wholehearted dedication. It is only too easy for us to judge others while ignoring our own failings. That is to miss the point of Christ's invitation.

Application
We live in a world that has vast and immediate systems of communication. One of the effects of this is that we know things that have happened across the world within minutes of them taking place. It would be nice to think that this would make us more aware of a shared destiny among all human beings. Sadly, the opposite is often the case. Each incident tends to make us react defensively, particularly if it highlights a struggle between ethnic or religious groups. We automatically think "our" group must be right and try to find ways of supporting our claim.

Jesus challenges such assumptions. Many of the groups we feel to be in some way less enlightened or less civilised than us may hold truths and understanding that we need humbly to listen to and appreciate rather than treat with disdain. If we are able to get inside the minds of those who seem most different from ourselves and acknowledge their generosity and goodness, at that point the doors of perception open in ourselves. As Dostoevsky experienced, not only do we see their goodness in relation to ourselves: that goodness acts as a key to unlock our hearts towards others.

Often we struggle to understand others. We make assumptions about their motives and morality, sometimes because of their actions but often just because of the group they belong to. In the end people share the same hopes and fears, the same mixture of drives to good and evil. It is ours to rejoice when they offer us evidence of their conquest of evil and their delight in what is good.

C

"Everyone… who humbles himself will be exalted."

Illustration

Imagine yourself arriving at a wedding reception. You enter the dining hall, its tables glistening with snowy-white tablecloths and the guests cheerfully moving towards their seats. Uppermost in your mind is the thought: where, I wonder, is my place?

One thing is certain: you wouldn't dream of marching up to the top table, unless, of course, you were certain that that's where your allotted place was. Far better to wander towards one of those tables near the door and have someone call out to you: "Come up here, you're on this table."

Gospel Teaching

In today's Gospel, Jesus isn't out to give us a lesson in etiquette. He's drawing a vital moral from the way people tend to "lower" themselves rather than risk embarrassment. He wants us to see that humility is of crucial importance in our lives as Christians; and so he tells us that those who humble themselves will be exalted. Genuine humility certainly isn't pretence, putting on an act, playing down our talents as a way of fishing for compliments. "Sorry, I can't sing," you say, trusting that someone will respond, "Of course you can, you sing like an angel."

A little girl in earnest conversation with her mother suddenly made the delightful comment: "Mum, I'm not pretending now, I'm 'reallying'." Humility is "reallying"; it is facing up to reality, to truth. The most basic reality of all is that we are God's creatures, and humility is the practical acknowledgement that everything I have and am comes from God, all is sheer gift. And if I happen to have some special talent, then my gratitude and my humility ought to be all the greater.

The saints were genuinely humble people because they were vividly aware of God's generosity towards them. St Teresa of Ávila, for example, explained that once she began to understand how much she had received from God, she wanted to fall on her knees in joy and wonder: she was filled with "a sense of unpayable debt". It's that sense of "unpayable debt" that's at the heart of humility: it sets us before God in an attitude of joy and gratitude and surrender; we belong completely to God. St Teresa also added: "I cannot understand how there is or can be humility without love."

Application

Genuine humility sparks off a deeper love of God; it also leads to a deeper respect for our fellow human beings. Facing up to God's reality is only a step away from discovering the reality that binds all human beings together: we all belong to what Jesus calls "the lowest place". No matter what our position in society, our education, our wealth or our natural gifts, we are all essentially equal, all paupers enriched by God. Since there's nothing we have not received, there's nothing that places us above others, nothing for us to boast about.

It's easy to look down upon certain people as our inferiors; perhaps that is why Jesus singles out those of his day who were regarded as second-class citizens – "the poor, the crippled, the lame, the blind" – and explains that they are the ones who are to be accorded special treatment and respect. It might be revealing to compile a list of the untouchables, the marginalised, the second-class citizens of our day – asylum seekers, perhaps, or people with AIDS, or prisoners – and ask ourselves honestly: do we look down upon them? Do we consider ourselves better than them?

"There is no cure for the proud man's malady," today's first reading insists, and there isn't, so long as he persists in his pride. If humility is "reallying", pride is living in a fantasy world, a make-believe world. The proud person is like the mouse that found itself on the tailgate of a farmer's wagon as it was being driven along a dusty path; looking back along the way it had come, the mouse struck its chest and said: "Wow, see the dust I've raised!" In wonderful contrast, the loveliest of all God's creatures proclaimed: "The Almighty has done great things for me. Holy is his name." Mary raised more dust, so to say, than any other human being, but she knew where her greatness came from. Let's humbly take our place with her as, in this Mass, we proclaim and magnify the Lord who has done such great things for us.

22nd Sunday in Ordinary Time

"Not as a slave any more, but… a dear brother."

Illustration

In 1833 William Wilberforce was buried among the great and good in Westminster Abbey, London. It was a posthumous honour richly deserved. Inspired by a deep Christian faith, Wilberforce had served as a politician for almost fifty years. He'd been an ardent supporter of several causes, including universal education and religious liberty; but above all he was renowned for his commitment to the abolition of slavery, even though he must often have felt almost alone in his struggle. Every year for eighteen years he raised the issue in the British Parliament and was rewarded when, just three days before his death, he was finally assured that a bill for the complete abolition of slavery in all British territories was to be passed by Parliament.

It may seem astonishing to us today that it took Christians so long to recognise the evils of slavery. Even St Paul seems never to have condemned it. In Paul's day, slavery was part and parcel of the social structures. Nonetheless, Paul in effect planted the seeds for the future destruction of slavery, first by insisting on the absolute equality of all people, slave or free, and secondly by urging Christians who possessed slaves to treat them compassionately. In today's liturgy we are given a delightful example of how he went about it.

Gospel Teaching

Paul's letter to Philemon is more like a postcard than a letter, as it is just twenty-five verses long. Eight of these verses appear in today's second reading. The letter concerns three people: Paul himself; a runaway slave called Onesimus; and the slave's master, Philemon. Onesimus had pocketed some of Philemon's money, escaped and headed for Rome, hoping to lie low in the great city.

At this time Paul was imprisoned in Rome, and one day the two men met. We do not know how the meeting came about but we do know its outcome. Onesimus the slave was baptised; he was, in Paul's beautiful words, "a child of mine, whose father I became while wearing these chains". Eventually, Paul persuaded Onesimus to return to his master Philemon, who was also a Christian; and, to make reconciliation easier, Paul wrote a brief letter, begging Philemon to receive Onesimus back – however, "not as a slave any more" but as "a dear brother".

All three men were guided by their Christian faith to live by new standards: Gospel standards. First Paul: he is an old man by this time, languishing in prison for the faith, and still anxious to help both Onesimus and Philemon to behave in a Christian way. Then there's Onesimus: his conversion means that he has to return to his master. Despite the message from Paul, still it must have seemed a crazy thing to do. Finally there's Philemon: because he is a Christian he is told by Paul not to behave as others might. The relationship between him and the slave can never be the same as it was. Onesimus has gone from being a runaway slave to being a brother.

Application

Not only are these ideas revolutionary, they are a practical application of today's Gospel. The way Jesus puts it – with the words about "hating" family members and even our own life – may sound shocking to our ears; but it is simply a powerful way of making the point that we cannot be true followers of Christ if we allow anyone or anything to come between us and him. Obviously, we may not be called literally to hate parents or children, or to get rid of all our possessions, but Jesus insists that being a Christian means that we have to be prepared sometimes to be different, to be the odd one out – like William Wilberforce, like Paul, Onesimus and Philemon.

So Jesus begs us not to be like the foolish men he describes. Have we really assessed what following him may mean – not just coming to Mass each week but trying to live out Gospel values during the rest of the week too? It's been said that Jesus came to comfort the disturbed and to disturb the comfortable. Maybe we have been disturbed a little today by the words of our readings, but a bit of that kind of disturbance may be no bad thing for any of us.

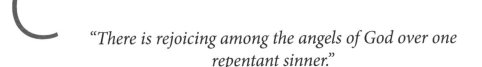

"There is rejoicing among the angels of God over one repentant sinner."

Illustration

Bishop William Gordon Wheeler, the Bishop of Leeds, England, from 1966 to 1985, often used to tell the story of how he once became lost while travelling to a speaking engagement. He was en route to St George's Hall in the city of Bradford, but completely lost his way. After driving round and round in the car, unable to find the right street, he eventually saw a young boy standing beside the road. So he stopped the car to ask the boy for directions. Winding down the window, he said to the boy, "Listen, I'm hopelessly lost; can you please tell me how to get to St George's Hall?" Instead of giving instructions, the boy looked puzzled and asked the bishop, "What do you want to go there for?" "Because I'm due to give a talk," replied Bishop Wheeler, "and I am already late." "What's the talk about?" the boy asked. "Well, it's about how to get heaven," said the bishop, "would you like to come and hear it?" "Me come and listen to you?" the boy replied. "How will you be able to tell me how to get to heaven when you don't even know the way to St George's Hall?"

Putting aside the humour of Bishop Wheeler's story, being lost can be a terrible and frightening experience. If we can't find the right direction or don't know the way back home, we can quickly feel anxious. If we somehow get separated from familiar people and places we can very soon start to panic.

Gospel Teaching

When Jesus wanted to help those around him come to a deeper understanding of God's searching love, he used the example of three things that were lost and then found again. These images teach us important truths, both about God and about ourselves.

The first image, of the lost sheep, reminds us that God cares about individuals. The details of people's lives matter to God and every single person is important. God so desires to include everyone that the majority must give way to the minority. The ninety-nine are left in order that the wayward stray might be found and brought safely home. The missing sheep is not punished by the shepherd. Rather, the shepherd joyfully lifts the sheep high on his shoulders, raising the one who was lost to a new dignity. He then calls others to rejoice in the homecoming.

The second image, the woman searching out the mislaid coin, reveals the extent of God's urgent longing that no one should be lost. The woman stops at nothing, putting incredible energy into finding the missing money.

Finally, Jesus tells the story of the lost son, the arrogant young man who rejects all that his father provides in order to do things his own way. Only when he is completely and utterly lost does he remember how different things had been, how different they could be if only he returned home. By describing this human father's patient waiting, his passionate forgiving embrace and his restoration of his child to his rightful place, Jesus teaches about his divine Father and a love that knows no limit.

In each of these stories Jesus reveals God's longing that those who are lost, those who have sinned, return home. God searches for us far more intensely than a shepherd seeks a lost sheep, a woman a lost coin, or even a father a lost son. Our heavenly Father will not rest until we are back where we belong, close to his heart. And when we are, there is rejoicing in heaven.

Application

Allowing ourselves to be found by God is not a one-off event, it's a lifelong process. Certainly we can make a decisive and fundamental choice to live a Christian life, but none of us is beyond the need for repentance.

We have in the sacrament of reconciliation a beautiful means of making these three parables come to life in our personal discipleship. Each time we go to confession we are lifted high again on the Good Shepherd's shoulders. Whenever we humbly confess our sins, the house of our heart is swept clean. When we receive absolution, we are embraced afresh by the Father as his precious daughter or son. Perhaps the fruit of hearing again these familiar stories might be that we find encouragement to seek the peace and joy of sacramental reconciliation. If there is rejoicing in heaven when a sinner repents, why not give the angels something to sing about?

C

"They will welcome you into the tents of eternity."

Illustration

What kind of people do you think Jesus spent most of his time with? Perhaps we tend to forget that Jesus spent much of his ministry among the outcasts of society, the people whom respectable religious citizens regarded as "dodgy". Perhaps we prefer to imagine that Our Lord dealt with nice, deserving people – people like us, we might like to think; and no doubt there were those in Luke's community who thought this too.

But in today's Gospel Luke relates a parable told by Jesus that is not "nice", but a tale of sharp dealing and shady practices – the story of those out to seize any opportunity to improve their lot, and not too concerned about how they did it. Yet this is an exploration of what we are truly like and how we should respond to the call of the Gospel.

Gospel Teaching

Today's Gospel is not about moral advice; instead it tells us how to live now in the hope of eternity. It is meant to engage with us and make us see that the Gospel is about a life-and-death decision, the most important we shall ever make. If we look at Luke's Gospel, we can see that he focuses on money more than any of the other Gospel writers. We see it right from his infancy narrative; in John the Baptist's teaching; in the parable of the prodigal son; in the unfavourable comparison of Jewish cities with the pagan Queen of Sheba and Nineveh; in the story of Dives and Lazarus; in Jesus' bitter controversies with the Pharisees, "lovers of money"; and right on to the betrayal of Jesus by Judas.

This Gospel was written for a world of intensely money-conscious city-dwellers. The majority were poor dependent clients of their wealthier patrons, but that web of interdependency was repeated endlessly up the chain to the emperor. The rich expected to give to the less well off, anything from the provision of public buildings, temples and baths, entertainments and a grain dole in times of famine, to various other needs. Many patrons made daily payments to their clients so they could eat, and the clients in return gave their patrons public honour and votes in local elections. It was a corrupt and venal world in which only the canny survived.

Jesus' story was intensely engaging to his hearers, for it was the stuff of their daily lives; it was about how they kept their heads above water amidst the dangerous currents of life in the city. The steward, who through his laziness has failed to perform as a fitting client of his master, seizes the initiative in order to guarantee himself a secure future when dismissed. He rewrites the loans of the two merchants indebted to his master, reducing the interest due on their loans. By so doing he has assumed the role of patron, making them into his clients, indebted to him for their futures; and so he has made them dependent upon him, required to help him out when he calls upon them to do so. The steward has established a new order of mutual responsibility in which the merchants "owe" him. He acts with barefaced effrontery both to swindle his master and pinch his clients. It was precisely what many of Jesus' hearers would have done; or alternatively they might have experienced having such things done to them.

Application

Jesus was intensely aware of these patterns of social obligation and speaks here of the radical action of one of the "wheeler-dealers" of his age. He uses it as an allegory for how we gain entry into the kingdom of God. He describes it not in spiritual terms, but by using an image that is vibrant and raw; not just for the holy few, but something the majority of the poor city-dwellers could recognise as they tried to survive among the sharp practices of their day. And Jesus says that the Gospel demands a similarly sharp response. We are reminded that we are all desperate people, urgently in need of God's grace. We are asked to bring to our faith all the cunning and graft that we adopt towards our most urgent earthly needs.

So what are we called to do, in response to what may seem strange and uncomfortable words of Jesus? We are called to respond to the urgency of the Gospel, for deep down we are often lazy stewards too, needing to be provoked to take that decisive leap of faith.

*"They have Moses and the prophets… let them
listen to them."*

Illustration

Pope Gregory the Great sent missionaries to England in AD 597 to convert the Angles and Saxons to the Christian faith. When Edwin, King of Northumbria, heard the Gospel message, he held a council of his nobles to discuss this new religion. One wise nobleman concluded the discussion: "It seems to me, your majesty, that our human life is like a banqueting hall. You are sitting at table feasting, with the warm fire blazing in the hearth, while outside the wintry storm rages. A sparrow enters through a window, flies the length of the hall, enjoying the light and warmth, and then flies out back into the cold wintry darkness from which it came. So with us. At birth we emerge from who knows where, and for a short time we live here on earth, with its light and comfort, but then we fly out back into the darkness. We know nothing of what went before and what comes after. If this new teaching can lighten the darkness for us, let us follow it."

Gospel Teaching

The unnamed rich man in our story is someone who has no interest in "what comes after". He sees no further than the present moment. He enjoys to the full the comforts and pleasures of this present life. He foresees no consequences to his lifestyle. He cannot conceive that there is a "before" or an "after". Or if there is, he simply does not believe that his afterlife will in any way be adversely affected by his earthly life.

Such beliefs were not uncommon at the time of Jesus. The Sadducees, who tended to be among the most affluent people in Jewish society, believed that at death everyone, good and bad alike, went to the shadowy underworld of the dead – Sheol, or Hades. They believed that there was neither reward nor punishment in the afterlife. The rich man in today's story clearly shares that outlook.

Unlike the early Angles and Saxons, he has absolutely no interest in the afterlife. In this way, he represents the mentality of many in modern society, with its "live for the moment" attitude and its strong emphasis on getting the most out of life for yourself. He would feel very much at home in our twenty-first-century materialist culture, which often defines people by how much they earn, or consume, or spend. It's not that he is unaware of the poor man at his gate, since, in Hades, he recognises Lazarus and calls him by name. He simply doesn't care – he cannot see beyond himself. He is totally caught up in his own pleasure. His lifestyle is one of conspicuous consumption. He does no harm to Lazarus, is not violent or abusive. He simply ignores him. And he thinks that such actions in this life have no meaning, no significance, no lasting consequences.

Application

The rich man believes that a person rising from the dead will convince his brothers to change their ways. Abraham is unconvinced. They have the Law of Moses and the prophets, who speak long and loud about the obligation to care for those who are poor. The point of this story is not simply to show that our actions have consequences in the afterlife – though clearly that is part of their message. The story points to a wider question about the meaning of life here and now – whom we listen to, whose values we choose to live by. The rich man ignores Moses and the prophets – he ignores God's vision for humanity. He chooses instead to look only to himself, to his own comfort. It is materialism taken to the extreme.

The Law, the prophets, the Gospel, challenge us to a deeper truth – to refuse to accept injustice, poverty, exploitation of those who are weak. They invite us to genuine love of neighbour – not just because of future reward, but simply because it is right in itself. Being truly human means living with a commitment to, and concern for, one's fellow human beings.

To reduce life to physical pleasure and consumerism is in fact to live an impoverished life. To live only for self, and purely for this life, is to cheapen what it means to be human. As our Anglo-Saxon wise man might say, this is the darkness which the light of the Gospel dispels. The Gospel reveals the true meaning of life: that practical love of neighbour leads to a fuller and more satisfying experience of life in the here and now, as well as in the life to come.

"God's gift was not a spirit of timidity."

Illustration

In the world of business there is a simple concept that is often quoted when trying to motivate people: "If you think something is going to happen then you are probably right."

If we convince ourselves that something is not going to work, or is impossible to achieve, then we are bound to make our thinking a reality, as there is no vision or real hope for a successful outcome. If, on the other hand, our sights are set on a project, however ambitious, and our energies are being invested to make it a reality, we are far more likely to achieve success and see our dreams realised.

Belief is a central part of every aspect of our world, even the business world. Entrepreneurs are people who are prepared to face difficult odds and invest their time, money and energy into believing in their project and the people who can help realise it. They are not afraid to ask others for help and support in order to achieve their aims, and they are not easily put off by failure or rebuttal. Such people stand in marked contrast with their competitors who do not appear to have the same belief, vision, drive and ability to enlist others to help in their enterprise.

Gospel Teaching

It is heartening to hear the apostles ask Jesus to increase their faith. These same apostles have the privilege of travelling around the countryside with Jesus, hearing him preach at first hand and seeing with their own eyes miraculous events. Even so, they still feel the need to ask the Lord to help them in the matter of faith.

Jesus' response is neither to lecture them on the weakness of their faith, nor to give them a quick seminar on the steps necessary for deepening their faith. He simply gives an example of what they would be capable of if they had even the smallest amount of faith.

St Paul echoes this teaching of Jesus, by reminding the community with Timothy that faith is a precious treasure that has been gifted to us. As such it is something to be guarded and looked after carefully. However, St Paul does not expect the community to guard the gift by their own efforts;

no, he reminds them that the Holy Spirit is within them to help them. This gift is not something that will diminish the individual, but rather it will enable, empower and strengthen the person who possesses it. Even though the community may experience trouble and strife, they are never to shrink from witnessing to the love of God, as it is the power of God itself that is to be relied upon.

Paul knows from his own personal experience what Jesus means when he says, "Were your faith the size of a mustard seed…" Paul has witnessed the power of God at work through his own missionary travels. He is therefore at pains to ensure that the newly established Christian communities know this for themselves and so continue to allow their faith to increase.

Application
Occasionally we may experience a lack of faith, or just assume that everyone else has more faith than we do. Let us take comfort that the apostles knew this experience, as did the early Christian communities. However, let us also learn that when the apostles and the early Christians really allowed their faith to take centre stage in their lives, they experienced the power and love of God in a very real way.

At the beginning of his pontificate, Pope Benedict XVI spoke of the fear that some people have at the thought of giving themselves to Christ. The fear is that by letting Christ into our lives, we might end up diminished or deprived. However, the Pope spoke of his conviction that the opposite is true: "If we let Christ into our lives we lose nothing, nothing, absolutely nothing of what makes life free, beautiful and great."

The scriptures remind us that faith is a gift, which has been entrusted to us. So precious is this gift that we are not expected to look after it on our own. We are asked to turn to the Holy Spirit to help us grow in faith. When was the last time we prayed for an increase in faith? The apostles obviously were not afraid to ask, so we too can have the courage to do so. After all, we are in the business of working for the building up of God's kingdom in our midst.

C

"One of them turned back praising God."

Illustration

A woman in her nineties used to take a taxi to Mass every Sunday morning because she was no longer able to get to church unaided. Very often she got the same taxi driver, and one Sunday morning he said to her, "Why do you bother coming to church every Sunday at your age?" She replied, "To say 'thank you'. Just to say 'thank you'."

That old woman had a very profound understanding of what we are doing when we come to Mass. Before all else we are saying "thank you". That in essence is what the Mass is – an act of thanksgiving. That's what the word "Eucharist" means. The meaning of the Mass is summed up in the dialogue before the Preface when we say, "It is right to give [the Lord] thanks and praise." And then in the Preface itself which begins with the words, "Father, all-powerful and ever-living God, we do well always and everywhere to give you thanks."

So we are here today at this Mass to say "thank you". What are we saying thank you *for*? If the taxi driver had asked the old woman that question, she might have said something like this: "I'm saying thank you for my life, for my long life. It's sometimes been hard; there have been bad times as well as good. But in times of hardship and difficulty I've always felt God was with me, supporting me. So I thank God for that. I say thank you for my late husband. He's long gone now, but he was a good man and a good father to our children. I say thank you for all my family, for my friends, for all the people I love. They have meant so much to me in my life. I say thank you to God for his Son Jesus Christ and for Mary his mother. I pray to them every day. It's such a joy to be able to do that. I say thank you for all the other people with me at Mass – especially the children. I love to watch them lighting candles and saying their own little prayers… I could go on and on. There's so much to thank God for."

Each of us could make our own list of reasons for giving thanks to God, but we don't usually think about all the things on that list every time we come to Mass. Nor is it necessary. What's important is that we come to Mass in a spirit of thankfulness.

Gospel Teaching

Jesus makes clear how important it is to give thanks in today's Gospel reading. He was astounded and hurt that only one of the ten lepers who were cured came back to give thanks to God.

They had pleaded with him to take pity on them. In telling them to go and show themselves to the priest, Jesus was responding to their plea. The priest had to confirm a cure before a leper could take his or her place in the community again. On the way to the priest the lepers found that they were cured, but only one came back to say "thank you". In fact Jesus uses the word "praise". He said, "It seems that no one has come back to give *praise* to God, except this foreigner." Praise and thanksgiving are intimately linked in the mind of Jesus. In both we acknowledge God's goodness to us.

Application

Thanksgiving is not an added extra. It is absolutely central to the life of a Christian. Without a spirit of thanksgiving, our Christian lives would be cold and lifeless. An attitude of mind in which thankfulness has no part is likely to lead to pettiness, resentment and cynicism. God takes a back seat in our lives and we begin to go our own way. Thankfulness, on the other hand, preserves a right relationship with God. If we are thankful, God is necessarily part of our lives. It is difficult to see how we could turn away from God permanently and irrevocably if we preserve an attitude of thankfulness. Even if we have serious sins we find it difficult to overcome, we will not be permanently separated from God if we can still acknowledge the Lord's love and goodness and thank him for it. To be thankful is to see reality clearly.

That's what we're doing today and every time we come to Mass. As the old woman said to the taxi driver, we have come to say "thank you"; just to say "thank you".

"Never lose heart."

Illustration

A university in the United States conducted an experiment on the effectiveness of prayer. Researchers collected information about a number of volunteers who were seriously ill in hospital. The details of half the patients were circulated to various religious groups around the world, to get them to pray for them. The other half of the patients, the control group, were not prayed for. None of the volunteers knew whether or not they belonged to the group who would be prayed for. The result of the experiment showed that those who were prayed for did not survive or recover any better than those who had not been prayed for. So why bother to pray at all?

Gospel Teaching

For the Israelites in today's first reading, the issue seems to have been straightforward: while Moses prayed, they were successful; when he stopped, they began to fail. So prayer works. It may seem from today's Gospel that Jesus too shares this mechanistic view of prayer. If, like the widow in the parable, you persist, God will give you what you ask for; give up, and you can forget it.

To us, such a view can seem simplistic and to fly in the face of experience. There is a paradox about prayer. Why does God, who loves us and knows our needs, want us to pray? Surely not in order to inform God about our misfortunes, since God already knows those things? Surely not to get the Lord to change his plans? That seems unlikely with a wise and loving God. And from experience we may perceive that it doesn't seem to be the case that God helps only those who do pray and refuses those who don't.

So why pray? Luke tells us that today's parable is about the need never to lose heart. We will never know this side of eternity why God seems to intervene in response to some prayers and not to others. The university experiment, of course, was unable to measure the possibility that God had answered the prayers, but in ways that had not been asked for or were not directly measurable, such as the effect on the patient, other than physical recovery.

But however God chooses to answer our prayers, prayer undoubtedly has the power to change and move us. When we pray, we open ourselves up to seeing the world through God's eyes, from God's perspective. It then becomes impossible for us to pray for peace and justice without acting to bring those things about. And similarly, we cannot pray with integrity for someone to get well, and then blithely ignore their practical needs. Often, God's response to prayer is quite simply to motivate us, the ones who are doing the praying, to act.

Application

Prayer always takes place in the context of a lived relationship with God. Prayer is never just about intercession, asking God for things, since that is to turn God into a kind of fairy godmother, arbitrarily answering or ignoring our requests. God is the sovereign Lord of all creation, including our lives. So when we pray, we always do so knowing that God wants only what is good for us. So the greatest prayer, the Our Father, asks simply: "Thy will be done." That is the basis of all our prayer. If we don't mean that, then any other prayers we make are in fact just wishes, hopes and fancies. But if we pray and truly believe that God's will, and God's will alone, will bring us happiness, then we will never lose heart in our prayer and in our relationship with God, whatever the apparent outcome of our prayer.

Always mystery surrounds our faith, because we live in a fallen world in which evil things happen. Our prayer is part of our faith-filled response to that evil. But we model our prayer on Jesus' own prayer in the Garden of Gethsemane: "Father, if you are willing, take this cup away from me. Nevertheless, let your will be done, not mine." That prayer was persistent but it was also trusting. This is what Paul calls the "wisdom that leads to salvation through faith in Christ Jesus". God does act to answer prayer, though sometimes in ways we never dreamed of. Jesus' prayer did not save him from the cross, but it did lead to resurrection. If we can pray with Jesus' faith, we will never lose heart; for if God's will is done, then our victory is assured and our prayers are answered.

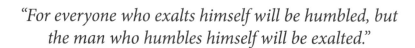

"For everyone who exalts himself will be humbled, but the man who humbles himself will be exalted."

Illustration

Rob was new to the area and when he first entered his local church he said he found it "very daunting walking into a church of five hundred people". Over several weeks he began to feel less of a stranger and welcomed the sign of peace, which gave an opportunity to greet and be greeted by people sitting near him. He especially liked the music that was led by the church's folk group. He had once been a reasonable singer and guitarist himself. As the weeks passed, he increasingly joined in the singing with gusto, so much so that members of the group began to notice him. One day a couple of them came over to him after the service and thanked him for his support. They invited him to join the group. One asked him if he had just moved into the neighbourhood.

Rob felt a wave of panic come over him. He hadn't been invited to join anything for some years, and he felt he couldn't just say "yes" and come along. He felt too much like an outsider. "I have recently moved into a flat in this area," he said nervously, "after a spell in prison." After a pause, he added, "I'm just trying to find my feet again." Was he imagining it, or did the smiles freeze? He sensed that they immediately regretted approaching him. He felt as if their friendliness and warmth towards him were withdrawn. "Well, if you feel you'd like to sing with us at any time, just let us know," one stammered. They moved to pack up their instruments. As he left the church he observed the heightened conversation and glances in his direction. He suspected he wouldn't be welcome again.

Gospel Teaching

Today's Gospel is one to which every believer is called to pay close attention, particularly those of us who are pillars of our parishes. The Pharisee and the tax collector in the story were both active believers who participated in Temple worship and said their daily prayers. Pharisees were serious-minded believers who had committed themselves to a life of regular prayer and observance of God's Law. They felt justified in thinking well of themselves. They tended to love only "good", respectable people like themselves and look down with contempt on sinners like the tax collectors, who were generally regarded as people of low moral standards. Because tax collectors worked for the pagan Romans, mixed with them and constantly handled their unclean money, they were in a state of ritual uncleanness.

The tax collector stays on the edge of the Temple court, not venturing into a prominent spot. In contrast to the proud Pharisee, the tax collector doesn't even lift his hands or his eyes heavenward. Instead, he pounds his chest, a sign of deep contrition. He cries out to God in despair, overwhelmed by the gulf separating him from the divine. Unexpectedly, it is not the devout Pharisee, but the penitent tax collector who is commended. The Lord accepts his sacrifice of a broken and contrite heart.

Application
Careful observance of religious dogma can breed pride. Believing in God is not enough. Rather, what really matters is what people believe about God and how their faith in God affects their view of themselves and of others. The Pharisees believed in a God who was quick to judge and condemn anyone who fell outside the norms of what they considered acceptable behaviour, and so they themselves were similarly quick to condemn. But Jesus teaches that those who arrogantly trust in themselves and despise others reject God, no matter how many their religious activities, or how worthy they may outwardly appear to be. Their worship tends to become self-centred, and, as they reject others, they make God in their own image. The musicians in our story who rejected the ex-prisoner might as well have got up in the morning and sung "How great thou art" to the mirror.

Let us learn from the tax collector the secret of worshipping in a manner that is acceptable to God. We are called to acknowledge our sinfulness and entrust ourselves to the generous mercy of God, which is bigger than any sins we might have committed. Jesus teaches us never to look down on our fellow sinners but to help them in their search for God. Our church communities are to be open and welcoming to all, especially to those at the margins of society, such as ex-offenders. God always opposes the proud, but gives grace to the humble.

"And he hurried down and welcomed him joyfully."

Illustration

On Boxing Day 2004 a tidal wave of immense proportions hit the coasts of Sri Lanka, Indonesia, India and Thailand. It was the result of one of the largest earthquakes ever recorded. It became known as the Asian tsunami and killed more than 200,000 people, devastating the homes and lives of many more. Tourists and local people, rich and poor – all were affected by this tremendous force of nature.

The compassionate response to this disaster was overwhelming as people from many different countries tried to help, donating more than US$7 billion. Charity events were held, or people just reached deep into their pockets to try to make a difference. Faced with this devastation, the human response was outstanding. It showed how compassion is a vital part of the human response to the world and to other people.

Gospel Teaching

Jesus had compassion. He comes across in today's Gospel reading as overflowing with concern and care for others. But, crucially, not just for the so-called "deserving". Jesus had compassion on those whom others despised. Zacchaeus was a tax collector. Even today those who collect taxes can find that they meet with hostility. Then, at the time of the Roman occupation, Zacchaeus' job meant that he was an outsider. Tax collectors were perceived as part of the system of oppression. They paid the Romans for the chance to collect tax, and were known for extorting larger amounts than were actually required by the Romans in order to make a profit.

Jesus invites himself to Zacchaeus' house, and everyone around them is surprised and even horrified. They all grumble. But Jesus has seen what nobody else seems to see. Zacchaeus is ready to make a change in his life. He had climbed a tree to see Jesus, which must have suggested to Jesus that actually Zacchaeus was looking for something. Zacchaeus' behaviour had made him an outcast in his own community. But as soon as Jesus greets him and goes to his house, Zacchaeus is ready to make restitution. He will not just pay back the money he has extorted, but four times more.

In Luke's Gospel this episode comes not long after the story of the rich young man who cannot give up his wealth. He has kept God's Law, but he cannot leave behind the security of wealth in order to experience fully the love of God. It is too difficult for him to answer Jesus' call.

Zacchaeus, in contrast, is ready. He knows that what Jesus is offering is worth so much more than the money he has. He has money, but it has not brought him happiness or fulfilment. He cannot depend on it to bring him peace. He chooses to depend on God, instead of on money.

Application

What is it in our lives that we need to change when Jesus comes to our house? If Jesus were coming to Sunday lunch, if he'd invited himself to our house as he did to Zacchaeus', what would he see? He has compassion on us, he loves us and he cares about us. But responding to this love with truth and honesty will often mean that we are called to change. Zacchaeus realised that he could trust and depend on Jesus. He could not carry on as he was, because he was damaging and hurting other people. Rather than condemning Zacchaeus, Jesus welcomes him; and this outpouring of love lights a spark in Zacchaeus – he is ready to change in response to Jesus' love.

What do we need to change? Are we full of compassion and love, or do we have a tendency to condemn and judge others? Are we welcoming and open – would we go to Zacchaeus' house? Or would we be among those in the crowd muttering about Jesus mixing with the wrong sort of people?

We are capable of compassion. You only have to look at the response to the catastrophe that was the tsunami to know that we can do it. But does it have to take a tsunami? We could change our behaviour a little at a time, taking gentle steps – or we might even have a massive change of heart like Zacchaeus. But change is necessary. We each know ourselves, and we know what our own temptations are. Let's try over the next few weeks to be ready to respond to God's love by making a change in our life – doing something positive in response to Jesus' call.

C

"Such inexhaustible comfort and such sure hope."

Illustration

In late May 1940 the evacuation of the British Army from the beaches of Dunkirk in France was under way. Desperate for ships to help with the evacuation, the Royal Navy called on all available vessels, including fishing craft and pleasure boats, to help lift the stranded men off the beaches. From the little fishing harbour of Leigh-on-Sea, in the Thames estuary, a local cockle-boat set out across the Channel to assist. It was crewed by two brothers and their cousin. As they set out that morning, the brothers said goodbye to their mother. "See you later," they said. Their mother said "goodbye"; and she never saw them again.

Out on the sea, as the men were returning, they hit a mine and their craft exploded. No boat, no boys. For the rest of her life, that mother never again said "goodbye" to anyone. She would say "cheerio" to people, and "see you soon", but never again would she use the word that she had said to her sons. It was too painful. It stirred up such sorrowful feelings in her. It was the long goodbye. This simple word "goodbye" is a blessing that we call down on each other when we part. God be with you till we meet again. Because that meeting, that reuniting, had not happened, that mother's word would hang in the air until she saw her sons again.

This world can be very cruel, and people lose loved ones unexpectedly. Then people can truly say, "There is no sorrow like my sorrow." The pain that we feel may ease with time, but it never goes away. It never leaves us completely. If death has the last word, then life is a sorry tale. All our goodness, all our strivings are ultimately rendered futile. Is this the way it really is?

Gospel Teaching

The Sadducees would say "yes". These people were the religious realists of their day. They believed in God as the creator of the world, but they did not accept any kind of afterlife. They thought that only a shadowy existence remained when this life was done, therefore this world was the only real agenda. So it made sense to get the best deal that you could for yourself in this present life. The good life beckoned. They could collaborate with the powers that be, and so come to share in the privileges that power can bring. Wealth, comfort, position, honour, esteem – all these, they thought, can be yours if you play your cards right and if you stop all this nonsense about life beyond the grave, and judgement, reward and punishment. The Sadducees were thoroughgoing pragmatists, sensible, common-sense realists.

Jesus is challenged by these powerful citizens, and his teachings on the afterlife are ridiculed and rebuffed. But Jesus has an answer for these people. They believe in God, whom they call "the God of Abraham". What kind of God is a "God of the dead"? No, God, if God exists at all, is God of the living, and death shall have no victory. When we die, we die in the Lord. God is greater than death, and greater than the tragedies that threaten to destroy our lives. The "goodbye" that we say in death is literally true. God is with us when we die, and takes us into the life of heaven.

Application

This is the faith that spurred St Paul on to spend his life preaching the Gospel of God's love. He had personally seen the risen Lord. His motivation was powerful. He would gladly spend himself and be spent for love of this Lord, and for the good news that he carried: Jesus Christ is risen from the dead.

This news can be an inexhaustible comfort for us, and a sure hope. It is unconquerable. Death has done its worst and has not won. So, as you live your lives in this world, think on the love God has for us and on the fortitude of Christ. Be brave and persevering, and practise God's love towards all. Faith is not given to everyone, but the grace of goodness and love is, since every human being is in God's image. Let our faith, then, light up the world around us, so that people can see the hope and love that is in Christ Jesus. Yes, God is a God of the living.

"Your endurance will win you your lives."

Illustration

"Beirut, Beirut," the song says. "City of the fragrance of flowers, why do you smell of gun-smoke and fire?" This song describes the tragedy of the Middle East, and was recalled by Robert Fisk, a British war correspondent, who had lived in that part of the world for more than thirty years. Fisk had lived with war all his adult life. "It is not the natural state of things," he said, "but after so many years of violence and of seeing people die, it seems as if it is the natural and normal state." Comparing life there, in the Middle East, with life in Europe, Fisk remarked how blessed and fortunate Europeans have been, these past decades, living in a condition of uninterrupted peace. As the world becomes more embroiled and polarised in new conflicts, perhaps those days of tranquillity are numbered.

This is a disturbing thought. For many of us, wars are events that are fought on foreign fields, and their sadnesses, though many, happen far away. Now, in these days of terrorism, the violence is coming closer to home. News bulletins bring us a daily diet of death, and the sunshine of our lives is clouded over with reports of carnage and destruction. We can become very depressed.

Many years ago, during another bombardment of Beirut, a man came out onto a bullet-scarred balcony of his apartment, and hung out his washing to dry in the sun. It was a beautiful moment. There, in the midst of bombs and bullets, a human being was letting us know that life goes on. The simple, daily tasks require to be done, and he was doing them. War is madness, and that man on the balcony was witnessing to wisdom.

Gospel Teaching

Today Jesus speaks to us about wisdom and witness. With his disciples he is looking at the splendour of the Temple in Jerusalem. It is a very impressive place. But one day soon, Jesus says, it will be no more. Not one stone will be left on another; all will be destroyed. From that particular calamity Jesus proceeds to speak of others, of wars and famines and earthquakes. Then things will come very close to home. Followers of Jesus will be persecuted and even put to death. It is a frightening list of disasters. But every crisis can be an opportunity, and that is precisely what Our Lord tells us.

The time of crisis is our opportunity to bear witness to the wisdom of God, and to the love of God. There is no need for us to go on a course to learn this wisdom. The Spirit of the Lord, living in us, will give us all the eloquence that we need. That eloquence does not have to take the form of words. It is the witness of a simple life, lived lovingly and devotedly, that will speak more powerfully than any words can ever do.

St Paul, writing to his disciples in Thessalonika, reminds them of the example of honest living that he gave to them. He worked and earned the food that he ate. He was not lazy. He lived in a spirit of solidarity with people. He did not allow circumstances to deflect him from this faithful way of life. Hostility from others is no excuse for us to be hostile ourselves. We are to persevere in goodness and holiness of life. We will leave judgement to the Lord. The sun that gives us warmth and good cheer is the same sun that can scorch and burn up objects under its relentless glare. God's justice will be like that, the prophet Malachi reminds us.

Application
In a time of war and conflict, it is very easy to be swept up in the general tumult and to become as aggressive and antagonistic as everyone around you. The demand is made that you stand up for your side, that you take sides. You will be condemned if you do not. You will be called a traitor to your own people. In such circumstances it is easy to be carried along by the general tide.

In his own life, Jesus faced hostility from all sides, Jews and Romans. Yet he had a wisdom and an eloquence that none of his enemies could resist or contradict. A reading of the Passion story shows this to be true. It is this example that we are called to follow, this spirit that we are to imbibe. So shall we win our lives.

C

"Today you will be with me in paradise."

Illustration

On 6th July 1535 the former Lord Chancellor of England, Thomas More, was led to his death on the scaffold in the Tower of London. Before he died, he is said to have cried out, "I die the king's good servant, but God's first." Thomas had given up a wealthy and powerful position because he objected to King Henry VIII's attack on the Church. Finally, he also gave up his life.

In 1886 in Uganda the young catechist Charles Lwanga and his companions were burned to death because they refused to obey the evil command of a bad king.

In the 1930s in Mexico many poor Mexicans died for their faith. They were being persecuted by a fiercely anti-Christian government. As they were being shot some of them cried out, "Hail, Christ the King!"

These three stories from three continents show us what it can mean to accept Jesus Christ as our Lord and King. It can sometimes bring us into conflict with the world around us, just as Jesus came into conflict with the world around him.

Today's feast was introduced by Pope Pius XI in 1925. It was a time of great stress in the world. In Europe, many nations were still badly wounded by the First World War. In Russia, atheistic Communism was already persecuting the Church. In Italy and Germany the unrest that led to ideas such as fascism and Nazism was growing. The Pope reminded the world that there is ultimately only one real ruler: God. God's rule is made most clear in the life, death and resurrection of our Lord Jesus Christ, Universal King. As Pope Pius XI said, when we all recognise "both in private and in public life, that Christ is King, society will at last receive the great blessings of real liberty, well-ordered discipline, peace and harmony".

Gospel Teaching

There are two sides to the kingship of Christ which must always be kept together. St Paul in today's second reading shows us the first side in a beautiful hymn from the early Church. The hymn describes the divine nature and authority of Christ. Christ transfers us by his power from the kingdom of darkness into his marvellous kingdom of light. But the hymn also mentions the other side to Christ's kingship, his suffering. Christ reconciles us and brings peace through his death on the cross.

In the Gospel reading we see how Jesus exercises the other side to his kingship through his sacrificial, loving death. By allowing himself to be mocked and tortured to death, Jesus overturns all our notions of earthly power. His kingly robe is the blood pouring down his body, his crown is a crown of thorns, and his throne is the cross. In Matthew's account of his passion, Jesus asks, "Do you think that I cannot appeal to my Father who would promptly send more than twelve legions of angels to my defence?" But Jesus chooses not to show his power in this way. No, his kingdom is not of this world.

As he is dying on the cross, Jesus acts as king by forgiving those who are killing him, because "they do not know what they are doing". We also have the beautiful story of the penitent thief. Like other outsiders in Luke's Gospel, he realises that Jesus is the Messiah of Israel, the Chosen One of God. He turns to Jesus, not to escape his mortal death, but to be healed of his sins. Jesus graciously grants his request with sovereign freedom: "Indeed, I promise you, today you will be with me in paradise."

Application
The good news is this: not only are we subjects of the crucified king but we also share his kingship. By right, Christ is priest, prophet and king. By our adoption through baptism, we come to have some share in those offices. As St Peter says in his first letter, we are "a chosen race, a royal priesthood, a consecrated nation, a people set apart".

We are all called to help build up the kingdom of God in this world, while never forgetting that the kingdom of God has still to come in its fullness. We can do this by living a sacramental life in the Church, by caring for those who are poor and marginalised, and by witnessing to Jesus quietly in our places of work and in our families. We are privileged to share in the kingly, creative power of Jesus, and so to be his fellow workers on earth.

Feasts and Solemnities

"My eyes have seen the salvation which you have prepared for all the nations to see."

Illustration

From his early childhood into his late teens, John received a present each Christmas from his aunt Marion. It took him a while to realise, but it was the same kind of present every year until his aunt died when he was seventeen. So it got to the stage when just to see the label on the parcel and read her name was enough to know it meant a pair of gloves, knitted slightly larger than last year's, in a mixture of brightly coloured wool. John became so used to his aunt's present that it was tossed aside on Christmas Day and left unwrapped. It would only be opened sometime in the New Year, perhaps when warmth was more important than style.

The celebration of Christmas seems a long way behind us. The trees have been taken down and the cribs put away. We have moved on in the life of Jesus, hearing Sunday by Sunday in the Gospel of how he was baptised, of how he called his disciples and began his adult ministry of preaching, teaching and healing. And yet, almost out of sequence, as if we had turned back the clock, we come today to this beautiful feast of the Presentation of the Lord. Like a present put on one side at Christmas, we now ponder again the significance of Jesus as God's greatest gift to the world. It's as if we've returned to unwrap something more of the mystery of Christ's birth.

Gospel Teaching

With Joseph, Mary and Jesus, we celebrate this feast and are joined by two other important people from the scriptures: Simeon and Anna. They represent every expectant heart, every person who ever longed for the promised Messiah to come. We hear how Jesus is consecrated to the Lord and, more than this, how he is consecrated with sacrifice as an act of cleansing and purification. For those who were wealthy this sacrifice was to be made with a year-old lamb; for those who were poor with a pair of turtledoves or two young pigeons. In their humble poverty, Joseph and Mary offer the two birds, for Jesus himself is the true Lamb of God who will take away the sins of the world.

What happened to Jesus had happened to countless thousands of other firstborn males, but the Gospel tells us that Jesus is not like any of these. He is the gift of God, in Simeon's words, a gift of salvation and light for the whole world. The redeemer once promised through the prophets is now embraced with joy. The words of Malachi have been fulfilled: "the Lord you are seeking will suddenly enter his Temple".

In bringing Jesus to the Temple, Mary and Joseph thankfully presented back to God the gift God had given them. This gesture of generous thanksgiving is the pattern of salvation and the way of all Christian living. The life that Jesus received, the very life for which his parents gave thanks, is the same life Jesus offered back to the Father. This too was accompanied with sacrifice, but a more costly and personal sacrifice in the temple that was Jesus' body, on a cross that pained his mother's soul.

On this feast, the reality of Jesus as Emmanuel, "God with us", is brought home once more. To free us, Jesus had to become one with us. As the letter to the Hebrews explains, Jesus fully shared our human condition. He is compassionate and trustworthy; because he knew temptation, he can help us when we are tempted. Jesus is truly light and hope for every person, for all time.

Application

In the ordination ceremony of priests and deacons there is a request that the one to be ordained come forward, and the candidate responds, "Present". The whole of Christian life, and every form of vocation, is about being "present"; not just about being there in time and place, but about being radically presented, gifted, to the Lord. Each of us has been presented to God through water and the Holy Spirit. In baptism we are caught up into the one perfect offering of Jesus to the Father: in his death we have died to sin; in his resurrection we have been reborn to everlasting life. The life we have been given by God is to be continually presented back, freely offered over in thankful service of Christ and our neighbour.

As gift we receive Christ; as gift we offer all to Christ; as gift we are called to share Christ as light and salvation for all.

"What will this child turn out to be?"

Illustration

At this time of year in the northern hemisphere, the days are at their longest, the nights at their shortest. Indeed, in the extreme north, the sun never sets. But as we head through summer, into autumn and winter, the daylight hours shorten until, in the very depths of winter, some places never see the sun at all.

The celebrations of the birth of John the Baptist and the birth of Jesus the Christ reflect these changes – this interplay between light and dark, waxing and waning, ending and beginning. John said of himself: "He must increase, I must decrease." And the seasons reflect this: from this day of celebrating the birth of John, the days now decrease as we draw closer to the birth of the Messiah, whose coming brings light to the world when it is at its darkest.

Gospel Teaching

There is something very self-effacing about John the Baptist. He's the best man rather than the groom; the forerunner, not the main event; the warm-up man, not the star attraction. Once he has completed his task of preparing the way for the Messiah, he steps back out of the limelight. John was very careful not to let attention be diverted to him. Paul quotes him as saying: "I am not the one you imagine me to be." There is a hidden quality about John, hinted at in today's reading from the prophet Isaiah: "The Lord… hid me in the shadow of his hand… and concealed me in his quiver." It is as if John were saying to us: "Don't focus on me. It's not the messenger who is important, but the message; not the singer, but the song."

St Paul reminds us that the simple content of John's song was to call people to repentance, to turn back to God – symbolised by baptism. In doing this, John has been called the conscience of Israel. A conscience can make us feel quite uncomfortable. Certainly, John comes across as a very challenging and uncompromising person. But his challenge is an important one for us to face; we are called to hear his message, that call of his addressed to each one of us: "Turn back to God, don't wander away from God, don't go your own way. It is God who gives life and salvation. Turn to God, trust God."

John was a fearless prophet – courageously speaking God's word to the people of his time. He did not court popularity or fame, but simply pointed out their faults to the people, challenging them to a better and more faithful way of life. John's birth was greeted with great joy. Even in the womb he leapt for joy at the nearness of the Messiah. Yet the end of his life was marked by violence and – perhaps most painfully for John himself – a questioning. From his prison he sent messengers to ask Jesus: "Are you the one who is to come, or are we to wait for another?" He was wondering whether, in the words of the prophet Isaiah, he had "toiled in vain".

Application

"What will this child turn out to be?" they asked when John was born. What he turned out to be is what we are also called to be. Like John, we are called to decrease, that Christ might grow within us. Like him, our task is to prepare a way for the Lord – by repenting, by turning away from the sin and self-centredness that are obstacles to his coming. John shows us what it means to let the Lord Jesus move to centre stage in our lives, so that our whole lives – words, actions, thoughts, values and lifestyles – can truly bear witness to the nearness of the Lord.

Like John, we may at times feel that we are toiling in vain. We question what difference it makes – to us or to others – that we are Christians. But we can also draw strength from John's faithfulness and courage. By our baptism and our daily commitment to God, we can invite Christ to grow within us, so that his light can dispel the darkness of our world. What are we to be? Like John, we are to prepare the way for the Lord, and bear witness to God's nearness and love. Jesus himself said of John: "Of all the children born of women, there has never been anyone greater than John the Baptist." May we, like John, allow the light of Christ to shine ever more brightly in our lives.

"And the gates of the underworld can never hold out against it."

Illustration

A sound you hear in the Filipino jungle is the whine of the chainsaw. Illegal cutting down of trees by rich lumber companies is a major industry. One morning in October 1991 a young priest, Fr Nery Satur, was driving his motorbike down a jungle road on the island of Mindanao when he was picked off by a sniper and killed. It was an act of revenge, and a warning, too. In church, Fr Nery had denounced the tree-cutters. Bare hillsides meant soil erosion, he said; the soil clogged the rivers, the rivers overflowed and his parishioners were drowned. The rivers carried the silt down to the ocean and killed the fish, and deprived poor fisherfolk of their living. All this, he said, was clean against the law of God.

On news of his murder, his bishop, Bishop Rosales, hastened to the scene of the shooting. Then he hit the national headlines. He publicly condemned the big business interests that had treated human life so lightly and so cruelly. He closed down every church in his diocese on the following Sunday. "There will be only one Mass," he said, "it will be at the cathedral: it will be the funeral Mass of this heroic young priest."

That bishop, a few years later, was made an archbishop, and was called to Rome on the feast of St Peter and St Paul to receive his pallium. (A pallium is a woollen mini-scarf that denotes a bishop-in-charge-of-other-bishops.) The pallium had been laid overnight on St Peter's tomb, and was conferred by the Pope himself. At that moment, was Archbishop Rosales thinking of young Fr Nery, murdered in the jungle for preaching the Gospel?

Gospel Teaching

This story illustrates the scripture we have heard today. The Catholic Church is a blend of Peter and Paul. Peter stands for the teaching and coordinating and governing that is undertaken by the Pope – and also by our local bishop. It is this strain of authority that holds the Church together. Sometimes we grouse about authority, and feel like rebelling against it. But it is necessary, because without it we would fall apart. "Whatever you bind on earth shall be considered bound in heaven." It's the way God wants things to be.

At the same time, however, Paul stands for the adventurous and missionary spreading of the Gospel, finding the words that suit the local circumstances, taking the risks, applying the Church's age-old teaching to the particular scene. "I have fought the good fight to the end; I have run the race to the finish." These words sound almost weary, as if Paul were saying, "All the mountains I've crossed, all the rivers I've forded, all the jails I've been in, all the beatings I've suffered, all this I have survived by the grace of God – 'and so I was rescued from the lion's mouth'." I haven't had much to do with the corridors of power, he says, I have been so taken up with these little communities in Turkey and Greece, and I have worn myself out in their service. And now, he says, I am waiting for the Lord to bring me into his heavenly kingdom.

Application

In a moment we shall say, in the Creed, "We believe in one holy catholic and apostolic Church." When we say this, we are affirming that this worldwide family to which we belong, this Catholic Church, with all its human shortcomings, is made and willed by God. This subtle blend of the static and the dynamic, the institutional and the missionary, is the way it's meant to be. Peter needs Paul and Paul needs Peter. It is the same Holy Spirit at work in both.

The Holy Spirit was with young Fr Nery when, in the name of justice, he publicly blamed the rich loggers, and the following morning paid the price on that dirt road through the trees. And he was equally with Archbishop Rosales years later in the sunshine of St Peter's Square when the Holy Father put the pallium round his neck. It is the same Holy Spirit who invites all of us, priests and people, to live our life in the Church and be proud of her and loyal to her. And it is the same Holy Spirit who gives us the certainty that the Lord will rescue us from all evil attempts against us, and bring us safely to his heavenly kingdom.

A
B
C

"This is my Son, the Beloved. Listen to him."

Illustration

When Susan learnt that cancer had returned to bones in her back after five years of remission, she decided to climb a mountain. She would scale one of the mountains near her home in Colorado, before facing the mountains of fear, loss of confidence and debilitating treatment that were to come. Weeks later, accompanied by her son – an experienced climber – and two family friends, she picked her way up the steep slope. After nearly four hours, they reached the summit. "When I stepped onto the top of that massive mountain," she said afterwards, "I was so overcome with emotion that I couldn't stop crying."

Susan was entranced by the miles of snow-capped mountains, pristine valleys and glacial lakes. When she listened to God speaking to her through creation, she "felt the peace of God which passes all understanding". This strengthened her when she came down from the mountain to face the struggles ahead.

Gospel Teaching

When Jesus realised that his passion and death were imminent, he too climbed a mountain with three people close to him – Peter, James and John. Mountains were regarded as places where the veil between heaven and earth was thin. This was certainly the case on Mount Tabor in southern Galilee, for, sure enough, as Jesus prayed his face shone like the sun and his clothes became, in the words of Mark's Gospel, "whiter than any earthly bleacher could make them". Not only that, but Moses and Elijah – the two great figures of the Old Testament – joined Jesus. Luke's Gospel tells us that the prophets confirmed and strengthened Jesus' decision to go to Jerusalem and face the cross.

When we hear this story, the focus is almost always on the shining Jesus revealing his divinity. Highlighted too is a flustered Peter, offering to build three tents for Jesus and the two prophets. He was still babbling on with this suggestion when a bright cloud enveloped the group and a voice spoke out. The words sound familiar because the same expressions were spoken when the heavens opened at Jesus' baptism. Then he was beginning his ministry. Now he is close to ending his ministry – and his life. The voice from heaven indicates that God is pleased with Jesus' acceptance of his suffering role. The one who is radiant with God's glory is the one who will soon suffer and die on another mountain.

What is not so well appreciated is that in this story we have one of the clearest and most neglected commandments of the scriptures. The only time God personally speaks to the disciples, what is said? God points them to Jesus and tells them to listen to him: "This is my Son, the Beloved. Listen to him." Peter's idea of keeping Jesus on the mountain in a tent is completely dismissed. At the very moment when it would seem that Jesus is emphasising his transcendence, he takes the apostles off the mountain and into a town, particularly to suffering people. In fact, his first act is to cure a boy racked by convulsions.

Application

Peter wants to hold on to a good thing, rather than go down the mountain and face the trials of life. But the command to listen creates the final dramatic tension of the story and suspense as to whether the disciples will indeed listen to Jesus as God's beloved Son. Like Peter, we all want to control God, to stay in a comfortable place for ever, far away from our own Jerusalem. Like Peter, we want to avoid the crosses of life as far as we can. But if we listen to Jesus, rather than doing all the talking, then uncomfortable challenges are presented to us in the way we practise our faith.

We have a lot of voices that we listen to today: voices on news programmes, celebrity viewpoints or influential people in our lives. But today God commands us to listen to Jesus. God calls us as a community to be people who attend to the words and actions of Jesus; people who read the Gospels and take Jesus at his word. If we do listen, we are likely to hear a very specific, counter-cultural, but life-affirming message, which brings good news. It is about God's love for us and the importance of showing compassion towards those who are vulnerable in society. Like Peter, we are called to learn the lesson of his mountain-top experience – to be quiet and listen to Jesus.

"The Almighty has done great things for me."

Illustration

Two very different sets of images might help us enter into the spirit and significance of this wonderful feast of Mary's assumption into heaven. The first set of images comes from a primary school. The children had been thinking about Our Lady, and their teacher had asked them to draw pictures of what she might have looked like. Most of their drawings showed Mary doing the kinds of things their own mums or grandmothers did. Some were sat down with the child Jesus on their knee. Others were walking, leading Jesus by the hand. One was carrying shopping bags; another was baking a cake. They were all shapes and sizes, with varying designs and a mixture of colours. Some looked like scarecrows; others were more glamorous, almost like pop stars. But what united them all was their ordinariness, their humanity. To the children, Mary was a woman like their own mother, even though they knew she was also very special as the mother of Jesus.

The second image comes from the magnificent cathedral church, the Minster, in York, England. The vaulted arches stretching up to the ceiling meet in a number of what are known as "bosses", carved and decorated with symbols of faith. In one of these bosses, above the entrance to the choir and the high altar, is an image of the assumption, dating from the fifteenth century. Beautifully coloured, it shows Mary crowned and ascending towards heaven in an oval garland of flowers, supported on either side by golden angels. Here is a very different Our Lady, one who seems other-worldly, almost beyond us.

Gospel Teaching

This celebration invites us to reflect on the different dimensions of Mary's life. At one and the same time, she is totally like us, she is as human as we are; and yet, unlike us, she followed Jesus perfectly and generously and now lives fully in his presence. Mary's earthly existence found its meaning and completion in her heavenly existence. And this transition is promised to every believer: we too, one day, will be present to Jesus, as Mary is present to Jesus. As a famous hymn puts it, Mary is a "light on earth's horizon". She is a sign of hope for us of the promise of our future glory.

This is what St Paul was speaking about when he wrote to the Corinthians. The magnificent consequence of the resurrection is that all will be brought back to life in Christ. Death has been destroyed, so that, in the fullness of time, all who have fallen asleep in Christ and belong to him will be raised to the heights of heaven. When Mary proclaimed her song of thanksgiving in the Magnificat, she gave praise for the great things God had done. God had called her, a lowly peasant-girl, and blessed her with a unique and awesome privilege. She was to be the mother of Jesus, the long-expected Messiah, the one whose very name means "God saves". It's impossible for us to know at what point Mary realised in her own life that the greatest thing God would do for her would be to raise her son from the dead. Jesus' resurrection is the key to understanding Mary's assumption.

Although all die, says St Paul, in Christ all will be brought back to life. The imagery in the book of the Apocalypse, of the woman giving birth to a son, has many different interpretations. However, Christians down the ages have seen in her a reflection of Mary, closely linked to the victory and power of God and the authority of Christ. This great victory of God in Christ is the risen life, won through the cross and the empty tomb. Mary's assumption is her full participation in this mystery of our faith.

Application
Elizabeth described Mary as "the most blessed" of all women. She was "blessed" not only because God had chosen her, but also because Mary believed that the promise made to her by God would be fulfilled. This promise, that Mary would give birth to God's Son, was the prelude to another promise: Jesus' promise that whoever lives and believes in him shall not die, but have eternal life. This promise is for everyone, for all of us here.

Mary's assumption – her being taken up, body and soul, into heavenly glory – is really a feast that flows out of Easter. It's her feast, but it's also our feast. It's a celebration in the life of Mary of what the resurrection ultimately means for us – fullness of life with Jesus in heaven.

"The Son of Man must be lifted up."

Illustration

We spend millions of pounds on buying cosmetics so that we can hide our bodily imperfections and make sure we conform to society's standard of beauty. But beauty is not just skin deep. There is a story about the late Queen Elizabeth the Queen Mother, who was sitting for her portrait when she was very elderly. When the painting was finished, one of her friends noticed that the artist had painted in the wrinkles on her face and asked her whether it would not be better to remove them. "No," the Queen Mother said firmly, "I earned those wrinkles."

Gospel Teaching

What were the last words Jesus spoke as he hung upon the cross? We read in St Mark that he cried out, "My God, my God, why have you deserted me?" But in St John's Gospel he says, "It is accomplished." The two Gospels emphasise different aspects of Jesus' passion.

Mark emphasises the terrible sense of pain and isolation Jesus experienced in his final suffering. After all, the punishment of crucifixion was seen in the ancient world as one of the most barbaric ever devised. The cross was a sign of fear and shame, something you would hide your face from. We have grown so familiar with seeing a crucifix as a piece of unremarkable church furniture that it can lose any shock value. If we are going to feel the terror that Jesus' death evoked, it might be more effective to imagine him burning to death in the electric chair.

St John does not deny the horror of the cross but he presents Jesus, not in lonely helplessness at the end but rather as one who is majestically in control of his actions and destiny. Jesus alone decides to take up his cross and to carry it unaided. And, as he dies, he sees his death as the final act of God's plan which is now completed.

John wants to present Jesus' death on the cross not as a defeat but rather as a victory. He does this by showing us that Jesus is raised up in two senses. When the cross is raised, Jesus does indeed hang on the cross; but he is also raised up as a king might be raised up on a throne. The cross becomes the means of his victory. Christ reigns on the throne of the cross.

Moses had raised up the brazen serpent so that those who had been bitten by serpents would be healed when they looked on the serpent that had now become the instrument of God's power. In the same way John presents Jesus on the cross as the source of eternal life. Those who look on him will have their hearts moved by this amazing divine love and come to believe.

Application

Just as there is a tendency to hide our wrinkles and other blemishes, there is also a reluctance to face the reality of death. We deny it. Some Christians have tried to hide the cross as the central symbol of our faith. "Can't we have something more cheerful? Why do we have to have an image of suffering at the centre of the church?"

Today's feast celebrates the finding of the true cross by St Helena during a pilgrimage she made to Jerusalem in the third century. There is something very down-to-earth about this feast: we venerate a piece of wood. Just as we cherish some object that belonged to a beloved relative or friend, so now we prize this wood stained by Christ's blood. It is not something magical, but rather a very concrete reminder of the depths that God plumbed in order to save us. Christ did not pretend that our suffering does not exist; his whole life was an expression of his care and compassion for those who were poor and outcast – the cross was a consequence of that love. We do not glory in suffering for itself, but we cherish the cross which is the most adequate symbol of God's love for us.

Having a crucifix in the house, making the sign of the cross at grace, venerating the cross on Good Friday – all are ways by which we can witness to the triumph of the cross in our daily lives. But most important of all is to witness to Christ's sacrificial love in our family or community and to show that we are grateful for the costly way he earned our salvation. By his wounds we were healed.

"Think of the love that the Father has lavished on us."

Illustration

A young priest was visiting his friend, an elderly man who had once been his parish priest. The old man, now living on his own in retirement, always welcomed a visit. Though well over eighty, he was still pretty sprightly – in mind as well as in body. He'd always been admired for his learning and for his goodness.

In the course of their conversation he explained, much to the young priest's surprise, that after many years of study he had come to the conclusion that there was only one convincing argument for the existence of God, so far as he was concerned. And that, he said, is holiness. "Ah yes," said the young priest, "the fact that down through the ages the Church has never ceased to produce great saints."

"Well, I know that's true, but it isn't exactly what I had in mind," replied the old man. "I was thinking rather of the sheer mass of goodness that I found among parishioners in all the parishes I've ever been in. So many men and women who had no special training – some of them not particularly bright – and yet you could see that the faith was firmly established in their hearts. They prayed, God really mattered to them, they became – well, quite simply, I suppose you'd say they became saints, though they didn't know it. But they were; and, I tell you now, they were always an inspiration to me."

Gospel Teaching

Many priests would express similar sentiments. Nor should that surprise us: by baptism we have been incredibly transformed. Already we are able to be "called God's children". And that, insists St John in our second reading, is not some kind of courtesy title: it is a fact, it "is what we are". It is a wondrous gift, which has been lavished upon us by the overflowing love of our heavenly Father.

And yet even that is only the start, the start of a process that is to continue until the day when we see our God face to face. On that day our full glory will be revealed, and no one, I suspect, will be more surprised than ourselves. As John explains, "we shall be like [God] because we shall see him as he really is". And in the first reading, we were given a

All Saints

glimpse of those who have reached their journey's end, that immense crowd "impossible to count, of people from every nation, race, tribe and language" who have remained faithful to God through every difficulty and who now praise and worship him.

In that throng there will surely be many of our own dear ones who have gone before us – parents perhaps, or children who died young, or people who knelt beside us in this very church, or next-door neighbours. The great truth, which was proclaimed boldly at the Second Vatican Council, is that "The Lord Jesus… preached holiness of life… to each and every one of his disciples no matter what their condition of life" (*Lumen Gentium*, 40). This is only another way of saying that we have all been called to be saints. The call to holiness, to sainthood, is open to everyone. It is what we were created for.

Application
It is a strange thing that while we would all be ready to claim that we are decent people, we'd probably be far less eager to speak of ourselves as holy people. Perhaps it's due to false modesty; perhaps it's because we think that the only saints are those who have been canonised by the Church; but perhaps above all it's because we haven't begun to appreciate the love the Father has lavished upon us. It's because of that love that we can humbly trust that we are even now on the way to becoming saints.

In the Gospel we heard the Beatitudes. Jesus is telling us where real happiness is, where the kingdom of heaven is to be found. It is, he says, with those who are "poor in spirit" and so know their need of God; who are strong enough to be gentle and merciful; who "hunger and thirst" for justice; who strive to be peacemakers; who because of their single-mindedness are "pure in heart". Today we thank God that such people are to be found in every parish and community – sometimes in the most unlikely places. At the same time we pray that the Mass, source of the Church's holiness, may enable us, despite our sins and unfaithfulness, to be numbered finally among the saints, the holy ones of God.

"I will give you rest."

Illustration

The small Greek island of Leros is part of the chain of Dodecanese islands which sit snugly in the Aegean Sea off the coast of Turkey. If you travel north from Platanos, the island's capital, the road follows the curve of the bay and eventually brings you to a village called Alinda with its sandy beach. Here, set back from the road, amidst the frivolity of swimmers and sunbathers, a tall cross rises up above the trees. It marks the site of a cemetery.

During the Second World War, Leros was the scene of bloody fighting. Although this particular battle is not widely known, the cemetery testifies to its impact. As you walk though the iron gates, there are rows of white gravestones, 183 in total, neatly set out on either side of the cross.

The grounds are immaculately kept by local Greek gardeners; the grass is trimmed and the paths are swept. The inscriptions on the graves give the names and ages of the deceased – often the age is startlingly young. Sometimes there is no name, just "A Soldier of the 1939-45 War". Despite being surrounded by a holiday resort, the cemetery is quiet and calm.

In a small cupboard set into the cemetery wall, there is a visitors' book. People from all around the world have written down their sentiments of remembrance and respect. The most moving ones are comments from relatives who have made the journey to see where their loved ones are buried. In simple, heartfelt words they write of their deep love for those who have died. They express their gratitude for all they gave, for their service and their sacrifice. They proclaim that those who have died will never be forgotten. They record their prayerful petitions that God might grant them rest and peace.

Gospel Teaching

In this Mass we remember all those who have died, whatever the circumstances, and especially members of our family and friends. As we do so, the words of Jesus from St Matthew's Gospel offer us sure and certain hope. The Gospel confirms that it is Jesus to whom God the Father has entrusted everything. Therefore, what he says is trustworthy; it brings reassurance.

The invitation that Jesus offers in the Gospel is true for the whole of life, but when placed in the context of our passing from this world to the next it carries a special significance. How wonderful it is to know that when our earthly life draws to its close Jesus desires that we enter into his peace. No matter what burdens may weigh us down, or how exhausted, confused, or unprepared we might be, the overriding concern of Jesus is that we share his life.

It is by his own dying and rising that Jesus makes real the vision of the prophet Isaiah. He shouldered our sins on the cross so that our own death might be destroyed and our hope of being saved could be fulfilled. In Christ we are forgiven and reconciled: he is gentle and humble of heart; he does offer rest for our souls and the souls of those we love. How important it is that we remember the hope we have in Jesus, in the power of his mercy and in his longing that we be at peace with him for ever.

Application

Each of us will carry in our hearts the memory of people we love who have now gone before us. Perhaps the loss of them is still very painful to recall; maybe we can think of them with a loving smile. Sometimes we are left with questions about their life or even doubts about their place with the Lord.

Whatever our feelings and emotions, we trust and hope in a God of love, a God who desires that everyone will be saved. Christ did not die for humanity because we are worthy of such a sacrifice. Christ died for us while we were sinners so that, unworthy though we are, we might be able to make our final journey home to him. The promise of new life which flows from the empty tomb underpins how we live and how we die.

So, with profound hope in the resurrection, let us remember all those who have died. Let us be grateful for what we have received from previous generations, especially for the love and kindness of our family and friends. And let us pray that the faithful departed will receive from Christ gentle mercy, rest for their souls and eternal peace.

"Christ died for us while we were still sinners."

Illustration

Deceased, expired, passed away, snuffed it, shuffled off this mortal coil: the list of expressions associated with dying is almost endless and reflects our unease with accepting this inevitable part of life. Our funeral customs can insulate us from facing death. Often, people die in institutions rather than in the familiar intimacy of their own homes. Funeral directors offer a service that can protect the bereaved from any of the practicalities of death. The whole process of having a funeral can be sanitised, even romanticised, with eulogies that bear little relation to the true character of the deceased. Doctors can offer drugs to take away the pain people feel when a loved one dies. Death is a reality that many of us are reluctant to face.

Gospel Teaching

Today's Gospel offers a stark presentation of the death of Jesus. This is no romantic picture of the heroic martyr dying for his beliefs. Mark's picture presents us with the full horror of Jesus' death, an event that was traumatic both for Jesus and his followers. There is a darkness about the scene, reflected in the darkness of the skies. Rather than a confident and self-assured Jesus, certain of victory, Mark portrays Jesus as entering into the full pain of death – the utter loneliness and isolation of it, feeling abandoned even by God. The vinegar-soaked sponge, probably offered as an anaesthetic, remains untouched, as Jesus drinks fully of the pain of death.

What is significant about Mark's presentation is that it is precisely at this moment, as Jesus dies with a final shout of agony, that Jesus is recognised for who he is – the Son of God. This is something that no human being has recognised before in Mark's Gospel, despite all the miracles Jesus had worked. Only now – when he dies in apparent defeat – is Jesus understood to be the Son of God. For Mark, it is the stark reality of Jesus' death that reveals the truth about Jesus – and so about humanity.

The tearing of the veil in the Temple is symbolic of the meaning of these events: in the death of Jesus, the barrier between God and God's people is removed. Somehow, through the death of Jesus, humanity and God are reunited. As Paul tells us: "we were reconciled to God by the death of his Son". By entering fully into the reality of the human condition – especially the reality of death – Jesus is able to bridge the gap that separates the divine and the human. It is achieved not by avoiding death, not by fast-forwarding to the more comfortable image of the empty tomb, but precisely by embracing the consequences of human sinfulness, by experiencing the death and separation from God which sin brings.

Application

Today's readings speak to us of the importance of facing reality. In this commemoration of All Souls, we acknowledge the reality of the human condition – that sinfulness and weakness are a part of every human life. We resist the temptation to canonise our loved ones, simply because they have died. Though we love them dearly, we avoid any false romantic memories of those who have died. We remember them today not because they were perfect, but because they were human – and so they need our prayers, just as we need theirs. To admit this is not to be disloyal to the memory of our loved ones, but it is to face the truth about God and humanity: Christ died for us while we were still sinners. And it is precisely this truth – as Paul tells us – that "proves that God loves us".

Today's Gospel and first reading complete the picture. Death is not the end. The sin and selfishness that lead to death are real – and need to be forgiven. But that is not the full story. Jesus has achieved our reconciliation – our peace – with God. He did rise again. Jesus' tomb – that very real place of death – is empty. And therefore so is our tomb. What God offers us – offers all our loved ones for whom we pray today – is the reality of the banquet of heaven, when all sadness and pain will be removed, and every one of our needs will be met. We shall live in the presence of God – the Temple veil is gone. The reality of death has been transformed by the truth of life everlasting for all who place their hope in Christ. And, as Paul says, that "hope is not deceptive". May the Lord lead us all – living and dead – to the reality of the resurrection.

"He will destroy Death for ever."

Illustration

In February 1943 a young student in Munich, twenty-one-year-old Sophie Scholl, was found guilty of treason for distributing leaflets at the university, against Hitler and against the war. Together with her brother and another friend, she was condemned to death and executed later that same day. As she stood before the judge and heard her fate, she contemplated the sadness of her short life. Sophie loved life and loved justice, and now it was all being taken from her. She looked at the judge and said wistfully, "It is such a fine, sunny day and I must go."

Forty years later another young student had cause to feel the same way about the beauty and the sadness of this world. The student was in Italy and had gone to visit the famous town of Monte Cassino. Site of a famous monastery, built on top of a hill, Cassino is also the place where a terrible battle in 1944 cost the lives of many thousands of soldiers. Three war cemeteries are dotted around the town: Allied, Polish and German.

After a pleasant lunch, the student and his companion went to visit the Allied cemetery. They walked along a country lane in glorious afternoon sunshine. All around, the blue hills of Italy encircled them. It was warm and bright and beautiful. Then as they crested an embankment their eyes were met by an endless sea of graves, row upon row of headstones. Stunned and shocked by what he saw, the student remembered the words of Sophie Scholl: "It is such a fine, sunny day and I must go."

Gospel Teaching

Similar feelings of sadness must have engulfed the little procession of people who came out from the village of Nain, to bury a young man and to comfort his poor mother, on the day that Jesus visited the place. The death of young ones is always a tragedy. Doubly so, in the case of a poor widow left behind with no one to support her. But on this day, as the procession winds its way out of the village, it is met by another procession making its way in – Jesus and his companions – and sorrow is turned into joy.

Jesus brings the sorrowful procession to a halt. He touches the coffin and stops the death march. Jesus is the Lord of life, St Luke tells us, and death shall not have the victory. Jesus speaks to the dead man; and the man is brought back to life. Jesus restores the son to his mother; and her life, too, is renewed. Jesus has made this day of death into "such a fine, sunny day". The Lord of life is here.

Later, when Jesus met his own death, they said about him, "He saved others, why can't he save himself?" St Paul answers that question for us. Jesus experienced in his own body all the evil of this world. He died for us, to save us and set us free. He trusted in God, his Father, and yielded up his spirit. Laid in a tomb, he was brought back to life by the finger of God. As if God said to him, "Young man, I tell you to get up." That is why Easter is for us such a fine and sunny day.

Application

Today, on this November day, the Church calls to mind, in the light of Easter sunshine, all the faithful who have departed this life and gone before us. There is sadness in remembering, because life is often so fine and sunny and our loved ones had to leave us. But there is joy in remembering too, because death has been defeated and our loved ones are with the Lord of life.

The resurrection of Jesus changes not only the situation of those who have died, but also the life of the Lord's followers in this world. Our hope of the world to come grasps hold of true life. We believe, we *know* that the Lord has put an end to death. In remembering those who have died, we look back fondly in love for our dear ones, and we look forward in fervent hope to the life of the world to come. In that moment Jesus will restore us and reunite us, one to another.

At Monte Cassino the restored abbey preaches from the mountain top this Gospel of everlasting life. When the day of our death approaches, may we say in faith, and without sadness, "It is such a fine, sunny day and I must go."

"My Father's house."

Illustration

A group of pilgrims from a parish in a run-down area of an industrial city in the north of England were in Rome, visiting the sacred places of the Eternal City. Their own parish church of St Mary's was a crumbling old building of faded beauty, destined to be demolished in just a few months. As the pilgrims entered St Peter's Basilica and marvelled at the awesome size and grandeur of the building, one of the elderly women of the party went up to the parish priest to express her admiration, and then added: "But Father, you have to go a long way to beat our old St Mary's!"

For her, St Peter's in Rome couldn't compete with the beauty of her battered old parish church. And of course she was absolutely right: for her, St Peter's was simply a building to be admired, not a church where she encountered God, nor a community that she belonged to.

Gospel Teaching

Today we celebrate the feast of the Dedication of St John Lateran, another of the major basilicas of the city of Rome. But, as the elderly pilgrim reminds us, we are not celebrating the bricks and mortar of that impressive church, but its heart, what it symbolises. What distinguishes this church from the hundreds of churches in Rome is that it is the Pope's own church, his cathedral as the bishop of that city. You could describe it as Rome's parish church. As such, what we celebrate today is what we hope to find in every parish church, in God's house: a place to worship and encounter God; a place of community where we give and receive support, love and encouragement in our journey of faith; a place where we are strengthened to be sent out as witnesses of Gospel joy.

Our first reading gives a very vivid picture of what a church is meant to be. The healing and medicinal waters flow out from the Temple, from the place of God's presence, for the salvation of the whole world, to bring life and healing. That is the role of parish communities, the role of the Church – to be the means by which God communicates his love and salvation to the world.

Parish communities are not like monasteries or convents – places that are set apart from the hustle and bustle of the outside world. They are situated very much in the heart of cities, towns and villages – at the centre of places where people live out their lives and their faith. As such, they are called to point to and incarnate the presence of God among God's people. They are called to be truly the house of God our Father – sources of life-giving water, places where people can come into contact with the healing and forgiving love of God through the community's celebration of the sacraments, and its ministry of compassion and outreach to the local area. It is not in essence the buildings that God inhabits. St Paul tells us specifically that *we* are the Church – we, the people, are God's temple, because God's Spirit is living among us.

Application

What incensed Jesus when he came to the Temple were the abuses that he found going on there, as people served their own interests instead of those of God and God's people. Jesus purified that Temple, he cleansed it of its corruption.

Today's feast of the Dedication of the Lateran Basilica reminds us that perhaps we too stand in need of purification, of a rededication. Today's readings invite us to become what we are – the body of Christ, the presence of God in the world. That means ridding ourselves of those things that prevent us from being able to encounter the presence of the living God, and which hide and obscure God's presence among us from outsiders.

Perhaps we ourselves need first to return to the healing waters of God's forgiveness as we turn away from sin, from greed and self-seeking, in order that we – God's temple – can truly function as the presence of God in the world. That means becoming not just communities of prayer, but individuals who live in the presence and knowledge of God. It is that familiarity and intimacy with God which should be the hallmark of every Christian community and each Christian individual. If we are to live in this way, Jesus calls us to be firmly founded on him: espousing his values, his zeal for God's house and God's people, having his passion to make the kingdom of God a reality.

Index of
Gospel Readings